Writing a Thesis Statement

Skill

A sentence that outlines the specific elements of the speech supporting the speech goal statement.

Use

To specify the main points of the speech.

Procedure

1. Write the specific speech goal.

2. Brainstorm potential parts or elements of that goal.

3. Select those elements that best develop the goal.

4. Write a complete sentence that best incorporates those elements.

Example

Sally writes her speech goal: "I want the audience to understand the three steps involved in shooting a jump shot." She then thinks of balance, holding the ball steady, squaring shoulders to the basket, bending knees, and delivering the ball smoothly. She selects squaring shoulders, balance, and smooth delivery. She then writes her thesis statement: "The three steps required to shoot a jump shot are to square yourself to the basket, balance yourself properly, and deliver the shot smoothly."

Enthusiasm

Skill

Using your voice and bodily action to show the audience that you are excited about the topic and your opportunity to talk with the audience about it.

Use

To ensure audience perception of the importance and relevance of the information to them.

Procedure

1. Make sure that you are truly excited about your topic.

2. As you speak, re-create your original feelings of excitement.

3. Focus on sharing that feeling of excitement with the audience.

Example

As Trisha was practicing her speech on Alberta, Canada, she refocused on her feelings of awe as she first saw mountain peak after mountain peak. She also reminded herself of how much she wanted her audience to actually "see" what she had experienced.

SKILL BUILDERS

Assertiveness

Skill	Use	Procedure	Example
Standing up for yourself and doing so in interpersonally effective ways that describe your feelings honestly and exercise your personal rights while respecting the rights of others.	To show clearly what you think or feel.	1. Identify what you are thinking or feeling. 2. Analyze the cause of these feelings. 3. Choose the appropriate skills necessary to communicate these feelings, as well as any outcome you desire, if any. 4. Communicate these feelings to the appropriate person. Remember to own your feelings.	When Gavin believes that he is being unjustly charged, he says, "I have never been charged for a refill on iced tea before—has there been a change in policy?"

Empathy

Skill	Use	Procedure	Example
Intellectually identifying with or vicariously experiencing the feelings, thoughts, or attitudes of another.	To create or promote a supportive climate.	1. Adopt an attitude of caring. 2. Concentrate on understanding the nonverbal as well as the verbal messages in order to ascertain his or her emotional state. 3. Try to feel with the person; try to recall or imagine how you would feel in similar circumstances; or try to understand what the person is feeling and allow yourself to experience your own feelings of concern, compassion, or sorrow.	When Jerry says, "I really feel embarrassed about wearing braces in college," Mary smiles ruefully and replies, "Yeah, it makes you feel like a little kid, doesn't it? I remember the things I had to put up with when I wore braces."

SKILL BUILDERS

Gatekeeping

Skill

A leader intrusion that is designed to achieve balance in group participation.

Use

To stimulate hesitant or reluctant members to contribute and to control overzealous members.

Procedure

1. Listen carefully to the discussion.

2. Note when some members are reluctant to share information or are unable to get the floor; also note when some members are dominating the discussion.

3. Phrase specific questions to reluctant members that require more than a yes-or-no answer; phrase statements that get talkative members to yield the floor without making them defensive.

Example

When Della notices that Maria seems to have something to say but can't get the floor, she might say, "Maria, I get the sense that you have something you've wanted to say here—tell us what you're thinking"; or when Della notices that Greg has talked three times in the last six turns even though there are five people in the group, she might say, "Greg, we want to hear what you have to say, but let's hear from those folks who haven't had a chance to be heard, and then we'll be sure to get back to you."

Questioning

Skill

A sentence phrased to get additional information.

Use

To initiate discussion, to focus discussion, to probe for information, or to deal with interpersonal problems.

Procedure

1. Listen carefully to the discussion.

2. Note the kind of information you want to get into the discussion.

3. Phrase specific questions that focus on achieving that particular goal.

4. Deliver them in a sincere tone of voice.

Example

When Connie says, "Well, it would be better if she weren't so sedentary." Jeff, seeing a need to probe for additional information, replies, "I'm not sure that we all understand what you mean by 'sedentary'—would you explain?"

Public Speaking

Brainstorming

Skill

An uncritical, nonevaluative process of generating associated ideas.

Use

To generate a list of specific topics from the subject areas you have identified.

Procedure

1. Label a column with your major or vocation, a hobby or activity, or a concern or issue.

2. Without trying to evaluate them, list at least twenty one- or two-word related ideas or topics.

3. Check the one topic that has special meaning to you or that seems particularly appropriate for your classroom audience.

Example

Under the column marked Tennis (a hobby), you might list rackets, balls, strokes, net play, tournaments, serving, stars, leagues, footwear, racket stringing, lobs, strategy, singles, doubles, forehand, backhand, overhead, surfaces, clay, grass. Then, from the list, you might select racket stringing.

Describing Behavior, Consequences, and Feelings

Skill	Use	Procedure	Example
Describing the basis of a conflict in terms of behavior, consequences, and feelings (b-c-f).	To help the other person understand the problem completely.	1. Own the message. 2. Describe the behavior that you see or hear. 3. Describe the consequences that result. 4. Describe your feelings.	Jason says, "I have a problem that I need your help with. When I tell you what I'm thinking and you don't respond (b), I start to think you don't care about me or what I think (c), and this causes me to get very angry with you (f)."

Group Communication

Problem Solving: Fact/Value Questions

Skill	Use	Procedure	Example
Arriving at a conclusion about a fact or value question.	A guide for groups to follow in arriving at conclusions to fact or value questions.	1. Clarify the specific fact or value question. 2. Analyze the question by determining the criteria that must be met to establish the fact or value. 3. Examine the facts to determine whether the subject meets those criteria.	Question: "Did Branson behave ethically in firing Peters?" The group then discusses and arrives at the criteria for determining whether a firing procedure is ethical. Then the group considers whether Branson's procedure met those criteria.

Problem Solving: Policy Questions

Skill	Use	Procedure	Example
Arriving at a solution to a policy question by following four steps.	A guide for groups to follow in finding solutions to policy questions.	1. Clarify the specific policy question. 2. Analyze the question by finding out the nature of the problem and determining the criteria that must be met to find an acceptable solution. 3. Brainstorm potential solutions. 4. Select the solution that best meets the criteria.	Question: "What should we do to increase alumni donations to the Department Scholarship Fund?" The group begins by discussing "Why are alumni not donating to the fund?" and asking "What criteria must be met to find an acceptable solution?" After brainstorming potential solutions, the group discusses each and selects the one or ones that best meet the criteria.

Paraphrasing

Skill	Use	Procedure	Example
Putting your understanding of the message into words.	To increase listening efficiency; to avoid message confusion; to discover the speaker's motivation.	1. Listen carefully to the message. 2. Determine what the message means to you. 3. Restate the message using your own words to indicate the meaning you have received.	Grace says, "At two minutes to five, the boss gave me three letters that had to be in the mail that evening!" Bonita replies, "If I understand you correctly, you were really resentful that the boss would dump important work on you right before closing time."

Supporting

Skill	Use	Procedure	Example
Making statements whose goals is to soothe, approve, reduce tension, or pacify the other by acknowledging that you understand what the other is feeling and you support that person's right to be feeling that way.	To help people feel better about themselves or what they have said or done.	1. Listen closely to what the person is saying. 2. Try to empathize with the dominant feelings. 3. Phrase a reply that is in harmony with the feelings you have identified. 4. Supplement your verbal response with appropriate nonverbal responses. 5. If it seems appropriate, indicate your willingness to help.	In response to Kendra's statement, "My new baby is so small, I hope I don't accidentally hurt her," Dr. Smith replies, "I can understand your fear; babies are so small and appear delicate."

Politeness

Skill	Use	Procedure	Example
Relating to others in ways that meet their need to be appreciated and protected.	To determine the degree of politeness necessary to achieve your objective.	1. Recognize when what you are planning to say is likely to be seen as a face-threatening act. 2. Consider how well you know each other, whether one person holds power over the other, and the risk of hurting the other person. 3. Construct the wording of a positive politeness or negative politeness statement based on the issues of relationship, power, and risk.	Chris thinks her boss did not consider all that he should have in determining her year's bonus. She might construct the following positive politeness statement: "Mr. Seward, I know that you take bonus decisions very seriously, and I know that you've been willing to talk about your decisions, so I was hoping you'd be willing to take a few minutes to discuss your decision on my bonus with me."

Writing Speech Goals

Skill	Use	Procedure	Example
A single statement that specifies the exact response the speaker wants from the audience.	To give direction to the speech.	1. Write a first draft. 2. Revise the draft until you have a complete sentence that states the specific response or behavior you want from your audience. 3. Make sure that the goal contains only one idea. 4. Revise the infinitive or infinitive phrase until it indicates the specific audience reaction desired. 5. Write at least three different versions of the goal.	Ken first writes, "I want my audience to know what to look for in buying a canine companion." As he revises, he arrives at the wording "I want my audience to understand four considerations in purchasing the perfect canine companion." Once Ken assures himself that the goal has a single focus and that the infinitive "to understand" indicates the preferred audience reaction desired, he then writes two differently worded goals to make sure that his first one is the best.

Recording Data

Skill	Use	Procedure	Example
Having a written record of information drawn from a source with complete documentation.	To provide information and its source in a speech or to report the documentation to anyone who might question the information's accuracy.	1. Indicate the topic in the upper-left-hand corner. 2. Record each factual statement or expert opinion on a separate four-by-six-inch or larger index card. Any part of the information that is quoted directly should be enclosed in quotation marks. 3. For a book, write the name of the author, the title, the publisher, the date, and the page number from which the information was taken. 4. For a periodical or newspaper, write the name of the author if one is given, the title of the article, the name of the periodical or newspaper, the date, and the page number from which the information was taken.	While gathering material for a speech on effects of electronic delivery services on mail delivery, Tamika found an article with relevant information. In the upper-left-hand corner of one four-by-six card, she wrote: U.S. Postal Service Record. Then she wrote the data she had discovered: In 1997, the U.S. Postal Service delivered 630 million pieces of mail a day and "raised its on-time rate for first-class letters to a remarkable 92%." Under the information, she wrote: John Greenwald, "Zapping the Post Office," *Time*, January 19, 1998, p. 40.

Foundations of Communication

Perception Checking

Skill

Making a verbal statement that reflects your understanding of the meaning of another person's nonverbal cues.

Use

To clarify the meaning of non-verbal behavior.

Procedure

1. Watch the behavior of another. Describe the behavior to yourself or aloud.

2. Ask yourself: What does that behavior mean to me?

3. Put your interpretation of the nonverbal behavior into words to verify your perception.

Example

As Dale frowns while reading Paul's first draft of a memo, Paul says, "From the way you're frowning, I take it that you're not too pleased with the way I phrased the memo."

Clarity—Specific, Concrete, Precise Words

Skill

Clarify meaning by narrowing what is understood from a general category to a particular group within that category, by appealing to the senses, or by choosing words that symbolize exact thoughts and feelings.

Use

To help the listener picture thoughts analogous to the speaker's.

Procedure

1. Assess whether the word or phrase used is less specific, concrete, or precise than it should be.

2. Pause to mentally brain-storm alternatives.

3. Select a more specific, con-crete, or precise word.

Example

Instead of saying "Bring the stuff for the audit," say "Bring the records and receipts from the last year for the audit." Or instead of saying "I was really cold," say "I nearly froze."

Interpersonal Communication

Describing Feelings

Skill

Putting an emotional state into words.

Use

For self-disclosure; to teach people how to treat you.

Procedure

1. Indicate what has triggered the feeling.

2. Mentally identify what you are feeling. Think specifically: Am I feeling hate? anger? joy?

3. Verbally own the feeling. Begin your statement with "I feel. . . ."

4. Verbally state the specific feeling.

Example

"As a result of not getting the job, I feel depressed and dis-couraged" or "Because of the way you stood up for me when Leah was putting me down, I'm feeling very warm and loving toward you."

Vocal Expressiveness

Skill

Using contrasts in pitch, volume, rate, and quality.

Use

To express the meanings you want audiences to get from the sentences you present.

Procedure

1. Identify the words you want to stress to best express your intended meaning.

2. Raise your pitch and/or increase your volume on key words.

Example

As Marquez thought about what he wanted to emphasize, he said, "You need to put your *left hand* at the *bottom* of the bat."

Spontaneity

Skill

Being responsive to the ideas of your speech.

Use

To ensure that your audience perceives your speech as a lively and fresh interaction even though it has been well practiced.

Procedure

1. Learn the ideas of your speech.

2. In each practice, allow yourself to express the ideas and their development in slightly different language.

Example

As Connie was talking about day care, she allowed herself to report a personal experience that she hadn't planned on using in the speech.

Eye Contact

Skill

Looking directly at members of the audience while you are talking to them.

Use

To strengthen the sense of interaction.

Procedure

1. Consciously look at the faces of groups of people in your audience while you are talking.

2. If your eyes drift away, try to bring them back.

Example

As Bill was talking about how people can sign up for tutoring other students, he was talking to people near the back of the room. When he looked down at his notes to make sure he had included all he wanted, he found himself continuing to look at his note card rather than at the audience. As he moved to the next point of his speech, he forced himself to look at people sitting in the front right of the room.

Communicate!

Communicate!

NINTH EDITION

Rudolph F. Verderber
Distinguished Teaching
Professor of Communication
University of Cincinnati

Wadsworth Publishing Company

I(T)P® An International Thomson Publishing Company

Belmont, CA ▪ Albany, NY ▪ Boston ▪ Cincinnati ▪ Johannesburg ▪ London ▪ Madrid ▪ Melbourne
Mexico City ▪ New York ▪ Pacific Grove, CA ▪ Scottsdale, AZ ▪ Singapore ▪ Tokyo ▪ Toronto

Executive Editor: Deirdre Cavanaugh
Development Editor: Sherry Symington
Assistant Editor: Megan Gilbert
Editorial Assistant: Matthew Lamm
Marketing Manager: Mike Dew
Advertising Project Manager: Cait Youngquist
Project Editor: Debby Kramer
Print Buyer: Barbara Britton
Permissions Editor: Robert Kauser
Production: Cecile Joyner/The Cooper Company
Designer: Ross Carron Design
Copy Editor: Margaret C. Tropp
Cover Design: Ross Carron Design
Cover Image: Hank Osuna
Compositor: American Composition & Graphics, Inc.
Printer: World Color/Taunton
Cover Printer: Phoenix Color Corp.
Photo credits appear on page 481.

Printed in the United States of America
3 4 5 6 7 8 9 10

For more information, contact Wadsworth Publishing Company, 10 Davis Drive, Belmont, CA 94002,
or electronically at http://www.wadsworth.com

International Thomson Publishing Europe
Berkshire House
168-173 High Holborn
London, WC1V 7AA, United Kingdom

International Thomson Editores
Seneca, 53
Colonia Polanco
11560 México D.F. México

Nelson ITP, Australia
102 Dodds Street
South Melbourne
Victoria 3205 Australia

International Thomson Publishing Asia
60 Albert Street
#15-01 Albert Complex
Singapore 189969

Nelson Canada
1120 Birchmount Road
Scarborough, Ontario
Canada M1K 5G4

International Thomson Publishing Japan
Hirakawa-cho Kyowa Building, 3F
2-2-1 Hirakawa-cho, Chiyoda-ku
Tokyo 102 Japan

International Thomson Publishing Southern Africa
Building 18, Constantia Square
138 Sixteenth Road, P.O. Box 2459
Halfway House, 1685 South Africa

Library of Congress Cataloging-in-Publication Data
Verderber, Rudolph F.
    Communicate! / Rudolph F. Verderber. —9th ed.
        p.   cm.
    Includes bibliographical references and index.
    ISBN 0-534-52074-X
    1. Communication.   I. Title.
P90.V43   1998
302.2—dc21   98-15334

 This book is printed on acid-free recycled paper.

Brief Contents

Contents

Preface

Instructors bring different approaches to teaching communication. Some tend to emphasize theory and research, while others focus on skills acquisition and practice. In this ninth edition of *Communicate!* I have tried to impart conceptual understanding of relevant theory and research, but I also believe such understanding is incomplete unless students can translate it into genuine communication competence.

Achieving communication competence is a goal that students of all ages and backgrounds can relate to and aspire to—something I try to acknowledge by treating readers with respect and using a diversity of examples.

With a combination of theory, skills practice, and competency evaluation, students reading this book (1) learn to understand the major concepts from communication theory and research, (2) become able to recognize how these concepts and theories provide a basis for communication skills, (3) have access to a range of communications skills and (4) begin to apply what they learn in class to real-life situations, thus increasing communication competence in all settings.

Strengths of the Text

The primary goal of this edition is to continue to emphasize the elements of communication competence in a way that is appealing both to the student learning the skills and to the instructor who is guiding that learning. A major challenge is to be sensitive to the burgeoning research in communication while still providing a manageable, coherent introduction that makes a real difference to the development of students' skills.

Thus, this revision emphasizes current trends in the field while preserving the qualities that previous users have said they find valuable:

- **Competency-based orientation** that shows students how to translate theory and research into communication behaviors.
- **A clear, concise writing style**
- **Ample examples**
- **Numerous suggestions for practice integrated within chapters**
- **Sensitivity to issues of gender and culture**
- **A reliable learning model** that is designed to give both instructors and students a consistent way to approach each new topic. To help you maximize what your students can accomplish during this course, this book uses a systematic learning model that consists of six integrated steps.

1. *Theoretical understanding.* Learning new skills begins with an understanding of how and why certain skills are effective. This book presents communication theories that provide the foundation for specific skills.

2. *Examples.* The second step of the learning model is the study of concrete examples of communication behavior that help bridge the gap between theory and practice. Specific examples enable students to identify effective skill usage.

3. *Steps involved in the performance of skills.* The third step of the learning model involves breaking down complex behaviors so that students can see the individual components of each skill. Thus, when a new skill is presented, the text describes the essential steps students will need to master in order to perform that skill.

4. *Practice in using skills.* The fourth step of the learning model involves putting the students' new-found knowledge of skills into practice. Throughout this book, exercises are presented that encourage students to try out the skills in familiar situations. In some of the exercises, individuals will practice alone; in other exercises, students are encouraged to practice the skills in interactions with class members, friends, or family members.

5. *Self-assessment.* The fifth step of the learning model involves a focus on self and commitment to change. To improve communication skills, students must first evaluate how well they currently perform. For each skill an individual selects to work on, he or she is invited to prepare a communication improvement goal statement that specifies a realistic plan for improvement. The elements of the goals statement are introduced in Chapter 1. Then at the end of each of the four major sections, or Parts, of the book, students are encouraged to write a goal statement to help them with their mastery of a key skill within that Part. Self-evaluation checklists help the students identify skills to work on.

6. *Review.* The final step of the learning model involves reviewing what has been learned. A summary of the chapter's content is provided at the end of each chapter.

Pedagogical Changes to This Edition

▪ **A new approach to text exercises** challenges students to work with the concepts and theories in a way that encourages creative and critical thinking while helping them to hone basic communications skills.

Think Critically exercises are designed to have students critically analyze what they have read by passing it through the filter of their own life experience.

Understand Yourself exercises ask the students to reflect on their motivations, behaviors, and values in order to see how who they are relates to others.

Observe and Analyze exercises require students to observe a specific event or series of events that are related to concepts they are learning. Then they are asked to analyze what happened, using the theories and concepts from the chapter.

Practice in Speech Preparation exercises help students with practical advice on how to apply the speech development principles discussed in the text.

- **Online research** is encouraged through exercises that guide students to the "virtual library" available through InfoTrac College Edition, which is offered to users of this text. This online tool gives students access to more than 600 periodicals.
- **Special features on ethics and diversity** highlight these important concepts for students while giving them compelling examples for reflection and analysis.

Reflect on Ethics exercises require students to think critically about ethical dilemmas common to communication.

Diverse Voices essays present personal accounts of diversity issues as they relate to communication.

- **Clearer presentation of skills** throughout the book ensures that students have all the tools they need to understand how to put theory into action.

Skill Builders boxes present the highest priority skills in a clear, easy-to-use format that includes the definition of the skill, a brief description of its use, the steps for enacting the skill, and a brief example that illustrates it.

A Skill Builders Chart in the front of the text groups the skills for easy reference and review.

- **Increased focus on research** is emphasized by up-to-date references throughout of the latest in communications scholarship as well as a clear presentation of classic theory.

Spotlight on Scholarship boxes offer summary descriptions of important contributions to the field of communications research.

Changes in Chapters

For those who are familiar with or have used the previous edition of *Communicate!*, here is a brief summary of the most significant content changes.

New Chapters

Chapter 7. Conversations. This new chapter covers topics ranging from the types and structures of conversation, the unwritten "rules" of conversation, to the skills of effective conversationalists. This chapter also emphasizes engaging in ethical dialogue and cultural variations. A "Test Your Competence" section presents sample conversation and analysis.

Chapter 9. Job Interviewing. This chapter, which was a module in the previous edition, is now a full chapter and appears in *Part Three, Interpersonal Communication*.

Revised Chapters

Part One, Foundations of Communication, provides a broad perspective on the discipline and shows how perceptions, verbal communication, and nonverbal communication are fundamental to all types of communication. Many chapters in this section have been reorganized and revised to better achieve these goals.

Chapter 1. Communication Perspective. The definition of communication has been sharpened while the discussions of the process of communication and the functions of communication have been retained. Increased emphasis on ethics has taken the form of a new section, "Communications Has Ethical Implications." Communications competence is elaborated further in the section on becoming a competent communicator and in the boxed *Spotlight on Scholarship* feature.

Chapter 2. Perception of Self and Others. The section on perception of self has been extensively revised to focus on self-concept and self-esteem.

Chapter 3. Verbal Communication. The discussion of how to increase message clarity has received major revision, and the sections on cultural and gender differences have been greatly expanded. The final section on speaking appropriately has a new section on profanity and vulgar expression.

Part Two, Interpersonal Communication has been revised to provide increased emphasis on specific skills that lead to interpersonal competence.

Chapter 6. Listening has been heavily revised and now incorporates both listening and responding. The section on understanding has been totally revised. For example, the discussion of empathy builds on a new definition and the discussions on questioning and paraphrasing have been streamlined to sharpen their focus.

Chapter 8. Communicating in Relationships. A section on examining disclosure and feedback ratios in relationships, featuring the Johari window, is new to this edition. The latter part of the chapter, dealing with managing conflict, has received major revision. For example, the discussion of how to deal with conflict has been reorganized around the headings of with-drawal, accommodation, forcing, compromising, and collaborating. Also new is a chart that contrasts the elements of styles. Another new section discusses communication skills that promote successful conflict management.

Chapter 11. Leadership in Groups. The discussion of the functions of leadership now has new sections on coaching others at work and on counseling. These new sections focus on broadening the context of leadership and making the concept of leadership more relevant to organizational settings.

Part Four, Public Speaking has been revised and reorganized to present the most recent scholarship while offering practical, easy-to-follow tips on honing skills.

Chapter 12. Topic and Goal. The section on audience analysis has been reorganized and now starts with a discussion of the kinds of audience data, and the section on writing a speech goal has been revised to make it easier for students to follow.

Chapter 13. Research. This chapter gives more detailed coverage of electronic resources for research. Also, the discussions of interviewing and surveys have been greatly expanded and the coverage of types of speech supporting information has been considerably revised.

Chapter 14. Organization. The section on selecting and stating main points has received major revision and the discussion on "Determining the Best Order" now focuses on topic order, time order, and logical reasons order.

Chapter 15. Adapting to Audiences Verbally and Visually now opens with a new section on "Developing Common Ground." Visual material that was in the old chapter on informative speaking has been moved forward to show that decisions about adaptation involve both visual and verbal considerations. The visual aids section now offers more information on computer graphics.

Chapter 16. Presenting Your Speech has received major revision. For example, the discussion of how to cope with communication anxiety has been heavily revised to give students more guidance in coping with nervousness. Also, the types of speech presentation—impromptu, manuscript, memorized, and extemporaneous—are now covered in the chapter opening, and the sections on conversational quality and rehearsing have been revised and reorganized. The chapter also now includes a sample speech with analysis and outline.

Chapter 17. Informative Speaking has received major revision, as well. For example, the section on principles of informing has been reordered to put greater emphasis on selecting information that is intellectually stimulating and a new section with an informative speech, analysis, and outline has been added.

Chapter 18. Persuasive Speaking has received considerable revision. The material on informative and persuasive speaking similarities and differences has been streamlined. The section on finding reasons has a new part on evaluating evidence and on recognizing fallacies.

Supplements

As a user of this text you also have access to a wealth of supplementary materials.

- **www.wadsworth.com/communications** This web site features a wealth of material linked directly to this text, along with valuable links to other communications sites.
- **InfoTrac College Edition** provides a "virtual library" of more than 600 periodicals (both scholarly and popular) to students for online research
- **CNN Hybrid Communication Today, Volume 1 Video Tape** A 60-minute video available with this text offers contemporary CNN news and feature stories that range from one to seven minutes in length. These can work as lecture launchers to stimulate class discussion.
- **Wadsworth Communication Library** offers a wealth of videotapes to choose from on a range of communications topics and includes coverage of such teaching issues as how to evaluate student speeches.
- **Web site assistance** is provided through the easy-to-use "Thomson World Class Course" that gives instructors a working template to build their own web site.
- **Text-specific PowerPoint** This tool offers professionally created text and images linked to the book, as well as the means to create your own slides. Available on cross-platform CD-ROM in either Windows or Macintosh format.
- **Instructor's Resource Manual** This includes a general discussion of the hybrid course, sample syllabi, lecture outlines, exam questions (multiple choice and essay) with page references and answer keys, assignments, checklists, critique sheets, and transparency masters. It also includes role-playing exercises and experiential learning exercises.
- **Computerized testing** With "World Class Testing Tools" instructors have access to a collection of test-creation, delivery, and classroom management tools, as well as all of the test questions in the Instructor's Resource Manual.

Acknowledgments

The ninth edition could not have been completed without the help of many people. I would like to acknowledge the help of my colleagues at various colleges and universities who offered prerevision suggestions or who read the completed manuscript for the ninth edition and offered many valuable suggestions: Robert L. Bohlken, Northwest Missouri State; Pam Broyles, Southern Nazarene University; Lori Carrell, University of Wisconsin-Oshkosh; Marcia D. Dixson, Indiana University–Purdue University, Ft. Wayne; Bruce Dorries, Winona State University; Dennis Dufer, St. Louis Community College; Michael H. Eaves, Valdosta State University; Linda L. Griffin, Edison Community College; Andrea J. Hanson, Clemson University; Robert L. Krizek, St. Louis University; Deleasa Randall, Ashland University; and Janice Stuckey, University of Montevallo.

Communicate!

one

Although you communicate in specific settings, principles and skills of perception, verbal communication, and nonverbal communication are common to all of them. This four-chapter unit provides a solid foundation on which to develop your skills in interpersonal communication, group communication, and public speaking.

I

FOUNDATIONS OF COMMUNICATION

OBJECTIVES

After you have read this chapter, you should be able to answer the following questions:

■ What is the definition of communication?

■ How does the communication process work?

■ What are the functions that make communication so important?

■ What principles underlie communication?

■ What is the measure of communication competence?

■ How does one write communication improvement goal statements?

1

Communication Perspective

As the selection committee deliberated, they felt they had four viable candidates for the position. "They all look good on paper," Carson said, "but I must admit I was especially impressed with the way Corrie Jackson presented herself to us. Not only did she have a clear vision for where we need to be five years from now, but also she explained that vision with precise, concrete statements. I was really convinced that she was on the right track. She gets my vote."

Your presence in this course may be far more important to you than you imagined when you chose (or were required) to take it, for communication effectiveness is vital to success in nearly every walk of life. For instance, of the seventeen factors most important in helping graduating college students obtain employment, one study found oral communication, listening ability, and enthusiasm (all of which are basic to this book) to be first, second, and third, respectively (Curtis, Winsor, and Stephens 1989, p. 11). So, whether you aspire to a career in business, industry, government, education, or almost any other field you can name, communication skills are likely to be a prerequisite to your success.

Communication is the process of sharing meaning, whether the context is informal conversation, group interaction, or public speaking. In this chapter, we will explain the process, its importance, its underlying principles, and means for increasing user competence in its three major settings.

The Communication Process

Communication is a process that includes context, participants, messages, channels, presence or absence of noise, and feedback.

Context

Context is the setting in which communication occurs—including what precedes and follows what is said. Communication contexts are (1) physical, (2) social, (3) historical, (4) psychological, and (5) cultural.

Physical context. The **physical context** of communication includes where it takes place, the environmental conditions (temperature, lighting, noise level), the distance between communicators, seating arrangements, and time of day. Each of these factors can affect the communication. For instance, the boss sitting behind her desk in her office talking with members of her staff creates a different atmosphere than if she talks with those same staff members while sitting around a table in the lunchroom.

Social context. The **social context** includes the nature of the relationships that exist between and among the participants. Whether communication takes place among family members, friends, acquaintances, work associates, or strangers influences what and how messages are formed, shared, and understood. For instance, most people change how they interact when talking with their parents or siblings as compared to how they interact when talking with their boss or their professor.

Historical context. The **historical context** includes the background provided by the previous communication episodes between the participants that influ-

How might the communication of these people in this setting differ from their communication in a work setting?

ences understandings in the current encounter. For instance, suppose one morning Chad tells Shelby that he will get the draft of the report that they had left for their boss to read. As Shelby enters the office that afternoon, she sees Chad and says, "Did you get it?" Another person listening to the conversation would have no idea what "it" is, but Chad may well reply, "It's on my desk." Shelby and Chad understand each other because of their earlier exchange.

Psychological context. The **psychological context** includes the moods and feelings each person brings to the communication. For instance, suppose Corinne is under a great deal of stress as she tries to finish a report due the next morning. If her husband jokingly suggests that she take a speed-typing course, Corinne, who is normally good-natured, may explode with an angry tirade. Why? Because her stress level provides the psychological context within which she hears this message and it taints what she understands.

Cultural context. The **cultural context** includes the beliefs, values, and norms that are shared by a large group of people (Lustig and Koester 1993, p. 41). In the United States the dominant cultural context is a European American one. The assumptions that one makes when interacting with others is that they share the beliefs, values, and norms that are common in Western European countries as they have been adopted and adapted to the American experience. But cultural contexts may include African American, Mexican American, Native American, Spanish American, and Asian American, as well as such nonethnic cultures as gay, middle-class, and corporate cultures, to name only a few. Thus, misunderstandings may occur on nearly any subject because of conflicting perspectives. Throughout this book we will encounter a series of "Diverse Voices"—excerpts from previously published articles chosen to expand your understanding of the richness in interpretations and expressions that is part of interpersonal communication.

Participants

The **participants**—the people communicating—are both senders and receivers during communication. As senders, we form messages and attempt to communicate them to others through verbal symbols and nonverbal behavior. As receivers, we process the messages and behaviors that we receive and react to them.

In general, it is easier for participants to communicate effectively when they share physical, social, psychological, intellectual, and cultural characteristics (Deaux, Dane, and Wrightsman 1993, p. 232). The more we perceive ourselves as being different, the more difficult our communication tends to be.

Messages

Communication takes place through the sending and receiving of **messages**, which include the elements of meanings and symbols, encoding and decoding, and form or organization.

Meanings and symbols. **Meanings** are the ideas and feelings that exist in your mind. You may have ideas about how to study for your next exam, what your career goal is, and whether taxes should be raised or lowered; you also may have feelings such as jealousy, anger, and love. The meanings you have within you, however, cannot be transferred magically into another's mind. To share these ideas and feelings, you form messages comprising both verbal symbols and nonverbal symbols.

Symbols are words, sounds, and actions that represent specific content meaning. As you speak, you choose words to convey your meaning. At the same time facial expressions, eye contact, gestures, and tone of voice—all nonverbal cues—accompany your words and also affect the meaning your listener receives from the symbols you use. As you listen, you use both the verbal symbols and the nonverbal cues to make sense of what is being said.

Encoding and decoding. The cognitive thinking process of transforming ideas and feelings into symbols and organizing them into a message is called **encoding** a message; the process of transforming another's messages back into one's own ideas and feelings is called **decoding**. Ordinarily you may not consciously think about the encoding and decoding processes. But the times when you have difficulty in communicating makes you aware of them. For example, if during a speech you see puzzled frowns, you may go through a conscious encoding process to select expressions that better convey your meaning.

Likewise, you may become aware of the decoding process when you must figure out the meaning of an unfamiliar word based on its use in a particular sentence.

The encoding process is made more difficult when verbal and nonverbal cues conflict. For instance, if a coworker says, "Yes, I'm very interested in the way you arrived at that decision," the meaning you decode will be very different if the person leans forward and looks interested or yawns and looks away.

The processes of encoding and decoding messages are at the heart of communication. For this reason, many of the skills presented in this book relate directly to improving how we form and interpret messages.

Form or organization.   When meaning is complex, we may need to organize it in sections or in a certain order. Message form is especially important in public speaking, when one person talks without interruption for a relatively long time. Elizabeth's coworkers will derive much more meaning from her Monday morning pep talk if her thoughts are organized than if she rambles on, randomly expressing whatever comes to mind. Even in the give-and-take of interpersonal conversation, however, form can affect the understanding of messages. For instance, when Yolanda's husband tells her about the apartment he looked at yesterday, she is likely to have a clearer picture if his description moves logically from room to room than if she has to piece together impressions communicated in a haphazard order.

Channels

A **channel** is both the route traveled by the message and the means of transportation. Messages are transmitted through sensory channels. Face-to-face communication has two basic channels: sound (verbal symbols) and light (nonverbal cues). However, people can and do communicate by any of the five sensory channels. A fragrant scent or a firm handshake may contribute as much to meaning as what is seen or heard. In general, the more channels used to carry a message, the more likely it is that the communication will succeed.

Noise

Noise is any external, internal, or semantic stimulus that interferes with the sharing of meaning.

External noise.   External noises are sights, sounds, and other stimuli in the environment that draw people's attention away from what is being said or done. For instance, while a person is giving directions on how to work the new food processor, your attention may be drawn away by the external noise of a radio playing an old favorite of yours. External noise can also be visual. Perhaps, while the person gives the directions, your attention is drawn momentarily to an attractive man or woman.

Internal noise.   Internal noises are thoughts and feelings that interfere with the communication process. Have you ever found yourself daydreaming during a lecture? Perhaps your mind wanders to thoughts of the dance you attended last night or to the argument you had with a friend this morning. If you have tuned out the words of the person with whom you are communicating and tuned into a daydream or a past conversation, then you have experienced internal noise.

Semantic noise. Semantic noises are the unintended meanings aroused by certain symbols inhibiting the accuracy of decoding. Suppose a friend describes a forty-year-old secretary as "the girl in the office." If you think *girl* is an odd and condescending term for a forty-year-old woman, you might not even hear the rest of what your friend has to say. Use of ethnic slurs, profanity, and vulgar speech can have the same effect.

Feedback

Feedback is the response to a message. Feedback indicates to the person sending a message whether and how that message was heard, seen, and understood. If the verbal or nonverbal response indicates to the sender that the intended meaning was not heard, the originator may try to find a different way of encoding the message in order to align the meaning that was understood with the initiator's original meaning. This reencoded message is also feedback because it gives meaning to the original receiver's response. In all of our communication, whether interpersonal, small-group, or public-speaking, we want to stimulate as much feedback as the situation will allow.

A Model of the Process

Let's look at a pictorial representation to see how the elements of communication interrelate. Figure 1.1 illustrates the transactional communication process in an interpersonal communication relationship. In the minds of the participants are meanings—thoughts or feelings that they intend to share. Those thoughts or feelings are created, shaped, and affected by the participants' total field of experience, including such specific factors as values, culture, environment, experiences, occupation, sex, interests, knowledge, and attitudes. To turn meaning into messages, participants encode a thought or feeling into words and actions and send it via sending channels—in this case, sound (speech) and light (nonverbal behavior).

Meanings that have been encoded into symbols are turned back into meaning by participants through the decoding process. This decoding process is affected by the participants' total field of experience—that is, by all the same factors that shape the encoding process.

The area around the participants represents the physical, social, historical, psychological, and cultural context; it includes the formal and informal rules in operation during the communication and the participants' prior relationships.

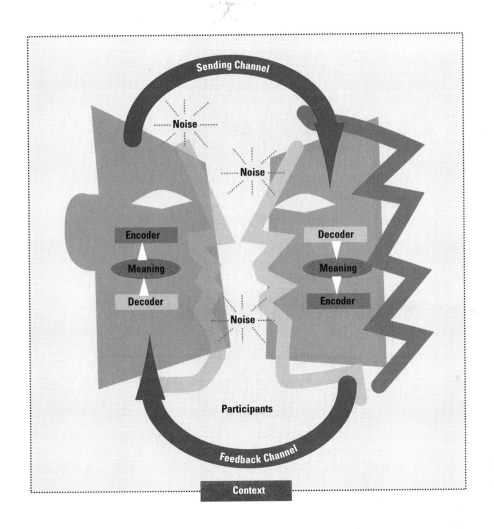

Figure 1.1
A model of communication between two individuals.

During the entire transaction, external, internal, and semantic noise may be occurring at various points, affecting the participants' ability to share meanings.

In a group or public-speaking situation, all these elements of communication operate simultaneously—and differently—for everyone present. As a result, communication in these settings is especially complex. Whereas some people focus on the speaker's message, others may be distracted by noise—whether external (the hum of the air-conditioning), internal (preoccupation with personal matters), or semantic (a reaction to the speaker's choice of words). Furthermore, all the participants bring their unique perspectives to the communication transaction. Less skillful communicators are oblivious of such factors and plunge ahead regardless of whether they are being understood or even heard. Skillful communicators attend to verbal and nonverbal feedback and adapt their words and nonverbal behavior until they are confident that their listeners have received the meanings they intend to share.

Functions of Communication

Communication serves several important functions in our lives.

1. **We communicate to meet needs.** Because we are by nature social animals, we need other people just as we need food, water, and shelter. Two people may converse happily for hours gossiping and chatting about inconsequential matters that neither remembers afterward. When they part, they may have exchanged little real information, but their communication has served the purpose of meeting the important need simply to talk with another human being.

2. **We communicate to enhance and maintain our sense of self.** Through our communication, we learn who we are, what we are good at, and how people react to how we behave. We explore this important function of interpersonal communication in detail in Chapter 2, "Perception of Self and Others."

3. **We communicate to fulfill social obligations.** We use such statements as "How are you doing?" to a person we sat next to in class last quarter and "What's happening?" or simply "Hi" when we pass people we know in order to meet social obligations. By saying "Hi, Josh, how's it going?" we acknowledge a person we recognize. By not speaking we risk being perceived as arrogant or insensitive.

4. **We communicate to develop relationships.** Not only do we get to know others through our communication with them, but more important, we develop relationships with them—relationships that grow and deepen or stagnate and wither away. We discuss how relationships begin and develop in Chapter 8, "Communicating in Relationships."

5. **We communicate to exchange information.** Some information we get through observation, some through reading, some through television, and a great deal through direct communication with others. Whether we are trying to decide how warmly to dress or whom to vote for in the next presidential election, all of us have countless exchanges that involve sending and receiving information. We discuss communication as information exchange in Chapter 7, "Conversations"; Chapter 10, "Participating in Small Groups"; and Chapter 17, "Informative Speaking."

6. **We communicate to influence others.** It is doubtful whether a day goes by in which you don't engage in such behavior as trying to convince your friends to go to a particular restaurant or support a political candidate, persuade your spouse to quit smoking, or (an old favorite) convince an instructor to change your course grade. We discuss the role of influencing others in Chapter 11, "Leadership in Groups" and Chapter 18, "Persuasive Speaking."

OBSERVE AND ANALYZE

Communication Functions

Keep a log of the various communication episodes you engage in today. Tonight, categorize each episode according to which of the six functions it served. Each episode may serve more than one function. Were you surprised by the variety of communication you engaged in even in such a relatively short period?

Communication Principles

Now that we have seen the elements that comprise the communication process and the functions it serves, we can turn to the principles that guide our communication. Six principles that affect our ability to communicate effectively are (1) communication has purpose, (2) communication is continuous, (3) communication messages vary in conscious encoding, (4) communication is relational, (5) communication has ethical implications, and (6) communication is learned.

Communication Has Purpose

When people communicate with one another, they have a purpose for doing so. As Kathy Kellermann, a leading researcher on interpersonal contexts, puts it, all communication is goal-directed whether or not the purpose is conscious (Kellerman 1992, p. 288). The purpose of a given transaction may be serious or trivial, but one way to evaluate the success of the communication is to ask whether it has achieved its purpose. When Beth calls Leah to ask whether she'd like to join her for lunch to discuss a project they are working on, her purpose may be to resolve a misunderstanding, to encourage Leah to work more closely with her, or simply to establish a cordial atmosphere. When Kareem shares statistics he has found with other members of student government to show the extent of drug abuse on campuses, his purpose may be to contribute information to a group discussion or to plead a case for confronting the problem of drug abuse. Depending on the speaker's purpose, even an apparently successful transaction

Frank and Ernest

Frank & Ernest reprinted by permission of NEA, Inc.

may fail to achieve its goal. And of course, different purposes call for different communication strategies.

Speakers may not always be aware of their purpose. For instance, when Jamal passes Tony on the street and says lightly, "Tony—what's happening?" Jamal probably doesn't consciously think, "Tony's an acquaintance and I want him to understand that I see him and consider him worth recognizing." In this case the social obligation to recognize Tony is met spontaneously with the first acceptable expression that comes to Jamal's mind. Regardless of whether Jamal consciously thinks about the purpose, it still motivates his behavior. In this case Jamal will have achieved his goal if Tony responds with an equally casual greeting.

Communication Is Continuous

Because communication is nonverbal as well as verbal, we are always sending behavioral messages from which others draw inferences or meaning. Even silence or absence are communication behaviors if another person infers meaning from them. Why? Because your nonverbal behavior represents reactions to your environment and to the people around you. If you are cold, you shiver; if you are hot or nervous, you perspire; if you are bored, happy, or confused, your face or body language will probably show it. As skilled communicators, we need to be aware of the messages, whether explicit or implicit, we are constantly sending to others.

Communication Messages Vary in Conscious Encoding

As we discussed earlier in this chapter, sharing meanings with another person involves encoding messages into verbal and nonverbal symbols. This encoding process may occur spontaneously, may be based on a "script" that you have learned or rehearsed, or may be carefully considered based on your understanding of the situation in which you find yourself (Reardon 1987, pp. 11–12).

For each of us there are times when our communication reflects a spontaneous expression of emotion. When this happens, our messages are encoded without much conscious thought. For example, when you burn your finger, you may blurt out "Ouch!" When something goes right, you may break out in a broad smile.

At other times, however, our communication is "scripted." R. P. Abelson (1976) defines a **script** as a "highly stylized sequence of typical events in a well understood situation" (p. 33). Thus, in some communication episodes we use conversational phrases that we have learned from our past encounters and judge to be appropriate to the present situation. To use scripted reactions effectively, we learn or practice them until they become automatic. Many of these scripts are learned in childhood. For example, when you want the sugar bowl but cannot reach it, you may say "Please pass the sugar," followed by "Thank you" when someone complies. This conversational sequence comes from your "table manners script," which you may have had drilled into you at home. Scripts enable us to use messages that are appropriate to the situation and are likely to increase our communication effectiveness. Because scripts are based on past experiences, many are culturally bound; that is, they are appropriate for a particular relationship in a certain situation within a specific culture. One goal of this text is to acquaint you with general scripts (or skills) that can be adapted for use in your communication encounters across a variety of relationships, situations, and cultures.

Messages may also be carefully constructed to meet the particular situation. Constructed messages are those that we encode at the moment to respond to the situation for which our known scripts are inadequate. These messages help us communicate both effectively and appropriately.

Effective public speakers know when to depart from their prepared script to respond creatively to audiences.

Creatively constructed responses are perhaps the ideal communication vehicle, especially in public-speaking settings. When you are able to both envision what you want to say and construct how you say it, you are likely to form messages through which your intended meaning can be shared. Another goal of this text is to help you become so familiar with a variety of message-forming skills that you can use them to construct effective and appropriate messages.

Communication Is Relational

Saying that communication is relational means that in any communication setting people not only share content meaning, they are also negotiating their relationship. For instance, when Laura says to Jennie "I've remembered to bring the map," she is not only reporting information; through the way she says it, she may also be communicating "You can always depend on me" or "I am superior to you—if it weren't for me we'd be missing an important document for our trip."

Two aspects of relationships can be negotiated during an interaction. One aspect is the affect (love to hate) present in the relationship. For instance, when José says "Hal, good to see you," the nonverbal behavior that accompanies the words may show Hal whether José is genuinely happy to see him (positive affect) or not. For instance, if José smiles, has a sincere sound to his voice, looks Hal in the eye, and perhaps pats him on the back or shakes hands firmly, then Hal will recognize the signs of affection. If, on the other hand, José speaks quickly, with no vocal inflection and a deadpan facial expression, Hal will perceive the comment as simply meeting some social expectation.

Another aspect of the relational nature of communication seeks to define who's in control (Watzlawick, Beavin, and Jackson 1967, p. 51). Thus, when Tom says to Sue, "I know you're concerned about the budget, but I'll see to it that we have money to cover everything," he can, through his words and the sound of his voice, be saying that he is "in charge" of finances—that he is in control. How Sue responds to Tom determines the true nature of the relationship. The control aspect of relationships can be viewed as complementary or symmetrical.

In a complementary relationship one person lets the other define who is to have greater power. Thus, the communication messages of one person may assert dominance while the communication messages of the other person accepts the assertion. In some cases the relationship is clarified in part by the nature of the context. For instance, in traditional American businesses most boss-employee relationships are complementary, with the boss in the control position. Likewise, most public-speaking relationships are complementary. People in the audience have come to hear what the speaker has to say and in so doing often consider the speaker's information as authoritative.

In a symmetrical relationship people do not "agree" about who is in control. As one person shows a need to take control, the other challenges the person's right and asserts his or her own power; or as one person abdicates power,

© Cable News Network, Inc.

Who's in control? Power in relationships is influenced by both verbal and nonverbal messages.

the other refuses to assume it. For example, Tom may say, "I think we need to cut back on credit card expenses for a couple of months," to which Sue may respond, "No way! I need a new suit for work, the car needs new tires, and you promised we could replace the couch." Here both people are asserting control.

Relational control is not negotiated in a single exchange, but is determined through many message exchanges over time. The interaction of communication messages, as shown through both language and nonverbal behavior, defines and clarifies the complementary or symmetrical nature of people's relationships. In complementary relationships open conflict is less prevalent than in symmetrical ones, but in symmetrical relationships power is more likely to be evenly shared.

Communication Has Ethical Implications

In encounters, we choose whether or not we will communicate ethically. **Ethics** are a set of moral principles that may be held by a society, a group, or an individual. For purposes of simplicity, in this section and throughout the book we will use the words *ethics* and *morals* interchangeably because there is not a *clear* differentiation between the two terms (Jaksa and Pritchard 1994, p. 4). Ethical principles are high standards that define honest and honorable methods and outcomes when dealing with others according to a particular moral code. For example, people who belong to animal rights groups believe it is immoral to use animals for research purposes. So for them it is unethical to buy cosmetic products that have been developed through animal testing.

Anyone discovered engaging in what a group believes to be immoral behavior is likely to be admonished by that society or group through social means. Your personal ethic is based on your belief and acceptance of what is considered moral by the communities or groups with which you most closely identify. So, when you behave ethically, you voluntarily act in a manner that complies with expected behavior. Why do people internalize morals and develop a personal ethic? Because most of us regard ourselves as accountable for our conduct, and even to some extent for our attitudes and character, and blame ourselves when we fall short of these ideal principles (Pritchard 1991, p. 39).

When we communicate, we cannot avoid making choices with ethical implications. To understand how our ethical standards influence our communication, we must recognize the ethical principles guiding our behavior. At various places in this text we will discuss a variety of ethical principles for interpersonal communication. Some of these principles are drawn from what is commonly accepted to be ethical behavior in the United States of America. Some of them come from what experts tell us will lead to trust and promote healthy relationships. As we discuss ethics, we will note where standards differ across cultures and between men and women and how these differences lead to alternative ethics.

Although people tend to cast discussion of ethics in either-or terms (*either* it is ethical *or* it is not), in most situations and with most behavioral choices we face, the question is *how* ethical a behavior is. In this book you will be asked to think about and discuss various ethical dilemmas. We will at times also look at ethical issues in terms of fairness, consideration, caring, and the like.

Communication Is Learned

Because communication appears to be a natural, inborn, unchangeable behavior, we seldom try to improve our skills however inadequate they may be. But communication is learned. Thus, throughout this text we will identify interpersonal, group, and public-speaking skills that will be valuable to you in all walks of life. In this next section we look at how you go about learning and improving your skills.

Becoming a Competent Communicator

Communication competence is the impression that communicative behavior is appropriate and effective in a given situation (Spitzberg 1997, p. 379). Communication is **effective** when it achieves its goals; it is **appropriate** when it conforms to what is expected in a situation. We create the perception that we are competent communicators through the verbal messages we send and the non-verbal behaviors that accompany them.

Since communication is at the heart of how we relate to one another, one of your goals in this course will be to learn those skills that will increase the likelihood that others will view you as competent. In the Spotlight on Scholarship that follows, we feature Brian Spitzberg on Communication Competence. Spitzberg believes that perceptions of competence depend in part on personal motivation, knowledge, and skills (Spitzberg 1997, pp. 381–386).

SPOTLIGHT ON SCHOLARSHIP

Brian Spitzberg, Professor of Communication at San Diego State University, on Communication Competence

Although Brian Spitzberg has made many contributions to our understanding of interpersonal communication, he is best known for his work in interpersonal communication competence. This interest in competence began when he was in graduate school at the University of Southern California. For an interpersonal communication seminar assignment he read the research that had been done on interpersonal competence. What struck him was that the research conclusions went in different directions. Some researchers treated competence as if it were a personality trait (some people had it, some didn't); others saw it as specific behaviors or a skill set that one could practice and apply in all settings. Spitzberg believed the time was ripe for someone to synthesize these perspectives into a comprehensive theory of competence. His final paper for the seminar was his first effort at trying to construct a competence theory.

Today the model of interpersonal communication competence that Spitzberg has formulated guides most of our thinking and research in this area. His theory views competence neither as a trait nor as a set of behaviors. Rather, he strongly emphasizes that interpersonal communication competence is a *perception* that individuals have about themselves or others. If competence is a perception, it follows that your perception of your interpersonal communication competence or that of your relationship partner would affect how you feel about that relationship. It seems reasonable to believe that people are more likely to be satisfied in a relationship when they perceive themselves and the other person as competent. According to Spitzberg, we make these competence judgments based on how each of us acts when we talk together. But what determines how we act in a particular conversation?

As Spitzberg was trying to organize his thinking about competence, he was taking another course in which he became acquainted with theories of dramatic acting that held that an actor's performance depends on the actor's motivation, knowledge of the script, and acting skills. He found that these same variables could be applied to communication competence.

Spitzberg's theory suggests that these three variables—motivation, knowledge, and skill—can be combined with context variables to explain our actions. How we behave in a conversation depends, first, on how personally *motivated* we are to have the conversation; second, on how personally *knowledgeable* we are about what behavior is appropriate in situations like this; and third, on how personally *skilled* we are at actually using the appropriate behaviors during the conversation. In addition, Spitzberg's theory suggests that context variables such as the ones discussed in this chapter also affect how we choose to act in a conversation and the perceptions of competence that they create.

Although Spitzberg formed most of these ideas while he was still in graduate school, he and others have spent the last fifteen years refining the theory, conducting programs of research based on his theory, and measuring the theory's effectiveness. The research has fleshed out parts of the theory and provided evidence of the theory's usefulness. As with the scientific study of any phenomenon, much of the hard work has been to develop ways of measuring the variables. Over the years Spitzberg has developed about a dozen specific instruments to measure parts of the theory. One of these measures, the Conversational Skills Rating Scale, has been adopted as the standard measure of interpersonal communication skills by the Speech Communication Association (a leading national organization of communication scholars, teachers, and practitioners).

Currently, Spitzberg teaches undergraduate courses in conflict management, research methods, and relational communication and graduate courses in communication competence and his latest research interest, the role communication incompetence plays in abusive and other dysfunctional relationships. This "dark side of communication" (such as how jealousy affects a relationship) has been the subject of a recent book.

Whether the situation is a first date or a job interview, a conflict with a roommate or an intimate discussion of your feelings, Spitzberg believes it is important that others perceive you to be competent. By understanding what leads to communication competence, you can work to develop your motivation, knowledge, and skills and increase the chances that you will be perceived as competent. In addition to the numerous articles that Spitzberg has published based on the results of his work, he has coauthored two books on interpersonal communication competence with William Cupach. For a list of some of Spitzberg's major publications, see the References at the end of this book.

First, as communicator motivation increases, communicator competence increases. That is, perceived competence depends in part on how much a person wants to make a good impression and communicate effectively. People are likely to be more motivated if they are confident and if they see potential rewards. Suppose Annette has the chance to give a speech. If she has confidence in her ability to speak effectively or if she thinks it is likely that her speech will achieve her goal, then her motivation to give the speech will be high.

Second, as communicator knowledge increases, communicator competence increases. In addition to being motivated, people also need knowledge about communication to be effective. The more people understand how to behave in a given situation, the more likely they are to be perceived as competent. We gain knowledge about how to interact by observing what others do, by asking others how we should behave, by engaging in formal study, and by learning through trial and error. For instance, Annette may be highly motivated to be a competent speaker, but she must also know how to prepare and present her speech in a way that will be effective. As our knowledge and understanding of interpersonal, group, and public-speaking skills increase, the likelihood that others will see us as competent is likely to increase as well.

Third, as communicator skill increases, communicator competence increases. People who are motivated to be effective and who have knowledge about communication must still act in ways that are consistent with their communication knowledge. Skills are goal-oriented actions or action sequences that we can master and repeat in appropriate situations. The more skills you have, the more likely you are to be able to structure your messages to be effective and appropriate. For instance, Annette must not only know how to prepare and deliver her speech, she must also be able to do so in front of the actual audience. The more practice she has had in using specific speaking skills, the more likely it is that she will be able to draw on these skills in real situations.

The combination of our motivation, knowledge, and skills leads us to perform confidently in our encounters with others. Based on how we perform, not only do we judge our own competence but our competence is also judged by others. The rest of this book is aimed at helping you increase the likelihood that you will be perceived as competent. In the pages that follow you will learn about theories of interpersonal, group, and public speaking that can increase your knowledge and your motivation. You will also learn how to perform specific skills, and you will be provided with opportunities to practice them. Through this practice, you can increase the likelihood that you can actually perform these skills.

As communication motivation, knowledge, and skill increase, communicator competence increases.

In the remainder of this book we will be discussing the development of communication skills in several communication settings and recommending that you write goal statements for improvement.

Communication Settings

In this book you will be introduced to skills that you can choose from to help you achieve communication competence in interpersonal conversation, problem-solving groups, and public-speaking settings.

Interpersonal communication involves interacting with one other person or in a small, informal aggregate of people. Talking to a friend on campus, chatting on the phone with a classmate about an upcoming test, arguing the merits of a movie with friends, soothing an intimate friend who has been jilted, discussing strategies for accomplishing tasks at work, interviewing for a job, and planning the future with a loved one are all forms of interpersonal communication.

Interpersonal communication focuses on listening and responding empathically, sharing personal information, holding effective conversations, and developing, maintaining, or improving relationships.

Problem-solving groups involve two or more people communicating with one another, in public or in private, to solve a problem or to arrive at a decision. For many of us, this kind of communication takes place in meetings.

Problem-solving group communication focuses on group interaction, problem solving and decision making, and leadership. Group communication is not a separate, unrelated activity, but one that builds on the foundation of interpersonal communication skills.

Public speaking means preparing and delivering relatively formal messages to audiences in a public setting. All the variables of communication are present in this one-to-many situation, but their use in public speaking differs greatly from their use in the other situations.

Public speaking involves determining goals, gathering and evaluating material, organizing and developing material, adapting material to a specific audience, and presenting the speech, as well as variations in procedure for information exchange and persuasion.

If you are like most people, you already make conscious or unconscious use of some of these skills that are necessary to function competently, whereas others are not currently part of your repertoire. Regardless of how accomplished you already are, careful study and practice can enhance your competence and enable you to better achieve your goals.

Developing Written Goal Statements

To get the most from this course, we suggest that you set personal goals to improve specific skills in your own interpersonal, group, and public communication repertoire by writing down formal communication goal statements.

Why written goal statements? A familiar saying goes, "The road to hell is paved with good intentions." Regardless of how serious you are about changing some aspect of your communication, bringing about changes in behavior takes time and effort. Writing specific goals makes it more likely that your good intentions to improve don't get lost in the busyness of your life.

Before you can write a goal statement, you must first analyze your current communication skills repertoire. We recommend that after you read each chapter and practice the skills described, you select one or two skills to work on. Then write down your goal statement in four parts.

1. **Describe the problem.** Setting a goal begins by analyzing a problem situation and determining what skills might help you the most. In this first part, then, describe specific circumstances in which you feel the skills of the chapter could help you. For example: "*Problem:* My boss consistently gives all the interesting tasks to coworkers, but I haven't spoken up because I'm unsure about my ability to describe my feelings."

2. **Describe the specific goal.** A goal is specific if it is measurable and you know when you have achieved it. For example, to deal with the problem just described, you might write, "*Goal:* To describe my feelings about task assignments to my boss."

3. **Outline a specific procedure for reaching the goal.** To develop a plan for reaching your goal, first consult the chapter that covers the skill you wish to hone. Then translate the general steps recommended in the chapter so that they apply to your specific situation. This step is critical because successful behavioral change requires that you state your objective in terms of specific behaviors you can adopt or modify. For example: "*Procedure:* I will practice the steps of describing feelings. (1) I will identify the specific feeling I am experiencing. (2) I will encode the emotion I am feeling accurately. (3) I will include what has triggered the feeling. (4) I will own the feeling as mine. (5) I will then put that procedure into operation when I am talking with my boss."

4. **Devise a method of determining when the goal has been reached.** Since a good goal is measurable, the fourth part of your goal-setting effort is to determine your minimum requirements for knowing when you have achieved a given goal. For example: "*Test of Achieving Goal:* This goal will be considered achieved when I have described my feelings to my boss on the next occasion when his behavior excludes me."

Once you have completed all four parts of this goal-setting process, you may want to have another person witness your commitment and serve as a consultant, coach, and support person. This gives you someone to talk to about your progress. A good choice would be someone from this class because he or she is in an excellent position to understand and help. (Also, perhaps you can reciprocate with your support for his or her goal statements in return.)

Problem: When I get up to speak in class or in the student senate, I often find myself burying my head in my notes or looking at the ceiling or walls.

Goal: To look at people more directly when I'm giving a speech.

Procedure: I will take the time to practice oral presentations aloud in my room. (1) I will stand up just as I do in class. (2) I will pretend various objects in the room are people, and I will consciously attempt to look at those objects as I am talking. (3) In giving a speech, I will try to be aware of when I am looking at my audience and when I am not.

Test of Achieving Goal: This goal will be considered achieved when I am maintaining eye contact with my audience most of the time.

Figure 1.2
Communication improvement plan.

At the end of each section, you will be challenged to develop a goal statement related to the material presented. Figure 1.2 provides another example of a communication improvement plan, this one relating to a public-speaking problem.

Summary

We have defined communication as the process of sharing meaning, whether the context is informal conversation, group interaction, or public speaking.

The elements of the communication process are context, participants, messages, channels, noise, and feedback.

Communication serves many functions. People communicate to meet needs, to enhance and maintain a sense of self, to fulfill social obligations, to develop relationships, to exchange information, and to influence others.

Our communication is guided by at least six principles. First, communication is purposeful. Second, interpersonal communication is continuous. Third, interpersonal communication messages vary in degree of conscious encoding. Messages may be spontaneous, scripted, or constructed. Fourth, interpersonal communication is relational, defining the power and affection between people. Relational definitions can be complementary or symmetrical. Fifth, communication has ethical implications. Sixth, and most important, interpersonal communication is learned.

Communication competence is the degree to which you and others perceive your communication as effective and appropriate. These perceptions depend in part on your personal motivation, knowledge, and skills.

Communication competence comes from learning to use skills effectively in interpersonal conversation, problem-solving groups, and public speaking. Since skills can be learned, developed, and improved, you can help enhance your learning this term by writing goal statements to systematically improve your skill repertoire.

OBJECTIVES

After you have read this chapter, you should be able to answer the following questions:

- What is perception?

- How does the mind select, organize, and interpret information?

- What is the self-concept, and how is it formed?

- What is self-esteem, and how is it developed?

- How do our self-concept and self-esteem affect our communication with others?

- What affects how accurately we perceive others?

- What are some methods for improving the accuracy of social perception?

2

Perception of Self and Others

As was traditional at State U., all new students were invited to an orientation party in the Black and Red Grill. This was Pat's first chance to meet many of the new transfer students. As people were chatting before the formal orientation began, Pat's attention was drawn to a person on the opposite side of the room whose eyes sparkled and lips parted in a welcoming style. While pretending to make small talk with others, Pat slowly maneuvered across the room to talk with this person.

Without rereading the scene just described, answer the following question: Is the person maneuvering across the room a man or a woman? Although the passage does not tell you, you may well have answered the question based on your perception of male or female behavior.

In this chapter we consider some basic concepts of sensory perception, how our perceptions of ourselves are formed and changed, how we perceive others, and how we can increase the accuracy of both our self-perception and our perceptions of others.

Sensory Perception

Perception is the process of selectively attending to sensory information and assigning meaning to it. Your brain selects information, organizes the information, and interprets and evaluates it.

Attention and Selection

Although we are subject to a constant barrage of sensory stimuli, we focus attention on relatively little of it. How we choose depends in part on our needs, interests, and expectations.

Needs. We are likely to pay attention to information that meets our biological and psychological needs. If you go to the grocery store when you're hungry (having a need for food), you are likely to be aware of far more that is available than if you've just eaten. (This is why those on a tight budget or on a diet should avoid food shopping on an empty stomach.)

Interests. We are likely to pay attention to information that pertains to our interests. For instance, you may not even recognize that music is playing in the background until you find yourself suddenly listening to some "old favorite." Similarly, when we're really interested in a person, we are more likely to pay attention to what that person is saying.

Expectations. Finally, we are likely to ignore information that violates our expectations. Take a moment to read the phrases in the triangles in Figure 2.1.

Figure 2.1
A sensory test of expectation.

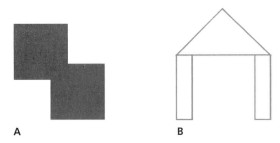

Figure 2.2
Principle of simplicity.

If you have never seen these triangles, you probably read "Paris in the springtime," "Once in a lifetime," and "Bird in the hand." But if you reexamine the words, you will see that what you perceived was not exactly what is written. Do you now see the repeated words? It's easy to miss the repeated word because we don't *expect* to see the word repeated. So, too, our expectations cause us to focus on or miss information that relates to our perceptions of ourselves and others.

Not only is our perception shaped by the stimuli we select to attend to, but it is also affected by the manner in which we organize those stimuli.

Organization of Stimuli

In order to organize stimuli, our brains are likely to follow principles of simplicity, pattern, proximity, and good form.

Simplicity.   One way to organize information is to seek ways to simplify it. Consider Figure 2.2.

Because of your need to simplify, you probably perceive A as overlapping squares rather than as a single eight-sided figure, and the shape in B as a triangle on legs or as a covered bridge. In other words, you are simplifying visual information into specific shapes that have meaning to you. So, too, we simplify complex data to form perceptions of others. Based on a quick perusal of someone's dress, stance, or facial expression, we may see her as "a successful businessperson," "a flight attendant," or "a soccer mom."

Pattern.   A second way to organize an abundance of information is to find familiar patterns. Look at Figure 2.3. Notice how you seek patterns to get meaning.

A   B   C

Figure 2.3
Principle of pattern.

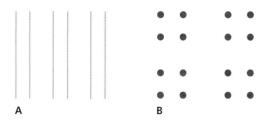

Figure 2.4
Principle of proximity.

In A, you probably perceive sets of horizontal parallel lines with the outer lines composed of "circles" and the inner lines of "dots." In B, you are likely to organize the figure by the shapes of the objects and perceive sets of vertical lines: circles, triangles, squares, and rectangles. In C, you are likely to organize the figure of twenty-five circles as an X formed by the filled-in circles. Why? Because your mind is looking for some organizational pattern to make sense out of the stimuli.

So, too, in dealing with people we seek patterns. For example, when you see a crowd of people, you may group them by gender (you may see them as groups of men and women), you may group them by age (you may see them as groups of children, adults, and elderly), or you may group them in some other way.

Proximity. A third way of organizing an abundance of information is to consider proximity—nearness in place, time, order, or occurrence. Two examples of visual proximity are shown in Figure 2.4. In A, you are likely to group the vertical lines as three sets of paired lines. In B, you will probably group the circles as four sets of four circles each. In these examples, your mind organizes the stimuli and groups those that are proximate.

We use proximity to organize our perception of people, too. For example, if you walk into a half-empty movie theater and see people sitting right next to each other, you will see them as groups distinct from other groups because they are nearer to each other than they are to some others.

Good form. A fourth way to organize information is to add information so that the result fits our experiences of good form. That is, we will organize stimuli to correspond to patterns we know, even if the stimuli we are attending to only roughly correspond to those patterns. For example, even if a visual stimulus has a gap in it, we are likely to see it as a closed figure. Look at Figure 2.5.

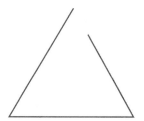

Figure 2.5
Principle of good form.

Did you organize the three lines and perceive them as a triangle, even though in good form a triangle is a closed figure? This principle explains why you may read a neon sign correctly although a portion is burned out, or why you may finish a sentence correctly even when the speaker leaves out a word.

Interpretation of Stimuli

As the brain selects and organizes the information it receives from the senses, it also **interprets** the information by assigning meaning to it. Look at the three sets of numbers below. What do you make of them?

A. 631 7348

B. 285 37 5632

C. 4632 7364 2596 2174

In each of these sets, your mind looked for clues to give meaning to the numbers. Since you use this pattern of numbers every day, there's a high probability of your interpreting A as a telephone number. How about B? This set may have been more of a puzzle to you. But there's a pretty good chance that you saw the set as a Social Security or ID number. And C? This set may have baffled you. But people who shop frequently may well have interpreted the set as a credit card number. Do you have a VISA or MasterCard? Take a look.

Although people believe strongly in the accuracy of their senses, their perceptions may well be inaccurate. The degree of inaccuracy varies from insignificant to profound, and communication based on inaccurate perception results in communication that can be misleading, unsuccessful, and even dangerous.

In the remainder of this chapter we will apply this basic information about perception to the study of perceptions of self and others.

Perception of Self: Self-Concept and Self-Esteem

Of the several related concepts that are used to describe our perception of ourselves, two that have direct impact on our communication are self-concept and self-esteem (Kolligan 1990, p. 273). In this section we will discuss self-concept, self-esteem, what determines whether these self-perceptions are accurate, and the part that these perceptions play when we communicate with others.

Forming and Maintaining a Self-Concept

Our **self-concept** is the idea or mental image that we have about our skills, our abilities, our knowledge, our competencies, and our personality. We form this mental image based on self-perception and on the reactions and responses of others.

PRACTICE IN CLASS

One Picture, Different Perceptions

Your instructor will ask for three volunteers, who will leave the classroom. One at a time, they will reenter the room and describe to the class a full-page magazine ad that the instructor has given them. On the basis of their descriptions, you are to form a mental picture of the people in the advertisement. As each volunteer describes the ad, write five adjectives about the person or persons in the picture. When all three have finished, your instructor will show you the ad.

a. What were the differences among the three descriptions?

b. Which of the three descriptions helped you form the most accurate picture? How did your image differ from the actual picture? How can you account for the differences?

c. Now that you have seen the picture, again write five adjectives about the person or persons in the picture. Did your five adjectives change after you actually saw the picture? If so, how and why?

Self-perception. We form impressions about ourselves partly from what we see. We look at a recent photograph and make judgments about our physical shape, dress, and facial expression. If we like what we see, we may feel good about ourselves. If we don't like what we see, we may try to change. Perhaps we will go on a diet, buy some new clothes, get our hair styled differently, or begin jogging. If we don't like what we see and are unable or unwilling to change, we may begin to develop negative feelings about ourselves.

Our self-perception may also result from our reactions to our experiences. Through experience, we learn what we are good at and what we like. If you can strike up conversations with strangers and get them to talk with you without causing yourself undue anxiety, you will probably perceive yourself as friendly, engaging, or interesting to talk with.

Interestingly, the first experience we have tends to have a greater effect in shaping our self-image than later ones (Centi 1981). For instance, teenagers who are rejected in their first effort at getting a date may become more reluctant to risk asking people out in the future. Regardless of the outcome of a single experience, if additional experiences produce results similar to the first experience, the initial perception will be strengthened.

In general, then, the more positive our response to the experiences we have—whether as a cook, lover, decision maker, student, worker, or parent—the more positive our self-image around that role becomes. Likewise, the greater the number of negative interpretations we make, the more negative is our self-concept in that role.

Reactions and responses of others. In addition to our self-perceptions, our self-concept is formed and maintained by how others react and respond to us. For example, if during a brainstorming session at work one of your coworkers tells you, "You're really a creative thinker," you may decide that this comment fits your image of who you are. Such comments are especially powerful in affecting your self-perception if you respect the person making the comment. The power of such comments is increased when the praise is immediate rather than delayed (Hattie 1992, p. 251). Thus, immediate responses from people we respect serve to validate, reinforce, or alter our perception of who and what we are.

Because our self-concepts begin to form early in life, information we receive from our families strongly shapes our self-concept (Demo 1987). One major responsibility of family members is to talk and act in ways that will help develop accurate and strong self-concepts in other family members. For example, the mom who says "Roberto, your room looks very neat; you are very organized" or the brother who comments "Kisha, lending Tomika five dollars really helped her out; you are very generous" are helping Roberto and Kisha to realize important parts of their personalities.

Unfortunately, in many families members damage each other's self-image and especially the developing self-concepts of children. Blaming, name-calling, and repeatedly pointing out another's shortcomings are particularly damaging.

UNDERSTAND YOURSELF

Self-Perceptions

How do you see yourself? On a blank sheet of paper, list the skills, abilities, knowledge, competencies, and personality characteristics that describe how you see yourself. To generate this list, try completing the following sentences: "I am skilled at . . . ," "I have the ability to . . . ," "I know things about . . . ," "I am competent at doing . . . ," and "One part of my personality is that I am. . . ." Complete these sentences over and over again, listing as many characteristics in each category as you can think of. What you have developed is an inventory of your self-concept.

When Dad shouts, "Terry, you are so stupid! If you had only stopped to think, this wouldn't have happened," he is damaging Terry's belief in his own intelligence. When big sister teases, "Hey, Dumbo, how many times do I have to tell you, you're too clumsy to be a ballet dancer," she is undermining her younger sister's perception of her gracefulness.

Developing and Maintaining Self-Esteem

Our **self-esteem** is our overall evaluation of our competence and personal worthiness (Mruk 1995, p. 21); it is our positive or negative evaluation of our self-concept. Our evaluation of our personal worthiness is rooted in our values and develops over time as a result of our experiences. As Mruk points out, self-esteem is not just how well or poorly we do things (self-concept), but the importance or value we place on what we do well or poorly. For instance, as part of his self-concept Fred believes that he is physically strong. But if he doesn't believe that physical strength is a worthwhile characteristic to have, and if he also believes that about the other characteristics he possesses, then he will not have high self-esteem. Mruk argues that it takes both the perception of having a characteristic and personally believing that the characteristic is of positive value to produce high self-esteem.

When we successfully use our skills, abilities, knowledge, or personality traits in worthwhile endeavors, we raise our self-esteem. When we are unsuccessful in using our skills, abilities, knowledge, competencies, or personality traits and/or when we use them in unworthy endeavors, we lower our self-esteem.

UNDERSTAND YOURSELF

Others' Perceptions

How do others see you? On a second sheet of paper, repeat the exercise you did before, only this time use the following statements: "Other people believe that I am skilled at . . . ," "Other people believe that I have the ability to . . . ," "Other people believe that I know things about . . . ," "Other people believe that I am competent at doing . . . ," and "One part of my personality is that other people believe that I am. . . ."

The feedback you get from your parents has an enormous influence on your self-concept and self-esteem.

Accuracy of Self-Concept and Self-Esteem

The reality or accuracy of our self-concept and self-esteem depends on the accuracy of our perceptions and how we process others' perceptions of us. Everyone experiences some success and failure and hears some praise and blame. If we attend more to successful experiences and positive responses, our self-concept may become overdeveloped and our self-esteem will become inflated. If, however, we perceive and dwell on negative experiences while giving little value to our positive experiences, or if we remember only the criticism we receive, our self-image may be poorly formed and we may have unduly low self-esteem. In neither case does our self-concept or self-esteem conform to reality.

The gap between our inaccurate self-perceptions and reality is called **incongruence** (Weiten 1995, p. 489). This incongruence is a problem because our perceptions of self are more likely to affect our behavior than our true abilities. For example, Sean may actually possess all the skills, abilities, knowledge, competencies, and personality characteristics for effective leadership, but if he doesn't perceive that he has these characteristics, he won't step forward when leadership is needed. Unfortunately, individuals tend to reinforce their self-perceptions by adjusting their behavior to conform with those perceptions. Therefore, people with high self-esteem tend to behave in ways that lead to more affirmation, while people with low self-esteem tend to act in ways that confirm the low esteem in which they hold themselves. The inaccuracy of the distorted picture of oneself becomes magnified through self-fulfilling prophecies and filtering messages.

Self-fulfilling prophecies. Self-fulfilling prophecies—events that happen as the result of being foretold, expected, or talked about—may be either self-created or other-imposed.

Self-created prophecies are those predictions you make about yourself. We often "talk ourselves into" success or failure. For example, Stefan sees himself as quite social and able to get to know people easily; he tells himself, "I'm going to have fun at the party tonight." As a result of his positive self-concept, he looks forward to encountering strangers and, just as he predicted, makes several new acquaintanceships and enjoys himself. Arthur, on the other hand, sees himself as unskilled in establishing new relationships; he tells himself, "I doubt I'll know anyone—I'm going to have a miserable time." Because he fears encountering strangers, he feels awkward about introducing himself and, just as he predicted, spends much of his time standing around alone and thinking about when he can leave.

Self-esteem has an important effect on the prophecies people make. For instance, people with positive self-esteem confidently prophesy that they can repeat successes; people with low self-esteem attribute their successes to luck and so prophesy that they will not repeat them (Hattie 1992, p. 253).

Other-imposed prophecies also affect your performance. For example, if a teacher tells Jon, "I can see that you have a terrific ability to remember details; I

How do you see yourself? A distorted self-concept can become a self-fulfilling prophecy.

know that you will be an outstanding member of the debate team," Jon is likely to believe this prophecy and will come to act in ways that are consistent with it. When teachers act as if their students are able, students "buy into" that expectation and succeed. Likewise, when they act as if students are not able, students may live "down" to these imposed prophecies. A lesson to be learned from this is that we should take care in what we say to others lest we place unnecessary limitations on them.

Filtering messages. A second way in which our self-perceptions can become increasingly distorted is through our filtering of what others say to us. Even though we may "hear" messages accurately (that is, our ears receive the messages and our brain records them), we do not listen to or perceive them equally. For example, suppose you prepare an agenda for your study group. Someone comments that you're a good organizer. If that is not part of your self-concept, you may not really hear the comment, you may ignore it, or you may reply, "Anyone could have done that—it was nothing special." On the other hand, if you think you are a good organizer, you will pay attention to the compliment and may even reinforce it by responding with something like, "Thanks, I've worked hard to learn to do this, but it was worth it. It comes in handy."

Changing self-concepts and self-esteem. Although self-concept and self-esteem are the basis for self-fulfilling prophesies and a filter we use for others' comments, at times others' comments will get past the filter and can begin to change the self-concept. Then, the newly changed self-perceptions begin to filter other concepts and are used as the basis of new self-created self-fulfilling prophesies. So, over the course of your life, your self-concept and self-esteem may change (Mruk 1995, p. 93).

The incredible growth of the self-help movement in the United States bears eloquent testimony to people's ability to work actively to develop self-perceptions that are congruent with their actual personal characteristics. For example, Alcoholics Anonymous and other twelve-step groups help members overcome inaccurate perceptions of self-worth by replacing self-conceptions such as "weak-willed" with more accurate self-descriptors.

In this book we consider many specific communication behaviors that are designed to increase your communication competence. As you begin to perfect and use these skills, you may receive positive responses to your behavior. If your self-esteem is low, these positive responses may change your self-concept and increase your self-esteem.

Presenting Ourselves

We also present our self-image and self-esteem to others through various roles we enact. A **role** is a pattern of learned behaviors that people use to meet the perceived demands of a particular context. For instance, during the course of a single day you may enact the roles of student, brother or sister, and salesclerk.

Roles that we enact may result from our own needs, relationships that we form, cultural expectations that are held for us, the groups we choose to be part of, and our own conscious decisions. For instance, if you are the oldest child in a large family, your parents may have cast you in a role that involves such functions as disciplinarian, brothers' and sisters' keeper, or housekeeper, depending on how they see family relationships. Or if your peers look on you as a "joker," you may go along by enacting your role, laughing and telling funny stories even though you really feel hurt or imposed on.

So, everyone enacts numerous roles each day. We may draw on different skills and attributes as we enact these roles. For instance, Samantha, who is perceived as a warm, quiet, sensitive person in her family group, may choose to enact the role of a boisterous "party animal" in a friendship group. With each new situation, we may test a role we know how to enact or we may decide to try to enact a new role.

The term **working self-concept** has been used to denote the specific aspects of one's identity that are activated by the role one is enacting at a particular time (Markus and Nurius 1986). The working self-concept changes as we change roles. "To some extent we become different people as we move from situation to situation" (Deaux, Dane, and Wrightsman 1993, p. 56).

The diversity of the roles we enact helps us to withstand stressful situations. For instance, if a person only enacted the role of student, he or she might be devastated by being forced to withdraw from school for a while. When that role of student ended, a large part of the person's self-concept would end as well. In contrast, a person who is the product of many roles is more protected from negative events. Thus, the person who also sees himself or herself as parent, friend, and salesclerk will have these roles (these parts of the self-concept) to identify with if he or she cannot be a student for a period of time.

Self-Concept, Self-Esteem, and Communication

Just as our self-concept and self-esteem affect how accurately we perceive ourselves, so too do they influence our communication by moderating competing internal messages in our self-talk and influencing our personal communication style.

1. **Our self-perceptions moderate competing internal messages.** When we are faced with a decision, we may be especially conscious of the different and often competing "voices" in our head. Listen to the conversation Corey had upon returning from a job interview.

   I think I made a pretty good impression on the personnel director—I mean, she talked with me for a long time. Well, she talked with me, but maybe she was just trying to be nice. After all, it was her job. No, she didn't have to spend that much time with me. And she really lit up when I talked about the internship I had at Federated. She said she was interested in my internship. But talking about it is not exactly telling me that it would make a difference in her view of me as a prospective employee.

   If Corey feels good about himself, he will probably conclude that the interviewer was sincere, and he'll feel good about the interview. If, on the other hand, he believes that he is unworthy, that he does not have the relevant skills and abilities to do a good job, he is more likely to "listen" to the negative voices in his head and conclude that he doesn't have a chance for the job.

2. **Our self-perception influences how we talk about ourselves with others.** If we feel good about ourselves, we're likely to communicate positively. For instance, people with strong self-concepts and higher self-esteem usually take credit for their successes by saying such things as "My suggestions helped the Kappa Xi Phi honorary service recruit new members, so I think I'm likely to be asked to run for president next year." Likewise, people with healthy self-perceptions are likely to defend their views even in the face of opposing arguments. For instance, when criticized Amber might say, "You

UNDERSTAND YOURSELF

Monitor Your Enacted Roles

For three days, record the various situations you experience. Describe the images you chose to project in each. At the conclusion of this three-day observation period, write an analysis of your self-monitoring. To what extent does your communication behavior differ and remain the same across situations? What factors in a situation seem to trigger certain behaviors in you? How satisfied are you with the images or "selves" that you displayed in each situation? Where were you most pleased? Least pleased?

**INFOTRAC
COLLEGE EDITION**

Some people believe that "the greater the discrepancy between a person's own assessment of his or her interpersonal style and the perception of others, the greater will be that individual's reported psychological stress."

What does research show? Using InfoTrac College Edition, look under the subject of *Self-evaluation; periodicals*. See

Amy VanBuren (1997), Awareness of interpersonal style and self-evaluation. *The Journal of Social Psychology*, 137, p. 429.

Can you find any additional related studies?

may not like my position, but I've thought this through carefully and believe that I have good reasons to support my views."

If we feel negatively about ourselves, we're likely to communicate negatively by downplaying our roles. For instance, Jan, who has low self-esteem, may comment to her friend David, "What I did probably wasn't that important to the company, so I don't deserve a raise and won't get one."

Why do some people put themselves down regardless of what they've done? If a person has low self-esteem, that person is likely to be unsure of the value of his or her contributions and expect others to view them negatively. As a result, perhaps, people with poor self-concepts or low self-esteem find it less painful to put themselves down than to hear the criticism of others. Thus, to preempt the likelihood that others will comment on their unworthiness, they do it first.

Cultural and Gender Differences

Culture influences perception and affects people's views of self. Most Americans share what is called the Western view of self—that the individual is an autonomous entity comprising distinct abilities, traits, motives, and values, and that these attributes cause behavior. Moreover, people with this Western view see the individual as the most basic social unit; to them, the notions of self-concept and self-esteem are built on the idea of independence from others and the value of discovering and expressing individual uniqueness.

Yet people in most of the rest of the world don't share this view. In Eastern cultures, where the family not the individual is the smallest social unit, the idea of self-concept is very different, as are the traits and behaviors that give rise to self-esteem. For instance, most Eastern (and Native American) cultures neither assume nor value independence. Rather, in these cultures the goal of human life is to maintain *interdependence* among individuals (Markus and Kitayama 1991, p. 19). To make this comparison more vivid, whereas Western culture espouses the maxim "It's the squeaky wheel that gets the grease," Eastern cultures, including Japanese, Chinese, and Australian, espouse the maxim "The nail that sticks up shall be hammered down."

In American culture, it seems important to socialize children away from helplessness and dependence in order to help them be more self-sufficient and independent. As a result, children come to value those personal characteristics that are associated with independence, deriving high self-esteem from them. In many other cultures, however, children are socialized toward greater dependence (Jordan 1991, p. 137). As a result, they develop higher self-esteem when they perceive themselves to be helpful, cooperative group members.

Likewise, in many societies men and women are socialized to view themselves differently and to value who they are based on whether their behavior corresponds to what is expected of their sex. If women are expected to be nurturing caregivers who attend to home and family life, then those women who perceive that they have the skills, abilities, knowledge, competencies, and personality characteristics needed to perform these jobs will have enriched self-concepts and high self-esteem. Women who do not have these attributes are likely to be less confident of who they are and to have lower self-esteem. In such societies, the more a person's self-concept includes those characteristics that are held to be "gender appropriate," the more likely the person is to have a rich self-concept and high self-esteem.

Perception of Others

When two people meet, their initial impressions of each other—based on physical characteristics and social behaviors, stereotyping, and emotional states—guide their behavior. As they interact, these perceptions will be reinforced, intensified, or changed.

Physical Characteristics and Social Behaviors

First impressions of people are often based on physical characteristics (facial features, height, weight, grooming, dress, and sound of voice) that help us to categorize them as friendly, courageous, intelligent, cool, or their opposites (Zebrowitz 1990, p. 44). For instance, in one study people assessed professional women dressed in jackets as more powerful than professional women dressed in other clothing (Temple and Loewen 1993, p. 345).

First impressions may also be based on a person's social behaviors. For instance, Sara, who has observed Gavin interrupting Yolanda, may consider him rude.

Women and men differ in the way they are likely to describe their perceptions of others. According to Leslie Zebrowitz (1990, p. 24), men and boys are more likely to describe others in terms of their abilities ("She writes well"), whereas women and girls are more likely to describe others in terms of their self-concepts ("She thinks she's a good writer"). Likewise, she sees gender differences in categorizing behaviors. Males' descriptions include more nonsocial activities ("She likes to fly model airplanes"), whereas females include more interpersonal interactions ("He likes to get together with his friends").

Such judgments of people are based on "implicit personality theories"—a set of assumptions people have developed about what physical characteristics and personality traits or behaviors are associated with one another (Deaux et al. 1993, p. 88).

Because your own implicit personality theory says that certain traits go together, you are likely to judge a person's other characteristics upon observing a single characteristic, trait, or behavior without further verification. This tendency is known as the **halo effect**. For instance, Heather sees Martina personally greeting and welcoming every person who arrives at the meeting. Heather's implicit personality theory correlates this behavior with warmth. She correlates warmth with goodness and goodness with honesty. As a result, she perceives that Martina is good and honest as well as warm.

In reality, Martina may be a con artist who uses her warmth to lure people into a false sense of trust. But if Martina is accused of stealing from the club treasury, Heather may leap to Martina's defense. Heather's action is based on a "positive halo."

We also use implicit personality theory to inaccurately impute bad characteristics. Unfortunately, as Hollman (1972) has found, negative information more strongly influences our impressions of others than does positive information. So, we are more likely to negatively halo than to positively halo.

Halo effects seem to occur most frequently under one or more of the following conditions: (1) when the perceiver is judging traits with which he or she has limited experience, (2) when the traits have strong moral overtones, and (3) when the perception is of a person that the perceiver knows well.

Given limited amounts of information, we tend to fill in details. This tendency leads to a second factor that affects social perception: stereotyping.

Stereotyping

Stereotypes are simplified and standardized perceptions—positive or negative—about the characteristics or expected behavior of members of an identifiable group (Deaux et al. 1993, p. 355). We are likely to develop generalized perceptions about any group we come in contact with. Subsequently, any number of perceptual cues—skin color, accent, style of dress, a religious medal, gray hair, or gender, for example—can lead us to project our generalized perception onto a specific individual.

Stereotyping contributes to perceptual inaccuracies by ignoring individual differences. For instance, if part of Dave's stereotype of personal injury lawyers is that they are unethical, then he will use this stereotype when he meets Denise, a highly principled woman who happens to be a successful personal injury lawyer. You may be able to think of instances in which you have been the victim of a stereotype based on your gender, age, ethnic heritage, social class, physical characteristics, or other qualities. If so, you know how hurtful the use of stereotypes can be.

If stereotypes lead to inaccurate perceptions and miscommunication, why do they persist? Stereotyping is a shortcut that enables us to confer order on the complex social world in which we interact (McCrae, Milne, and Bodenhausen 1994, p. 45). In addition, we believe that stereotypes are helpful (Deaux et al. 1993, p. 94). Although people may learn to go beyond a stereotype in forming opinions of individuals, stereotypes provide a "working hypothesis." That is, when we encounter a new person who we determine is from a particular race or culture, we can reduce our uncertainty by attributing the characteristics of our stereotype to the person. We relate to the person based on the stereotype until we get sufficient information to enable us to perceive the person as an individual (Jones 1990, p. 110).

As these examples suggest, stereotyping and prejudice go hand in hand. **Prejudice** is a negative attitude toward members of a group (Weiten 1995, p. 674). For instance, when Laura discovers that Wasif, a man she has just met, is a Muslim, she might stereotype him as a chauvinist. If she is a feminist, she may use this stereotype to prejudge him and assume that he will expect women to be subservient. If she acts on her prejudice, she may abruptly end her conversation with him. So without really having gotten to know Wasif, Laura may decide that she does not like him.

People are likely to maintain their stereotypes and prejudices even in the face of evidence that disproves them. Suppose that Lou, an older man, stereotypes all young men who wear earrings as unreliable. When Lou meets Phil, a young man with a double-pierced ear, Lou will presume that Phil is unreliable. If Phil demonstrates that he is a reliable fellow, Lou is likely to see Phil as an exception and continue to use his unaltered stereotype when he meets other earring-wearing men.

Racism, sexism, ageism, and other -isms are beliefs that the behaviors or characteristics of one group are inherently superior to those of other groups, thus giving the "superior" group the right to discriminate against the "inferior" group (Dovidio et al. 1996, p. 279). This discrimination may take the form of leaving more space between you and another person on a bus, on a plane, in a lounge, or at a counter in a restaurant—a space wider than the space you would leave if the person you were sitting next to were of your race, sex, age, or ability. Or discrimination may be telling jokes, laughing at jokes, or encouraging repetition of jokes that demean women. It may be ignoring the presence or the worth of another person's comments because that person is of another race, the opposite sex, older, or disabled. We may say, "But I didn't mean anything by what I did"; however, our behavior will be perceived negatively, and it will seriously harm our attempts to communicate.

Emotional States

A final factor that affects how accurately we perceive others is our emotional state at the time of the interaction. Based on the findings in his studies, Joseph Forgas (1991) has concluded that "there is a broad and pervasive tendency for people to perceive and interpret others in terms of their (own) feelings at the time" (p. 288). If, for example, you learn that you got the internship you applied for, your good mood brought on by your good fortune is likely to spill over so that you perceive other things and other people more positively than you might have under different circumstances. If, on the other hand, you receive a low grade on a paper you thought was well written, your perceptions of people around you are likely to be colored by your disappointment or anger over the grade.

Our emotions also cause us to engage in selective perceptions, ignoring inconsistent information. For instance, if Donna sees Nick as a man with whom

THINK CRITICALLY

Racist and Sexist Talk

Describe the last time you found yourself in a situation where someone told a racist or sexist joke or made a racist or sexist remark. How did you react? How did others present react? If you are dissatisfied with how you reacted, write a script for how you wish you had reacted.

Arturo Madrid on Social Perception

Arturo Madrid served as president of the Tomas Rivera Center, a national institute for policy studies on Hispanic issues. In this selection, Madrid describes the conflicting experiences of those who see themselves as different from what has stereotypically been described as "American." Experiencing oneself and being perceived as "other" and "invisible" are powerful determinants of one's self-concept and form a very special filter through which one communicates with others.

My name is Arturo Madrid. I am a citizen of the United States, as are my parents and as were my grandparents and my great-grandparents. My ancestors' presence in what is now the United States antedates Plymouth Rock, even without taking into account any American Indian heritage I might have.

I do not, however, fit those mental sets that define America and Americans. My physical appearance, my speech patterns, my name, my profession (a professor of Spanish) create a text that confuses the reader.

I am very clearly the *other*, if only your everyday, garden-variety domestic *other*. I've always known that I was the *other*, even before I knew the vocabulary or understood the significance of otherness.

Despite the operating myth of the day, school did not erase my *otherness*. The true test was not our speech, but rather our names and our appearance, for we would always have an accent, however perfect our pronunciation, however excellent our enunciation, however divine our diction. That accent would be heard in our pigmentation, our physiognomy, our names. We were, in short, the *other*.

Being the *other* is feeling different, it is awareness of being distinct, it is consciousness of being dissimilar. Otherness results in feeling excluded, closed out, precluded, even disdained and scorned.

Being the *other* involves a contradictory phenomenon. On the one hand, being the *other* frequently means being invisible. On the other hand, being the *other* sometimes involves sticking out like a sore thumb. What is she/he doing here?

If one is the *other*, one will inevitably be seen stereotypically; will be defined and limited by mental sets that may not bear much relation to existing realities.

There is sometimes a darker side to otherness as well. The *other* disturbs, disquiets, discomforts. It provokes distrust and suspicion. The *other* frightens, scares.

For some of us being the *other* is only annoying; for others it is debilitating; for still others it is damning. For the majority otherness is permanently sealed by physical appearance. For the rest otherness is betrayed by ways of being, speaking, or of doing.

The first half of my life I spent downplaying the significance and consequences of otherness. The second half has seen me wrestling to understand its complex and deeply ingrained realities; striving to fathom why otherness denies us a voice or visibility or validity in American society and its institutions; struggling to make otherness familiar, reasonable, even normal to my fellow Americans.

Excerpted from Arturo Madrid, "Diversity and Its Discontents," in Intercultural Communication: A Reader, *7th ed., eds. Larry A. Samovar and Richard E. Porter (Belmont, CA: Wadsworth, 1994), pp. 127–131. Reprinted by permission of Black Issues in Higher Education.*

she would like to develop a strong relationship, she will focus on the positive side of Nick's personality and tend to overlook or ignore the negative side that is apparent to others.

Our emotions may also affect our attributions (Forgas, Bower, and Moylan 1990, p. 809). **Attributions** are reasons we give for others' behavior. In addition to making judgments about people, we attempt to construct reasons why people behave as they do. According to attribution theory, what we determine—rightly or wrongly—to be the causes of others' behavior has a direct impact on our perceptions of them. For instance, suppose that a coworker with whom you had a noon luncheon appointment has not arrived by 12:20. If you like and respect your coworker, you are likely to attribute his lateness to something external: an important phone call at the last minute, the need to finish a job before lunch, or some accident that may have occurred. If you are not particularly fond of your coworker, you are likely to attribute his lateness to something internal: forgetfulness, inconsiderateness, or malicious intent. In either case, your causal attribution further affects your perception of the person.

Like prejudices, causal attributions may be so strong that they resist contrary evidence. If you don't particularly care for the person, when he does arrive and explains that he had an emergency long-distance phone call, you are likely to disbelieve the reason or discount the urgency of the call. Being aware of the human tendency toward such cognitive biases can help you correct your perceptions and thus improve your communication.

Cultural and Gender Differences

Members of the opposite sex or people from different cultures talking with each other are likely to experience difficulty sharing meaning because they approach the world from different perspectives. But you don't have to cross national borders to encounter different cultures. As we mentioned earlier, the United States contains many different cultures. Moreover, differences can be experienced across generations, regions, social classes, even neighborhoods, so the need for awareness and sensitivity in applying our communication skills doesn't depend on someone's being from another country or otherwise so markedly "different" from ourselves.

When we are confronted with strangers of the opposite sex, people from different cultures, or differently able people, we tend to see these differences as barriers to communication because they tend to create uncertainty. The more one person differs from another, the less either person is able to predict the behavior of the other. When people are uncertain about how another person will behave, they become anxious. Some people express their fear by withdrawing or becoming compliant; others mask their fear with aggressive behavior. Clearly, none of these behaviors improves communication. All of these cultural and gender differences argue for a greater need to confront our ignorance about what people are thinking, feeling, and valuing. In the final part of this chapter

How might stereotypes of age and gender prevent these people from being perceived as they actually are?

we focus on procedures that will enable us to improve our social perceptions of people regardless of their culture or gender.

Improving Social Perception

Because inaccuracies in perception are common and influence how we communicate, improving perceptual accuracy is an important first step in becoming a competent communicator. The following guidelines can aid you in constructing a more realistic impression of others as well as in assessing the validity of your own perceptions.

1. **Question the accuracy of your perceptions.** Questioning accuracy begins by saying, "I know what I think I saw, heard, tasted, smelled, or felt, but I could be wrong. What else could help me sort this out?" By accepting the possibility of error, you may be motivated to seek further verification. In situations where the accuracy of perception is important, take a few seconds to double-check. It will be worth the effort.

2. **Seek more information to verify perceptions.** If your perception has been based on only one or two pieces of information, try to collect further information before you allow yourself to form an impression so that you can increase the accuracy of your perceptions. At least note that your perception is tentative—that is, subject to change. You can then make a conscious effort to collect more data in order to determine whether the original perception is accurate.

   The best way to get information about people is to talk with them. Unfortunately, we tend to avoid people we don't know much about. It's OK to be unsure about how to treat someone from another culture or someone who is disabled. But rather than letting your uncertainty hold you back, ask the person for the information you need to be more comfortable.

3. **Realize that perceptions of people may need to be changed over time.** People often saddle themselves with perceptions that are based on old or incomplete information, yet find it easier to stick with a perception, even if it is wrong, than to change it. Willingness to change means making an effort to observe this person's behavior at other times without bias and being prepared to modify your perception if the person's behavior warrants it. It takes strength of character to say to yourself or others, "I was wrong." But communication based on outdated, inaccurate perceptions can be more costly than revising your perceptions.

TEST YOUR COMPETENCE

Factors Leading to Misperceptions of Others

For the following situation, list each of the factors discussed in this section that have contributed to the inaccuracy of the initial perception of the other person. Be able to defend your answers in class.

Amanda was depressed. Her daughter was having problems in school, she had just been informed that her work hours were being cut back, and her mother was facing possible surgery. On her way home from campus, she stopped at the dry cleaner to pick up her laundry. There was a new man working the counter. From looking at him, Amanda could tell he was quite old. She thought to herself that he could be a problem. When she requested her laundry, he asked to see her claim check. Because no one had ever asked her for a claim check before, Amanda told him, she had started throwing them away. "Well," the man firmly replied, "I'm not able to give you clothes without a claim check. It's store policy." After demanding to see the manager and being informed that she had left for the day, Amanda stormed out of the store. "I'll fix him," she fumed to herself. "It's just like an old man to act so rigidly!"

4. **Use perception checking to verify conclusions you've drawn.** A perception check is a verbal statement that reflects your own understanding of the meaning of another person's nonverbal cues. Perception checking calls for you to (1) watch the behavior of the other person; (2) ask yourself, "What does that behavior mean to me?"; and (3) put your interpretation of the behavior into words to verify whether your perception is accurate.

In each of the following examples, the final sentence is a perception check.

Vera comes walking into the room with a completely blank expression. She neither speaks to Ann nor acknowledges that she is in the room. Vera sits on the edge of the bed and stares into space. Ann says, "Vera, I get the feeling that something has happened to put you in a state of shock. Am I right? Is there something I can do?"

Ted, the company messenger, delivers a memo to Erin. As Erin reads the note, her eyes brighten and she breaks into a smile. Ted says, "Hey, Erin, you seem really pleased. Am I right?"

Cesar, speaking in short, precise sentences with a sharp tone of voice, gives Bill his day's assignment. Bill says, "From the sound of your voice, Cesar, I can't help but get the impression that you're upset with me. Are you?"

PRACTICE IN CLASS

Perception-Checking Role-Play

Working in groups of three, A and B should role-play a situation while C observes. During the conversation, A should intentionally give off various nonverbal cues to his or her feelings. B should use perception checking to determine if his or her perception of A's behavior is accurate. When they have finished, C should discuss the behaviors observed and analyze the effectiveness of B's perception checks. The exercise continues until each person in the group has a chance to be A, B, and C. After completing the exercise, the participants should discuss how the skill of perception checking affected the accuracy of the communication.

Perception checking brings the meaning that was received through nonverbal cues into the verbal realm, where it can be verified or corrected. For instance, when Bill says, "I can't help but get the impression that you're upset with me. Are you?" Cesar may say (1) "No, whatever gave you that impression?" in which case Bill can further describe the cues that he received; (2) "Yes, I am," in which case Bill can get Cesar to specify what has caused the feelings; or (3) "No, it's not you; it's just that three of my team members didn't show up for this shift." If Cesar is not upset with him, Bill can deal with what caused him to misinterpret Cesar's feelings; if Cesar is upset with him, Bill has the opportunity of changing the behavior that caused Cesar to be upset. Even though you may be correct most of the time in identifying another person's feelings, if you do not do a verbal perception check, you are still guessing what the other person is really feeling.

You will want to check your perceptions whenever the accuracy of your understanding is important (1) to your current communication, (2) to the relationship you have with the other person, or (3) to the conclusions you draw about that person. Most of us use this skill far too little, if at all.

Although perception checking may not always eliminate defensive behavior, its use can help you reduce the likelihood of misinterpreting another's nonverbal cues and thus the likelihood of defensiveness. As with most skills, to become competent you must practice.

SKILL BUILDERS   Perception Checking

Skill

Making a verbal statement that reflects your understanding of the meaning of another person's nonverbal cues.

Use

To clarify the meaning of non-verbal behavior.

Procedure

1. Watch the behavior of another. Describe the behavior to yourself or aloud.

2. Ask yourself: What does that behavior mean to me?

3. Put your interpretation of the nonverbal behavior into words to verify your perception.

Example

As Dale frowns while reading Paul's first draft of a memo, Paul says, "From the way you're frowning, I take it that you're not too pleased with the way I phrased the memo."

Summary

Perception is the process of gathering sensory information and assigning meaning to it. Our perceptions are a result of our selection, organization, and interpretation of sensory information. Inaccurate perceptions cause us to see the world not as it is but as we would like it to be.

Self-concept means the idea or mental image that you have about your skills, your abilities, your knowledge, your competencies, and your personality. Self-esteem is the degree to which you have a favorable impression of who you are. The inaccuracy of a distorted picture of oneself becomes magnified through self-fulfilling prophecies and filtering messages. Our self-concept and self-esteem moderate competing internal messages in our self-talk, influence our perception of others, influence our personal communication style, and affect how we present ourselves to others in the roles that we play.

Perception also plays an important role in forming impressions of others. Factors that are likely to influence our social perceptions are physical characteristics and social behaviors, stereotyping, and emotional states. Because research shows that the accuracy of people's perceptions and judgments varies considerably, your communication will be most successful if you do not rely entirely on your impressions to determine how another person feels or what that person is really like. You will improve (or at least better understand) your perceptions of others if you take into account physical characteristics and social behaviors, stereotyping, and emotional states.

You can learn to improve perception if you actively question the accuracy of your perceptions, seek more information to verify perceptions, talk with the people about whom you are forming perceptions, realize that perceptions of people need to change over time, and check perceptions verbally before you react.

Perception Checking

Write a well-phrased perception check for each of the following situations:

Franco comes home from the doctor's office with a pale face and slumped shoulders. Glancing at you with a forlorn look, he shrugs his shoulders.

You say:

As you return the tennis racket you borrowed from Liam, you smile and say, "Here's your racket." Liam stiffens, grabs the racket, and starts to walk away.

You say:

Natalie comes dancing into her room with a huge grin on her face.

You say:

In the past, your adviser has told you that almost any time would be all right for working out your next term's schedule. When you tell her you'll be in Wednesday at 4 P.M., she pauses, frowns, sighs, and says "Uh" and nods.

You say:

Compare your written responses to the guidelines for effective perception checking suggested earlier. Edit your responses where necessary in order to improve them. Now say them aloud. Do they sound "natural"? If not, revise them until they do.

Corpex, a large out-of-town corporation that had just bought out Rustown's major factory, decided to move its headquarters there and to expand the current plant, creating hundreds of new jobs.

Rustown inhabitants had mixed reactions to this takeover. They were excited by the increased business that was expected, but they knew that many of the new factory managers as well as some of the new employees were African Americans. Rustown had never had a black family in its community, and some of the townspeople openly worried about the effect African Americans would have on their community.

At work on the first day, Otis Carr, one of the Corpex managers who had agreed to move to Rustown, noticed that the workers seemed very leery of him, but by the end of the first week the plant was running smoothly and Otis was feeling the first signs of acceptance. On Monday morning of the next week, Otis accidentally overhead a group of workers talking on their break, trading lies about African Americans, using vulgarities and racist slurs, and repeating negative stereotypes.

A bit shaken, Otis returned to his office. He had a problem. He recognized his workers' prejudices, but did not know how to change them. He wanted to establish good work relationships with his workers for the sake of the company, but he also wanted to create a good working atmosphere for other African Americans who would be coming to Rustown. What should Otis do?

Devise a plan for Otis that would be effective and ethical.

OBJECTIVES

After you have read this chapter, you should be able to answer the following questions:

◼ What is the relationship between language and meaning?

◼ What is the difference between the denotative and the connotative meanings of words?

◼ How can you improve your language usage so that it is more precise, specific, and concrete?

◼ How can you use the skills of dating and indexing generalizations to increase the accuracy of your messages?

◼ What happens when people use language that is inappropriate for the situation?

◼ How can you phrase messages so that they are perceived as appropriate for the situation?

Verbal Communication

"**K**yle, why do you keep obfuscating the plan?"

"Now just a minute, Derek. There's no need for you to get obscene with me. I may not have looked at the job the same way you did but I wouldn't, uh . . . I'm not going to lower myself to repeat your language!"

"Obfuscating" means confusing. What in the world did Derek mean when he accused Kyle of "obfuscating the plan"? And why did Kyle think that Derek was talking obscenely? Many years ago, I. A. Richards (1965, p. 3) observed that communication is "the study of misunderstanding and its remedy." And in this instance we have a classic example of misunderstanding. The remedy? Clearer and more appropriate language.

Whether you're trying to iron out a problem with a friend or explain your views on reducing domestic violence in a group discussion or a public speech, your effectiveness will depend on your verbal and nonverbal communication usage. In this chapter we discuss verbal communication: how people use language; the relationship between language and meaning, with emphasis on denotation, connotation, and cultural and gender differences; and the skills that help us speak clearly and appropriately.

The Nature and Use of Language

Language is the body of words and the system for their use in communicating that are common to the people of the same community or nation, the same geographical area, or the same cultural tradition. Each language community has a body of words that have commonly understood meanings to the people who are members of that community. Likewise, each language has a grammar and a syntax that work to create a system whereby specific strings of words will be interpreted similarly by people in that language community.

Although language communities vary in the words that they use and in their grammar and syntax systems, all human languages serve the following similar purposes.

1. **We use language to designate, label, define, and limit.** For instance, if you ask me to tell you about my neighbor, and I respond by saying that my neighbor is "a chemistry major," I will have limited your understanding of my neighbor to his intellectual pursuits. If instead I had chosen to say that my neighbor is "a scratch golfer," I would have limited your understanding of my neighbor differently. The point is, whatever words I choose, I will only capture a particular characteristic—part of that person—so that the person who is listening will only perceive part of the totality that is my neighbor. In short, as we use language we not only designate and define, we also limit the meaning that will be understood.

2. **We use language to evaluate.** Language scholars emphasize that language is inherently value-laden: We give the things we talk about a positive or negative slant simply by the words we use to refer to them (Richards 1965, p. 3). For instance, if you see Hal taking more time than others to make a

THINK CRITICALLY

Labeling and Limiting

Imagine that you are going with a friend to a party where you are to meet Terrance, who was your friend's best friend in high school. Suppose that your friend has only told you either (1) that Terrance is a Ph.D. student in anthropology at Harvard or (2) that Terrance is a "Big Brother" and regularly volunteers with Habitat for Humanity. Would you have any different expectations of Terrance the Harvard Ph.D. student versus Terrance the Big Brother and volunteer? If each description of Terrance was accurate, how would your expectations change?

decision, you could describe Hal as either "thoughtful" or "dawdling." Likewise, an evaluation is implicit when someone chooses to refer to the object on the grill as "prime filet mignon" or "dead animal flesh." Because there is an evaluative component to much of our language choice, we need to select our words carefully so that we do not unintentionally offend others.

3. **We use language to discuss things outside our immediate experience.** Language enables us to speak hypothetically, to talk about past and future events, and to communicate about people and things that are not present. Through language, we can discuss where we hope to be in five years, analyze a conversation two acquaintances had last week, or learn about the history that shapes the world we live in. Language enables us to learn from others' experiences, to share a common heritage, and to develop a shared vision for the future.

4. **We can use language to talk about language.** We can use language to discuss how we phrased a question and whether better phrasing would have resulted in a more precise question and thus a more informative answer. For instance, if your friend said that Dr. Ball's lectures are boring, you might say, "I think the word *complicated* describes Dr. Ball's lectures more accurately than *boring*."

Although the purpose of language is to help members of language communities understand and relate to each other, the very process of using language carries the rich possibility for creating misunderstanding. To understand this outcome you need to understand how language conveys meaning.

Language and Meaning

On the surface, the relationship between language and meaning seems perfectly clear: We select the correct word, and people will interpret our meanings correctly. In fact, the relationship between language and meaning is not nearly so simple for two reasons: Language must be learned, and the use of language is a creative act.

First, we are not born knowing a language. Rather, each generation within a language community learns the language anew from older members. But each generation may learn only a portion of the words used by the previous generation or may only learn some of the word meanings used by previous generations, because some words and meanings are no longer useful for conveying meaning.

In addition, younger generations will invent new words or assign different meanings to the words they learn. For instance, such words as *mediagenic* (attractive and appealing to viewers and readers of the news media) and *hip-hop* (street subculture including rap) have come into common usage to express ideas that were unthinkable to your grandparents.

PRACTICE IN CLASS

Verbal Description

Choose three members of the class who are willing to volunteer to describe a picture to the rest of the class. Have two of the three volunteers leave the room. The instructor will give the remaining volunteer the picture and ask this person to describe it to the rest of the class. When this person has finished, the instructor should have a second volunteer reenter the room, look at the picture, and describe it to the class. When the second person has finished, do the same thing with the third volunteer. As the volunteers are describing the picture, notice how their descriptions differ. Do they use the same words? Do they describe the picture in the same order? How does your mental picture of what is being described change from one description to the next? In what ways does this exercise exemplify the creativeness we all use when forming verbal messages?

Language must be learned, and the use of language is a creative act.

Changes also occur because of the need to create words to communicate perceptions. If we encounter a situation that no word in our vocabulary can describe, we are likely either to form a new word or to use an old word in a new way to describe it. Likewise, if we see an object that is different from any object we have a word for, we choose a new word to label it. Speakers of English in the 1940s would have been puzzled by the expression *couch potato*, for example, because only recently have we used this term to describe people who are chronic television viewers.

The Denotative and Connotative Meaning of Words

When Melissa tells Trish that her dog has died, what Melissa means is dependent on both word denotation and connotation.

Denotation. Denotation is the direct, explicit meaning people agree to give to a word; in short, denotation is the meaning given in a dictionary. Denotatively, when Melissa says her dog has died, her meaning is clear: Her domesticated canine has passed from physical life. But in some situations even the denotative meaning of a word may not really be clear. First, dictionary definitions reflect current and past practice in the language community; second, they use words to define words; and third, each dictionary author is engaging in the creative act of communicating. The end result is that words are defined differently in various dictionaries and may include multiple meanings that change over time.

Moreover, meaning may vary depending on the context in which the word is used. For example, the dictionary definitions of *gay* include both having or showing a merry, lively mood and homosexual. Thus, **context**—the position of a word in a sentence and the other words around it—has an important effect on correctly interpreting which denotation of a word is meant. Not only will the other words and the syntax and grammar of a verbal message help us to understand the denotative meaning of certain words, but so will the situation in which they are spoken. Whether the comment "He's really gay" is understood to refer to someone's sexual orientation or to his merry mood may depend on the circumstances in which it is said.

Connotation. Whereas *denotation* refers to the standard dictionary definition of a word, *connotation* is the feelings or evaluations associated with the word. A word's connotation may be even more important to our understanding of meaning.

C. K. Ogden and I. A. Richards (1923) were among the first scholars to consider the misunderstandings that result from the failure of communicators to realize that their subjective reactions to words are a product of their life experiences. For instance, when Melissa tells Trisha that her dog has died, Trisha's understanding of the message depends on the extent to which her feelings about pets and death—her connotations of the words—correspond to the feelings that Melissa has about pets and death. Melissa, who sees dogs as truly indispensable friends, may be trying to communicate a true sense of grief; Trish, who doesn't particularly care for pets in general and dogs in particular, may miss the sense of Melissa's statement.

Why should you understand the relationship of denotation and connotation to message meaning? Because the only message that counts is the message that is understood, regardless of whether it is the one you intended.

Meaning Varies across Subgroups in the Language Community

As we mentioned earlier, a language community may include within it subgroups with unique cultures. Hecht, Collier, and Ribeau (1993) point out, "Cultural groups define themselves in part through language, and members establish identity through language use" (p. 84). Subgroups thus develop variations on the core language that allows them to share the meanings that are unique to their cultural experiences. Because people from different cultures approach the world from different perspectives, they are likely to experience difficulty sharing meaning when they talk with each other. As the Diverse

OBSERVE AND ANALYZE

Denotative Meanings

1. Compile a list of ten slang or "in" words. Discuss how the meanings you assign to these words differ from the meanings your parents or grandparents assign to them (for example, "He's bad!").

2. Write your own definition of each of the following words; then go to a dictionary and check how closely your definition matches the dictionary's.

building	justice
love	ring
success	band
glass	peace
freedom	honor

PRACTICE IN CLASS

Connotative Meanings

Working with others in groups, select several common nouns such as *college* and *industry*. Each person should list at least five adjectives that he or she associates with the word. When you have finished, compare the results. In what ways are your meanings (the connotations the words have for you) different?

Cultural traditions influence how we learn and interpret language.

Voices feature shows, one of the most confounding aspects of language and its interpretation for people from different cultures is the use of idioms.

In addition to subgroups based on race, religion, and national origin, we are also experiencing an unprecedented growth in subgroup cultures and language communities associated with generation, social class, and political interests. The need for awareness and sensitivity in applying our communication skills doesn't depend on someone's being an immigrant or from a different ethnic background. Rather, the need for being aware of potential language differences is important in every type of communication. Developing our language skills so that the messages we send are clear and sensitive will increase our communication effectiveness in every situation.

Increasing Message Clarity

Message clarity is improved by reducing ambiguity and confusion. Compare the clarity of the following two descriptions of the same incident: (1) "Some nut almost got me a while ago." (2) "An older man in a banged-up Honda Civic ran the light at Calhoun and Clifton and almost hit me while I was waiting to turn left at the cross street." You can clarify your language by selecting specific, concrete, and precise words and by dating and indexing generalizations.

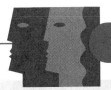

That's Greek to Me: Between a Rock and a Hard Place in Intercultural Encounters

by Wen-Shu Lee

In addition to word connotation, idiomatic language (an expression in the usage of a language that is peculiar to itself either grammatically or in having a meaning that cannot be derived from the conjoined meanings of its elements) also makes communication between and among cultures difficult. This excerpt both exemplifies the concept of an idiom and shows why its use is frustrating to people of different cultures.

There are four reasons why idioms should be an important subject in intercultural communication. First, idioms are figurative in nature. Second, figurative meanings often cause comprehension problems for people from different cultures. Third, we do not explain idioms completely. Finally, idioms open up an avenue to interpersonal closeness. Let me explain these related reasons in detail for you.

First, an idiom and its meaning often do not match because they have a *figurative* rather than a *literal* relationship. The meaning of an idiom is rarely predictable from its constituent components; consider, "bought the farm," "get your feet wet," "get your hands dirty," "a wild goose chase," "like a duck on a June bug." Like the "It's Greek to me" example, "bought the farm" has no literal relationship with "someone died," and "like a duck on a June bug" has no literal relationship with "I will confront you immediately with what you have done."

Second, communication breakdowns often occur when people use idioms in communicating with those who do not comprehend the idiomatic meaning. For people who use idioms "naturally," the figurative link between an idiom and its meaning often goes unnoticed. But this link becomes problematic for those who do not share the life-world with the idiom users. This problem is more easily solved by those who speak English as a first language (hereafter, L1 speakers) than those who speak English as a second language (hereafter, L2 speakers). For example, a young college student, Susan, living in San Jose uses "Check it out,

there's a stud muffin" with her friend, Jenny, while shopping with her Mom. Her mother, an L1 speaker in her fifties who does not share the life-world of "college life" with Susan and Jenny, may ask "What do you mean by a 'stud muffin'?" knowing that it is an expression among young people that she is not familiar with. But if Susan and Jenny are shopping with an L2 speaker, Huei-Mei, the problem becomes more complex. She may not hear "stud muffin" clearly. Or, she may hear the idiom but remain quiet about it, suspecting that her English is not good enough. Even if she has the courage to ask for the meaning of "stud muffin," Huei-Mei may still have a hard time linking "a handsome guy" with "a male breeding horse" and "English breakfast food." Finally, even if she knows the linguistic meaning of "stud muffin," she may use it in an inappropriate relational context. For example, she may want to compliment her handsome seminar professor: "Professor Spano, you are a stud muffin." Therefore, the study of idioms is important to intercultural communication competence.

Third, as is apparent in the "stud muffin" example, a complete explanation of an idiom requires a linguistic discussion about the meaning of idiom words and a relational discussion about the association between the two people who use an idiom together. Most of us engage in a linguistic explanation but leave out the relational one. For example, Susan forgets to tell Huei-Mei that "stud muffin" is used between friends (usually females) to comment on a third person, a handsome male. We do not use it with someone who has a formal, professional relationship with us. Huei-Mei, as a result, needs to know that one should not use "stud muffin" with a professor. For this reason, we need to study idiom explanations more carefully in intercultural encounters.

Finally, idioms hold one of the keys to interpersonal closeness. Idioms are commonly used in informal situations between casual acquaintances, friends, and pals. The ability to use idioms accepted by a group may not guarantee closeness, but it can increase the possibilities of shortening interpersonal distance if so desired. That is, if people from different cultural backgrounds can use each other's idioms, formal and awkward discomfort may be replaced by a sense of informality and even closeness. This may facilitate intercultural relationships in a variety of contexts—interpersonal relationships between classmates and friends, working relationships in a company, and teaching-learning relationships in the classroom.

Excerpted from Wen-Shu Lee, "That's Greek to Me: Between a Rock and a Hard Place in Intercultural Encounters." From Intercultural Communication: A Reader, *8th ed., eds. Larry A. Samovar and Richard E. Porter (Belmont, CA: Wadsworth, 1997), pp. 213–221. Reprinted by permission of the author.*

Specificity, Concreteness, and Precision in Language Use

Specific words clarify meaning by narrowing what is understood from a general category to a particular group within that category. The first words that come to mind as we try to express our thoughts are often general and abstract, allowing the listener to choose from many possible images rather than picturing the single, focused image that the speaker has. The more listeners are called on to provide their own images, the more likely they are to see meanings that are different from what we intend.

For instance, if Nevah says that Ruben is a "blue-collar worker," you may picture an unlimited number of occupations that fall within this broad category. If, instead, she says he's a "construction worker," the number of possible images you can picture is reduced. But if she says Ruben is a "bulldozer operator," the image snaps into focus and is likely to align with the one she intended you to have.

Think of a continuum going from most general to most specific. In the previous example, the continuum goes from blue-collar worker to construction worker to construction vehicle operator to bulldozer operator. Figure 3.1 provides another illustration of this continuum.

Concrete words are not only specific, but are also likely to appeal to our senses—to conjure up a picture. Often we can see them, hear them, smell them. Consider the word *speak*. This is a general/abstract term. To make it more concrete, we can use words such as *mumble, whisper, bluster, drone, jeer,* or *rant*. Say these words aloud. Notice the different sound of your voice when you say *whisper* as opposed to *bluster, jeer,* or *rant*.

Finally, we seek words that are **precise**—that most accurately or correctly capture the sense of what we are saying. Suppose I seek the most precise word to describe Phillip's speech. I might say, "Phillip blustered. Well, to be more

"See what I mean? You're never sure just where you stand with them."

precise, he ranted." Notice now that we are not moving from the general to the specific—both words are quite specific; nor are we moving from abstract to concrete—both words are concrete. Here we are concerned with precision in meaning. *Blustering* means talking in a way that is loudly boastful; *ranting* means talking in a way that is noisy or bombastic. So, what we're considering here is shades of meaning: Depending on how the person was talking, *bluster-*

Art
Painting
Oil painting
Impressionist oil painting
Renoir's *La Promenade*

Figure 3.1
Levels of specificity.

Synonyms

One good way to increase specificity, concreteness, and precision is to play "synonyms." Think of a word, then list words that mean about the same thing. For example, some synonyms for *happy* are *glad*, *joyful*, and *pleased*. When you have completed your list, refer to a book of synonyms, such as *Roget's Thesaurus*, to find other words. Then write what you think is the meaning of each word, focusing on the shades of difference in meaning among the words. When you are done, look up each word, even those whose meaning you are sure of. The goal of this exercise is to select the most specific, concrete, or precise word to express a given idea.

ing or *ranting* would be the more precise word. Let's try another one. "Susan laughed at my story—well, to be more precise, she chuckled." A *laugh* is a loud show of mirth; a *chuckle* is a more gentle sound expressing suppressed mirth. Similar? Yes—but with a different shade of meaning.

While specific, concrete, and precise words enable us to reduce ambiguity and sharpen meaning through individual words, at times we can achieve greater clarity by adding a detail or an example. For instance, suppose Linda says, "Rashad is very loyal." Because the meaning of *loyal* (faithful to an idea, person, company, and so on) is abstract, to avoid ambiguity and confusion Linda might add, "He never criticizes a friend behind her back." By following up her use of an abstract concept with a concrete example, Linda makes it easier for her listeners to "ground" their idea of this personal quality in a concrete or "real" experience.

In the examples that follow, notice how the use of specific, concrete, and precise language in the right-hand column improves the clarity of the messages in the left-hand column.

The senator brought *several things* with her to the meeting.	The senator brought *recent letters from her constituency* with her to the meeting.
He lives in a *really big house*.	He lives in a *fourteen-room Tudor mansion*.
The backyard has *several different kinds* of trees.	The backyard has *two large maples, an oak, and four small evergreens*.
Morgan is a *fair grader*.	Morgan *uses the same standards for grading all students*.
Many students *aren't honest* in class.	Many students *cheat on tests* in class.
Judy *hits* the podium when she wants to emphasize her point.	Judy *pounds on* the podium when she wants to emphasize her point.

Developing Our Ability to Speak More Clearly

Being able to speak more clearly requires us to build our working vocabulary and to brainstorm to generate word choices from our active vocabulary.

Vocabulary building. As a speaker, the larger your vocabulary, the more choices you have from which to select the word you want; as a listener, the larger your vocabulary, the more likely you are to understand the words used by others.

One way to increase your vocabulary is to study one of the numerous vocabulary-building books available in most bookstores. You might also study magazine features such as "Word Power" in *The Reader's Digest*. By completing this monthly quiz and learning the words with which you are not familiar, you can increase your vocabulary by as many as twenty words per month.

A second way to increase your vocabulary is to take note of any words that people use in their conversations with you that you are not able to define precisely. For instance, suppose you hear, "I was inundated with phone calls today!" If you can't define *inundated*, you could ask the speaker to clarify this usage. "Excuse me, but I'm not sure what you mean by *inundated*." Or you can write it down, look up its meaning at the first opportunity, and then go back over what you heard to see whether the dictionary meaning matches what was said. Most dictionaries define *inundated* using synonyms such as *overwhelmed* or *flooded*. If you then say to yourself, "She was inundated—overwhelmed or flooded—with phone calls today," you are likely to remember that meaning and apply it the next time you hear the word. You can follow the same procedure when you read. As you are reading today's assignments for your courses, circle any words whose meanings you are unsure of. After you have finished the assignment, look up the circled words in the dictionary. If you follow this practice faithfully, you will soon notice an increase in your vocabulary.

Mental brainstorming. Having a larger vocabulary won't help your speaking if you don't have a procedure for using it. One way to practice accessing choices from your memory is to brainstorm during practice sessions and later in conversation. **Brainstorming** is an uncritical, nonevaluative process of generating alternatives. Suppose someone asks you how well preregistration is working. You might initially say, "Preregistration is awful." If you don't think that *awful* is the right word, you might quickly brainstorm alternatives such as *frustrating*, *demeaning*, *cumbersome*, and *annoying*. Then you could say, "What I really meant to say is that preregistration is overly cumbersome."

Or suppose you are talking about a basketball game. On first thought you might simply say, "They played really sloppy ball." Stop. What words would be more concrete than *sloppy*? What specific part or parts of their play was ineffective? As a result of brainstorming you might be able to correct yourself and say, "What I meant to say is that passes were intercepted repeatedly because they were thrown too hard."

Clearly stating our verbal messages is hard work, but as you build your vocabulary and learn to mentally brainstorm you will find that you are able to make such adjustments in everyday conversation. At times you will want to make adjustments in midsentence, as in the following examples:

> "To move these things, we'll need a van—I'm sorry, I don't mean van, I mean one of those extra-large station wagons."

> "I think that many of the boss's statements are very [split-second pause while thinking: I want the word that means 'know-it-all'] dogmatic."

TEST YOUR COMPETENCE

Brainstorming

Set up a tape recorder and talk about a course you're taking, a game or a movie you saw. As you're talking, when you come to a key word or phrase, assess whether that word or phrase is specific, precise, or concrete enough that your message would be correctly understood. If you think not, pause momentarily to brainstorm alternative word choices, and then use the more specific, precise, or concrete word.

SKILL BUILDERS   Clarity—Specific, Concrete, Precise Words

Skill	Use	Procedure	Example
Clarify meaning by narrowing what is understood from a general category to a particular group within that category, by appealing to the senses, or by choosing words that symbolize exact thoughts and feelings.	To help the listener picture thoughts analogous to the speaker's.	1. Assess whether the word or phrase used is less specific, concrete, or precise than it should be. 2. Pause to mentally brainstorm alternatives. 3. Select a more specific, concrete, or precise word.	Instead of saying "Bring the stuff for the audit," say "Bring the records and receipts from the last year for the audit." Or instead of saying "I was really cold," say "I nearly froze."

"Mike was just a jerk yesterday—well, I guess I mean he was inconsiderate."

"I agree Pauline is a tough manager, but I think she's a good one because she is fair—she treats everyone exactly alike."

When we are relaxed and confident, our word choice usually flows smoothly and is likely to be most effective. When we are under pressure, however, our ability to select the best symbols to convey our thoughts is likely to deteriorate. People sometimes think one thing and say something entirely different. For example, a math professor might say, "We all remember that the numerator is on the bottom and the denominator is on the top of the fraction,

TEST YOUR COMPETENCE

Specific, Concrete, and Precise Words

1. For each word listed, find three words or phrases that are more specific or more concrete.

implements	building	nice	education
clothes	colors	chair	bad
happy	stuff	things	car

2. Make the following statements clearer by editing words that are not precise or not specific and concrete.

"You know I love basketball. Well, I'm practicing a lot because I want to get better."

"Paula, I'm really bummed out. Everything is going down the tubes. You know what I mean?"

"Well, she just does these things to tick me off. Like, just a whole lot of stuff—and she knows it!"

"I just bought a beautiful outfit—I mean, it is really in style. You'll love it."

"I've really got to remember to bring my things the next time I visit."

so when we divide fractions. . . ." "Professor," a voice from the third row interrupts, "you said the numerator is on the bottom and. . . ." "Is that what I said?" the professor replies. "Well, you know what I meant!" Did everyone in the class know? Probably not.

You will really know that you have made strides in improving specificity, precision, and concreteness when you find that you can form clear messages even under pressure.

Dating Information

Because nearly everything changes with time, it's important that we **date** the information we communicate by telling when it was true. Not dating our communications leads to inaccuracies that can be dangerous. For instance, Parker says, "I'm going to be transferred to Henderson City." Laura replies, "Good luck—they've had some real trouble with their schools." On the basis of Laura's statement, Parker may worry about the effect his move will have on his children. What he doesn't know is that Laura's information is five years old! Henderson City may still have problems, but then it may not. Had Laura replied, "Five years ago, I know they had some real trouble with their schools. I'm not sure what the situation is now, but you may want to check," Parker would look at the information differently.

To date information, (1) consider or find out when the information was true and (2) verbally acknowledge it. Consider each of the examples that follow. The statements on the left are undated; those on the right are carefully dated.

Palm Springs is really popular with the college crowd.	When we were in Palm Springs *two years ago*, it was really popular with the college crowd.
Professor Powell brings great enthusiasm to her teaching.	Professor Powell brings great enthusiasm to her teaching—at least she did *last quarter* in communication theory.
The Beast is considered the most exciting roller coaster in the country.	*Five years ago*, the Beast was considered the most exciting roller coaster in the country.
You think Mary's depressed? I'm surprised. She seemed her regular high-spirited self when I talked with her.	You think Mary's depressed? I'm surprised. She seemed her regular high-spirited self when I talked with her *the day before yesterday*.

We have no power to prevent change. But we can verbally acknowledge the reality of change and date the statements we make, thereby increasing the effectiveness of our messages.

Indexing Generalizations

Generalizing allows people to use what they have learned from one experience and apply it to another. So, when Glenda learns that tomatoes and squash grow better if the ground is fertilized, she *generalizes* that fertilizing will help all of her vegetables grow better. You'll recall from the previous chapter, however, that misuse of generalization contributes to perceptual inaccuracies because it ignores individual differences. Thus, just because men have greater strength in general than do women does not mean that Max (one man) is stronger than Barbara (one woman).

Indexing generalizations is the mental and verbal practice of acknowledging individual differences while still allowing us to draw on generalizations. The concept of indexing is borrowed from mathematics, where it is used to acknowledge individual elements in a group by assigning each a unique number (called subscripts). We mentally index by assigning a number to each member of a class or group. So in the class of men, we have man_1 (Fred), man_2 (Darnell), man_3 (William), and so forth; in the class of Chevrolets, we have $Chevrolet_1$ (a blue Nova), $Chevrolet_2$ (a red Corvette), $Chevrolet_3$ (a white Nova), and so forth. The purpose of this mental process is to remind us that although we may group like persons, objects, or ideas together based on some common characteristic (man, Chevrolet), each member is unique and not an exact replica of the others (Fred is different from Darnell, and a Nova is not a Corvette).

In order to index generalizations in your conversation, first consider whether what you want to say is about a specific object, person, or place or whether it is a generalization about a class to which the object, person, or place belongs; then, if what you want to say is a generalization about the class, qualify it appropriately so that your assertion does not go beyond the evidence that supports it.

In the examples that follow, the statements on the left are overgeneralizations; the statements on the right have been indexed.

Because men are stronger than women, Max is stronger than Barbara.	*In general*, men are stronger than women, so Max is probably stronger than Barbara.
State's got to have a good economics department; the university is ranked among the top twenty in the nation.	Because State is ranked among the top twenty schools in the nation, the economics department should be a good one, *although it may be an exception*.
Jack is sure to be outgoing; Don is, and they're both Joneses.	Jack is likely to be outgoing because his brother Don is (they're both Joneses), *but Jack could be different*.
Your Chevrolet should go 50,000 miles before you need a brake job; Jerry's did.	Your Chevrolet may well go 50,000 miles before you need a brake job; Jerry's did, *but of course, all Chevrolets aren't the same*.

All people generalize at one time or another, but by indexing statements, we can avoid the problems that hasty generalization sometimes creates.

Cultural Differences Affect Verbal Communication

Because language and culture are inseparable, in this section we look at three dimensions of culture that help explain differences in connotations of language.

Individualism/collectivism. One major dimension that theorists use to explain similarities and differences in language and behavior is individualism versus collectivism (Gudykunst and Matsumoto 1996, p. 21). Members of individualistic and collectivistic cultures learn different values that affect their behavior. **Individualistic cultures** tend to value uniqueness and to emphasize the goals of individuals over those of the group. Members of these cultures are more likely to look after themselves and their immediate families. Individualistic cultures generally include those of western Europe and the United States. In contrast, **collectivistic cultures** tend to value harmony and solidarity and to emphasize group goals over those of individuals. Members of these cultures are more likely to belong to in-groups or collectives that are supposed to look after them in exchange for their loyalty to the group (Hofstede 1991, p. 67). Collectivistic cultures include many nations of Asia, Africa, and South America.

Individualistic cultures tend to use **low-context communication,** meaning that information is (1) embedded mainly in the messages transmitted and (2) presented directly. Collectivistic cultures tend to use **high-context communication,** in which people (1) expect others to know how they're thinking and feeling and (2) present messages indirectly. Thus, low-context cultures operate on the principle of saying what you mean and getting to the point, whereas high-context cultures communicate in ways that are often ambiguous and indirect (Gudykunst and Matsumoto 1996, pp. 29–30). In a low-context culture, "Yes" means "Affirmative, I agree with what you have said." In a high-context culture, "Yes" may mean "Affirmative, I agree with what you have said," or it may mean "In this setting it would embarrass you if I said 'No,' so I will say 'Yes' to be polite, but I really don't agree and you should know this, so in the future don't expect me to act as if I have agreed with what you said." Typically, people from Asian cultures are comfortable talking for hours without clearly expressing an opinion; they can be suspicious of direct verbal expressions of love and respect. In contrast, people from low-context cultures prize clear and direct communication.

Uncertainty avoidance. Although we all live in a world of uncertainty, societies respond to this uncertainty differently. Nations with **low uncertainty avoidance** accept uncertainty; they are tolerant of differing behavior and opinions. A society with **high uncertainty avoidance** sees a high level of anxiety among its people—nervousness, stress, and aggressiveness. These societies seek to maximize security and minimize risk, with little tolerance for deviant ideas and behaviors.

Masculinity/femininity. Hofstede (1983, p. 85) refers to those societies that require people to maintain rigid sex roles as **masculine cultures**. In these societies, men take more assertive and dominant roles and women more service-oriented and caring roles. These societies also emphasize materialism and acquisitivism. Hofstede refers to **feminine cultures** as those that allow both men and women to take different roles. In these societies, the emphasis is on relationships, concern for others, and overall quality of life.

In summary, compared to other national cultures, United States culture is the highest of all countries on individualism, well below average on uncertainty avoidance, and well above average on masculinity.

This analysis considers national cultures—the differences between and among countries. But we also need to note that different cultures are represented in nearly every country. Within the United States in particular are a multitude of cultures that differ from each other even when they speak the same language. People who speak different languages expect to have some problem communicating and thus seem willing to take extra care. Surprisingly, misinterpreting word meaning can be more of a problem for two people from different cultures who are speaking the *same language* because they tend to believe that words mean the same things in other cultures. For example, if a person says that the government wants what is "best for the people," it would seem that others should have no difficulty understanding the words. Yet "best for the people" can and does mean many different things depending on one's politics, governmental form, priorities, and so on. When someone from another culture uses a word and you perceive that word as particularly important to understanding, you might ask for concrete examples so that you can be sure of what the person means.

Gender Differences Affect Verbal Messages

There is no evidence to suggest that the differences that have been identified between women's message construction patterns and those of men cause "problems" for either group (Canary and Hause 1993, p. 141). Nevertheless, a number of specific differences between women's and men's speech patterns have been found, and understanding what has led to them has intrigued scholars.

Edwin and Shirley Ardener argue that the language differences between men and women is a result of the male-biased culture of the United States. Because men have created the meanings for language, the feminine voice has been "muted." As a result, women are less expressive in public situations than men are and monitor their own communications more intensely than do men (Littlejohn 1996, pp. 239–240). Julia Wood (1997, p. 167) explains the differences in language usage in terms of the differences in psychological orientation that men and women acquire in growing up. Because women establish gender identity by seeing themselves as "like" or connected to mother, she argues, they come to see communication as a primary way of establishing and maintaining relationships with others. Whichever theory is more accurate, Pearson, West, and Turner (1995, pp. 94–108) summarize several differences in language usage between men and women:

1. Women tend to use both more intensifiers and more hedges than men. **Intensifiers** are words that modify other words and serve to strengthen the idea represented by the original word. According to studies of the actual speech practices of men and women, women are more likely to use words such as *awfully*, *quite*, and *so* (as in "It was quite lovely" or "This is so important"). **Hedges** are modifying words that soften or weaken the meaning of the idea represented by the original word. According to the research, women are likely to make far greater use of such words as *somewhat*, *perhaps*, or *maybe* (as in "It was somewhat interesting that . . ." or "It may be significant that . . .").

2. Women add "tag" questions to their sentences more frequently than men do. Tag questions are questions that ask the other person to confirm or affirm the statement that has preceded it, as in "That was a really sad song, wasn't it?" or "The meeting is on Wednesday, isn't it?" Even though we all use tag questions at times when we are not certain or when we are trying to get more information, women tend to use them more frequently than men. One consequence of this speech pattern is that women tend to be perceived as both less dogmatic and more "wishy-washy" than men.

Although research has found specific language differences between men and women, it is important not to overgeneralize. Some men use verbal patterns that are more characteristically female, and some women use characteristically male patterns.

Speaking Appropriately

During the past several years in the United States, we have had frequent discussions and disagreements about "political correctness." Colleges and universities have been at the forefront of this debate. Although several issues germane to the debate go beyond the scope of this chapter, at the heart of this controversy is the question of what language behaviors are appropriate—and what language behaviors are inappropriate.

Speaking appropriately means choosing language and symbols that are adapted to the needs, interests, knowledge, and attitudes of listeners in order to avoid language that alienates them. Through appropriate language we communicate our respect and acceptance of those who are different from us. In this section, we discuss specific strategies that will help you to craft appropriate verbal messages.

Formality of Language

Language should be appropriately formal for the situation. In an interpersonal setting, we are likely to use more informal language when we are talking with our best friend and more formal language when we are talking with our parents. In a group setting, we are likely to use more informal language when we are talking with a group of our peers and more formal language when we are talking with a group of managers. In a public-speaking setting, we are likely to use more formal language than in either interpersonal or group settings.

One type of formality in language that we usually observe is the manner by which we address others. In formal settings we address others by their titles followed by their surnames unless they invite us to do something else. So in business settings or at formal parties, it is appropriate to call people "Mr. X," "Ms. B," "Rabbi Z," "Dr. S," or "Professor P." In addition, we generally view it as appropriate to refer to those older than we are, those of higher status, or those whom we respect by title and surname unless otherwise directed.

Jargon and Slang

Appropriate language should be chosen so that jargon and slang do not interfere with understanding. We form language communities as a result of the work we do, our hobbies, and the subcultures with which we identify. But we can forget that people who are not in our same line of work, do not have the same hobbies, or are not from our group may not understand language that seems to be such a part of our daily communication. For instance, when a computer hacker gets into a conversation with a computer-illiterate friend about the Internet, the hacker is likely to lose her friend if she talks to him in the language of "browsers," "downloading," and "websites." If, however, the hacker recognizes her friend's level of sophistication, she can work to make her language appropriate by discussing ideas in words that her friend understands. In short, anytime you are talking with people outside your specific language community, you need to carefully explain, if not abandon, the technical jargon or slang.

Shoe by Jeff MacNelly; reprinted by permission of Tribune Media Services.

Profanity and Vulgar Expressions

Appropriate language does not include profanity or vulgar expressions. There was a time when uttering "hell" or "damn" would have resulted in severe punishment for children and social isolation for adults. Today, unfortunately, we tolerate commonplace profanities and vulgarities, and in many subcultures their use is common. Under the influence of film and television writers who aim to titillate and entertain, we have become inured to these expressions. In fact, it is common to hear elementary-school children utter strings of "four-letter words" in school hallways and lunchrooms and on the playground.

Why do people swear and engage in coarse language? DeKlerk (1991, p. 165) suggests that swearing is one way of asserting independence by breaking adult taboos. In a society that prizes adulthood and independence, the tendency to use increasingly vulgar and profane language at increasingly younger ages is not surprising. Despite this trend in our society, however, we believe that profane and vulgar language continues to be inappropriate in most settings and even in informal conversation is offensive to many people, although our current social conventions may preclude them from saying so.

Unfortunately, profanity and vulgarity are habits that are easily acquired and hard to extinguish. In fact, an alarming number of people use such language as filler expressions that add little or no meaning to the content of the message but are liberally peppered into the verbal message out of habit. Thus, for some folks the ubiquitous "f--k" has come to serve the same purpose as "like" and "you know."

What does the use of profanity communicate? When used infrequently, profanity and vulgar expressions communicate strong emotions for which there may be no other appropriate words. Profanity and vulgarity are meant to shock and to communicate one's deep disgust or contempt. When profanity and vulgarity are used frequently, others assume that the person using these expressions intends them to threaten or intimidate. Unfortunately, with far too many people profanity and vulgarity have lost all meaning, indicating only their inability to express their thoughts or feelings at any but the basest and most ignorant level. Competent communicators avoid using profanity or vulgarity, because its use is more likely to damage than to strengthen relationships.

Sensitivity

Language is appropriate when it is sensitive to usages that others perceive as offensive. Some of the mistakes in language that we make result from using expressions that are perceived as sexist, racist, or otherwise biased—that is, any language that is perceived as belittling any person or group of people by virtue of their sex, race, age, handicap, or other identifying characteristic. Two of the most prevalent linguistic uses that communicate insensitivity are generic language and nonparallel language.

UNDERSTAND YOURSELF

Profanity and Vulgarity

How much do you use profanity and vulgarity? Has your usage increased, decreased, or remained the same since you have started college? Does your use of profanity and vulgarity change depending on who you are speaking with? If so, articulate the decision rules that seem to guide your behavior. Overall, how comfortable are you with how frequently you use profanity and vulgarity in your verbal messages?

**THINK
CRITICALLY**

Sexist Language

Develop nonsexist alternatives for the following terms:

fireman	foreman	serviceman
brakeman	airman	stewardess
craftsman	repairman	councilman
doorman	coed	waitress
bellman	anchorman	freshman
night watchman		

Generic language. Generic language uses words that may apply to only one sex, race, or other group as though they represent all people. This usage is a problem because it linguistically excludes a portion of the population it ostensibly includes. Let's consider some examples.

1. **Generic *he*.** Traditionally, English grammar called for the use of the masculine pronoun *he* to stand for the entire class of humans regardless of sex. Under this rule, standard English called for such usage as "When a person shops, *he* should have a clear idea of what *he* wants to buy." Even though these statements are grammatically correct, they are now considered sexist because they inherently exclude females. Despite traditional usage, it would be hard to maintain that we picture people of both sexes when we hear the masculine pronoun *he*.

    Guideline: Do not construct sentences that use only male pronouns when no specific gender reference is intended. You can avoid this construction in one of two ways. First, you can use plurals. For instance, instead of saying "Because a doctor has high status, his views may be believed regardless of topic," you could say "Because doctors have high status, their views may be believed regardless of topic." Second, you can use both male and female pronouns: "Because a doctor has high status, his or her views may be believed regardless of topic." These changes may seem small, but they may mean the difference between alienating or not alienating the people with whom you are speaking.

2. **Generic *man*.** A second problem results from the traditional reliance on the use of generic *man*. Many words have become a common part of our language that are inherently sexist in that they seem to apply to only one gender. Consider the term *man-made*. What this really means is that a product was produced by human beings, but its underlying connotation is that a male human being made the item. In past generations this masculine generalization may have been appropriate, but today that is no longer the case. Using such terms when speaking about all human beings is troubling, but using them to describe the behavior or accomplishments of women (as in "Sally creates and arranges man-made flowers") is ludicrous.

    Guideline: Avoid using words that have built-in sexism, such as *policeman, postman, chairman, man-made,* and *mankind.* For most expressions of this kind, you can use or create suitable alternatives. For instance, for the first three examples, you can use *police officer, mail carrier,* and *chairperson.* For *man-made,* you might substitute *synthetic.* For *mankind,* you may need to change the constructions—for example, from "All of mankind benefits" to "All the people in the world benefit."

Nonparallel language. Nonparallel language occurs when terms are changed because of the sex, race, or other group characteristic of the individual. Because it treats groups of people differently, nonparallel language is also belittling. Two common forms of nonparallelism are marking and unnecessary association.

1. **Marking** means adding sex, race, age, or other designations unnecessarily to a general word. For instance, *doctor* is a word representing any person with a medical degree. To describe Jones as a doctor is to treat Jones linguistically as a member of the class of doctors. For example, you might say, "Jones, a doctor, contributed a great deal to the campaign." If, however, you referred to "Jones, a woman doctor" (or a black doctor, or an old doctor, or a handicapped doctor), you would be marking. Marking is offensive to some people because you may appear to be trivializing the person's role by laying emphasis on an irrelevant characteristic. For instance, if you say "Jones is a really good female doctor" (or black doctor, or old doctor, or handicapped doctor), you may be intending to praise Jones. However, your listeners may interpret the sentence as saying that Jones is a good doctor for a woman (or a black, or old, or handicapped person) but not necessarily as good as a male doctor (or a white, young, or able-bodied doctor).

   Guideline: Avoid markers. If it is relevant to identify a person by sex, race, age, and so on, do so, but leave such markers out when they are irrelevant. One test of whether a characteristic is relevant and appropriate is whether you would mention the person's sex, race, or age (and so on) regardless of what sex, race, or age the person happens to be. It is relevant to specify "female doctor," for example, only if in that context it would be equally relevant to specify "male doctor." In general, leave sex, race, age, and other markers out of your labeling.

2. **Unnecessary association** occurs when you emphasize a person's association with another when you are not talking about the other person. Very often you will hear a speaker say something like "Gladys Thompson, whose husband is CEO of Acme Inc., is the chairperson for this year's United Way campaign." In response to this sentence, you might say that the association of Gladys Thompson with her husband gives further credentials to Gladys Thompson. But using the association may be seen to imply that Gladys Thompson is important not because of her own accomplishment but because of her husband's. The following sentence is a more flagrant example of unnecessary association: "Don Jones, the award-winning principal at Central High School, and husband of Brenda Jones, local state senator, is chairperson for this year's Minority Scholarship campaign." Here Brenda Jones's occupation and relationship to Don Jones is clearly irrelevant. In either case, the pairing takes away from the person who is supposed to be the focus.

   Guideline: Avoid associating a person irrelevantly with others. If the person has done or said something noteworthy, you should recognize it without making unnecessary associations.

Avoiding Insensitive Language

You've heard children shout, "Sticks and stones may break my bones, but words will never hurt me." But, whether we admit it or not, words do hurt—

sometimes permanently. This inappropriate language is not only insensitive but, in many instances, unethical as well. Think of the great personal damage done to individuals throughout history as a result of being called "hillbilly," "nigger," "fag," or "yid." Think of the fights started by one person calling another's sister or girlfriend a "whore." Of course, we all know that it is not the words alone that are so powerful; it is the context of the words—the situation, the feelings of the participants, the time, the place, or the tone of voice. You may recall circumstances in which a friend called you a name or used a four-letter word to describe you and you did not even flinch; you may also recall other circumstances in which someone else made you furious by calling you something far less offensive.

We should always be aware that our language has repercussions. When we do not understand or are not sensitive to our listeners' frame of reference, we may state our ideas in language that distorts the intended communication. Many times a single inappropriate sentence may be enough to ruin an entire interaction. For instance, if you say "And we all know the problem originates downtown," you may be alluding to the city government. However, if your listeners associate downtown not with the seat of government but with the residential area of an ethnic or social group, the sentence will have an entirely different meaning to them. Being specific will help you avoid such problems; recognizing that some words communicate far more than their dictionary meanings will help even more.

Very few people can escape all unfair language. By monitoring your usage, however, you can guard against frustrating your attempts to communicate by assuming that others will react to your language the same way you do, and you can guard against saying or doing things that offend others and perpetuate outdated sex roles, racial stereotypes, and other biased language.

How can you speak more appropriately? (1) Assess whether the word or phrase used is less appropriate than it should be. (2) Pause to mentally brainstorm alternatives. (3) Select a more appropriate word.

Summary

Language is a system of symbols used for communicating. Through language, we designate, label, define, and limit; we evaluate; we talk about things outside our immediate experience; and we talk about language itself.

You will be a more effective communicator if you recognize that language symbols are arbitrary, that language is learned and is creative, and that language and perception are interrelated.

The denotation of a word is its dictionary meaning. Despite the ease with which we can check a dictionary meaning, word denotation can still present problems because most words have more than one dictionary meaning, changes

REFLECT ON ETHICS

One day after class, Heather, Terry, Paul, and Martha stopped at the Student Union Grill. After they had talked about class for a few minutes, the conversation shifted to students who were taking the class.

"By the way," Paul said, "do any of you know Porky?"

"Who?" the group responded in unison.

"The really fat guy who was sitting a couple of seats from me. We've been in a couple of classes together—he's a pretty nice guy."

"What's his name?" Heather asked.

"Carl—but he'll always be Porky to me."

"Do you call him that to his face?" Terry asked.

"Aw, I'd never say anything like that to him—I wouldn't want to hurt his feelings."

"Well," Martha chimed in, "I'd sure hate to think that you'd call me 'skinny' or 'the bitch' when I wasn't around."

"Come on—what's with you guys?" Paul retorted. "You trying to tell me you never talk about another person that way when they aren't around?"

"Well," said Terry, "maybe a couple of times—but I've never talked like that about someone I really like."

"Someone you like?" queried Heather. "Why does that make a difference? Do you mean it's OK to trash-talk someone so long as you don't like him?"

1. Sort out the ethical issues in this case. How ethical is it to call a person you supposedly like by an unflattering name that you would never use if the person was in your presence?

2. From an ethical standpoint, is whether you like a person or not what determines when such name-calling is OK?

in meanings occur faster than dictionaries are revised, words take on different meanings as they are used in different contexts, and meanings can become obscured as words become more abstract.

The connotation of a word is the emotional and value significance the word has for the listener. Regardless of how a dictionary defines a word, we carry with us meanings that stem from our experience with the object, thought, or action the word represents.

You can improve your clarity of language by selecting the most specific, concrete, and precise word possible and by dating and indexing generalizations.

Cultural differences in language result from similarities and differences in behavior between cultures that are individualistic or collectivistic, have low or high uncertainty avoidance, and are more masculine or feminine. Gender differences in language usage may result from cultural muting of the feminine voice. Women tend to use more intensifiers, hedges, and tag questions than men do.

Speaking appropriately means using language that adapts to the needs, interests, knowledge, and attitudes of the listener and avoiding language that alienates. Inappropriate, unethical language can be minimized by avoiding such exclusionary usages as generic *he* and generic *man* and by eliminating such non-parallel usages as marking and unnecessary association.

OBJECTIVES

After you have read this chapter, you should be able to answer the following questions:

- What are the types of body motions that have communication functions?

- What is paralanguage?

- What are the elements of paralanguage, and how does each affect message meaning?

- How do clothing, touching behavior, and use of time affect self-presentation?

- How is communication affected by the use of physical space?

- How do temperature, lighting, and color affect communication?

- What are three ways you can improve the messages you communicate through your nonverbal behavior?

4

Nonverbal Communication

Marsha Collins steps into Houston's office and says, "I'm not going to be able to meet with you to talk about the report you wrote because I'm swamped with work."

In a speech to her constituents, Stephanie Morris, a candidate for Congress says, "I want you to know I am committed to the needs of the people of this district."

How will Houston take Marsha Collins's excuse? How much faith will Stephanie Morris's constituents have in her commitment? In both cases, the answers will rest largely on how the listeners interpret the speakers' vocal inflections, facial expressions, and gestures. In reality, the meaning of any communication is based on both the content of the verbal message and the interpretation of the nonverbal behavior that accompanies and surrounds the verbal message.

In this chapter, we provide a framework for analyzing and improving nonverbal communication behavior in all contexts. We begin by studying the nature of nonverbal behavior and the way verbal and nonverbal communication messages interrelate. We then look at the major types of nonverbal communication: body motions, paralanguage, self-presentation, and management of the environment.

The Nature of Nonverbal Communication Behavior

Nonverbal communication behaviors are those bodily actions and vocal qualities that typically accompany a verbal message and are usually interpreted as intentional. They are used with regularity among members of a given culture or speech community, and they have agreed-upon interpretations in that culture or speech community (Burgoon 1994, p. 231).

When we say that nonverbals are interpreted as intentional, we mean that people act as if they are intended even if they are performed unconsciously or unintentionally (Burgoon 1994, p. 231). So, when Anita says "I've had it" as she slams a book down on the table, we interpret the loudness of her voice and the act of slamming the book down as intentionally emphasizing the meaning of her words.

Likewise, when we refer to agreed-upon interpretations in a culture or speech community, we recognize that although people from around the world use many of the same nonverbal cues, they may interpret them differently. For instance, a smile may mean a positive experience, or it may mean enjoyment of personal contact, or it may simply be a means of saving face in an uncomfortable situation.

In addition to bodily actions and vocal qualities that accompany verbal messages, nonverbal communication also includes the messages sent by our use of physical space and our choices of clothing, furniture, lighting, temperature, and color.

As we will see, we communicate nonverbally even when we aren't speaking; our nonverbal behaviors are seen as well as heard. And because our nonverbal behavior is often reactive, it may be used as a guide to the nature and depth of our feelings. In fact, it is often our nonverbal behavior that others regard as the true measure of our feelings.

Because much of what is considered appropriate nonverbal behavior depends on culture, after we have discussed each category in terms of the dominant U.S. culture, we will describe some important alternative ways in which nonverbal communication behavior is interpreted in other cultures and communities.

Body Motions

Of all nonverbal behaviors, you are probably most familiar with body motions: the use of eye contact, facial expression, gesture, and posture to communicate.

Communication between Able-bodied Persons and Persons with Disabilities

by Dawn O. Braithwaite and Charles A. Braithwaite

Our nonverbal reactions are particularly informative when we find ourselves in situations that make us uncomfortable, such as talking with people from other cultures, other religions, or different socioeconomic levels, and perhaps especially when talking with people with disabilities. This excerpt is designed not only to increase our sensitivity, but also to provide some specific guidelines for communication.

Jonathan is an articulate, intelligent, thirty-five-year-old professional man who has used a wheelchair since he became a paraplegic at age twenty. He recalls taking an able-bodied woman out to dinner at a nice restaurant. When the waitress came to take their order, she looked only at his date and asked, in a condescending tone, "And what would *he* like to eat for dinner?" At the end of the meal the waitress presented Jonathan's date with the check and thanked her for her patronage.

[Scenarios like this] represent common experiences for people with physical disabilities and are indicative of what often happens when disabled and able-bodied people communicate.

The passage of the Americans with Disabilities Act (ADA), a "bill of rights" for persons with disabilities, highlighted the fact that they are now a large, vocal, and dynamic group within the United States. Disabled people represent one group within American culture that is growing in numbers. Persons with disabilities constitute as much as 7 percent of the population.

In the past, most people with disabilities were sheltered, and many were institutionalized; but today they are very much a part of the American mainstream. Each of us will have contact with people who have disabilities within our families, among our friends, or within the workplace.

As for able-bodied persons who communicate with disabled persons, this intercultural perspective leads to the following proscriptions and prescriptions:

Don't:

assume persons with disabilities cannot speak for themselves or do things for themselves.

force your help on persons with disabilities.

avoid communication with persons who have disabilities simply because you are uncomfortable or unsure.

use terms like "handicapped," "physically challenged," "crippled," "victim," and so on, unless requested to do so by persons with disabilities.

assume that a disability defines a person.

Do:

assume persons with disabilities can do something unless they communicate otherwise.

let persons with disabilities tell you if they want something, what they want, and when they want it. If a person with a disability refuses your help, don't go ahead and help anyway. The goal is to give the person with the disability control in the situation.

remember that persons with disabilities have experienced others' discomfort before and understand how you might be feeling.

use terms like "*people* with disabilities" rather than "disabled people." The goal is to stress the person first, before introducing their disability.

treat persons with disabilities as *persons first*, recognizing that you are not dealing with a disabled person but with *a person* who *has* a disability. This means actively seeking the humanity of the person you are speaking with, and focusing on the person's characteristics instead of the superficial physical appearance. Without diminishing the significance of a physical disability, you can selectively attend to many other aspects of a person during communication.

Excerpted from Dawn O. Braithwaite and Charles A. Braithwaite. "Understanding Communication of Persons with Disabilities as Cultural Communication." From Intercultural Communication: A reader, *8th ed., eds. Larry A. Samovar and Richard E. Porter (Belmont, CA: Wadsworth, 1997), pp. 154–164. Reprinted by permission of the authors.*

Eye Contact

Eye contact, also referred to as **gaze,** is the way we look at people with whom we are communicating. Eye contact serves many functions in our communication. Its *presence* shows that we are paying attention. *How* we look at a person also reveals a range of emotions such as affection, anger, or fear. Intensity of eye contact may also be used to exercise dominance (Pearson, West, and Turner 1995, p. 121). We describe people in love as looking "doe-eyed"; we comment on "looks that could kill"; and we talk of someone "staring another person down."

Through eye contact we also monitor the effect of our communication. By maintaining eye contact, you can tell whether people are paying attention to you, whether they are involved in what you are saying, and whether what you are saying is eliciting feelings.

The amount of eye contact differs from person to person and from situation to situation. Studies show that although people generally look at each other as they talk, talkers hold eye contact about 40 percent and listeners nearly 70 percent of the time (Knapp and Hall 1992, p. 298).

We generally maintain better eye contact when

- we are discussing topics with which we are comfortable.
- we are genuinely interested in a person's comments or reactions.
- we are trying to influence the other person.

Conversely, we tend to avoid eye contact when

- we are discussing topics that make us uncomfortable.
- we lack interest in the topic or person.
- we are embarrassed, ashamed, or trying to hide something.

Because of its importance in public speaking, we will talk more about eye contact in Chapter 16, Presenting Your Speech.

PRACTICE IN CLASS

Body Motions

Working with a partner, have a two-minute conversation entirely through body motions. At the end of the two minutes, each of you should write a "script" of what messages were conveyed and understood. Compare your scripts. How accurately did you communicate? Which of the body motion categories were most helpful in conveying meaning? Where there were inaccuracies, can you identify why? What kinds of information did you find easiest to communicate nonverbally? What kinds of information did you feel the greatest frustration in communicating?

Facial Expression ✳

Facial expression is the arrangement of facial muscles to communicate emotional states or reactions to messages. Three sets of muscles affect the brow and forehead; the eyes, eyelids, and root of the nose; and the cheeks, mouth, remainder of the nose, and chin. Our facial expressions are especially important in conveying the six basic emotions of happiness, sadness, surprise, fear, anger, and disgust that are recognized across cultures (Ekman and Friesen 1975, pp. 137–138).

Gesture ✳

Gestures are the movements of hands, arms, and fingers that we use to describe or to emphasize. When a person says "about this high" or "nearly this round," we expect to see a gesture accompany the verbal description. Likewise, when a person says "Put that down" or "Listen to me," a pointing finger, pounding fist, or some other gesture often reinforces the point. People do vary, however, in the amount of gesturing that accompanies their speech; some people "talk with their hands" far more than others.

Posture ✳

Posture is the position and movement of the body. Changes in posture can also communicate. For instance, suddenly sitting upright and leaning forward are movements that show increased attention; standing up may signal "I'm done now"; turning one's back to the other conveys a redirection of attention away from the other person.

How Body Motions Are Used ✳

Body motions in general and gestures in particular help us considerably in conveying meaning (Ekman and Friesen 1969).

1. **Body motions may be used to take the place of a word or phrase.** We could make a considerable list of the **emblems** (nonverbal symbols that take the place of words) that we use frequently. For instance, thumbs up means "everything is go"; first and second fingers held in a V shape means "peace" or "victory"; shaking the head from side to side means "no" and up and down means "yes"; shrugging the shoulders means "maybe," "I don't care," or "I don't know."

    In many contexts, emblems are used as a complete language. **Sign language** refers to systems of body motions that include sign languages of the deaf and alternate sign languages used by Trappist monks in Europe and the women of Australia (Leathers 1992, p. 75).

2. **Body motions may be used to illustrate what a speaker is saying.** We use gestures to illustrate in at least five ways:

- To *emphasize* speech. A man may pound the table in front of him as he says, "Don't bug me."

- To show the *path* or *direction* of thought. A professor may move her hands on an imaginary continuum when she says, "The papers ranged from very good to very bad."

- To show *position*. A waiter may point when he says, "Take that table."

- To *describe*. A person may use her hands to indicate size as she says, "The ball is about three inches in diameter."

- To *mimic*. A person may nod his head as he says, "Did you see the way he nodded?"

3. **Body motions can display the verbal expression of feelings.** These *affect (emotional) displays* will take place automatically and are likely to be quite noticeable. For instance, if you stub your toe on a chair as you drag yourself out of bed in the morning, you are likely to grimace in pain. Occasionally we are fooled by these displays when people purposely deintensify or overreact. For example, a baseball player may remain stone-faced when he is hit by a wild pitch and refuse to rub the spot where he has been struck; conversely, a youngster may howl "in pain" when her older sister bumps her by accident.

4. **Body motions may be used to control or regulate the flow of a conversation or other communication transaction.** We use shifts in eye contact, slight head movements, shifts in posture, raising of eyebrows, and nodding of the head to tell a person when to continue, to repeat, to elaborate, to hurry up, or to finish. Effective communicators learn to adjust what they are saying and how they are saying it on the basis of such cues.

5. **Body motions may be used to relieve tension.** As we listen to people and watch them while they speak, they may scratch their head, tap their foot, or wring their hands.

Cultural Variations ❀

Several cultural differences in body motions are well documented.

Eye contact. Whereas a majority of people in the United States and other Western cultures expect those with whom they are communicating to "look them in the eye," in many societies avoiding eye contact communicates respect and deference (Martin and Nakayama 1997, p. 149). For instance, in Japan, people direct their gaze to a position around the Adam's apple, not directly into the other's eyes. Chinese, Indonesians, and rural Mexicans lower their eyes as a sign of deference; to them, too much direct eye contact is a sign of bad manners. Arabs, in contrast, look intently into the eyes of the person with whom they are talking for long periods; to them, direct eye contact demonstrates keen interest.

UNDERSTAND YOURSELF

Body Motions

Describe the body motions you use most frequently when you speak. Are they used as emblems, illustrators, affect displays, conversation regulators, or tension relievers? Are they effective in helping you convey your message? Are they habits that distract from your message?

Gestures, such as this V for victory sign, may have other meanings in other cultures.

There are also differences in use of eye contact among subcultures of the United States. For instance, African Americans use more continuous eye contact than European Americans when they are speaking but less when they are listening (Samovar and Porter 1995, p. 195).

Gestures, movements, and facial expression. People of other cultures also show considerable differences in use of gestures, movements, and facial expression. Gestures in particular can assume completely different meanings. For instance, forming a circle with the thumb and forefinger—the OK sign in the United States—means zero or worthless in France, a symbol for money in Japan, a curse in some Arab countries, and an obscene gesture in Germany, Brazil, and Australia (Axtell 1991, p. 47). Displays of emotion also vary. For instance, in some Eastern cultures, people have been socialized to deintensify emotional behavior cues, whereas members of other cultures have been socialized to amplify their displays of emotions. The cultural differences that are related to emotional displays are often reflected in the interpretation that can be given to facial expressions (Davitz 1964, p. 14).

Gender Variations

Men and women also show differences in their use of nonverbal communication behavior (Canary and Hause 1993, p. 141).

Eye contact. In the United States, women tend to have more frequent eye contact during conversations than men do (Cegala and Sillars 1989). Women tend to hold eye contact more than men regardless of the sex of the person they are interacting with (Wood 1997, p. 198).

Facial expression and gesture. Women tend to smile more than men, but their smiles are harder to interpret. Men's smiles generally mean positive feelings, whereas women's smiles tend to be general expressions of affiliation and friendliness (Pearson, West, and Turner 1995, p. 122). Gender differences in the use of gestures are so profound that people have been found to attribute masculinity or femininity on the basis of gesture style alone (Pearson, West, and Turner 1995, p. 126). Women are more likely to keep their arms close to their body, are less likely to lean forward, play more often with their hair or clothing, and tap their hands more often than men.

Success in male-female relationships is often measured by accuracy in encoding and decoding nonverbal messages. For instance, Noller (1987) found that couples with a high degree of marital satisfaction were likely to be accurate in decoding each other's nonverbal messages and in predicting whether or not their spouse would correctly decode their messages. Noller goes on to say that the inability of many men to correctly interpret the meaning of women's nonverbal behaviors suggests that men need more work in communication skills training (p. 173).

Paralanguage

Paralanguage is the nonverbal "sound" of what we hear—*how* something is said. We will first describe the four vocal characteristics that comprise paralanguage and then discuss how vocal interferences can disrupt message flow.

Vocal Characteristics

By controlling the four major vocal characteristics—pitch, volume, rate, and quality—we can complement, supplement, or contradict the meaning conveyed by the language of our message.

Pitch is the highness or lowness of tone. People tend to raise and lower vocal pitch to accompany changes in volume. They may also raise the pitch when they are nervous or lower the pitch when they are trying to be forceful.

UNDERSTAND YOURSELF

Vocal Characteristics

What happens to your voice in stressful situations? When does your pitch go up? Down? When do you talk loudly? Softly? Fast? Slowly? How aware of these changes are you?

PRACTICE IN CLASS

Paralanguage

Groups should create various situations to role-play. Have two or three members of the group role-play a situation for about four minutes. The rest of the group should observe and make notes of changes in paralanguage (pitch, rate, volume, and vocal quality) usage by each participant over the course of the conversation. Continue to role-play until each member of the group has both participated and observed.

Volume is loudness or softness of tone. Whereas some people have booming voices that carry long distances, others are normally soft-spoken. Regardless of their normal volume level, people vary their volume depending on the situation and the topic of discussion.

Rate is the speed at which a person speaks. People tend to talk more rapidly when they are happy, frightened, nervous, or excited and more slowly when they are problem-solving out loud or are trying to emphasize a point.

Quality is the sound of the voice. Each human voice has a distinct tone. Some voices are raspy, some smoky, some have bell-like qualities, while others are throaty. Moreover, each of us uses a slightly different quality of voice to communicate a particular state of mind. We may associate complaints with a whiny, nasal quality; seductive invitation with a soft, breathy quality; and anger with a strident, harsh quality.

Some of us have developed vocal habits that lead others to consistently misinterpret what we say. For instance, some people have cultivated a tone of voice that causes others to believe they are being sarcastic when they are not. If you have concerns about your vocal characteristics, talk them over with your professor. Your professor can observe you and make recommendations for additional help should you need it.

Vocal Interferences

Although most of us are occasionally guilty of using some **vocal interferences** (extraneous sounds or words that interrupt fluent speech), these interferences become a problem when they are perceived by others as excessive and when they begin to call attention to themselves and so prevent listeners from concentrating on meaning. The most common interferences that creep into our speech include "uh," "er," "well," "OK," and those nearly universal interrupters of Americans' conversation, "you know" and "like."

Vocal interferences may initially be used as "place markers" designed to fill in momentary gaps in speech that would otherwise be silence. In this way we indicate that we are not done speaking and it is still our "turn." Thus, we may use an "um" when we need to pause momentarily to search for the right word or idea. Although the chance of being interrupted may be real (some people will seek to interrupt at any pause), the intrusion of an excessive number of fillers can lead to the impression that you are unsure of yourself or confused about what you are trying to say.

Equally prevalent, and perhaps even more disruptive, is the overuse of "you know" and "like." The "you know" habit may begin as a genuine way to find out whether what is being said is already known by others. Similarly, the use of "like" may start from making comparisons such as "Tom is hot; he looks like Denzel Washington." Soon the comparisons become shortcuts as in "He's like really hot!" Finally, the use of "like" becomes pure filler: "Like, he's really cool, like I can't really explain it, but I'll tell you he's like wow!"

Curiously, no matter how irritating the use of "you know" or "like" may be to listeners, they are unlikely to verbalize their irritation. Yet your habitual use of these fillers can prove to be a handicap in many settings. For example, excessive use of vocal interferences during job interviews, at work, or in class can adversely affect the impression that you make.

By practicing the following steps, you can limit the occurrence of vocal interferences in your speech.

1. **Train yourself to hear your interferences.** Even people with a major problem seem to be unaware of the interferences they use. You can train your ear in one of two ways:

    a. Tape-record yourself talking for several minutes about any subject—the game you saw yesterday, the course you plan to take next term, or anything else that comes to mind. Before you play it back, estimate the number of times you think you peppered your speech with "um," "uh," "you know," and "like." Then compare the actual number with your estimate. As your ear becomes trained, your estimates will be closer to the actual number.

    b. Have a close friend listen to you and raise a hand every time you use "um," "uh," "you know," or "like." You may find the experience traumatic or nerve-racking, but your ear will soon start to pick up the vocal interferences as fast as the listener.

2. **Practice to see how long you can go without using a vocal interference.** Start out by trying to talk for fifteen seconds. Continue to increase the time until you can talk for two minutes without an interference. Meaning may suffer; you may spend a disproportionate amount of time avoiding interferences. Still, it is good practice.

3. **Mentally note your usage of interferences in conversation.** You will be making real headway when you can recognize your use of interferences in normal conversation without affecting the flow. When you reach this stage, you are well on your way to limiting your use of interferences.

Self-Presentation

People learn a great deal about us based on how we choose to present ourselves through our choices in clothing and personal grooming, our use of touching, and the way we treat time.

PRACTICE IN CLASS

Recognizing and Eliminating Vocal Interferences

Work in groups. Each person in the group should try to talk continuously for two minutes. Each person selects her or his own topic—for example, a current event in the news, a critique of a recent movie, or a description of a job/course problem. Whenever the speaker uses a vocal interference, the other members of the group should raise their hands. One group member should be assigned the task of counting and recording the number of times that hands are raised (if two hands are raised at the same time, count it as only one vocal interference). Give everyone two chances. Work to eliminate vocal interferences.

What is this woman expressing through her use of touchng behavior?

© Cable News Network, Inc.

Clothing and Personal Grooming

Choice of clothing and personal grooming will communicate a message; you need to determine what message you want to send and then dress and groom yourself accordingly. Lawyers and business managers understand the power of dress and grooming. For instance, an attorney knows that a person charged with drug peddling would be foolish to show up in the courtroom wearing the local gang starter jacket, heavy gold chains, oversized pants, and a backwards-facing baseball cap. Similarly, business managers generally have a clear idea of the images they want their businesses to project and may have a dress and personal grooming code for employees.

Many young people consciously choose clothing styles and personal grooming behaviors that stretch Western norms of acceptability. From "retro" fashions to hip-hop styles, from blue hair and nail colors to dreadlocks and mohawks, from tattooing to body piercing, more and more people are choosing to use their clothing and appearance to differentiate themselves from some groups and to identify closely with others.

While each of us has the *right* to express our individuality and to communicate our political feelings in our dress and personal grooming, we must realize that when we stretch norms and conventions, we create barriers. Part of being a skilled communicator is realizing that meaning depends as much on the receiver's perceptions as it does on our own intentions.

Poise

Poise refers to assurance of manner. As much as 20 percent of the population experiences a high degree of nervousness when encountering strangers, speaking in groups, and in public-speaking settings (Richmond and McCroskey 1989). For most people, nervousness decreases as they gain confidence in their ability to function well in the particular setting. Mastery of the skills discussed in the rest of this text should help you cope with the nervousness you might face in different communication situations.

Touch

Through **touch**—the use of hands, arms, and other body parts to pat, hug, slap, kiss, pinch, stroke, hold, embrace, and tickle—we communicate a variety of meanings. In Western culture, we shake hands to be sociable and polite, we pat a person on the back for encouragement, we hug a person to show love, we clasp raised hands to demonstrate solidarity. Our touching can be gentle or firm, perfunctory or passionate, brief or lingering. And how we touch can communicate our power, our empathy, our understanding.

People differ in their touching behavior and in their reactions to unsolicited touch from others. Some people like to touch and be touched; other people do not. Women tend to touch others less than men do, but women value touching more than men do. Women view touch as an expressive behavior that demonstrates warmth and affiliation, whereas men view touch as instrumental behavior so that touching females is considered as leading to sexual activity (Pearson, West, and Turner 1995, p. 142).

Although U.S. culture is relatively noncontact-oriented, the kinds and amounts of touching behavior within our society vary widely. Touching behavior that seems innocuous to one person may be perceived as overly intimate or threatening by another. Touch that is perceived to be OK in private may embarrass a person when done in public or with a large group of people. What you communicate by touching may be perceived positively or negatively (Burgoon, Walther, and Baesler 1992, p. 259). Thus, if you want to be perceived as sensitive and caring, it is a good idea to ask the other before touching.

Time

A less obvious aspect of our self-presentation is how we manage and react to others' use and management of what Edward T. Hall (1959) calls **informal time**, including duration, activity, and punctuality (p. 135).

Duration is the amount of time we regard as appropriate for certain events or activities. For instance, we may think a sermon should last 20 minutes and a typical class 50 minutes. When the duration of that event or activity differs

UNDERSTAND YOURSELF

Touch Orientation

Are you a "touchy-feely" type of person? Where does your touch orientation come from? Are others in your family similar in their reaction to touch? What kinds of touching behavior do you associate with power plays? with expressions of concern? with love? How often do you use touching behavior? How do you respond to the touching behaviors of others? What do you do when someone is using more touch behavior than you are comfortable with?

INFOTRAC COLLEGE EDITION

Touching behavior can be perceived as interpersonally comforting or harassing. Using the InfoTrac College Edition subject guide, enter the term "touch." Look for an article that considers the nature of the behaviors that shed light on the difference between these two perceptions.

significantly from our expectations, we begin to attribute meaning to that difference. For example, if we are told that our job interview will take one hour and it is over in twenty minutes, we may conclude that we didn't get the job. Similarly, if the interview stretches to two hours, we may believe that we are in strong contention for the job. Since our use of time creates its own meanings, we need to be sensitive to polite conventions about the "appropriate duration" of events and activities.

Activity refers to what people perceive should be done in a given time period. Many of us work during the day, sleep at night, eat a light meal around midday, and so on. When someone engages in behavior at a time that we deem inappropriate, we are likely to react negatively. For instance, Susan, who prides herself on being available to her employees, may well be put off when Sung Lei calls her at home during the dinner hour to discuss a presentation that is to be delivered at the end of the month. While Sung Lei may think she is presenting herself as organized and interested in her work, Susan may view her as rude and insensitive.

Punctuality is the extent to which one adheres strictly to the appointed or regular time. In many respects it may be the dimension of informal time that is most closely related to self-presentation. If you make an appointment to meet your professor in her office at 10 A.M., her opinion of you may differ depending on whether you arrive at 9:50, at 10:00, at 10:10, or at 10:30. Similarly, your opinion of her will differ depending on whether she is there or not at the appointed time. In the United States, strict punctuality is the dominant cultural imperative. When a date is made or an appointment set, you are normally expected to be prompt or risk having your early or late arrival be interpreted as meaningful.

Cultural Variations in Self-Presentation

Just as the meaning of body motions and paralanguage are culturally determined, so, too, are self-presentation behaviors.

Touch. In some cultures lots of contact and touching is normal behavior, while in other cultures individual space is respected and frequent touching is not encouraged. "People in high contact cultures evaluate 'close' as positive and good, and evaluate 'far' as negative and bad. People in low contact cultures evaluate 'close' as negative and bad, and 'far' as positive and good" (Gudykunst and Kim 1992, p. 178). According to the research that has been done, Latin America and the Mediterranean countries are high-contact cultures, northern European cultures are medium to low in contact, and Asian cultures are for the most part low-contact cultures. The United States, which is a country of immigrants, is generally perceived to be medium contact, though there are wide differences among individual Americans because of their family heritage.

Time. A particularly important area of difference concerns perceptions of time. Some cultures, including the dominant culture of the United States, view time **monochronically**; that is, they see time as compartmental, irreversible, and one-dimensional—a scarce resource to be "spent," "saved," and "budgeted." As a result, in the United States, being even a few minutes late may require you to acknowledge your lateness. Being ten to fifteen minutes late usually requires an apology, and being more than thirty minutes late is likely to be perceived as an insult requiring a great deal of explanation to earn the person's forgiveness (Samovar and Porter 1995, p. 206).

People from other cultural backgrounds, such as those from Latin America, Asia, or the Middle East, tend to view time **polychronically**, a view that sees time as continuous and involves engaging in several activities at the same time. To those with a polychronic view of time, the concept of "being late" has no meaning. One arrives when one has completed what came before. In Latin American or Arab cultures, for instance, it is not unusual for either person to be more than thirty minutes late, and neither is likely to expect or offer an apology (Gudykunst and Kim 1992, p. 178). Although the dominant culture in the United States is monochromatic in the extreme, within some of our Latin American and African American subcultures a polychromatic view of time still influences behavior.

Communication through Management of Your Environment

In addition to the way we use body motions, paralanguage, and self-presentation cues, we communicate nonverbally through the physical environment in which our conversations occur, including the space we occupy, the temperature of the surroundings, the lighting levels, and the colors used in the interior decorations.

Space

As a study, space includes permanent structures, the movable objects within space, and informal space.

Management of permanent structures. Permanent structures are the buildings in which we live and work and the parts of those buildings that cannot be moved. Although we may not have much control over their creation, we do exercise control in our selection of them. For instance, when you rent an apartment or buy a condominium or a home, you consider whether or not it is in tune with your lifestyle. People who select a fourth-floor loft may view themselves differently from those who select one-room efficiencies. Doctors, lawyers, and other professionals usually search with care to find homes that fit the image they want to communicate.

UNDERSTAND YOURSELF

Time Orientation

How do you use time? Recall an incident when the duration of an event violated your expectation for appropriate length. How did this violation affect what you thought of the person or what the other person thought of you? Do you have certain activity patterns that you consider important to follow? For example, do you have a set schedule for studying? doing your laundry? eating meals? How do you react when others have schedules that are drastically different? How important is it to you that you be punctual? Do you expect others to observe the same punctuality behavior? How does your opinion of others change when they continually deviate from your preferred level of punctuality?

OBSERVE AND ANALYZE

Cultural Differences in Self-Presentation

Interview or converse with two international students from different countries. Try to select students whose cultures differ from one another and from the culture with which you are most familiar. Develop a list of questions related to the self-presentation behaviors discussed here. Try to understand how people in the international student's country differ from you in their use of nonverbal self-presentation behaviors. Prepare to share what you have learned with your classmates.

In addition, specific features affect our communication within that environment. For instance, people who live in apartment buildings are likely to become better acquainted with neighbors who live across the hall and next door than those who live on other floors. Similarly, people who share common space like laundry facilities or garages are more likely to become acquainted than those who do not.

Management of movable objects within space. Whether the space is a dormitory room, a living room, a seminar room, or a classroom, we have the opportunity to arrange and rearrange movable objects to achieve the effect we want. In a classroom, for example, arranging chairs in rows facing the lectern establishes a lecture format, whereas grouping chairs in small circles suggests that the class will work on group projects. A boss's office arranged so that the boss sits behind the desk and the employee's chair is on the other side of that desk says, "Let's talk business—I'm the boss and you're the employee." If the employee's chair is at the side of the desk (creating an absence of a formal barrier), the arrangement says, "Don't be nervous—let's just chat."

Management of informal space. Managing **informal space** involves the space around us at the moment. In the dominant U.S. culture, four distinct distances represent what most people consider appropriate or comfortable in various situations (Hall 1969):

■ **Intimate distance,** up to eighteen inches, is appropriate for private conversations between close friends.

Many executives use the arrangement of their office furniture to communicate their status nonverbally.

Differing concepts of informal space: While you might find it rude for nonintimates to get this close to you in conversation, these men would find it rude if you backed away.

- **Personal distance,** from eighteen inches to four feet, is the space in which casual conversation occurs.
- **Social distance,** from four to twelve feet, is where impersonal business such as job interviews is conducted.
- **Public distance** is anything more than twelve feet.

Of greatest concern to us is the intimate distance—the distance we regard as appropriate for intimate conversation with close friends, parents, and younger children. If you have become uncomfortable because a person you were talking with was standing too close to you, you are already aware of how attitudes toward intimate space influences people's conversation. People usually become uncomfortable when "outsiders" violate this intimate distance. For instance, in a movie theater that is less than one-quarter full, people will tend to leave one or more seats between themselves and others whom they do not know. If in such a setting a stranger sits right next to you, you are likely to feel uncomfortable or threatened and may even move away.

Intrusions into our intimate space are acceptable only in certain settings, and then only when all involved follow the unwritten rules. For instance, people will tolerate being packed into a crowded elevator or subway and even touching others they do not know, provided that the others follow such "rules" as standing rigidly, looking at the floor or the indicator above the door but not making eye contact with others. These rules also include ignoring or pretending that they are not touching. Only occasionally will people who are forced to invade each others intimate space acknowledge the other as a person. Then they are

THINK CRITICALLY

Permanent Structures and Communication

Consider where you live. Which of your neighbors do you know well? How did you happen to meet them? Does your experience confirm what you have just read? If not, what other factors seem to account for what you have experienced?

SPOTLIGHT ON SCHOLARSHIP

Judee K. Burgoon, Professor of Communication, University of Arizona, on Nonverbal Expectancy Violations Theory

With seven books and more than 150 articles and book chapters to her credit, Judee K. Burgoon is a leading scholar who has helped to shape how we now think about nonverbal com-

munication. Her fascination with nonverbal behavior dates back to a graduate school seminar assignment at the University of West Virginia, where she was asked to find out what was known about proxemics, the study of space. From that assignment, she says, "I just got hooked. Nonverbal is more elusive and difficult to study, and I've always enjoyed a challenge!"

At the time, scholars believed that the road to interpersonal success lay in conforming one's behaviors to social norms about the distances that are appropriate for certain types of interactions and the types of touch that are appropriate for certain people in certain relationships. Thus, people would be successful in their interactions as long as they behaved in accord with these norms. Encouraged by one of her professors to "look for the counterintuitive," Burgoon's research showed that there were situations in which violations of these norms resulted in positive, rather than negative, consequences. For example, in settings where two people were not well acquainted and one of them began "flirting" by moving closer to the other, thus "violating" that person's space, the other person did not always react by moving away from the violator as expected. In fact, at times the person seemed to welcome the violation and at times may even have moved closer. Similarly, she noticed that touching behavior that violated social norms was sometimes rejected and at other times accepted.

To explain what she saw happening, Burgoon developed and began to test what she called "expectancy violation theory," which is based on the premise that we have strong expectations about how people ought to behave when they interact with us. Whether they meet our expectations not only affects how we interact with them, but also affects such outcomes as how competent, credible, and influential we perceive them to be and what we think of our relationship. She found that how we interpret a violation depends on how we feel about the person. If we like the person, we are likely to read the nonverbal violation as positive ("Gee, she put her arm around me—that means she's really interested in me"); if we don't like the person, we are likely to read the same nonverbal violation as negative ("He better take his arm off me, this is a clear case of harassment"). And because we have become sensitized to the situation, the violations will be subject to strong evaluations ("Wow, I really like the feel of her arm around my waist" or "He's making me feel really uncomfortable"). As Burgoon continued to study violations, she discovered that when a person we really like violates our expectations, we are likely to view the interaction as even more positive than we would have if the person had conformed to our expectations. Over the years, numerous research studies by Burgoon and her students have provided strong support for expectancy violation theory.

Burgoon's scholarship has developed like a river. Her first work was a narrow stream with a focus on proxemics that grew with expectancy violation theory to include all of nonverbal behavior and continues to branch. Presently, in one stream of work, she is studying what determines how people adapt their behavior when they experience any type of communication violation. Why and when do they reciprocate the violation (if someone shouts, you shout back) or compensate for it (if someone comes too close to you, you step back)? In a second stream, Burgoon is focusing on a specific type of expectancy violation: deception. Here she is trying to sort out the role that nonverbal behavior plays in deceitful interactions. Finally, she has begun a stream of work whose purpose is to identify the essential properties of interpersonal communication that are different from the properties of media communication. Whatever branch her research takes, Judee Burgoon brings the same readiness to challenge the current thinking that has been the hallmark of her work. For complete citations of many of her recent publications in these areas, see the references listed at the end of this book.

In addition to teaching a number of courses, Burgoon serves as Director of Graduate Studies, where her role of helping students learn how to conduct research and formulate theory gives her great satisfaction. "Mentoring others is among the major gratifications of doing research. The fun is to teach others what I was taught: Always challenge the current assumptions."

likely to exchange sheepish smiles or otherwise acknowledge the mutual invasion of intimate distance. In the Spotlight on Scholarship, we feature Judee Burgoon, who has focused a great deal of her research on the effects of such intrusions into our intimate space. Her findings develop and test what she calls "expectancy violation theory."

Interpersonal problems occur when one person's use of space violates the behavioral expectations of another. For instance, Jaron may come from a family that conducts informal conversations with others at a range closer than the eighteen-inch limit that many European Americans place on intimate space. When he talks to a colleague at work and moves in closer than eighteen inches, the coworker may back away from him during the conversation. Unfortunately, there are times when one person intentionally violates the space expectations of another. When the violation is between members of the opposite sex, it can be considered sexual harassment. Don may, through violations of informal space, posture, movements, or gestures, appear to "come on" to Donnice. If Donnice does not welcome the attention, she may feel threatened. In this case, Don's nonverbal behavior can be construed as sexual harassment. In order to avoid perceptions of harassment, people need to be especially sensitive to others' definitions of intimate space.

Besides our intimate or personal space, which moves when we move, we are likely to look at certain space as our **territory**—as space over which we may claim ownership—whether or not we are currently occupying it. If Marcia decides to eat lunch at the company commissary, the space at the table she selects becomes her territory. Suppose that during lunch Marcia leaves her territory to get butter for her roll. The chair she left, the food on the table, and the space around that food are "hers," and she will expect others to stay away. If, when she returns, Marcia finds that someone at the table has moved a glass or a dish into the area that she regards as her territory, she is likely to feel resentful.

Many people stake out their territory with markers. For example, Ramon arrives early for the first day of class, finds an empty desk, and puts his back-

OBSERVE AND ANALYZE

Management of Movable Objects

Rearrange the furniture in your dorm room or in one room of your house so that you change the primary focus of the room. Record your own reactions to the new arrangement. Observe how other people react to the changes you have made. Compare them to your written reactions.

pack at the side on the floor and his coat on the seat. He then makes a quick trip to the restroom. If someone comes along while Ramon is gone, moves his backpack and coat, and sits down at the desk, that person is violating what Ramon has marked as his territory.

As a student of nonverbal communication, however, you understand that other people may not look at either the space around you or your territory in quite the same way as you do. That the majority of U.S. residents have learned the same basic rules governing the management of space does not mean that everyone shares the same respect for the rules or treats the consequences of breaking the rules in the same way. For example, members of rival street gangs may "punish" those who violate their territories with beatings or worse. Thus, it is important to be observant so that you can be sensitive to how others react to your behaviors.

Temperature, Lighting, and Color ✻

Three other elements of the environment that can be controlled and that "send messages" affecting communication are temperature, lighting, and color.

Temperature can stimulate or inhibit effective communication by altering peoples' moods and changing their levels of attentiveness. Do you sometimes have difficulty listening to a teacher in a hot, stuffy classroom? Or have you found that you become "edgy" when you're cold?

Lighting also adds meaning to communication messages. In lecture halls and reading rooms, bright light is expected—it encourages good listening and comfortable reading. By contrast, in a chic restaurant, a music listening room, or a television lounge, you expect the lighting to be soft and rather dim, which makes for a cozy atmosphere and invites intimate conversation (Knapp and Hall 1992, p. 72). We often change the lighting level in a room to change the mood and indicate the type of interaction that is expected. Bright lights encourage activity and boisterous conversations; softer lighting levels calm and soothe, encouraging quiet and more serious conversations.

Color may stimulate both emotional and physical reactions. For instance, red excites, blue comforts and soothes, yellow cheers and elevates moods. Professional interior designers who understand how people react to colors may choose blues when they are trying to create a peaceful, serene atmosphere for a living room, but decorate a playroom in reds and yellows.

In addition, specific colors may convey information about people and events. For instance, youth gangs often use colors to signal membership. So in some communities gang members wear bandannas or other articles of clothing in a specific color.

Cultural Variations in Management of Environment ✻

As you would expect, the environments in which people feel comfortable depend on their cultural background. In the United States, where we have ample land, many people live in individual homes or in large apartments. In other countries, where land is scarce, people live in more confined spaces and can feel "lonely" or isolated in larger spaces. In Asia, most people live in spaces that by our standards would feel quite cramped. Similarly, people from different cultures have different ideas about what constitutes appropriate distances for various interactions. Recall that in the dominant culture of the United States, personal or intimate space is eighteen inches or less. In Middle Eastern cultures, however, men move much closer to other men when they are talking (Samovar and Porter 1995, p. 202). Thus, when an Arab man talks with a man from the United States, one of the two is likely to be uncomfortable. Either the American will feel uncomfortable and invaded, or the Arab will feel isolated and too distant for serious conversation. We also differ in the temperature ranges that we find comfortable. People who originate from warmer climates can tolerate heat more than people who originate in cooler climates. Even the meanings that we assign to colors vary by national culture and religion. In India, white not black is the color of mourning, and Hindu brides wear red.

UNDERSTAND YOURSELF

Personal Territory

Do you have your own place at the family dinner table? What happens if you find someone else sitting in your place? Make a mental list of the other "territories" you "own."

REFLECT ON ETHICS

After the intramural mixed-doubles matches on Tuesday evening, most of the players adjourned to the campus grill for a while to have a drink and chat. Marquez and Lisa sat down with Barry and Elana, whom they had lost to that night largely because of Elana's improved play. Although Marquez and Lisa were only tennis friends, Barry and Elana had been going out together for much of the season.

After some general conversation about the tournament, Marquez said, "Elana, your serve today was the best I've seen it this year."

"Yeah, I was really impressed. And as you saw, I had trouble handling it," Lisa added.

"And you're getting to the net a lot better, too," Marquez added.

"Thanks, guys," Elana replied in a tone of gratitude. "I've really been working on it."

"Well, aren't we getting the compliments today?" sneered Barry in a sarcastic tone. Then after a pause, he said, "Oh, Elana, would you get my sweater—I left it on that chair by the other table."

"Come on Barry, you're closer than I am," Elana replied.

Barry got a cold look on his face, moved slightly closer to Elana, and said emphatically, "Get my sweater for me, Elana—now."

Elana backed away from Barry as she said, "OK, Barry—it's cool," and quickly got the sweater for him.

"Gee, isn't she sweet?" Barry said to Marquez and Lisa as he grabbed the sweater from Elana.

Lisa and Marquez both looked down at the floor. Then Lisa glanced at Marquez and said, "Well, I'm out of here—I've got a lot to do this evening."

"Let me walk you to your car," Marquez said as he stood up.

"See you next week," they both said in unison as they hurried out the door, leaving Barry and Elana alone at the table.

1. Analyze Barry's nonverbal behavior. What was he attempting to achieve?
2. How do you interpret Lisa's and Marquez's nonverbal reactions to Barry?
3. Was Barry's behavior ethically acceptable? Explain.

OBSERVE AND ANALYZE

Managing the Environment

Choose two or more sites of the same type (such as restaurants, apartments, dorm rooms, or doctors' offices). Visit each site, and observe and record the seating arrangements, temperature, lighting, and use of color at each site. Also observe the communication behavior of the people at the site.

Describe the sites in writing, and discuss how the environmental factors affected the behavior of the people at each site.

Summary

Nonverbal communication refers to how people communicate through the use of body motions, paralanguage, self-presentation cues, and the physical environment.

Perhaps the most familiar methods of nonverbal communication are what and how a person communicates through body motions and paralanguage. Eye contact, facial expression, gesture, and posture are four major types of body motions. Body motions act as emblems, illustrators, affect displays, conversation regulators, and tension relievers. Likewise, a person's vocal characteristics (volume, rate, pitch, and quality) as well as vocal interferences (such as "ah," "um," "you know," and "like") help us interpret the meaning of the verbal message.

Although verbal and nonverbal communication work together best when they are complementary, nonverbal cues may replace or even contradict verbal symbols. Generally, nonverbal communication is more to be trusted when verbal and nonverbal cues are in conflict.

Through self-presentation cues, such as clothing, touching behavior, and use of time, people communicate about themselves and their relationship to others. The physical environment is often overlooked, even though we set the tone for conversations and nonverbally communicate through it. The choices people make in their permanent spaces, the way they arrange the objects in those spaces, and the way they control or react to temperature, lighting, and color contribute to the quality and meaning of the communication episodes that occur.

SELF-REVIEW

Establishing a Communication Foundation from Chapters 1 to 4

What kind of communicator are you? The following analysis looks at ten specific behaviors that are basic to effective communication. On the line provided for each statement, indicate the response that best captures your behavior: 1, never; 2, rarely; 3, occasionally; 4, often; 5, almost always.

_____ When I speak, I tend to present a positive image of myself. (Ch. 2)

_____ In my behavior toward others, I look for more information to confirm or negate my first impressions. (Ch. 2)

_____ Before I act on perceptions drawn from people's nonverbal cues, I seek verbal verification of their accuracy. (Ch. 2)

_____ My conversation is helped by a large vocabulary. (Ch. 3)

_____ I speak clearly, using words that people readily understand. (Ch. 3)

_____ When I am speaking with people of different cultures or of the opposite sex, I am careful to monitor my word choices. (Ch. 3)

_____ I tend to look at people when I talk with them. (Ch. 4)

_____ Most of my sentences are free from such expressions as "uh," "well," "like," and "you know." (Ch. 4)

_____ I consider the effect of my dress on others. (Ch. 4)

_____ I try to control my environment in ways that help my communication. (Ch. 4)

Based on your responses, select the communication behavior that you would most like to change. Write a communication improvement goal statement similar to the sample contract in Chapter 1 (page 24). If you would like verification of your self-analysis before you write a goal, have a friend or coworker complete this same analysis for you.

Interpersonal communication is your informal interaction with others. Talking to a friend on campus, chatting on the phone with a classmate about an upcoming test, arguing the merits of a movie with friends, soothing an intimate friend who has been jilted, discussing strategies for accomplishing tasks at work, interviewing for a job, and planning the future with a loved one are all forms of interpersonal communication.

Effective interpersonal communication conveys our sensitivity to others and to the situation. One goal of effective interpersonal communication is to maintain relationships, and forming verbal messages that accurately convey our ideas and feelings while not offending the other person is key to our success.

Effective interpersonal communication empowers us. People who can clearly express their ideas, beliefs, and opinions become influential and exert control over what happens to them and to others that they care about. When we accurately and precisely encode our thoughts, others gain a better appreciation for our position. Their understanding and appreciation make it more likely that they will respond in ways that are consistent with our needs.

Effective interpersonal communication helps us manage the impressions we create. Presenting ourselves in such a way that others will respect and trust us is important in both public and private settings—whether we're communicating in a professional setting, where our interpersonal skills are vital to getting a job, holding a position, or rising in an organization, or in a private setting where we're trying to build and maintain relationships.

In this part we discuss sharing personal information, listening and responding with empathy and understanding, holding effective conversations, building and maintaining relationships, and interviewing. With an increased repertoire of interpersonal communication skills, you can select the ones that are most appropriate for the particular communication situation.

two

INTERPERSONAL COMMUNICATION

OBJECTIVES

After you have read this chapter, you should be able to answer the following questions:

- What do we mean by self-disclosure?
- What are some guidelines for disclosing?
- When and how does one describe feelings?
- What are the differences between displaying feelings and describing feelings?
- What are the differences among passive, aggressive, and assertive responses?
- How can you assert yourself appropriately?
- How can you improve your effectiveness in giving praise and constructive criticism?

5

Self-Disclosure and Feedback

"**C**huck, when that interviewer at the grocery store asked you whether you'd rather have stuffing than potatoes, you said 'yes'! We've been married more than twenty years, and I'm just now learning that you like stuffing more than potatoes."

"Well, I'm sorry, Susan," Chuck said sheepishly.

"Chuck," Susan asks, "are there other things that you like or don't like that you haven't told me about during these more than twenty years?"

"Well, probably."

"Chuck—why aren't you telling me about these things?"

"Well, I don't know, Susan. I guess I didn't think they were all that important."

"Not important? Chuck, almost every night that I cook we have potatoes. And frankly, I hate potatoes. I wouldn't care if I never saw a potato again. Now I find out you like stuffing better!"

"Sue, why didn't you ever tell me that you don't like potatoes?"

"Well, I, uh-uh . . ."

Poor Chuck—poor Susan—all those years! But is their experience all that unusual? Do we take the time to tell others what we're really thinking and feeling? For a lot of people, the answer is a resounding *no*.

Because the self-disclosure and feedback processes are fundamental to healthy relationships, in this chapter we will take a closer look at these concepts, and we will elaborate on the skills associated with each. More specifically, we will discuss self-disclosure, disclosing feelings, owning feelings, giving personal feedback, and assertiveness.

Self-Disclosure

Almost all effective interpersonal communication requires some degree of self-disclosure. In the broadest sense, **self-disclosure** means sharing biographical data, personal ideas, and feelings. Statements such as "I was 5-foot-6 in seventh grade" reveal biographical information—facts about you as an individual. Biographical disclosures are the easiest to make, for they are, in a manner of speaking, a matter of public record. By contrast, statements such as "I don't think prisons ever really rehabilitate criminals" disclose personal ideas and reveal what and how you think. And statements such as "I get scared whenever I have to make a speech" disclose feelings. In terms of accuracy in understanding of self and others, it is this last sense in which most people think of self-disclosure—that is, revealing personal information about self that the other person does not know.

Self-disclosure is at the heart of what is called "social penetration theory." The term **social penetration** was coined by Irwin Altman and Dalmas Taylor (1973). Initially, they thought that the self-disclosure pattern in a relationship moved steadily from shallow to deeper and more personal. Recently, however, their research has shown that levels of self-disclosure are cyclical. Relational partners go back and forth between achieving more intimacy by disclosing more and developing distance by refraining from disclosure. This cycle is the process through which they manage the tension between the needs for privacy and connection (Altman 1993, p. 27).

Although knowing a person better may well result in closer interpersonal relations, learning too much too soon about a person may result in alienation. If what we learn about another person causes us to lose trust in the person, our affection is likely to wane—hence the saying "Familiarity breeds contempt." Because some people fear that their disclosures could have negative rather than positive consequences for their relationships, they prefer not to disclose.

So while self-disclosure usually helps people become more comfortable with each other, unlimited self-disclosure may have negative effects. By far the most consistent finding of the research on self-disclosure is that self-disclosure has the greatest positive effect on relationships when it is reciprocated (Berg and Derlega 1987, p. 4). This finding suggests that the amount of self-disclosure in a relationship should be approximately equal.

Guidelines for Appropriate Self-Disclosure

So, what should be disclosed, and when, in a relationship? Following are some guidelines for determining an appropriate amount of self-disclosure in interpersonal encounters.

1. **Self-disclose the kind of information you want others to disclose to you.** When people are getting to know others, they begin by sharing information that is seen as normally shared freely among people with that type of relationship in that culture. At early stages in the relationship, this level of disclosure might include information about hobbies, sports, school, and views on current events. One way that people signal an interest in moving a relationship to a deeper level is when they take the risk of disclosing something normally perceived as inappropriate for the level that the relationship has been on. So if you are trying to achieve more intimacy, you will need to "risk" disclosing. But remember, if the other person does not reciprocate, you need to consider whether continued disclosure is appropriate.

2. **Self-disclose more intimate information only when you believe the disclosure represents an acceptable risk.** There is always some risk involved in disclosing, but as you gain trust in another person, you perceive that the disclosure of more revealing information is less likely to have negative consequences. Incidentally, this guideline explains why people sometimes engage in intimate self-disclosure with bartenders or with people they meet while traveling. They perceive the disclosures as safe (representing reasonable risk) because the person either does not know them or is in no position to use the information against them. Unfortunately, some people apparently lack the kinds of relationships with family and friends that would enable them to make these kinds of disclosures to them.

3. **Continue intimate self-disclosure only if it is reciprocated.** Based on the research, it appears that people expect a kind of equity in self-disclosure (Derlega, Metts, Petronio, and Margulis 1993, p. 33). When it is apparent that self-disclosure will not be returned, you should seriously consider limiting the amount of disclosure you make. Lack of reciprocation generally suggests that the person does not feel the relationship is one in which extensive self-disclosure is truly appropriate. When the response to your self-disclosure tells you that the disclosure was inappropriate, ask yourself what led to this effect. You can learn from a mistake and avoid making the same kind of mistake in the future.

4. **Move self-disclosure to deeper levels gradually.** Because receiving self-disclosure can be as threatening as giving it, most people become

PRACTICE IN CLASS

Self-Disclosure Guidelines

The following exercise will help you recognize the variations in what people see as appropriate self-disclosure and provide you with a useful base of information from which to work. Label each of the following statements L (low risk), meaning you believe it is appropriate to disclose this information to almost any person; M (moderate risk), meaning you believe it is appropriate to disclose this information to persons you know fairly well and with whom you have already established a friendship; H (high risk), meaning you would disclose such information only to the few friends you have great trust in or to your most intimate friends; or X (unacceptable risk), meaning you would disclose it to no one.

_____a. Your hobbies, how you like best to spend your spare time

_____b. Your preferences and dislikes in music

_____c. Your educational background and your feelings about it

_____d. Your personal views on politics, the presidency, and foreign and domestic policy

_____e. Your personal religious views and the nature of your religious participation

_____f. Habits and reactions of yours that bother you at the moment

_____g. Characteristics of yours that give you pride and satisfaction

continued on p. 105

uncomfortable when the level of disclosure exceeds their expectations. As a relationship develops, the depth of disclosure increases as well.

5. **Reserve intimate or very personal self-disclosures for ongoing relationships.** Disclosures about fears, loves, and other deep or intimate matters are most appropriate in close, well-established relationships. When people disclose deep secrets to acquaintances, they are engaging in potentially threatening behavior. Making such disclosures before a bond of trust is established risks alienating the other person. People are often embarrassed by and hostile toward others who try to saddle them with personal information in an effort to establish a relationship where none exists.

Cultural and Gender Differences

As we might expect, levels of self-disclosure and appropriateness of disclosure differ from culture to culture. The United States is considered an informal culture (Samovar and Porter 1995, p. 105). As a result, Americans tend to disclose more about themselves than people from other cultures. Levels of formality are based on how people dress, forms of address, and levels of self-disclosure. Germany, for instance, a country that is like the United States in many ways, has a much higher degree of formality. Germans are likely to dress well even if just visiting friends or going to school. They also use formal titles in their interactions with others. And they have fewer close friends. A German proverb states, "A friend to everyone is a friend to no one." Japan is another country that has a much higher degree of formality.

Particularly in the beginning stages of a friendship, such cultural differences can easily lead to misperceptions and discomfort if the people involved are unaware of them. For instance, a person from the United States may perceive an acquaintance from an Eastern culture as reserved or less interested in pursuing a "genuine" friendship, whereas the acquaintance may see the person from the United States as discourteously assertive or embarrassingly expressive about personal feelings and other private matters. Being aware of cultural differences can help us recognize when we need to check out our perceptions instead of assuming that everyone shares the standards of appropriateness and the verbal and nonverbal cues we are used to in our own culture.

©1995 Baby Blues Partnership. Distributed by King Features Syndicate.
Reprinted with special permission of King Features Syndicate, Inc.

Given the differences in culture, can we assume that disclosure always deepens relationships? Gudykunst and Kim (1992) have discovered that, across cultures, when relationships become more intimate, self-disclosure increases. In addition, they found that the more partners self-disclosed to each other, the more they were attracted to each other and the more uncertainty about each other was reduced (p. 202).

Consistent with conventional wisdom, women tend to disclose more than men, are disclosed to more than men, and are more aware than men of cues that affect their self-disclosure (Pearson, West, and Turner 1995, p. 164). But of course, this generalization is not true in all cases (Hill and Stull 1987, p. 95). In their discussion of differences in disclosure, Pearson, West, and Turner (1995, p. 164) suggest several reasons why women tend to disclose more. Women may disclose more because they are expected to (a kind of self-fulfilling prophecy), because self-disclosing is more important to women, and because the results are more satisfying to women. Interestingly, both men and women report that they disclose more intimate information to women (Stewart, Cooper, Stewart, and Friedley 1996, p. 110).

Differences in learned patterns of self-disclosure can create misunderstandings between men and women, especially in intimate relationships. In *You Just Don't Understand*, Deborah Tannen (1990) argues that one way to capture the differences between men's and women's verbal styles is to use the terms *report-talk* and *rapport-talk*. Her point is that men in our society are more likely to view conversation as "report-talk"—a way to share information, display knowledge, negotiate, and preserve independence. In contrast, women are more likely to use "rapport-talk"—a way to share experiences and establish bonds with others. When men and women fail to recognize these differences in the way they have learned to use conversation, the stage is set for misunderstandings about whether or not they are being truly open and intimate with one another. "Learning about style differences won't make them go away," Tannen remarks, "but it can banish mutual mystification and blame (p. 48)."

_____h. The actions you have most regretted taking in your life and why

_____i. The main unfulfilled wishes and dreams in your life

_____j. Your guiltiest secrets

_____k. Your views on the way a husband and wife should live their marriage

_____l. What to do, if anything, to stay fit

_____m. The aspects of your body you are most pleased with

_____n. The features of your appearance you are most displeased with and wish to change

_____o. The person in your life whom you most resent and the reasons why

Optional: Working in groups of five, discuss your labeling of the statements. The goal of the discussion is not to make any of the disclosures, only to discuss why or why not you would make them, and under what circumstances. The purpose of the discussion is to see how people differ in what they view as acceptable disclosure.

Disclosing Feelings

At the heart of intimate self-disclosure is sharing your feelings with someone else. And sharing feelings is a risky business. Why is this so? When we share our feelings about something important, we are generally giving someone else potent knowledge about us that they might use to harm us. Yet all of us experience feelings and have to decide whether and how to disclose them. Obviously, one option is to withhold or mask our feelings. If we do decide to disclose our feelings, we can display them or we can describe them.

Multiculturalism and Self-Disclosure

by Shawn McDougal

In this excerpt Shawn McDougal questions the ways in which we use our racial identities to mask important cultural differences. He suggests that real multicultural understanding is possible only when we are willing to risk and to disclose honestly.

I'd like to take a little time to say a few things about multiculturalism. I'm sure (and I hope!) I'll catch flames for some of what I have to say here, but isn't a willingness to expose oneself to vigorous ridicule or criticism a necessary precondition of saying anything valuable or meaningful?

I've been more and more aware recently of a certain misunderstanding that a lot of people have about culture.

Race does not equal culture. Culture does not equal race. Although they may be correlated, they are not the same, and this confounding of the two is an unfortunate fallacy in our popular thinking about race, identity, and culture that really limits us from having a truly culturally diverse experience with each other.

What happens when people confuse something like race with culture is a false-culture, a false self-consciousness. People deceive themselves into playing roles—identity games—that don't reflectively and consciously speak to their true culture, their life-curves. They adopt ritualized patterns of behavior and interaction that don't allow any space for honest and open self-reflection. We see the results of this self-deceiving shallowness in the culture of conformity; people adopt the latest fashionable lifestyle(s) uncritically—they just want to fit in. Their culture is the false-culture of whatever happen to be the latest fads. Their thinking is the stereotyped thinking of the herd. They hide their personal-biographical differences behind a facade of uniformity. They end up reducing their unique and problematic selves to easy to swallow (and to stereotype) images: "It's a black thing . . . ," "My background is suburban," "I had typical Asian parents . . . ," etc. (What the hell are typical

Asian parents? Is the "black thing" of Jamaican immigrants the same as that of transplants from Alabama? Do wealthy suburbanites live like working-class suburbanites?)

False-culture, or false self-consciousness, doesn't lead to any real cultural exchange for two reasons. First, because people only bring their superficial/stereotypical selves to their general relations with each other, the cultures that end up getting negotiated and "understood" in their communion/communication are devoid of precisely those gritty, hard-to-reduce, problematic aspects of their personal experience that have shaped them on their profoundest levels.

This discomfort with problematic culture is manifest here at Williams College in the way people tend to stick tightly to groups of people they are most comfortable with (and least challenged by). Social groups here most often seem to be comprised solely of people who already have very similar backgrounds to each other. Further, even if a group is "multicultural," it is usually so in exactly the false-culture sort of way: it is made up of people from different backgrounds who submerge any problematic aspects of themselves beneath some stereotyped group identity. People resist talking in depth about their various personal-biographies. It is as if being "black" or "Asian" or "queer" or "middle class" says it all.

The second reason that false-culture inhibits cultural exchange follows from the subjective-experiential nature of culture: for an individual to communicate his or her culture requires that he or she has some reflective awareness of how his or her life has been shaped. Someone who doesn't reflect on their experiences can't communicate those experiences to other people.

In short: Although I might meet someone who has a radically different background than my own, unless we talk about more than our favorite sports teams or current love-interests, there is no real cultural exchange going on. And if we only think about the present and the future, and we don't reflectively think about our pasts, any

cultural exchange is empty and false. Any "multiculturalism" based on false and simplistic notions of culture is not multiculturalism at all, but some convenient and ultimately valueless substitute.

Excerpted from Shawn McDougal, "Mistaken Notions of Multiculturalism Limit Communication and Self-Reflection," The Williams Record, Vol. 107, no. 21 (1993), p. 3. Reprinted by permission of Shawn McDougal.

Withholding or Masking Feelings

In our culture, **withholding feelings**—that is, denying them by keeping them inside and not giving any verbal or nonverbal cues to their existence—is considered unhealthy and generally regarded as an inappropriate means of dealing with feelings. Withholding feelings is best exemplified by the good poker player who develops a "poker face"—a neutral look that is impossible to decipher, always the same whether the player's cards are good or bad. Unfortunately, many people use poker faces in their relationships, so that no one knows whether they are hurt, excited, or saddened. For instance, Doris feels very nervous when Anitra stands over her while Doris is working on her report. When Anitra says, "That first paragraph isn't very well written," Doris begins to seethe, yet says nothing—she withholds her feelings.

Psychologists believe that habitually withholding feelings can lead to physical problems such as ulcers and heart disease, as well as psychological problems such as stress and depression. Moreover, people who withhold feelings are often perceived as cold, undemonstrative, and not much fun to be around.

Is withholding ever appropriate? When a situation is inconsequential, you may well choose to withhold your feelings. For instance, a stranger's inconsiderate behavior at a party may bother you, but there is often little to be gained by disclosing your feelings about it. You don't have an ongoing relationship with the person, and you can deal with the situation simply by moving to another part of the room. In the example of Doris's seething at Anitra's behavior, however, withholding could be costly to both parties because Doris's feelings of irritation and tension are likely to affect their working relationship as well as Doris's well-being.

Displaying Feelings

Displaying feelings is expressing feelings through facial reactions, body responses, or paralinguistic reactions. Although displays of feelings may be accompanied by verbal messages, the feelings themselves are expressed in non-

In general, men tend to disclose their feelings less than women, but this varies by individual and cultural tradition.

verbal behavior. Cheering over a great play at a sporting event, howling when you bang your head against the car doorjamb, and patting a coworker on the back for doing something well are all displays of feelings.

Displays are usually appropriate when the feelings you are experiencing are positive. For instance, when your friend Gloria does something nice for you and you experience a feeling of joy, giving her a big hug is appropriate; when your supervisor gives you an assignment you've wanted, a big smile with your "Thank you" is an appropriate display of your feeling of appreciation. In fact, many people need to be more demonstrative of good feelings than they typically are. The bumper sticker "Have you hugged your kid today?" reinforces the point that people we care about need open displays of love and affection.

Displays become detrimental to communication when the feelings you are experiencing are negative—especially when the display of a negative feeling appears to be an overreaction. For instance, when Anitra says to Doris, "That first paragraph isn't very well written," if Doris displays her feelings of resentment by shouting, "Who the hell asked you for your opinion?" such a display will no doubt embarrass and offend Anitra and short-circuit their communication. Although displays of negative feelings may make you feel better temporarily, they are likely to be bad for you interpersonally.

Displays of feelings often serve as an escape valve for very strong emotions. In this way they may be a more healthy approach than withholding feelings because they "get them out of our system." Unfortunately, especially with negative emotions, these displays can often damage our relationships or cause stress in our relational partners. In many families, children learn to "stay out of Dad's way if he's in a bad mood" because they have experienced the power of Dad's emotional displays. Rather than displaying our emotions, we can use the self-disclosure skill of describing feelings to help us share our feelings with others in a manner that does not damage our relationships or cause stress.

Describing Feelings

Describing feelings is naming the emotion you are feeling without judging it. Describing feelings increases the chances of positive interaction and decreases the chances of short-circuiting lines of communication. Moreover, describing feelings teaches others how to treat us by explaining the effect of their behavior. This knowledge gives them the information they need to determine the appropriateness of that behavior. Thus, if you tell Paul that you feel flattered when he visits you, your description of how you feel should encourage him to visit you again. Likewise, when you tell Tony that you feel very angry when he borrows your jacket without asking, he is more likely to ask the next time. Describing your feelings allows you to exercise a measure of control over others' behavior simply by making them aware of the effects their actions have on you.

Many times, people think they are describing when in fact they are displaying feelings or evaluating the other person's behavior. For instance, Doris may believe her outburst, "Who the hell asked you for your opinion?" is a description of feelings. The Test Your Competence exercise at the end of this section focuses on your awareness of the difference between describing feelings and either displaying feelings or expressing evaluations.

If describing feelings is so important to effective communication, why don't more people do it regularly? There seem to be at least five reasons why many people don't describe feelings.

1. **Many people don't have a very good vocabulary of words for describing the various feelings they experience.** People can sense that they are angry; however, they may not be able to distinguish between feeling annoyed, betrayed, cheated, crushed, disturbed, envious, furious, infuriated, outraged, or shocked. Each of these terms describes a slightly different aspect of what many people lump together as anger. A surprising number of shades of meaning can be used to describe feelings, as shown in Figure 5.1. If you are to become more effective in describing your feelings, you may first need to work to develop a better "vocabulary of emotions."

Words Related to *Angry*

agitated	annoyed	bitter	cranky
enraged	exasperated	furious	hostile
incensed	indignant	infuriated	irked
irritated	mad	offended	outraged
peeved	resentful	riled	steamed

Words Related to *Helpful*

agreeable	amiable	beneficial	caring
collegial	compassionate	constructive	cooperative
cordial	gentle	kindly	neighborly
obliging	supportive	useful	warm

Words Related to *Loving*

adoring	affectionate	amorous	aroused
caring	charming	fervent	gentle
heavenly	passionate	sensitive	tender

Words Related to *Embarrassed*

abashed	anxious	chagrined	confused
conspicuous	disconcerted	disgraced	distressed
flustered	humbled	humiliated	jittery
overwhelmed	rattled	ridiculous	shamefaced
sheepish	silly	troubled	uncomfortable

Words Related to *Surprised*

astonished	astounded	baffled	bewildered
confused	distracted	flustered	jarred
jolted	mystified	perplexed	puzzled
rattled	shocked	startled	stunned

Words Related to *Fearful*

afraid	agitated	alarmed	anxious
apprehensive	bullied	cornered	frightened
horrified	jittery	jumpy	nervous
petrified	scared	shaken	terrified
threatened	troubled	uneasy	worried

Words Related to *Disgusted*

afflicted	annoyed	nauseated	outraged
repelled	repulsed	revolted	sickened

2. **Many people believe that describing their true feelings will make them too vulnerable.** It is true that if you tell people what hurts you, you risk their using the information against you when they want to hurt you on purpose. So it is safer to act angry than to be honest and describe the hurt you feel; it is safer to appear indifferent than to share your happiness and risk being made fun of. Nevertheless, as the old saying goes, "Nothing ventured,

Words Related to *Hurt*

abused	awful	cheated	deprived
deserted	desperate	dismal	dreadful
forsaken	hassled	ignored	isolated
mistreated	offended	oppressed	pained
piqued	rejected	resentful	rotten
scorned	slighted	snubbed	wounded

Words Related to *Belittled*

betrayed	defeated	deflated	demeaned
diminished	disparaged	downgraded	foolish
helpless	inadequate	incapable	inferior
insulted	persecuted	powerless	underestimated
undervalued	unfit	unworthy	useless

Words Related to *Happy*

blissful	charmed	cheerful	contented
delighted	ecstatic	elated	exultant
fantastic	giddy	glad	gratified
high	joyous	jubilant	merry
pleased	satisfied	thrilled	tickled

Words Related to *Lonely*

abandoned	alone	bored	deserted
desolate	discarded	empty	excluded
forlorn	forsaken	ignored	isolated
jilted	lonesome	lost	rejected
renounced	scorned	slighted	snubbed

Words Related to *Sad*

blue	crestfallen	dejected	depressed
dismal	dour	downcast	gloomy
heavyhearted	joyless	low	melancholy
mirthless	miserable	moody	morose
pained	sorrowful	troubled	weary

Words Related to *Energetic*

animated	bold	brisk	dynamic
eager	forceful	frisky	hardy
inspired	kinetic	lively	peppy
potent	robust	spirited	sprightly
spry	vibrant	vigorous	vivacious

Figure 5.1
A list of more than 200 words that can describe feelings.

nothing gained." If you don't take reasonable risks in your relationships, you are unlikely to form lasting and satisfying relationships. For instance, if Pete calls you by a derogatory nickname and you tell Pete that calling you by that nickname embarrasses you, Pete has the option of calling you by that name when he wants to embarrass you. But if he is ethical and cares about you, he is more likely to stop calling you by that name. And if you

Describing and sharing feelings can be difficult for many people.

don't describe your feelings, Pete is probably going to continue calling you by that name simply because he doesn't realize that you don't like it. By saying nothing, you reinforce his behavior. The level of risk varies with each situation, but if you have healthy relationships, you will more often improve a relationship by describing feelings than hurt it by doing so.

3. **Many people believe that if they describe feelings, others will make them feel guilty about having such feelings.** At a tender age, we all learned about "tactful" behavior. Under the premise that "the truth sometimes hurts," we learn to avoid the truth by not saying anything or by telling "little" lies. Perhaps when you were young, your mother said, "Don't forget to give grandma a great big kiss." At that time, you may have blurted out, "Ugh— it makes me feel yucky to kiss grandma. She's got a mustache." If your mother then responded, "That's terrible! Your grandma loves you. Now you give her a kiss and never let me hear you talk like that again!" you probably felt guilty for having this "wrong" feeling. Yet the thought of kissing your grandmother did make you feel "yucky," whether it should have or not. In this case, the issue was not your having the feelings but the way you talked about them.

4. **Many people believe that describing feelings causes harm to others or to a relationship.** If it really bothers Fyodor when his girlfriend, Lana, bites her fingernails, Fyodor may believe that describing his feelings may hurt her feelings so much that it will drive a wedge into their relationship. So it's better if Fyodor says nothing, right? Wrong! If Fyodor says nothing, he's still going to be irritated by Lana's behavior. In fact, as time goes on, Fyodor's irritation will probably cause him to lash out at Lana for other things because he can't bring himself to talk about the behavior that really bothers him. Lana will be hurt by Fyodor's behavior, which she won't understand. By not describing his true feelings, Fyodor may well drive a wedge into their relationship anyway. But if Fyodor describes his feelings to Lana in a nonjudgmental way, she might try to quit biting her nails; they might get into a discussion in which he finds out that she has tried but just can't seem to stop, and he may be able to help her in her efforts to stop; or Fyodor might come to see that it really is a small thing, and it may not bother him as much. In short, describing feelings yields a better chance of a successful outcome than does not describing them.

5. **Many people come from cultures that teach them to hide their feelings and emotions from others.** In some cultures, harmony among the group or in the relationship is considered more important than individuals' personal feelings. People from such cultures may not describe their feelings out of concern for the health of the group.

To describe your feelings, use the following steps: (1) Indicate what has triggered the feeling. The feeling results from some behavior, so identify the behavior. (2) Mentally identify what you are feeling; be specific. This sounds easier than it sometimes is. When people experience a feeling, they sometimes

SKILL BUILDERS   Describing Feelings

Skill	Use	Procedure	Example
Putting an emotional state into words.	For self-disclosure; to teach people how to treat you.	1. Indicate what has triggered the feeling. 2. Mentally identify what you are feeling. Think specifically: Am I feeling hate? anger? joy? 3. Verbally own the feeling. Begin your statement with "I feel. . . ." 4. Verbally state the specific feeling.	"As a result of not getting the job, I feel depressed and discouraged" or "Because of the way you stood up for me when Leah was putting me down, I'm feeling very warm and loving toward you."

display it without thinking about it. To describe a feeling, you must be aware of exactly what you are feeling. The vocabulary of emotions provided in Figure 5.1 can help you develop your ability to select specific words to describe your feelings. (3) Verbally own the feeling. Begin your statement with "I feel. . . ." (4) Verbally state the specific feeling.

Here are two examples of describing feelings:

"Thank you for your compliment [trigger]; I [the person having the feeling] feel gratified [the specific feeling] that you noticed the effort I made."

TEST YOUR COMPETENCE

Statements that Describe Feelings

In each of the following sets of statements, place a D next to the statement or statements in each set that describe feelings:

1. a. That was a great movie!
   b. I was really cheered up by the story.
   c. I feel this is worth an Oscar.
   d. Terrific!
2. a. I feel you're a good writer.
   b. Your writing brings me to tears.
   c. [You pat the writer on the back] Good job.
   d. Everyone likes your work.
3. a. Yuck!
   b. If things don't get better, I'm going to move.
   c. Did you ever see such a hole?
   d. I feel depressed by the dark halls.
4. a. I'm not adequate as a leader of this group.
   b. Damn—I goofed!
   c. I feel inadequate in my efforts to lead the group.
   d. I'm depressed by the effects of my leadership.
5. a. I'm a winner.
   b. I feel I won because I'm most qualified.
   c. I did it! I won!
   d. I'm ecstatic about winning that award.

Answers

1. b. (a) is evaluative; (c) is an evaluation dressed in descriptive clothing—using the word *feel* does not mean the person is truly describing feelings; (d) is a display.
2. b. (a) is evaluative (there's that word *feel* again); (c) is a display; (d) is evaluative.
3. d. (a) is a display; (b) is the result of feelings but not a description of feelings; (c) is an evaluation in question form.
4. c and d. (a) is evaluative; (b) is evaluative; (c) is similar to (a) except that here the feeling is described, not stated as an evaluation.
5. d. (a) is evaluative; (b) is a display; (c) is a display.

"When you criticize my cooking on days that I've worked as many hours as you have [trigger], I [the person having the feeling] feel very resentful [the specific feeling]."

To begin with, you may find it easier to describe positive feelings: "You know, your taking me to that movie really cheered me up" or "When you offered to help me with the housework, I really felt delighted." As you gain success with positive descriptions, you can try describing negative feelings attributable to environmental factors: "It's so cloudy; I feel gloomy" or "When the wind howls through the crack, I get really jumpy." Finally, you can move to negative descriptions resulting from what people have said or done: "When you step in front of me like that, I get really annoyed" or "When you use that negative tone while you are saying that what I did pleased you, I feel confused."

THINK CRITICALLY

Describing Feelings

Using each word in Figure 5.1, say "I feel . . . " and try to identify the feeling this word would describe. Which of these words are meaningful enough to you that you could use them to help make your communication of feelings more precise?

Owning Feelings and Opinions

Owning feelings or opinions (or crediting yourself) means making "I" statements to identify yourself as the source of a particular idea or feeling. An "I" statement can be any statement that has a first-person pronoun, such as *I*, *my*, *me*, or *mine*. "I" statements help the listener understand fully and accurately the nature of the message. Consider the following paired statements:

"Advertising is the weakest department in the corporation."

"Everybody thinks Collins is unfair in his criticism."

"It's common knowledge that the boss favors anything that Kelly does."

"Nobody likes to be laughed at."

"I believe advertising is the weakest department in the corporation."

"It seems to me that Collins is unfair in his criticism."

"In my opinion, the boss favors anything that Kelly does."

"Being laughed at embarrasses me."

Each of these examples contrasts a generalized or impersonal account with an "I" statement.

Instead of owning their feelings and opinions and honestly disclosing them as such, people often express their thoughts and feelings in impersonal or generalized language or attribute them to unknown or universal sources. Why do people use vague referents to others rather than owning their ideas and feelings? There are two basic reasons.

1. **To strengthen the power of their statements.** Saying "Everybody thinks Collins is unfair in his criticism" means that if listeners doubt the statement, they are bucking the collective evaluation of countless people. Of course, not everybody knows and agrees that Collins is unfair. In this

PRACTICE IN CLASS

Describing Feelings

Working with at least one other person, role-play typical situations (for example, Tom's roommate borrows Tom's car without asking permission; the roommate comes into the room later and, giving Tom the keys, says, "Thanks for the car"), and then describe your feelings. After you have finished, have the other person or people describe their feelings in response to the same situation. Continue the exercise until each member of the group has had two or three chances to practice describing feelings.

UNDERSTAND YOURSELF

Owning Ideas and Feelings

Under what circumstances are you likely to take credit for your own ideas and feelings? When are you likely to attribute them to some generalized other?

instance, the statement really means that one person holds the belief. Yet because people think that their feelings or beliefs will not carry much weight, they may feel the need to cite unknown or universal sources for those feelings or beliefs.

2. **To escape responsibility.** Similarly, people use collective statements such as "everybody agrees" and "anyone with any sense" to escape responsibility for their own feelings and thoughts. It seems far more difficult for a person to say "I don't like Herb" than it is to say "No one likes Herb."

The problem with such generalized statements is that at best they are exaggerations and at worst they are deceitful and thus unethical. Being both accurate and honest with others requires taking responsibility for our own feelings and opinions. We all have a right to our reactions. If what you are saying is truly your opinion or an expression of how you really feel, let others know, and be willing to take responsibility for it. Otherwise, you may alienate people who would have respected your opinions or feelings even if they didn't agree with them.

PRACTICE IN CLASS

Communicating Feelings

Form groups of six. Choose a controversial conversational topic that is of interest to all members of the group and about which there is a diversity of feelings in the group. Appoint one person to be observer. The five participants will hold a ten-minute conversation on the topic. The observer is to keep track of the number of times that participants attribute their thoughts and feelings to a generalized other versus the number of times they attribute thoughts and feelings to themselves by making "I" statements. Observers should also note when (if) participants describe their feelings as opposed to displaying or withholding them. When the time is up, the observer should discuss his or her observations with the participants.

Giving Personal Feedback

Sometimes in our interactions and relationships with others it is appropriate to comment on how the other person's message or behavior is affecting their relationships with other people or is affecting them. Responses of this type are generally referred to as "giving personal feedback." When we highlight positive behavior and accomplishments, we give positive feedback through praise. When we need to identify negative, harmful behavior and actions, we can provide negative feedback through constructive criticism.

Praising

Too often the positive things people say and do are not acknowledged by others. Yet, as you'll recall from our earlier discussion of self-concept, not only our behavior but our view of who we are—our identity—is shaped by how others respond to us. Praise can be used to reinforce positive behavior and help another to develop a positive self-concept. By praising we can provide feedback to others that what they have said or done is commendable.

Praising is describing the specific positive behavior or accomplishment of another and the effect of that behavior on others. Praise is not the same as flattery. When we flatter someone, we use excessive compliments that are insincere in order to ingratiate ourselves. When we praise, our compliments are in line with the behavior or accomplishment. We express only admiration that we genuinely feel. Finally, when we praise, our purpose is to inform the other, not to curry favor. For praise to achieve its goal and not be perceived as mere flattery, we need to focus the praise on the specific action and make sure that the message is worded so that it is in keeping with the significance or value of the accomplishment or behavior. If a child who tends to be forgetful remembers to return the scissors he borrowed, that behavior should be praised so that it is reinforced. Saying "You're so wonderful, you're on top of everything" reinforces nothing, because it is an overly general statement that doesn't identify a particular behavior or accomplishment. Overly general statements can be perceived as flattery. However, gushing "Oh, you remembered to return the scissors! I'm so-ooo grateful. That was just unbelievably thoughtful of you—I can't wait to tell your Mommy about this! She will be so proud of you," is overkill that even a five-year-old will probably perceive as insincere flattery. In this case, simply saying "Thanks for putting the scissors back where they belong—I really appreciate that" would be appropriate. This response acknowledges the accomplishment by describing the specific behavior and the positive feeling of gratitude that the behavior has caused. Following are two more examples of appropriate praising.

Behavior: Sonya takes responsibility for selecting and buying a group wedding present for a friend. The gift is a big hit.
Praise: "Sonya, the present you chose for Stevie was really thoughtful. Not only did it fit our price range, but Stevie really liked it."

Accomplishment: Cole has just received a letter inviting him to a reception at which he is to receive a scholarship award given for academic accomplishments and community service work.
Praise: "Congratulations, Cole. I'm proud of you. It's really great to see that the effort you put into studying, as well as the time and energy you have devoted to the Second Harvest Food Program and Big Brothers, is being recognized and valued.

While praising responses don't "cost" much, they are valuable and generally appreciated. Not only does praising provide information and acknowledge the worth of another person, but it can also deepen our relationships because it increases openness. To increase your effectiveness at praising, try to follow these steps: (1) Make note of the specific behavior or accomplishment that you want to reinforce. (2) Describe the specific behavior and/or accomplishment. (3) Describe the positive feelings or outcomes that you or others experience as a result of the behavior or accomplishment. (4) Phrase the response so that the level of praise appropriately reflects the significance of the behavior or accomplishment.

Giving Constructive Criticism

Even though research on reinforcement theory has found that people learn faster and better through positive rewards such as praise, there are still times

PRACTICE IN CLASS

Writing Praise Responses

Class members should each bring to class four 3- by 5-inch cards on which they have described four real situations in which a praising response would be appropriate. Each card should contain a precise description of the praiseworthy behavior or accomplishment, along with the name of the class member who wrote it. Class members should form groups of four. The cards should be collected and redistributed so that each group is working with cards that were not prepared by members of that group. Each group should then work together to phrase an appropriate praising response for each situation described on the cards they receive. When the group is satisfied with a response, it should write this response on the back of the card, along with the names of those who worked on the response. When all groups have finished the task, the cards should be returned to their original creators. Each class member should read the praising responses provided by the group, then comment in writing on how well the response seems to follow the guidelines for effective praising. Cards, responses, and comments should then be returned to the group for discussion.

OBSERVE AND ANALYZE

Expressing Criticism

Think about the last time you criticized someone's behavior. Which, if any, of the guidelines for constructive feedback did you follow or violate? If you were to do it again, what would you say differently?

when personal feedback needs to address negative behaviors or actions. Obviously it's best to give this type of feedback when a person specifically asks for it. Even when people don't ask, however, we sometimes need to provide another with constructive criticism. **Constructive criticism** is describing the specific negative behaviors or actions of another and the effects that these behaviors have on others.

Although the word *criticism* can be interpreted to mean "harsh judgment," the skill of constructive criticism is based not on judgment, but rather on empathy. When we give another constructive criticism, we begin by trying to empathize with the person and to forecast what his or her reaction to our feedback is likely to be. Research shows that well-given feedback can actually strengthen relationships and improve interactions, but feedback that is not empathically grounded or is poorly understood is likely to hurt relationships and lead to defensive interactions (Tracy, Dusen, and Robinson 1987).

Before you give constructive feedback, you should not only make sure that the person is interested in hearing it, but you should also restrict your comments to recent behavior that a person can do something about. If you don't know whether a person wants to hear what you have to say, ask. For instance, you might ask a group chairperson, "Are you interested in hearing my comments about the way you handled the meeting?" Remember, however, that even if the answer is yes, you must proceed carefully.

You will be more effective in responding with constructive criticism if you proceed in the following ways:

1. **Describe the behavior by accurately recounting precisely what was said or done without labeling the behavior good or bad, right or wrong.** By describing behavior, you lay an informative base for the feedback and increase the chances that the person will listen receptively. Feedback that is preceded with detailed description is less likely to be met defensively. Your description shows that you are criticizing the behavior rather than attacking the person, and it points the way to a solution. For example, if DeShawn asks, "What did you think of the visuals I used when I delivered my report?" instead of saying, "They weren't very effective," it would be better to say something like, "Well, the type on the first two was kind of small, and they were a little hard to read." This criticism does not attack DeShawn's self-concept, and it tells him what he needs to do to be more effective.

2. **Preface a negative statement with a positive one whenever possible.** When you are planning to criticize, it is a good idea to start with some praise. Of course, common sense suggests that superficial praise followed by crushing feedback will be seen for what it is. In the preceding example, one could say, "Well, the charts and graphs were useful, and the color really helped us to see the problems, but the words on the first two overheads were a little small, and they were hard to read." Here the praise is relevant and

significant. If you cannot preface feedback with significant praise, don't try. Prefacing feedback with empty praise will not help the person accept your feedback.

3. **Be as specific as possible.** The more specifically you describe the behavior or the actions, the more effectively a person will be able to understand what needs to change. In the situation just discussed, it would not have been helpful to say, "Some of the slides were kind of hard to read." This comment is so general that DeShawn would have little idea of what to change. Moreover, he may infer that every overhead needs to be redone.

4. **When appropriate, suggest how the person can change the behavior.** Since the focus of constructive criticism is helping, it is appropriate to provide the person with suggestions that might lead to positive change. So in responding to DeShawn's request for feedback, one might add, "When I make overheads, I generally try to use 18 point type or larger. You might want to give that a try." By including a positive suggestion, you not only help the person with honest information, you also show that your intentions are positive.

Assertiveness

Assertiveness means standing up for ourselves in interpersonally effective ways that exercise our personal rights while respecting the rights of others. Assertiveness may focus on describing feelings, giving good reasons for a belief, or suggesting a behavior or attitude we think is fair, without exaggerating for dramatic effect or attacking the other individual. We can understand the specific qualities of assertive behavior best if we contrast it with other ways of interacting when our rights or feelings are in danger of being violated or ignored.

Contrasting Methods of Expressing Our Needs and Rights

When we believe our needs or rights are being ignored or violated by others, we can choose to behave in one of three ways: passively, aggressively, or assertively.

Passive behavior. People behave passively when they are reluctant to state their opinions, share feelings, or assume responsibility for their actions. Thus, instead of attempting to influence others' behavior, they often submit to other people's demands, even when doing so is inconvenient, against their best interests, or violates their rights. For example, when Bill was uncrating the new color television set he purchased at a local department store, he noticed a

---

PRACTICE IN CLASS

Giving Constructive Feedback

In groups of four, consider the following two situations. Work out an appropriate phrasing of constructive feedback for each. Then share your phrasings of the feedback with others in your group. Which of the wordings best meets the guidelines for constructive feedback?

1. You have been driving to school with a fellow student whose name you got from the transportation office at school. You have known him for only three weeks. Everything about the situation is great except that he drives too fast for you.

2. A good friend says "you know" more than once every sentence. You like her very much, but you see that others are beginning to avoid her. She is very sensitive and does not usually take feedback well.

We often have to assert ourselves. The key is not to fall into aggressive behavior. He seems to be crowding her (aggressive), but she's setting limits (assertive).

scratch on the left side of the set. If Bill is upset about the scratch but nevertheless keeps the set without trying to influence the store to replace it, he is behaving passively.

Aggressive behavior. People who behave aggressively lash out at the source of their discontent with little regard for the situation or for the feelings, needs, or rights of those they are attacking. Aggressiveness should not be confused with assertiveness. Unlike assertive behavior, aggressive behavior is unethical. It is judgmental, dogmatic, fault-finding, and coercive. Most receivers of aggressive messages, regardless of the relationship, are likely to feel hurt by them (Martin, Anderson, and Horvath 1996, p. 24).

Suppose that after discovering the scratch on his new television set, Bill stormed back to the store, grabbed the first clerk he found, loudly demanded his money back, and accused the clerk of being a racist for intentionally selling him damaged merchandise. Such aggressive behavior might or might not be successful in getting the damaged set replaced, but it would certainly not be an ethical influence attempt.

Assertive behavior. As we have noted, behaving assertively means standing up for oneself in an interpersonally effective way. The difference between assertive behavior and passive or aggressive behavior is not the original feeling behind the response but the way in which we choose to react as a result of what has happened. If Bill chose an assertive response, he would still be angry about bringing home a damaged set. But instead of either doing nothing or verbally assaulting the clerk, Bill might call the store and ask to speak to the clerk from whom he had purchased the set. When the clerk answered, Bill would describe the condition of the TV set and his feelings on discovering a large scratch on the cabinet when he uncrated the set. He would then go on to say that he was calling to find out what to do to return the damaged set and get a new one. Whereas aggressive behavior might also achieve Bill's purpose of getting a new television set, the assertive behavior would achieve the same result at lower emotional costs to everyone involved.

Examples of Passive, Aggressive, and Assertive Responses

It is inevitable that our interpersonal exchanges will often involve the need to assert ourselves. For this reason, and because so much difficulty in relationships stems from ineffective responses to adversity, learning to distinguish among passive, aggressive, and assertive responses is a key interpersonal skill. To highlight the contrast among these response styles, let's examine situations in which the issue is the quality of interpersonal relations.

At work. Tanisha works in an office that employs both men and women. Whenever the boss has an especially interesting and challenging job to be done, he assigns it to a male coworker whose desk is next to Tanisha's. The boss has never said anything to Tanisha or to the male employee that would indicate he thinks less of Tanisha or her ability. Nevertheless, Tanisha is hurt by the boss's behavior.

Passive: Tanisha says nothing to the boss. She's very hurt by what she feels is a slight, but swallows her pride.
Aggressive: Tanisha marches into her boss's office and says, "Why the hell do you always give Tom the plums and leave me the garbage? I'm every bit as good a worker, and I'd like a little recognition!"
Assertive: Tanisha arranges a meeting with her boss. At the meeting, she says, "I don't know whether you are aware of it, but during the last three weeks, every time you had a really interesting job to be done, you gave the job to Tom. To the best of my knowledge, you believe that Tom and I are equally competent—you've never given me any evidence to suggest that you thought less of my work. But when you 'reward' Tom with jobs that I perceive as plums and continue to offer me routine jobs, it hurts my feelings. Do you understand my feelings about this?" In this statement, she has both described her perception of the boss's behavior and her feelings about that behavior.

OBSERVE AND ANALYZE

Passive, Aggressive, and Assertive Behavior

For the next day or two, observe people and their behavior. Make note of situations in which you believe people are behaving in passive, aggressive, or assertive ways. Which of the ways seem to help the people achieve what they want? Which of the ways seem to maintain or even improve their interpersonal relationship with the other person or other people?

If you were Tanisha's boss, which of her responses would be most likely to achieve her goal of getting better assignments? Probably the assertive behavior. Which of her responses would be most likely to get her fired? Probably the aggressive behavior. And which of her responses would be least likely to "rock the boat"? Undoubtedly the passive behavior—but then she would continue to get the boring job assignments.

With a friend.   Dan is a doctor doing his residency at City Hospital. He lives with two other residents in an apartment they have rented. Carl, one of the other residents, is the social butterfly of the group. It seems whenever he has time off, he has a date. But like the others, he's a bit short of cash. He doesn't feel a bit bashful about borrowing clothes or money from his roommates. One evening, Carl asks Dan if he can borrow his watch—a new, expensive watch that Dan received as a present from his father only a few days before. Dan is aware that Carl does not always take the best care of what he borrows, and he is very concerned about the possibility of Carl's damaging or losing the watch.

Passive: "Sure."

Aggressive: "Forget it! You've got a lot of nerve asking to borrow a brand-new watch. You know I'd be lucky to get it back in one piece!"

Assertive: "Carl, I know I've lent you several items without much ado, but this watch is special. I've had it only a few days, and I just don't feel comfortable lending it. I hope you can understand how I feel."

What are likely to be the consequences of each of these behaviors? If he behaves passively, Dan is likely to worry the entire evening and harbor some resentment of Carl even if he gets the watch back undamaged. Moreover, Carl will continue to think that his roommates feel comfortable lending him anything he wants. If Dan behaves aggressively, Carl is likely to be completely taken aback by his explosive behavior. No one has ever said anything to Carl before, so he has no reason to believe that he can't borrow whatever he likes. Moreover, the relationship between Dan and Carl might become strained. But if Dan behaves assertively, he puts the focus on his own feelings and on this particular object—the watch. His response isn't a denial of Carl's right to borrow items, nor is it an attack on Carl. It is an explanation of why Dan does not want to lend this item at this time.

In a social situation.   Kim has invited two of her girlfriends and their dates to drop by her dormitory room before the dance. Shortly after the group arrives, Nick, who has come with Ramona, Kim's best friend, reaches into his pocket for a flask of whiskey, takes a large sip, and passes it to Kim. Kim knows that alcohol is strictly off-limits in the dorm and, moreover, is concerned about anyone in the group drinking before driving.

Passive: Muttering "Uh, well," Kim pretends to take a sip and then passes the flask on.

Aggressive: "Nick, that's really stupid, bringing whiskey into my dorm room. Can't anybody here have a good time without drinking, or are you all lushes? Now get out of here before somebody notices, and take the bottle with you."

Assertive: "Nick, Ramona probably didn't tell you that drinking isn't allowed in the dorm. Besides, I'd feel a lot more at ease if we all stayed sober to drive to the dance. So I'd appreciate it if you would take the whiskey out to the car. We can have a great time without getting into trouble or risking an accident."

Again, let's contrast the three behaviors. In this case, the passive behavior is not at all in Kim's interests. Kim knows the dormitory rules, and even if no one finds out, she'll feel uncomfortable because she did nothing to protect her friends from taking a needless risk with their safety. But the aggressive behavior is hardly better. She knows nothing about Nick, but her outburst assumes bad intentions not only from Nick but also from her friends. If Nick is at all inclined to be belligerent, her method is only going to incite him and damage her relationship with Ramona besides. The assertive behavior presents the issue firmly—the dorm rules must not be violated, especially since it is her room—and her feelings about the group's safety are described firmly but pleasantly. She also follows up with her original intent in getting together—to have a good time.

Characteristics of Assertive Behavior

Now let's consider some of the characteristics of behaving assertively that are illustrated or implied in the examples.

1. **Owning feelings.** In all cases, the assertive statement acknowledged that the thoughts and feelings were those of the person making the statement.

2. **Avoiding confrontational language.** In none of the cases did the speaker act aggressively by using threats, evaluations, or dogmatic language.

3. **Using specific statements directed to the behaviors at hand.** In each case, potential issues could have been raised. For instance, Dan could have brought up Carl's untrustworthiness, but in the particular situation, he chose to focus on the issue that was most relevant—his feelings about a special possession.

4. **Maintaining eye contact and firm body position.** People will not be perceived as being firm if they shift gaze, look at the floor, sway back and forth, hunch over, and use other signs that may be perceived as indecision or lack of conviction.

5. **Maintaining a firm but pleasant tone of voice.** Whereas aggressiveness is signaled with yelling or harsh tones, assertiveness is shown through steady, firm speech at a normal pitch, volume, and rate.

6. **Avoiding hemming and hawing.** Recall the passive example in which Kim says, "Uh, well." Vocalized pauses and other nonfluencies are other signs of indecisiveness.

INFOTRAC COLLEGE EDITION

As we have seen, assertiveness is sometimes perceived as aggressiveness. Using the InfoTrac College Edition subject guide, enter the term "assertiveness." Look for an article that considers the importance of behaving assertively without becoming aggressive.

7. **Speaking clearly.** Sometimes when people have something uncomfortable to say, they mutter so that what they have to say is almost unintelligible. Again, lack of clarity will be seen as indecision.

It's important to recognize that being assertive will not always achieve your goals. The skills discussed in this book are designed to increase the probability of achieving interpersonal effectiveness. Just as with self-disclosure and describing feelings, however, there are risks involved in being assertive. For instance, some people will label any assertive behavior as "aggressive." But people who have difficulty asserting themselves often do not appreciate the fact that the potential benefits far outweigh the risks. Remember, our behavior teaches people how to treat us. When we are passive—when we have taught people that they can ignore our feelings—they will. When we are aggressive, we teach people to respond in kind. By contrast, when we are assertive, we can influence others to treat us as we would prefer to be treated.

Following are some useful guidelines for practicing assertive behavior: (1) Identify what you are thinking or feeling. (2) Analyze the cause of these feelings. (3) Choose the appropriate skills to communicate these feelings, as well as the outcome you desire, if any. (4) Communicate these feelings to the appropriate person. If you have trouble taking the first step to being more assertive, try beginning with situations in which you are likely to have a high potential for success (Alberti and Emmons 1995).

Cultural Variations

Although assertiveness can be thought of as a basic human need, assertive behavior is primarily practiced in Western cultures. In Asian cultures, how one is seen is often considered more important than asserting one's beliefs or rights, and a premium is often placed on maintaining a formally correct standard of social interaction. For people from these cultures, maintaining "face" and politeness may be more important than achieving personal satisfaction. On the other hand, in Latin and Hispanic societies, men especially are frequently taught to exercise a form of self-expression that goes far beyond the guidelines presented here for assertive behavior. In these societies, the concept of "machismo" guides male behavior. Thus, the standard of assertiveness appropriate in our dominant culture may seem inappropriate to people whose cultural frame of reference leads them to perceive it as aggressive or weak.

For this reason, with assertiveness—just as with any other skill—we need to be aware that no single standard of behavior ensures we will achieve our goals. Although what is labeled appropriate behavior varies across cultures, the results of passive and aggressive behavior seem universal. Passive behavior can cause resentment, and aggressive behavior leads to fear and misunderstanding. When talking with people whose culture, background, or lifestyle differs from your own, you may need to observe their behavior and their responses to your statements before you can be sure of the kinds of behavior that are likely to communicate your intentions effectively.

OBSERVE AND ANALYZE

Learning to Respond Assertively

Identify five situations in the past in which you were nonassertive or aggressive. Try to write the dialogue for each situation. Then substitute an assertive response for the nonassertive or aggressive reaction you expressed in each case.

Reasons for Nonassertiveness

If assertiveness is the best way to achieve our goals, why are some people less likely to assert themselves? Probably for one or more of the following reasons:

1. **They fear reprisal.** People sometimes do not assert themselves because they are afraid that the person they are dealing with will punish them or withhold some reward. Is this fear justified? Certainly, there will be times when you are penalized for being assertive. Some people with power are very defensive and will react accordingly if they think you are threatening their security. For instance, if Adolfo's boss is giving him more to do than Adolfo thinks is fair, Adolfo may be reluctant to assert his position because his boss may decide not to reward him in the future. Often people let others run over them because they think that giving in will help them secure some other reward they seek.

2. **They are insecure about their knowledge or expertise.** Sometimes people are unassertive because they downplay their own knowledge or expertise in whatever subject is being considered. For instance, when buying cars, clothing, or other goods, people are often intimidated by the salesperson because they assume the person is more knowledgeable about the product. Of course, salespeople are not always masters of information; their primary skill is often persuasiveness rather than knowledge. More important, you are the expert when it comes to your own needs, wants, and tastes. No one needs to feel intimidated by the possibility of being shown up by another person's knowledge. Whether buying a coat, having the car repaired, or consulting a physician, a customer has a perfect right to ask questions about what is happening and why, and to look out for his or her own best interests.

3. **They question their self-worth.** Some people do not assert themselves because they question their self-worth. Perhaps because of their socialization in childhood or because of perceived failures as adults, they lack confidence in their own thoughts and feelings. Suppose Marcus receives a C on a term paper. As he reads his paper over, he's sure that what he said was worth more than a C. He thinks about going in to talk to his professor but says to himself, "He's not going to listen to me—I'm just a student." Is this a realistic appraisal? Maybe. It is also possible that Marcus generally doubts his ability to argue on his own behalf when his judgment differs from those of other people.

TEST YOUR COMPETENCE

Assertive Responses

For each of the following situations, write a passive or aggressive response, and then contrast it with a more appropriate assertive response.

You come back to your dorm, apartment, or house to type a paper that is due tomorrow, only to find that someone else is using your typewriter.
Passive or aggressive response:
Assertive response:

You're working at a store part-time. Just as your hours are up and you are ready to leave (you want to rush home because you have a nice dinner planned with someone special), your boss says to you, "I'd like you to work overtime, if you would. Martin's supposed to replace you, but he just called and can't get here for at least an hour."
Passive or aggressive response:
Assertive response:

During a phone call to your parents, who live in another state, your mother says, "We're expecting you to go with us when we visit your uncle on Saturday." You were planning to spend Saturday working on your résumé for an interview next week.
Passive or aggressive response:
Assertive response:

You and your friend made a date to go dancing, an activity you really enjoy. When you meet, your friend says, "If it's all the same to you, I thought we'd go to a movie instead."
Passive or aggressive response:
Assertive response:

SKILL BUILDERS Assertiveness

Skill	Use	Procedure	Example
Standing up for yourself and doing so in interpersonally effective ways that describe your feelings honestly and exercise your personal rights while respecting the rights of others.	To show clearly what you think or feel.	1. Identify what you are thinking or feeling. 2. Analyze the cause of these feelings. 3. Choose the appropriate skills necessary to communicate these feelings, as well as any outcome you desire, if any. 4. Communicate these feelings to the appropriate person. Remember to own your feelings.	When Gavin believes that he is being unjustly charged, he says, "I have never been charged for a refill on iced tea before—has there been a change in policy?"

4. **They believe it is not worth the time or effort.** Sometimes people are not assertive because they believe that it takes too much work to be assertive. Occasionally, it does. If, however, you habitually find yourself thinking or saying it's not worth the time or effort to assert your thoughts and feelings, you may be offering an excuse that reflects anxiety or lack of self-confidence. Being assertive does take both work and practice, especially at first—but you will find that the rewards are worth it. Occasionally, you may find a champion who will look out for your interests. Usually, however, you are the only one who can or will represent your position.

5. **They accept others' expectations.** For example, a number of American women exhibit passive behavior because they accept the social stereotype that women should be accepting, warm, loving, and deferential to men. Regrettably, too many people see any signs of assertiveness as "unfeminine." Fortunately, however, the stereotype that perpetuates such passive behavior is no longer as influential as it once was, and many women who have spent the better portion of their lives being passive now recognize the value of learning to be assertive. Of course, socially conditioned passive behavior is not restricted to women. We may be socialized to be unassertive for many reasons, whether we are male or female.

Summary

Self-disclosure statements reveal information about yourself that is unknown to others. Several guidelines can help us decide when self-disclosure is appropriate.

Three ways to disclose our feelings are to withhold them, display them, or skillfully describe them.

Instead of owning our own feelings and ideas, we often avoid disclosure by making generalized statements. The skill of making "I" statements can help us to more honestly assume ownership of our ideas and feelings.

Personal feedback builds relationships by providing information to others about their behavior and its effects that they do not currently understand. Positive feedback is accomplished through praising. Negative feedback can be delivered effectively by using the skill of constructive criticism.

Assertiveness is the skill of stating our ideas and feelings openly in interpersonally effective ways. Passive people are often unhappy as a result of not stating what they think and feel; aggressive people get their ideas and feelings heard, but may create more problems for themselves because of their aggressiveness. When people do not assert themselves, it is likely to be because they fear reprisal, they are insecure about their knowledge or expertise, they question their self-worth, they believe it is not worth the time or effort, or they accept others' expectations. And as we might expect, appropriateness of assertiveness varies across cultures.

Some of the characteristics of behaving assertively are owning feelings, avoiding confrontational language, using specific statements directed to the behaviors at hand, maintaining eye contact and firm body position, maintaining a firm but pleasant tone of voice, avoiding hemming and hawing, and speaking clearly.

REFLECT ON ETHICS

Maria Sanchos, a Mexican American graduate of Yale Law School, was excited to be assigned to the Local Employee Fraud Team (LEFT), whose job it was to design a system to uncover theft on the job for the Comptel Corporation. Maria found the company of her other five associates pleasant, except for Theresa Waterson, the leader of the group, whose social skills were as bad as the stereotypical queen bee. Maria wondered why she, of all people, had been appointed to head the project. Maria found herself increasingly angered by Theresa's views on issues of affirmative action and abortion. Several times she felt like confronting Theresa on these issues, but Maria felt that the harmonious relationship of the group was at stake, and she didn't want to risk losing the group's cohesiveness.

Although Maria was able to control herself in most settings, she began to be critical of Theresa's views during group meetings, harshly pointing out what she considered to be illogical thinking and openly upbraiding Theresa for her mistakes. When one of the men on the task force privately confronted her, she considered trusting him with her problem, yet she unconsciously feared that self-disclosure would make her weak, particularly to a white male. Several days later, when the two other women in the group confronted her about her behavior toward Theresa, Maria broke down and told them her problem.

1. What are the ethical issues in this case?
2. Did Maria behave ethically in this situation?
3. If you were one of the women advising Maria, what would you recommend that she do?

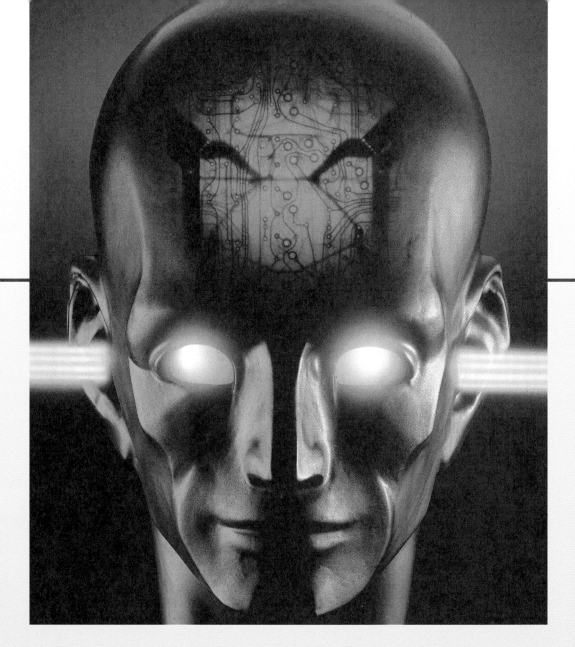

OBJECTIVES

After you have read this chapter, you should be able to answer the following questions:

- What are the five concepts involved in listening?
- How can you focus your attention?
- What is empathy?
- How can you ask questions to increase understanding?
- How can you paraphrase both the content and intent of another's message?
- What are three devices for remembering information?
- How can you evaluate inferences?
- How can you make appropriate supporting statements?
- How can you give reasonable alternative interpretations of events?

Listening

Sue says to Dan, "I'm going to be with the film crew on location and won't be able to pick up Marsha at 3:30, so you will have to pick her up." Catching a reference to the film crew, Dan nods and says "OK." At 4:15 he casually answers the phone, only to hear Marsha say, "Dad, aren't you picking me up?"

Margot tells Jack, "I need you to run 25 on regular-size paper with a blue cover page and 75 on legal-size paper with a yellow cover page." Later in the day, when Jack brings the forms, Margot notices that the 25 with a blue cover are on legal-size and the rest with a yellow cover are on regular-size paper. When Margot says, "Jack, I said 25 on regular size and 75 on legal size," Jack replies, "Oh, I'm sorry, I mixed it up."

Are you a good listener? Even when you're under pressure? Or do you sometimes find that your mind wanders when others are talking to you? **Listening**—"the process of receiving, attending to, and assigning meaning to aural and visual stimuli" (Wolvin and Coakley 1996, p. 69)—is a fundamental skill that affects the quality of the conversations that we have and shapes the course of the relationships that we create and maintain. The fact is that in our daily communication we may spend more of our time listening than we do speaking, reading, and writing combined (Barker et al. 1980, p. 103). Yet after 48 hours, most listeners can remember only about 25 percent of what they heard (Steil, Barker, and Watson 1983). In this chapter we'll consider the concepts of attending, understanding, remembering, analyzing critically, and responding empathically.

Attending

Attending is the perceptual process of selecting and focusing on specific stimuli from the countless stimuli reaching the senses. Recall from Chapter 2 that we attend to information that interests us and meets physical and psychological needs. But to be a good listener, we have to train ourselves to attend to what people are saying regardless of our interest or needs.

Let's consider four techniques for consciously focusing attention.

1. **Get physically and mentally ready to listen**. Oftentimes poor listening results from our failure to get ready to listen physically, even though we know what we should be doing. For instance, when we've been told that the next bit of information will be on the test, we are likely to sit upright in our chairs, lean slightly forward, cease any extraneous physical movement, and look directly at the professor.

   Likewise, when we're really listening, we know that mentally we need to focus attention, blocking our miscellaneous thoughts that constantly pass through our minds. Although what you're thinking about may be more pleasant to attend to than what someone is saying to you, you must compel yourself to focus on what is being said.

2. **Make the shift from speaker to listener a complete one.** Unlike the classroom, where you are supposed to listen continuously for long stretches, in conversation you are called on to switch back and forth from speaker to listener so frequently that you may find it difficult at times to make these shifts completely. If, instead of listening, you spend your time rehearsing what you're going to say as soon as you have a chance, your listening effectiveness will take a nosedive. Especially when you are in a heated conversation, take a second to check yourself—are you preparing speeches instead

One Big Happy by Rick Detorie. By permission of Rick Detorie and Creators Syndicate.

of listening? Shifting from the role of speaker to that of listener requires constant and continuous effort.

3. **Hear a person out before you react.** Far too often, we stop listening before the person has finished speaking because we "know what a person is going to say"; yet our "knowing" is really only a guess. Accordingly, cultivate the habit of always letting a person complete his or her thought before you stop listening or try to respond.

   In addition to ceasing to listen prematurely, we often let a person's mannerisms and words "turn us off." For instance, we may become annoyed when a speaker mutters, stammers, or talks in a monotone. Likewise, we may let a speaker's language or ideas turn us off. Are there any words or ideas that create bursts of semantic noise for you, causing you to stop listening attentively? For instance, do you have a tendency to react negatively or tune out when people speak of *gay rights*, *skinheads*, *welfare frauds*, *political correctness*, or *rednecks*? To counteract this effect, try to

What "noise" might be occurring in this communication, including the sounds of construction, his assumptions about a female boss, and her assumptions about male coworkers?

OBSERVE AND ANALYZE

Attending

Select an information-oriented program on your public television station (such as "NOVA," "News Hour with Jim Lehrer," or "Wall Street Week"). Watch at least fifteen minutes of the show while lounging in a comfortable chair or while stretched out on the floor with music playing on a radio in the background. For the next fifteen minutes, make a conscious effort to use the guidelines for increasing attentiveness. Then, contrast your listening behaviors. What was different in the second segment from the first. What were the results of those differences?

let a warning light go on when a speaker trips the switch to your emotional reaction. Instead of tuning out or getting ready to fight, be aware of this "noise" and work that much harder to listen objectively. If you can do it, you will be more likely to receive the whole message accurately before you respond.

4. **Adjust to the listening goals of the situation.** Listening is similar to reading in that you need to adjust *how* you listen to whether your goal is primarily enjoyment or whether it is understanding, evaluating, or responding to comfort another.

When your goal is primarily "pleasure listening," you can afford to listen without much intensity. People often speak of "vegging out in front of the tube," which usually means "listening" to comedy or light drama as a means of passing time pleasurably. Unfortunately, many people approach all situations as if they were listening to pass time. Yet how we listen should change qualitatively with the level of difficulty of the information.

Suppose that instead of watching a situation comedy, you turn to an information program on PBS—perhaps "NOVA" or "Frontline." Now you will likely decide that instead of just passing time, your goal is understanding or critical analysis. In listening situations such as attending to directions (how to get to a restaurant), to instructions (how to shift into reverse in a foreign car), to explanations (a recounting of the new office procedures), to messages intended to guide behavior or seek your advice, the intensity of your "listening" needs to increase.

Understanding

Understanding is decoding a message accurately by assigning appropriate meaning to it. Sometimes we don't understand because people use words that are outside our vocabulary or use them in a way that we don't recognize.

Fully understanding what a person means requires **active listening**—using specific techniques to ensure your understanding, including empathizing, asking questions, and paraphrasing.

Empathizing

Empathizing is intellectually identifying with or vicariously experiencing the feelings, thoughts, or attitudes of another. When we empathize, we are attempting to understand and/or experience what another understands and/or experiences. In order to do this, generally we try to put aside our own feelings, thoughts, and attitudes in order to "try on" the feelings, thoughts, and attitudes of another. The three approaches that people use when they are empathizing are empathic responsiveness, perspective taking, and sympathetic responsiveness (Weaver and Kirtley 1995, p. 131).

Empathic responsiveness occurs when you experience an emotional response parallel to, and as a result of, observing another person's actual or anticipated display of emotion (Stiff et al. 1988, p. 199). For instance, when Monique tells Heather that Brad broke off their engagement, Heather will have used empathic responsiveness if she senses the sadness that Monique is feeling and experiences a similar sense of loss.

Perspective taking—imagining yourself in the place of another—is the most common form of empathizing (Zillmann 1991). In our example, if Heather personalizes the message by picturing herself being told that her engagement is off, anticipates and experiences her own emotions were this to occur, and then assumes that Monique must be feeling the same way that Heather would feel in this situation, she is exemplifying perspective taking.

Sympathetic responsiveness is your feeling of concern, compassion, or sorrow for another because of the other's situation or plight. Some scholars call this "emotional concern" (Stiff et al. 1988) while others use the more common term "sympathy" (Eisenberg and Fabes 1990). Sympathetic responsiveness differs from the other two approaches in that you don't attempt to experience the feelings of the other, but rather you translate your intellectual understanding of what the speaker has experienced into your own feelings of concern, compassion, or sorrow for that person. Heather has sympathy for Monique when she understands that Monique is sad and disappointed, but instead of trying to feel Monique's emotions or experience how she herself would feel in a similar situation, Heather feels concern and compassion for her friend. Because of this difference, many scholars differentiate sympathy from empathy.

Although people vary in their ability to empathize, most of us have to learn to increase our empathy. The first step in increasing empathy is to take the time and make the effort to care about others. **Caring** simply means paying serious attention to what others are saying and to what they might be feeling as they speak. To do this, you set aside your own thoughts and feelings in order to put yourself in the *other* person's shoes.

The second step in increasing empathy is to observe others' behavior carefully in order to "read" their nonverbal messages. When a person begins speaking, silently pose two questions to yourself: (1) What emotions do I believe this person is experiencing right now? (2) What cues is the person giving that I am using to draw this conclusion? Consciously asking these questions helps you focus your attention on the nonverbal aspects of messages, where most of the information on the person's emotional state is conveyed.

How accurately can a person read others' emotions from their nonverbal behavior? Research studies have shown that when we concentrate, we can be very good at recognizing such primary emotions as happiness, sadness, surprise, anger, and fear (greater than 90 percent accuracy) and quite good at recognizing

---

UNDERSTAND YOURSELF

Empathy Approaches

1. Which of the three approaches to empathy do you find yourself relying on most?

2. Under what circumstances would it be difficult for you to use each of the three approaches to empathy?

3. When Janine appears to ignore Tasha's feelings of sadness over the death of the dog that she's had since third grade, Tasha says to Janine, "You've got about as much empathy as a rock." Disregarding the appropriateness of her comment, what does Tasha mean by such a statement? Should Janine be concerned about such an assessment? Why?

INFOTRAC COLLEGE EDITION

Using InfoTrac College Edition, under the subject of "empathy," click on periodical references. Look for the following article and ones like it. Marilyn Cram Donahue (1997). Empathy: Putting yourself in another's shoes. *Current Health 2* Vol. 24, Nov. p. 22. In this and other articles, what kinds of behaviors are recommended for helping us increase our empathy?

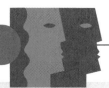

DIVERSE VOICES

Growing Up with Privilege and Prejudice

by Karen K. Russell

Although some of our most insensitive responses to others are made thoughtlessly, it doesn't lessen the sting of our words. Karen Russell shows us what it is like to be on the receiving end of hostile responses—and demonstrates dramatically the need to increase our levels of empathy for the experience of others.

I am a child of privilege (my father is Bill Russell, center for the Boston Celtics dynasty that won 11 championships in 13 years). In so many ways, I have been given every opportunity—good grade schools, college years at Georgetown, the encouragement to pursue my ambitions. I have just graduated from Harvard Law School. My future looks promising. Some people, no doubt, will attribute any successes I have to the fact that I am a black woman. I am a child of privilege, and I am angry.

How am I supposed to react to well-meaning, good, liberal white people who say things like: "You know, Karen, I don't understand what all the fuss is about. You're one of my good friends, and I never think of you as black." Implicit in such a remark is, "I think of you as white," or perhaps just, "I don't think of your race at all." Racial neutrality is a wonderful concept, but we are a long way from achieving it. In the meantime, I would hope that people wouldn't have to negate my race in order to accept me.

Last year, I worked as a summer law associate, and one day a white lawyer called me into her office. She told me, laughing, that her secretary, a young black woman, had said that I spoke "more white than white people." It made me sad; that young woman had internalized all of society's negative images of black people to the point that she thought of a person with clear diction as one of "them."

I am reminded of the time during college that I was looking through the classifieds for an apartment. I called a woman to discuss the details of a rental. I needed directions to the apartment, and she asked me where I lived. I told her I lived in Georgetown, to which she replied, "Can you

believe the way the blacks have overrun Georgetown?" I didn't really know how to respond. I said, "Well, actually, I can believe that Georgetown is filled with blacks because I happen to be black." There was a silence on the other end. Finally, the woman tried to explain that she hadn't meant any harm. She was incredibly embarrassed, and, yes, you guessed it, she said, "Some of my best friends are. . . . " I hung up before she could finish.

I was afraid to come back to Boston. My first memory of the place is of a day spent in Marblehead, walking along the ocean shore with a white friend of my parents. I must have been 3 or 4 years old. A white man walking past us looked at me and said, "You little nigger." I am told that I smiled up at him as he went on: "They should send all you black baboons back to Africa." It was only when I turned to look at Kay that I realized something was wrong.

I think my brothers and I may have been spared some of the effects of racism because my father was a celebrity. But I know that his position also made us a bit paranoid. Sometimes it was hard to tell why other kids liked us, or hated us, for that matter. Was it because we had a famous father? Was it because we were black?

How will I deal with racism in my life? I have no brilliant solution. On a personal level, I will ask people to explain a particular comment or joke. When I have trouble hailing a cab in New York, as frequently happens—cabbies "don't want to go to Harlem"—I will copy down the medallion numbers and file complaints if necessary. On the larger level, I will work with others to confront the dilemma of the widening gap between the black middle class and the black lower class, a gap that must be closed if my generation is to advance the cause of racial equality.

Like many middle-class children who grew up accustomed to a comfortable lifestyle, I will also have to work to balance the desire for economic prosperity with the desire to realize more idealistic goals.

If I do ever find a man and get married, will we want to raise our kids in a black environment? Sometimes I really regret that I didn't go to an all-black college. When I was in high school on Mercer Island, I didn't go out on dates. A good friend was nice enough to escort me to my senior prom. I don't know if I want my kids excluded like that. If it hadn't been my race, it might have been some-

thing else; I guess a lot of people were miserable in high school. Yet, I have to wonder what it would be like to be the norm.

I am concerned about tokenism. If I am successful, I do not want to be used as a weapon to defeat the claims of blacks who did not have my opportunities. I do not want someone to say of me, "See, she made it. We live in a world of equal opportunity. If you don't make it, it's your own fault."

Excerpted from Karen K. Russell, "Growing Up with Privilege and Prejudice." From New York Times Maga-zine, 136 (June 14, 1987): 69-74. © 1987 by The New York Times Company. Reprinted by permission.

contempt, disgust, interest, determination, and bewilderment (80 to 90 percent accuracy) (Leathers 1992, p. 42).

To further increase the accuracy of reading emotions, you can use the skill of perception checking—especially when the other person's culture is different from your own. Once you have understood the emotions that the other person is feeling, you can then choose the type of empathic response you wish to use.

In order to become more effective at empathizing with another, (1) adopt an attitude of caring; (2) concentrate on understanding the nonverbal as well as the verbal messages in order to ascertain his or her emotional state; and (3) try to feel with the person, recall or imagine how you would feel in similar circumstances, or understand what the person is feeling so that you can experience your own feelings of concern, compassion, or sorrow.

Questioning

Active listeners are willing to question to help them get the information they need to understand. A **question** is a response designed to get further information or clarify information already received. And although you may have asked questions for as long as you can remember, you may notice that at times your questions either don't get the information you want or irritate, fluster, or cause defensiveness. We can increase the chances that our questions will get us the information we want and reduce negative reactions if we observe the following guidelines.

SKILL BUILDERS   Empathy

Skill	Use	Procedure	Example
Intellectually identifying with or vicariously experiencing the feelings, thoughts, or attitudes of another.	To create or promote a supportive climate.	1. Adopt an attitude of caring. 2. Concentrate on understanding the nonverbal as well as the verbal messages in order to ascertain his or her emotional state. 3. Try to feel with the person; try to recall or imagine how you would feel in similar circumstances; or try to understand what the person is feeling and allow yourself to experience your own feelings of concern, compassion, or sorrow.	When Jerry says, "I really feel embarrassed about wearing braces in college," Mary smiles ruefully and replies, "Yeah, it makes you feel like a little kid, doesn't it? I remember the things I had to put up with when I wore braces."

1. **Phrase your questions specifically.** Determine what specific additional information or clarification you want. Suppose Maria says to you, "I am totally frustrated. Would you stop at the store on the way home and buy me some more paper?" At this point, you may be a bit confused and need more information to understand what Maria is asking you. But if you respond "What do you mean?" you are likely to add to the confusion, because Maria, who is already uptight, won't know precisely what it is you don't understand. Specific questions are of several types.

   You can ask questions to get more information on important details. "What kind of paper would you like me to get, and how much will you need?"

   You can ask questions to clarify the use of a term. "Could you tell me what you mean by 'frustrated'?"

   You can ask questions to clarify the cause of the feelings the person is expressing. "What's frustrating you?"

   Determine whether the information you need is more detail, clarification of a word or idea, or information on the cause of feelings or events, and then phrase your question accordingly.

Increasing empathy includes reading nonverbal messages and asking questions to clarify.

2. **Phrase questions as complete sentences.** Under pressure, our tendency is to use one- or two-word questions that may be perceived as curt or abrupt. For instance, suppose Miles says, "Molly just told me that I always behave in ways that are totally insensitive to her needs." Instead of asking "How?" you might ask "Did she give you specific behaviors or describe specific incidents when this happened?" Curt, abrupt questions often seem to challenge the speaker instead of focusing on the kind of information the respondent needs to understand the statement. By phrasing more complete questions, the questioner shows the respondent that he or she has been heard.

3. **Monitor your nonverbal cues so that they convey genuine interest and concern.** Ask questions in a tone of voice that is sincere—not a tone that could be interpreted as bored, sarcastic, cutting, superior, dogmatic, or evaluative. We need to constantly remind ourselves that the way we speak may be even more important than the words we use.

4. **Put the "burden of ignorance" on your own shoulders.** In order to minimize defensive reactions, especially when the speaker is under stress, phrase your questions to put the burden of ignorance on your own shoulders. Preface your questions with a short statement that suggests that any problem of misunderstanding may be the result of *your* listening skills. For instance, when Drew says, "I've really had it with Malone screwing up all the time," you might say, "Drew, I'm sorry, I'm missing some details that would help

OBSERVE AND ANALYZE

Empathizing

1. Recall the last time you treated someone as an object rather than a person. Describe the incident. Analyze why you acted in this way. Was it something about the person? the situation? How might you have changed this interaction if you were to do it over again?

2. Recall the last time you effectively empathized with another person. Write a short analysis of the episode. Be sure to cover the following: What was the person's emotional state? How did you recognize it? What were the nonverbal cues? Verbal cues? What type of relationship do you have with this person? How long have you known the person? How similar is this person to you? Have you ever had a real or vicarious experience similar to the one the person was reporting?

me understand your feelings better. What kinds of things has Malone been doing?"

Following are two more examples that contrast inappropriate with more appropriate questioning responses.

Tamara: "They turned down my proposal again!"

Art: *Inappropriate:* "Well, did you explain it the way you should have?" *(This question is a veiled attack on Tamara in question form.) Appropriate:* "Did they tell you why?" *(This question is a sincere request for additional information.)*

Renee: "With all those executives at the party last night, I really felt strange."

Javier: *Inappropriate:* "Why?" *(With this abrupt question, Javier is making no effort to be sensitive to her feelings or to understand them.) Appropriate:* "Gee, what is it about your bosses' presence that makes you feel strange?" *(Here the question is phrased to elicit information that will help Javier understand and may help Renee understand as well.)*

In summary, to increase your effectiveness at asking questions, (1) note the kind of information you need to increase your understanding of the message; (2) phrase specific, complete-sentence questions that focus on getting that information; (3) deliver your questions in a sincere tone of voice; and (4) especially in stressful situations, put the burden of ignorance on your own shoulders.

Paraphrasing

In addition to being skilled questioners, active listeners are also adept at **paraphrasing**—putting your understanding of the message into words. For example, during a meeting with his professor to discuss his performance on the first exam, Charley says, "Well, it looks like I really blew this first test—I had a lot of things on my mind." If the professor responds by saying, "If I understand you correctly, there were things happening to you that took your mind away from studying," she is paraphrasing.

Paraphrases may focus on content, on feelings underlying the content, or on both. In the previous example, the professor's response, "If I understand you correctly, there were things happening to you that took your mind away from studying," is a content paraphrase. It focuses on the denotative meaning of the message. If, as Charley began to speak, the professor noticed that he dropped his eyes, sighed, and slowly shook his head, and she said, "So you were pretty upset with your grade on the last test," her response would be a feelings paraphrase.

In real-life settings, we often don't distinguish clearly between content and feelings paraphrases, so our responses may well be a combination of both.

The following example includes all three types of paraphrases for the same statement.

Statement: "Five weeks ago, I gave the revised manuscript of my independent study to my project adviser. I felt really good about it because I thought the changes I had made really improved my explanations. Well, yesterday I stopped by and got the manuscript back, and my adviser said he couldn't really see that this draft was much different from the first."

Content paraphrase: "Let me see if I'm understanding this right. Your adviser thought that you hadn't really done much to rework your paper, but you put a lot of effort into it and think this draft was a lot different and much improved."

Feelings paraphrase: "I sense that you're really frustrated that your adviser didn't recognize the changes you had made."

Combination: "If I have this right, you're saying that your adviser could see no real differences, yet you think your draft was not only different but much improved. I also get the feeling that your adviser's comments really irk you."

Some of the best times to paraphrase are when

- You need a better understanding of a message—in terms of content, feelings, or both—before you can respond appropriately.
- What the person has said is important, and misunderstanding the message will have serious consequences.
- The message was long and contained several complex ideas.
- What the person has said seems controversial or seems to have been said under emotional strain, and there is a chance that the person did not mean what was actually said.

SKILL BUILDERS Paraphrasing

Skill	Use	Procedure	Example
Putting your understanding of the message into words.	To increase listening efficiency; to avoid message confusion; to discover the speaker's motivation.	1. Listen carefully to the message. 2. Determine what the message means to you. 3. Restate the message using your own words to indicate the meaning you have received.	Grace says, "At two minutes to five, the boss gave me three letters that had to be in the mail that evening!" Bonita replies, "If I understand you correctly, you were really resentful that the boss would dump important work on you right before closing time."

■ When you are speaking in a language that is not your native language or talking with people in a language that is not their first.

In summary, to paraphrase effectively, (1) listen carefully to the message, (2) determine what the message means to you, and (3) if you believe a paraphrase is necessary, restate the message using your own words to indicate the meaning (content, feelings, or both) that you have received.

TEST YOUR COMPETENCE

Questions and Paraphrases

Provide an appropriate question and paraphrase for each of the following statements. To get you started, the first conversation has been completed for you.

1. **Luis:** "It's Dionne's birthday, and I've planned a *big* evening. Sometimes I think Dionne believes I take her for granted—well, after tonight she'll know I think she's something special!"
   Question: "What specific things do you have planned?"
   Content paraphrase: "If I'm understanding you, you're planning a night that's going to be a lot more elaborate than what Dionne expects on her birthday."
   Feelings paraphrase: "From the way you're talking, I get the feeling you're really proud of yourself for making plans like these."

2. **Angie:** "Brother! Another nothing class. I keep thinking one of these days he'll get excited about something. Professor Romero is a real bore!"
   Question:
   Content paraphrase:
   Feelings paraphrase:

3. **Guy:** "Everyone seems to be talking about that movie on Channel 5 last night, but I didn't see it. You know, I don't watch much that's on the 'idiot box.'"
   Question:
   Content paraphrase:
   Feelings paraphrase:

4. **Kaelin:** "I don't know if it's something to do with me or with Mom, but lately she and I just aren't getting along."
   Question:
   Content paraphrase:
   Feelings paraphrase:

5. **Aileen:** "I've got a report due at work and a paper due in management class. On top of that, it's my sister's birthday, and so far I haven't even had time to get her anything. Tomorrow's going to be a disaster."
   Question:
   Content paraphrase:
   Feelings paraphrase:

Remembering: Retaining Information

Remembering is being able to retain information and recall it when needed. Yet too often we forget what we've heard almost immediately. For instance, you can probably think of many times when you were unable to recall the name of a person to whom you had been introduced just moments earlier. Three techniques that can help you improve your ability to remember information are repeating, constructing mnemonics, and taking notes.

Repeating Information

Repetition—saying something two, three, or even four times—helps listeners store information in long-term memory by providing necessary reinforcement (Estes 1989, p. 7). If information is not reinforced, it will be held in short-term memory for as little as twenty seconds and then forgotten. So, when you are introduced to a stranger named Jack McNeil, if you mentally say, "Jack McNeil, Jack McNeil, Jack McNeil, Jack McNeil," you increase the chances that you will remember his name. Likewise, when a person gives you the directions, "Go two blocks east, turn left, turn right at the next light, and it's in the next block," you should immediately repeat to yourself, "two blocks east, turn left, turn right at light, next block—that's two blocks east, turn left, turn right at light, next block."

Constructing Mnemonics

Constructing mnemonics helps you put information in a form that is more easily recalled. A **mnemonic device** is any artificial technique used as a memory aid. One of the most common ways of creating a mnemonic is to take the first letters of a list of items you are trying to remember and forming a word. For example, an easy mnemonic for remembering the five Great Lakes is HOMES (*H*uron, *O*ntario, *M*ichigan, *E*rie, *S*uperior).

When you want to remember items in a sequence, try to form a sentence using the words themselves, or using words with the same first letters as the items you are trying to remember. For example, when you first studied music, you may have remembered the lines on the treble clef (EGBDF) with the saying "*E*very *g*ood *b*oy *d*oes *f*ine." (And for the treble clef spaces, you may have used the word FACE.)

Taking Notes

Although note taking would be inappropriate in most casual interpersonal encounters, it represents a powerful tool for increasing your recall of information from telephone conversations, briefing sessions, interviews, and business meetings. Note taking not only provides a written record that you can go back

TEST YOUR COMPETENCE

Listening Test

Have a friend assume the role of a fellow worker on your first day in an office job and read the following information to you once, at a normal rate of speech. As the friend reads the instructions, take notes. Then give yourself the test that follows, answering true or false, without referring to your notes. Then repeat the quiz, but this time use your notes. How much does your score improve? Although the temptation is great to read this item to yourself, try not to. You will miss both the enjoyment and the value of the exercise if you do.

Since you are new to the job, I'd like to fill you in on a few details. The boss probably told you that typing and distribution of mail were your most important duties. Well, they may be, but let me tell you, answering the phone is going to take most of your time. Now about the typing. Goodwin will give you the most, but much of what he gives you may have nothing to do with the department—I'd be careful about spending all my time doing his private work. Mason doesn't give much, but you'd better get it right—she's really a stickler. I've always asked to have tests at least two days in advance. Paulson is always dropping stuff on the desk at the last minute.

The mail situation sounds tricky, but you'll get used to it. Mail comes twice a day—at 10 A.M. and at 2 P.M. You've got to take the mail that's been left on the desk to Charles Hall for pickup. If you really have some rush stuff, take it right to the campus post office in Harper Hall. It's a little longer walk, but for really rush stuff, it's better. When you pick up at McDaniel Hall, sort it. You'll have to make sure that only mail for the people up here gets delivered here. If there is any that doesn't belong here, bundle it back up and mark it for return to the campus post office.

Now, about your breaks. You get ten minutes in the morning, forty minutes at noon, and fifteen minutes in the afternoon. If you're smart, you'll leave before the 10:30 classes let out. That's usually a pretty crush time. Three of the teachers are supposed to have office hours then, and if they don't keep them, the students will be on your back. If you take lunch at 11:45, you'll be back before the main crew goes.

Oh, one more thing. You are supposed to call Jeno at 8:15 every morning to wake him. If you forget, he gets very upset. Well, good luck. (348 wds)

Without Notes	With Notes	
_____	_____	1. Where are you to take the mail that does not belong here?
_____	_____	2. How often does mail come?
_____	_____	3. When should you be back from lunch?
_____	_____	4. What is Paulson's problem with work?
_____	_____	5. Who gives the most work?
_____	_____	6. What's the problem with Goodwin's request to do work?
_____	_____	7. What are your main jobs, according to the boss?
_____	_____	8. Where are you to take outgoing mail?
_____	_____	9. Where is the post office?
_____	_____	10. How many minutes do you get for your morning break?
_____	_____	11. What is the preferred time to take your lunch?
_____	_____	12. Who are you supposed to give a wake-up call?

Answers:
1. Harper Hall 2. Twice a day 3. 12:25 4. Last minute 5. Goodwin 6. Not work-related 7. Typing, distributing mail 8. Charles Hall 9. Harper Hall 10. 10 11. 11:45 12. Jeno

to, but also forces you to take a more active role in the listening process (Wolvin and Coakley 1996, p. 239). In short, when you are listening to complex information, take notes.

What constitutes *good notes* will vary depending on the situation. Useful notes may consist of a brief list of main points or key ideas plus a few of the most significant details. Or they may be a short summary of the entire concept (a type of paraphrase) after the message is completed. For lengthy or rather detailed information, however, good notes likely will consist of a brief outline of what the speaker has said, including the overall idea, the main points of the message, and key developmental material. Good notes will vary in number of words depending on the importance of details. For good notes of the information-packed Listening Test on the previous page, see Figure 6.1.

Analyzing Critically

Critical analysis is the process of determining how truthful, authentic, or believable you judge information to be. For instance, when a person tries to convince you to vote for a particular candidate for office or to support efforts to legalize RU 486 (the so-called "abortion pill"), you will want to listen critically to these

---

OUTLINE

Duties
    Typing and distribution of mail most important
    Answering phone take most time

Typing
    Goodwin will give most
        Question spending time on his private work
    Mason not give much
        Get it right—she's really a stickler
    Ask for tests 2 days in advance
        Or get stuck by Paulson at last minute

Mail
    10 and 2
    Take the mail on the desk to Charles Hall
    Take rush stuff to the campus post office in Harper Hall
    Sort mail you pick up at McDaniel Hall—bundle what
        doesn't belong and mark it for return to campus post office

Breaks
    10 minutes morning—take before 10:30
    40 minutes noon—take at 11:45

Extra
    Call Jeno 8:15   (112 words)

Figure 6.1
Outline.

PRACTICE IN CLASS

Note Taking

Working in groups, have each
person in class select a newspaper
or magazine article and prepare a
two-minute reading of it. As each
person reads, everyone in class
takes notes. At the end of each
reading, class members compare
notes and discuss why they chose
to write what they did.

messages so as to determine how much you agree with the speaker and how you
wish to respond. If you fail to listen critically to the messages you receive, you
risk inadvertently concurring in ideas or plans that may violate your own values, be counterproductive to achieving your goals, or be misleading to others
(including the speakers) who value your judgment.

Critical analysis requires that you distinguish factual statements from inferences and then evaluate the quality of inferences.

Distinguishing Factual Statements from Inferences

Factual statements are those whose accuracy can be verified or proven; **inferences** are claims or assertions that are based on observation or fact but are not
necessarily true. Distinguishing factual statements from inferences means being
able to tell the difference between statements that can be accepted on face value
and statements that require proof.

Suppose someone says, "Cesar received an A in geology; he must have studied hard." If we can document that Cesar received an A in geology, then saying
so is a factual statement. "He must have studied hard," however, is an inference
that must be proven. Cesar may have studied hard to earn his grade, but it is
also possible that geology comes easily to Cesar and that he had already learned
much of the material in his high school physical science course.

So, when we hear statements such as "Better watch it; *Carl is really in a bad
mood today*—did you see the way he was scowling?" or "I know you're hiding
something from me; *I can tell it in your voice*," or "*Olga and Kurt are having
an affair*—I've seen them leave the office together nearly every night," we know
that each of the italicized portions is an inference.

Evaluating Inferences

Critical listeners evaluate inferences by examining the context in which they
occur. An inference is usually presented as part of an argument; that is, a person
makes a claim (or inference) and then presents other statements in support of
the claim. Take the following simple argument: Joyce says, "Next year is going
to be a lot easier than the past year. I got a $200-a-month raise, and my hus-
band's been relieved of some of the extra work he's had to do while they were
looking for a replacement for Ed." The statements "I got a $200-a-month
raise" and "my husband's been relieved of some of the extra work he's had to
do while they were looking for a replacement for Ed" are both factual statements that can be documented. The claim "Next year is going to be a lot easier
than the past year" is an inference—a statement that requires support to validate it. Notice that Joyce's inference suggests that she believes there is a relationship between her claim and the facts she presents. Her argument is based on
the assumption that more money per month and less work for her husband will
make the year easier because it will relieve stress.

The critical listener asks at least three questions when evaluating any inference:

1. Is there factual information to support the inference? Perhaps there is no supporting information; perhaps there is not enough; or perhaps the supporting information is inaccurate. In our example, Joyce does have factual statements for support: She received a raise, and her husband has less work to do.

2. Is the factual support relevant to the inference? Perhaps the actual or implied statement of relevance is logically weak. In our example, "increased income" is one kind of information that is relevant to "having an easier time." At this stage it would appear that Joyce does have the makings of a sound argument; however, we need to ask a third question.

3. Is there known information that would prevent the inference from logically following the factual statements? Perhaps there is information that is not accounted for that affects the likelihood of the inference. If we learn that getting the $200-a-month raise involves extra duties for Joyce, then we still might question whether the year is likely to be "easier" than the last one.

Let us consider one more example. Dan says, "This is a great time to buy a car; interest rates are at the lowest point they've been in three years." The inference is that this is a great time to buy a car.

1. Does Dan give any support for the inference? Yes.

2. Is the support relevant to the inference? Yes—interest rates are a factor in determining whether the time is right for car buying.

3. Is there known information that would prevent the conclusion's following from the data? If other indicators showed that we were entering a period of recession, that information might be more important to the decision than the level of interest rates.

For many of us, the most difficult of the three questions to answer is the second one: "Is the factual support relevant to the inference?" This question is difficult to answer because the listener must be able to verbalize a statement that shows the relevance. Recall that in the first example, Joyce never said anything like "A raise and a reduction of work are two criteria for predicting that next year will be a lot easier." Because the relevance is more often implied than stated, we must learn to phrase it.

To phrase the relationship between support and inference, ask yourself, "What can I say that would make sense for this inference to follow from this material?" For instance, suppose Hal says, "I see frost on the grass—I think our flowers are goners." To establish the relevance of the supporting fact "frost on the grass" to the claim "our flowers are goners," you might say, "The presence of frost means that the temperature is low enough to freeze the moisture on the grass; if it's cold enough to freeze the moisture on the grass, it's cold enough to kill Hal's flowers." This statement makes sense because we can demonstrate a relationship between frost and the death of unprotected flowers.

Let's take another example. Gina says, "I studied all night and only got a D on the first test—I'm not going to do any better on this one."

This statement suggests that Gina sees relevance between the amount of study time before a test and the grade. We could phrase the implied relevance by saying, "Since the time of study before the test, which determines the grade, can be no greater, Gina can't improve her grade."

In this case, the relevance seems questionable. Her reasoning suggests that the only factor in determining a grade is the amount of study time before the test. Experience would suggest that many other factors, such as previous time studying and frame of mind, are of equal if not greater importance.

In short, you are listening critically when (1) you question whether the inference is supported with meaningful factual statements, (2) you question whether the stated or implied relevance between the support and the inference makes sense, and (3) you question whether there is any other known information that lessens the quality of the inference.

TEST YOUR COMPETENCE

Distinguishing Fact from Inference

Read the following story only once. Then, without referring back to the story, evaluate each witness's statement as either F (fact) or I (inference).

Two people came hurrying out of a bank with several large bundles, hopped into a long black car, and sped away. Seconds later, a man rushed out of the bank, waving his arms and looking quite upset. You listen to two people discuss what they saw.

_____ a. "The bank's been robbed!"

_____ b. "Yes, indeed—I saw the robbers hurry out of the bank, hop into a car, and speed away."

_____ c. "It was a long black car."

_____ d. "The men were carrying several large bundles."

_____ e. "Seconds after they left, a man came out of the bank after them—but he was too late, they'd already escaped."

Answers: a. I   b. I   c. F   d. I (men?)   e. I

Responding Empathically to Give Comfort

When we respond empathically to give comfort, we not only show that we have understood a person's meaning, but we also affirm the person's right to his or her feelings. In addition, comforting statements are likely to soothe, console, reassure, and cheer up. Research on comforting suggests that people who use comforting strategies in their communication are perceived as more sensitive, concerned, and involved. Over the years, much of the most significant research on comforting has been conducted by Brant Burleson and colleagues, featured in this chapter's Spotlight on Scholarship.

In the section on Understanding, we discussed two important empathic responses: questioning and paraphrasing. In this section, we look primarily at the kinds of responses that both show empathy and give comfort.

Supporting

Supporting responses are comforting statements whose goal is to affirm, soothe, console, reassure, reduce tension, or pacify. Most of all, supporting responses show that we care about people and what happens to them. Effective supporting statements demonstrate that the listener empathizes with a person's feelings, whatever their direction or intensity (Burleson 1994, p. 5). In fact, comforting or supporting is considered one of the most important communication skills (Samter 1994, p. 200).

Supporting positive feelings. We all like to treasure our good feelings; when we share them, we don't want them dashed by listeners' inappropriate or insensitive responses. Supporting positive feelings is generally easy, but still requires some care. Consider the following example.

Kendra (hangs up the telephone, does a little dance step, and turns to Selena): "That was my boss. He said that he'd put my name in for a promotion. I didn't believe he would really choose me!"

TEST YOUR COMPETENCE

Evaluating Inferences

For each of the following statements, ask and answer the following three questions: (1) Is the inference supported with meaningful factual statements? (2) Does the stated or implied relevance between the support and the inference make sense? (3) Is there any other known information that lessens the quality of the inference? Remember that to evaluate an inference properly, you must phrase a reasoning link to tie the supporting information to the inference.

a. "The chess club held a raffle, and they made a lot of money. I think we should hold a raffle, too."

b. "Chad is aggressive, personable, and highly motivated—he ought to make a good salesman."

c. "Three of my students last year got A's on this test, five the year before, and three the year before that. There certainly will be some A's this year."

d. "I saw Kali in a maternity outfit—she must be pregnant."

e. "Listen, I like the way Darren thinks, Solomon is an excellent mathematician, and Marco and Ethan are two of my best students. All four are Alpha Alphas. As far as I'm concerned, the Alphas are the group on campus with academic strength."

f. "If Greg hadn't come barging in, I never would have spilled my iced tea."

g. "Maybe that's the way you see it, but to me when high city officials are caught with their hands in the till and when police close their eyes to the actions of people with money, that's corruption."

h. "Krista wears her hair that way and guys fall over her—I'm getting myself a hairdo like that."

SPOTLIGHT ON SCHOLARSHIP

Brant Burleson, Professor of Communication at Purdue University, on Comforting

The seeds of Brant Burleson's interest in comforting behavior were sown during his undergraduate days at the University of Colorado at Boulder, where he was taught that all communication is persuasion. This proposition did not square with Burleson's own experiences. As a child of the fifties who came of age during the emotion-filled sixties, Burleson had witnessed lots of hurt and conflict. But he had also seen people engaging in altruism and acts of comforting. These comforting acts, he reasoned, were not aimed at changing anyone's opinion or behavior, but were simply done to help the other person. So when he entered graduate school at the University of Illinois, Burleson began to study formally how individuals comfort others. He wanted to establish scientifically whether comforting messages were important and whether they made a difference. Since graduate school, Burleson's work has done much to accomplish this goal.

In his research, Burleson has carefully defined comforting strategies as messages that have the goal of relieving or lessening the emotional distress of others. He has limited his work to looking at how we comfort others who are experiencing mild or moderate sadness or disappointment as a result of everyday events. He has chosen not to study comforting in situations where there is extreme depression or grief because of extraordinary events. He has also chosen to limit his work to the verbal strategies that we use when we comfort. Burleson's care in defining the "domain" of his work is important. By carefully stating the type of emotional distress he is concerned with, and by

clearly identifying the limits of his work, Burleson enables those who read his work to understand the types of situations to which his finding apply.

Early on, Burleson worked with James L. Applegate, who had developed a way of judging the sophistication of particular comforting messages. Sophisticated messages were seen as those that acknowledge, elaborate, and legitimize the feelings of another person. Sophisticated comforting strategies are also more listener-centered (aimed at discovering how the distressed person feels), less evaluative, more feeling-centered, more likely to accept the point of view of the other person, and more likely to offer explanations for the feelings being expressed by the other person.

More recently, Burleson and others who study comforting have turned their attention to understanding the results of comforting. Previous research has judged comforting messages only on the extent to which they reduce the immediate distress that a person is feeling. Burleson believes that the effects of comforting extend beyond this simple instrumental effect. He theorizes that effective comforting should also help the other person cope better in the future. Skilled comforting should also benefit the comforter. Burleson believes that when we effectively comfort others, we increase our own self-esteem, and we become better liked by the person we comfort and by those who see us effectively comfort others. Finally, Burleson believes that those who are effective at comforting others are likely to have better long-term relationships. A growing list of research studies, some conducted by Burleson and his colleagues, provides support for his theory. For complete citations of many of his and his colleagues' publications, see the References at the end of this book.

Periodically, professors take a break from the rigors of the classroom and the day-to-day activities of a college professor to "go back to school" on what is called a sabbatical. Recently, Burleson completed a yearlong sabbatical at the University of Illinois. Believing that the primary goal of future research on comforting should be to increase our understanding of how comforting messages affect the emotional states of others, Burleson studied theories and research on emotion and the factors that lead to emotional distress.

Through a program of reading and meetings with leading scholars, Burleson enhanced his expertise in this area. Today, Burleson is using the knowledge he gleaned during this sabbatical as he conducts studies that will help him better explain how comforting messages work.

Kendra's statement requires an appropriate verbal response. To provide one, Selena must appreciate the feeling people get when they receive good news, or she must envision how she would feel under the same circumstances. Selena responds:

Selena: "Kendra, way to go, girl! That's terrific! I am so happy for you. You really seem excited."

In this case, Selena's response gives her approval for Kendra to be excited. Her response also shows that is happy because Kendra seems happy.

Supporting responses like Selena's are much needed. Think of times when you have experienced an event that made you feel happy, proud, pleased, soothed, or amused and needed to express those feelings. Didn't it further your good feelings when others recognized your feelings and affirmed your right to have them?

Supporting (giving comfort) when a person experiences negative feelings. When a person has had an unfortunate experience and is in the midst of or is recalling unpleasant emotional reactions, an effective supporting statement provides much-needed comfort. By acknowledging the person's feelings and supporting his or her right to those feelings, you can help further the person's progress toward working through the feelings.

For some people, making appropriate responses to painful or angry feelings is very awkward and difficult. But when people are in pain or when they are feeling justifiably angry, they need to be comforted by appropriate supporting statements. Because it can be difficult to provide comfort when we are ill at ease, we need to practice and develop skill in making appropriate supporting statements.

An appropriate comforting statement shows empathy and sensitivity, and may show a willingness to be actively involved if need be. Consider the following example.

Bill: "My sister called today to tell me that Mom's biopsy came back positive. She's got cancer, and it's untreatable."

UNDERSTAND YOURSELF

Sharing Good Feelings

Recall an occasion when you were feeling especially happy, proud, or pleased and chose to share your feelings with someone else. Whom did you choose? Why did you choose this person? How did the person react? What effect did that reaction have on your immediate feelings? On your relationship with that person? If you had a similar situation, would you choose to tell the same person?

Dwight: "Bill, you must be in shock. I'm so sorry that this is happening. Do you want to talk about it? Is there anything I can do to help you right now?"

Notice how Dwight begins by empathizing: "Bill, you must be in shock." He continues with statements that show his sensitivity to the seriousness of the situation: "I'm so sorry that this is happening." Finally, he shows that he really cares: He is willing to take time to talk about it, and he asks whether he can do anything for Bill.

Let's contrast this example with one that seems to be supportive but is really inappropriate.

Jim (comes out of his boss's office clutching the report he had been so sure he would receive praise for): "Jacobs tore my report apart. I worked my tail off, tried to do everything he asked, and he just threw it back in my face and told me to redo it."

Aaron (who has not read the report): "Jim, I can see why you're angry. You deserved praise for what you did!"

Such a response would certainly have supporting qualities—Jim might feel soothed—but supporting that "takes a person's side" can have unintended side effects, especially when Aaron is in no position to judge whether the report did in fact deserve praise. Instead, Aaron would do better to focus his supporting response on how hard Jim worked and, therefore, why Jim may be feeling overly angered. For example,

Aaron: "He rejected it? After you worked all that overtime, I can see why you're so upset."

Giving empathic support is not the same as making statements that aren't true or only telling people what they want to hear. When supportive statements are out of touch with the facts, they can encourage behavior that is actually destructive. So when offering comfort through supporting statements, be sure that you don't inadvertently set the person up.

Making appropriate supporting responses can be most difficult in situations of high emotion and stress. Sometimes, the best supporting response is a nonverbal one. Consider the following situation.

With a few seconds left in the basketball game and her team trailing by one point, Jory steals the ball, dribbles down the court for an uncontested layup, and misses. The gun sounds, ending the game. Teary-eyed, Jory walks off the floor, looks at the coach, and shouts with anger, "I blew it! I lost us the game!"

How should the coach react? A first reaction might be to say "Don't feel bad, Jory." But Jory obviously does feel bad, and she has a right to those feelings. Another response might be "Hey, Jory, you didn't lose us the game," but in fact Jory's miss did affect the outcome. Jory is unlikely to find this response helpful because it is inaccurate. At this moment, perhaps the best thing the coach can do is to put an arm around Jory and give a comforting squeeze that says, "It's OK, I understand." Later, the coach might say, "Jory, I know you feel bad, but without your steal, we wouldn't even have had a chance to win." Still, for the moment, Jory is going to be difficult to console.

Some people think that comforting supportive statements are easier for females or even are more of a female skill. But Derlega, Barbee, and Winstead (1994, p. 147) found in their laboratory study that males are as good as females in providing achievement-related support (for example, being passed over for a promotion). Even for relationship problems, which are often thought to be female strengths, they do as well. Whether you're a male or a female, you can learn to give effective supportive responses.

In summary, to make effective supporting statements, (1) listen closely to what the person is saying, (2) try to empathize with the dominant feelings, (3) phrase a reply that is in harmony with the feeling you have identified, (4) supplement your verbal response with appropriate nonverbal responses, and (5) if it seems appropriate, indicate your willingness to help.

Interpreting

Interpreting responses are those that offer a reasonable or alternative explanation for an event or circumstance with the goal of helping another to understand the situation from a different perspective.

Especially when people's emotions are running high, they are likely to see only one of a number of possible explanations. Consider the following situation.

THINK CRITICALLY

Comforting Responses

Think of the last time you told someone about an event or circumstance in which you felt scared, hurt, disappointed, or angry. Did the person try to comfort you? If so, report what was said. Did the person try to offer alternative interpretations for what had happened? Did this help you? If so, how? If not, why not? What can you learn from this experience that will help you improve your response skills?

SKILL BUILDERS   Supporting

Skill	Use	Procedure	Example
Making statements whose goals is to soothe, approve, reduce tension, or pacify the other by acknowledging that you understand what the other is feeling and you support that person's right to be feeling that way.	To help people feel better about themselves or what they have said or done.	1. Listen closely to what the person is saying. 2. Try to empathize with the dominant feelings. 3. Phrase a reply that is in harmony with the feelings you have identified. 4. Supplement your verbal response with appropriate nonverbal responses. 5. If it seems appropriate, indicate your willingness to help.	In response to Kendra's statement, "My new baby is so small, I hope I don't accidentally hurt her," Dr. Smith replies, "I can understand your fear; babies are so small and appear delicate."

Travis returns from his first date with Natasha, a woman he has been interested in for some time. He plops down on the couch, shakes his head, and says, "Well, that was certainly a disaster! We had a great dinner and saw a really good show, and when I get to her door, she gives me a quick little kiss on the cheek, says, 'Thanks a lot,' and rushes into the house. We didn't even have much time to talk about the play. I guess I can chalk that one up. It's clear she's really not interested in me."

Travis is interpreting Natasha's behavior negatively—he sees her action as a rejection of him. Martin, Travis's roommate, has been listening to him. Although he does not know what Natasha thinks, he perceives that Travis is only seeing one explanation for these events and he might be comforted by seeing other possible explanations. So Martin says,

"You're right, her behavior was a bit abrupt, but maybe she's had bad experiences with other guys—you know, ones who tried to go too far too fast—so she wasn't really trying to reject you, she was just trying to protect herself."

Whose interpretation is correct? It remains to be seen. Remember, you are not a mind reader—you cannot know for sure why something was done or said. Your primary goal when interpreting is to help a person look at an event from a different point of view. As with supporting statements, it is important to offer interpretation only when they seem plausible and worth considering. The point is not merely to soothe the person's feelings but to help the person see a possibility he or she has overlooked. Since most events can be interpreted in more

---

TEST YOUR COMPETENCE

Supporting and Interpreting

For each of the following situations, supply one supporting and one interpreting response.

1. **Statement:** "The milk is all gone! I know there was at least half a carton last night. I'll bet Jeff guzzled it all before he left for work. What did he expect me to put on my corn flakes, root beer? All my brother ever thinks about is himself!"
   Supporting response:
   Interpreting response:

2. **Statement:** "My manager must be trying to fire me or get me to quit. He told me that my error rate was higher than average, so he wants me to go downtown to headquarters and take another ten hours of training on my own time."
   Supporting response:
   Interpreting response:

3. **Statement:** "I just got a call from my folks. My sister was in a car accident and ended up in the hospital. They say she's OK, but told me the car was totaled. But I don't know whether she's really all right or whether they just don't want me to worry."
   Supporting response:
   Interpretive response:

Since most events can be interpreted in many ways, we can support one another by offering alternatives to negative interpretations.

than one way, we can be supportive of others by helping them to see alternative explanations for the things that happen to them. When we do this, we not only comfort them, but we can also help them understand what has happened.

Let's consider two additional examples of appropriate interpreting responses.

Karla: "I just don't understand Deon. I say we've got to start saving money, and he just gets angry with me."

Shelley: "I can understand why his behavior would concern you [a supportive statement prefacing an interpretation]. Perhaps he feels guilty about not being able to save money or feels resentful that you seem to be putting all the blame on him."

Micah: "I just don't believe Bradford. He says my work is top-notch, but I haven't had a pay raise in over a year."

Khalif: "I can see why you'd be frustrated, but maybe it has nothing to do with the quality of your work—maybe the company just doesn't have the money."

	Good Listeners	**Bad Listeners**
ATTENDING	Attend to important information	May not hear what a person is saying
	Ready themselves physically and mentally	Fidget in their chairs, look out the window, and let their minds wander
	Listen objectively regardless of emotional involvement	Visibly react to emotional language
	Listen differently depending on situations	Listen the same way regardless of the type of material
UNDERSTANDING	Assign appropriate meaning to what is said	Hear what is said, but either are unable to understand or assign different meaning to the words
	Seek out apparent purpose, main points, and supporting information	Ignore the way information is organized
	Ask questions to get information	Fail to anticipate coming information
	Paraphrase to solidify understanding	Seldom or never review information
	Seek out subtle meanings based on nonverbal cues	Ignore nonverbal cues

Both of these examples follow the guidelines for providing appropriate interpreting responses: (1) Listen carefully to what a person is saying. (2) Think of other reasonable explanations for the event or circumstance, and decide which alternative seems to best fit the situation as you understand it. (3) Phrase an alternative to the person's own interpretation—one that is intended to help the person see that other interpretations are available. (4) When appropriate, try to preface the interpretive statement with a supporting response.

Figure 6.2 summarizes how good listeners and poor listeners deal with the five aspects of listening: attending, understanding, remembering, analyzing critically, and responding empathically.

	Good Listeners	**Bad Listeners**
REMEMBERING	Retain information	Interpret message accurately but forget it
	Repeat key information	Assume they will remember
	Mentally create mnemonics for lists of words and ideas	Seldom single out any information as especially important
	Take notes	Rely on memory alone
ANALYZING CRITICALLY	Listen critically	Hear and understand message but are unable to weigh and consider it
	Separate facts from inferences	Don't differentiate between facts and inferences
	Evaluate inferences	Accept information at face value
RESPONDING EMPATHICALLY	Provide supportive comforting statements	Pass off joy or hurt; change the subject
	Give alternate interpretations	Pass off hurt; change the subject

Figure 6.2
A summary of the five aspects of listening.

REFLECT ON ETHICS

Janeen always disliked talking on the telephone—she thought it was an impersonal form of communication. Thus, college was a wonderful respite because when friends would call her, instead of staying on the phone she could quickly run over to their dorm or meet them at a coffeehouse.

One day, during reading period before exams, Janeen received a phone call from Barbara, an out-of-town friend. Before she was able to dismiss the call with her stock excuses, she found herself bombarded with information about old high school friends and their whereabouts. Not wanting to disappoint Barbara, who seemed eager to talk, Janeen tucked her phone under her chin and began straightening her room, answering Barbara with the occasional "uh-huh," "hmm," or "wow, that's cool!" As the "conversation" progressed, Janeen began reading through her mail and then her notes from class. After a few minutes, she realized there was silence on the other end of the line. Suddenly very ashamed, she said, "I'm sorry, what did you say? The phone . . . uh, there was just a lot of static."

Barbara replied with obvious hurt in her voice, "I'm sorry I bothered you, you must be terribly busy."

Embarrassed, Janeen muttered, "I'm just really stressed, you know, with exams coming up and everything. I guess I wasn't listening very well—you didn't seem to be saying anything really important. I'm sorry. What were you saying?"

"Nothing 'important,'" Barbara answered. "I was just trying to figure out a way to tell you. I know that you were friends with my brother Billy, and you see, we just found out yesterday that he's terminal with a rare form of leukemia. But you're right, it obviously isn't really important." With that, she hung up.

1. How ethical was Janeen's means of dealing with her dilemma of not wanting to talk on the phone but not wanting to hurt Barbara's feelings?
2. Identify ways in which both Janeen and Barbara could have used better and perhaps more ethical interpersonal communication skills. Rewrite the scenario incorporating these changes.

Summary

Listening is an active process that involves attending, understanding, remembering, analyzing critically and responding empathetically. Effective listening is essential to competent communication.

Attending is the process of selecting the sound waves we consciously process. We can increase the effectiveness of our attention by (1) getting ready to listen, (2) making the shift from speaker to listener a complete one, (3) hearing a person out before reacting, and (4) adjusting our attention to the listening goals of the situation.

Understanding is the process of decoding a message by assigning meaning to it. Understanding requires empathy, intellectually identifying with or vicariously experiencing the feelings, thoughts, or attitudes of another. We can increase our ability to empathize through caring and concentrating. A key to understanding is to practice active listening: Look for or create an organization for the information, ask questions, and paraphrase.

Remembering is the process of storing the meanings that have been received so that they can be recalled later. Remembering is increased by rehearsing information, looking for and storing information by an organizational pattern, grouping information to make it easier to remember, and, when feasible, taking notes.

Analyzing critically is the process of separating fact from inference and judging the validity of the inferences made. A fact is a verifiable statement; an inference is a conclusion drawn from facts. You are listening critically when you question (1) whether the inference is supported with meaningful factual statements, (2) whether the reasoning statement that shows the relationship between the support and the inference make sense, and (3) whether there is any other known information that lessens the quality of the inference.

Responding empathetically gives comfort. Comforting responses give people information about themselves or their behavior. Comforting can be accomplished through supporting and interpreting responses. When we are supportive, we soothe, approve, reduce tension, or pacify the other by acknowledging that we understand what the other is feeling and support that person's right to those feelings. When we use interpreting responses, we offer a reasonable alternative explanation for an event or circumstance, with the goal of helping another to understand the situation from a different perspective.

OBJECTIVES

After you have read this chapter, you should be able to answer the following questions:

■ What is a conversation?

■ How does a social conversation differ from a problem-consideration conversation?

■ What are some conversational rules, and what are their distinguishing features?

■ What is the cooperative principle?

■ What are the maxims of the cooperative principle, and how does each apply to conversation?

■ What are the skills associated with effective conversations?

■ What guidelines regulate turn-taking behavior?

■ What is conversational coherence, and how can it be achieved?

■ Why is politeness important in conversation?

Conversations

As Claude got into the car, he casually asked Phyllis, "How'd things go today?"

"Oh," Phyllis said as she shrugged her shoulders, "Mindy lost her ball, but Ken found it."

"That was nice of him."

"Well, I guess saying Ken found it isn't quite accurate—actually his foot found it. Luckily, the fall didn't hurt him too badly."

"What do you mean, the fall didn't hurt him too badly?" Claude asked, totally confused.

"Well, Dr. Scott says a break like that is often less troublesome than a sprain."

"Ken broke a bone, and you say he's not hurt too badly?" Claude replied incredulously.

"In comparison to the picture window," Phyllis said indignantly. "The lamp went through it."

"What does that have to do with Ken's falling?"

"Everything! When Ken fell, he landed on Rover, who leaped up out of a sound sleep and bumped into the lamp . . ."

"Which fell through the picture window," Claude finished. "Is that all?"

"Yes . . . unless Mrs. Parker decides to sue."

"Our baby-sitter? Sue about what?" Claude shouted.

"Calm down, Claude. I just knew you'd get all excited about this. See, when the lamp crashed through the window, Mrs. Parker jumped up to see what had happened and reinjured her back. But I doubt she'll sue. I offered to pay for her operation. But enough about this. How'd your day go?"

Conversations are the building blocks of good interpersonal relationships. In fact, as Steven Duck's work shows (see the accompanying Spotlight on Scholarship), how we talk with one another may be the most important variable in starting and building relationships. When conversations go well, they are informative, stimulating, and often just good fun. Yet, like Claude and Phyllis's, some conversations can be quite frustrating. By understanding how conversation works and by taking advantage of its dynamics, we all can become more skillful in the everyday talks we have with others.

SPOTLIGHT ON SCHOLARSHIP

Steven Duck, Daniel and Amy Starch Research Professor and Chair of the Communication Studies Department at the University of Iowa, on Personal Relationships

What began as a personal curiosity about the friendships he developed as a college student has turned out to be the focus of Steven Duck's lifelong work. He was curious about why some people who  meet become close friends while others remain acquaintances, and he selected this topic for a research paper assigned in one of his undergraduate classes. At that time, Duck's hypothesis was that people who have similar attitudes are likely to become attracted to each other and to become friends. Over the years, his understanding of how relationships are formed, developed, and maintained has changed considerably. In fact, in Duck's work you can see how scholars develop and test theories, only to replace them with more meaningful theories.

Many of Duck's breakthroughs in relationship theory came from his interdisciplinary studies in psychology, sociology, family studies, and communication, where he gained even deeper understanding of relationships. Duck saw his experience as so important that he founded the International Network on Personal Relationships and two inter-

national conferences on the subject to promote interdisciplinary scholarship.

Although many disciplines have contributed to how Duck views relationships, he believes his move to the University of Iowa, where he encountered colleagues whose backgrounds were in rhetoric, caused a fundamental shift in his thinking. Based on discussions with these colleagues, who assume that people are connected to one another through language, Duck began to see that conversations and talk were more than the instrument through which a relationship is developed.

Duck's early theories were based on the premise that what makes a relationship "work" is the degree of similarity among the personalities, backgrounds, and other characteristics of the participants. He saw talk as simply the channel through which these similarities are uncovered. This model can be seen in the operation of most dating services. Clients with similar profiles are "matched" and come together to talk to each other in order to learn about their similarities. Then presto, the relationship develops. Although people with many similarities often don't develop lasting relationships, this premise dominated the thinking on personal relationships for many years.

In his 1994 article in the *Handbook of Interpersonal Communication* (2d ed.), Duck first proposed a revision to his original premise. He argued that we "do" our relationships as we interact. Conversational statements such as "I just don't enjoy talking with him," "I really feel like she listens to me and understands," "We seem to have a lot in common, but we just can't seem to connect," and "We've gotten good at talking things out so that we work through our differences and both feel good about it" are not simply statements about the communication in the relationship—they are statements about the relationship itself.

Thus, according to Duck's new model, when two people begin to date, the way their relationship develops depends most directly on *how* they talk to each other, not simply whether they have similar personalities. If this is so, then from a practical standpoint, it is important to pay attention to *how* we say things and to *how* we respond to what others say. So while a dating service may be a convenient way to meet new people with similar interests, whether and what kind of a relationship develops depends on how the two people get along as they talk.

Duck thinks that it is time for scholars to focus more of their analysis on people's everyday talk in their ordinary conversations, rather than on what he calls the "peaks and valleys," because such everyday talk is at the heart of understanding how relationships grow, stabilize, and change. In addition, he believes that more theory and research should be directed to examining unhealthy relationships—for example, understanding "enemyship" as well as friendship.

Duck, a British citizen who received his Ph.D. from the University of Sheffield in 1971, has taught in the United States for twelve years. Over the years, he has authored or edited thirty-two books and hundreds of articles and papers on personal relationships. Currently, he teaches an advanced course in interpersonal communication for undergraduates, a seminar on personal relationships for graduate students, and a research methods course for both groups. For a list of some of Duck's major publications, see the References at the end of the book.

Whether we are trying to improve a relationship that is already pretty good or trying to figure out what went wrong in a relationship that is "on the rocks," by understanding the conversational strategies involved, we are better equipped to manage our relationships more effectively.

In this chapter, we define conversation and discuss its primary characteristics, the types and structure of conversation, the rules that conversations follow, the cooperative principle that helps explain how conversation works, and the skills of effective conversation. Finally, we offer a competence test of conversation and supply a sample conversation and analysis for your consideration.

Characteristics of Conversation

Conversations are informal interchanges of thoughts and feelings that usually occur in face-to-face settings in which any individual has an equal right to initiate talk, interrupt, respond, or refuse to do any of these (Wilson 1989, pp. 7, 20). So, students talking before class begins are holding "conversations." On the other hand, discussions between students and professor during class are not conversations because student rights are controlled—the professor sets the limits and the nature of the responses.

Robert Nofzinger (1991, pp. 3–5) suggests that conversations have three primary characteristics. First, conversation is fully *interactive*, echoing Wilson's point that at least two people exchange messages and take turns in sequence. Second, conversation is *locally managed*, meaning that those involved determine topic, who will speak, in what order, and for how long. Third, conversational topics are *mundane*, meaning they are about subjects that are commonplace and practical. Conversation fills the role of meeting participant needs, exchanging information, influencing behavior, and providing a building block for effective relationships.

If the results of a conversation are positive, people will tend to seek each other out in hopes that additional conversations will be positive as well. If, for instance, Dan meets Carl at a party and both of them consider the talk they have about politics stimulating, they're likely to look forward to later conversations.

If the results of a conversation are negative, people will tend to avoid each other and not invest time or energy in further attempts to develop a relationship. If, for instance, when Dan and Carl met they couldn't seem to find anything they both wanted to talk about, or Dan thought that Carl only wanted to brag about his accomplishments, or Carl thought that Dan didn't really know much about politics, they'd be unlikely to look for additional opportunities to talk.

Types and Structure of Conversation

Whether conversations are short or long, they have some structure. In this section we'll consider two common types of conversational situations: social conversation and problem-consideration conversation.

Social conversations are largely spontaneous, with no preplanned agenda. For instance, when Connie, Jeff, Wanda, and Trevor have dinner, they might hold conversations that at times involve all four and at other times involve two sets of two. During dinner they might spend nearly the entire time talking about

the upcoming presidential election, or they might talk about a new movie, a television series, last week's football game, politics, what a friend wore to a party they all attended, and several other topics. In all instances, the conversations would be held primarily to meet the conversationalists' interpersonal needs and would function to build or maintain the relationships among them.

In contrast, **problem-consideration conversations** are conversational episodes in which participants arrange to meet to discuss a specific problem or potential course of action. For instance, if Glen is concerned about attendance at a poker game that he and Susan have been playing in on a semiregular basis over the year, he may call Susan to help him generate some ideas about what can be done to increase the likelihood that enough people will show so they can play instead of watching a video to pass the time.

The Structure of Social Conversations

The structure of a social conversation, in which people talk spontaneously with no preplanned agenda, goes something like this. A topic is introduced and is accepted or rejected. If others accept it, it will be discussed until the participants feel the topic has been played out or until another topic is introduced. If the topic is rejected, someone else will introduce a different topic. At that point, the process recycles.

Suppose Donna and Juanita attend a play together. As they find their seats about fifteen minutes before the play is set to begin, their conversation may proceed as follows:

> **Looking around, Donna says, "They really did an Art Deco thing with this place, didn't they?"**
>
> **"Yeah . . . Hey," Juanita says as she surveys the audience, "it looks as if this is going to be a sellout."**
>
> **"Certainly does—I see people in the last row of the balcony."**
>
> **"I thought this would be a popular show. It was a hit when it toured Louisville . . . and I hear the attendance has been good all week."**
>
> **Agreeing with Juanita, Donna adds, "Lot's of people I've talked with were trying to get tickets."**
>
> **"Well it's good for the downtown."**
>
> **"Yeah," Donna says as she glances at the notes on the cast. After a few seconds, she exclaims, "I didn't know Gloria VanDell was from Cincinnati!"**

Notice what happened. Donna introduced the topic of decorative style. Juanita acknowledges the point, but chooses not to discuss it. Instead she chooses a different topic. Donna accepts the topic with a parallel comment. Juanita introduces information about what had happened in Louisville. The conversation lasts for two more turns. Then Donna introduces a new topic.

PRACTICE IN CLASS

Social Conversation

As a class, move all chairs to the perimeter of the room. Then position yourselves to form two circles, one inside the other. Each circle must have the same number of people. Those in the outer circle should face inward; those in the inner circle should face outward. Your instructor will direct you to move two, three, or four people to your left and begin a conversation with the person now facing you. When instructed to do so, move around the circle and begin another conversation. As you do this exercise, be aware of the flow of the conversation. Be prepared to discuss the experience with your classmates.

For the remainder of time before the show starts, Juanita and Donna could converse on one or more topics, sit and read their programs, or engage in some combination of conversing and reading.

The Structure of Problem-Consideration Conversation

In problem-consideration conversation, one person initiates the conversation on a topic that requires deliberation. This type of conversation is more orderly than social conversation and may have as many as five parts.

1. **Greeting and small talk.** Problem-consideration conversations usually open with some kind of greeting followed by a very brief conversation on social topics, just to establish rapport. Julia sees Shawna strolling across campus and knows that, since they have each just finished their last class, this would be a good time to get her ideas on what to do about Patterson. So she says, "Hey, girl, what'cha doing?" When Shawna walks over to her, Julia might not begin by jumping to the real topic, but might start with something less important. "How'd your Art History test go?" And the two of them might talk one or two rounds about the test before Julia transitions to the problem she really wants to discuss.

2. **Topic introduction and statement of need for discussion.** In the second stage, the real topic is introduced. Julia says, "Shawna, I'm glad I ran into you. We need to talk about what we can do to try to get Patterson to change the date our presentation is due." This stage may also suggest a time limit. "Have you got a few minutes? I was hoping to hear your ideas about what we might say to Patterson."

Skills in problem-consideration conversations allow us to resolve difficulties with others while enhancing our relationships.

3. **Information exchange and processing.** The conversation then revolves around sharing information, generating alternatives, discussing advantages and disadvantages of different options, and so on. At this point, the conversation will probably not be rationally organized. The conversationalists may move from subtopic to subtopic and circle back again. For instance, Julia and Shawna may begin to brainstorm strategies for getting Patterson to delay the assignment, at some point one of them may tell the other about a friend's experience with Patterson, and they may disagree about the merits of one possibility versus others. Although Julia and Shawna may talk about how they were really "bummed out" when Patterson "sprung" the assignment on them, or joke about how poorly they are likely to perform if they have to meet the current deadline, the theme of their conversation will relate to the issue at hand—that is, how to delay their presentation.

4. **Summarizing decisions and clarifying next steps.** After talking for a while, people often try to get some closure on the topic by summarizing their accomplishments. For instance, after Julia and Shawna have shared different strategies for getting Patterson to delay the assignment and given their reactions to each, Shawna might say something like, "We've discussed several strategies, but I think I like the idea of focusing on the importance of having enough time to do a good job on the assignment." If Julia has the same reading, she'll say or do something that in effect says, "Yeah, I agree that's our best shot." Once they agree, then one of them might double-check the next steps to be taken. "Well, then, why don't you call Patterson and schedule an appointment for us to talk with him before the next class?" But if Julia thinks they haven't reached agreement, she can say something like, "Well, I'm not sure. I still think we ought to talk with him about _____." Then Shawna and Julia will need to circle back and continue to discuss the pros and cons of each strategy or effect some sort of compromise before moving forward.

5. **Formal closing.** Once the conversationalists have discussed the issue and clarified the next steps that will be taken, they are ready to end the problem-consideration conversation. Endings enable the conversationalists to either move to a social conversation, begin a new problem consideration, or simply disengage from one another. The formal closing often includes showing appreciation for the conversation. For instance, Shawna might say, "I'm glad we took some time to share ideas—I think we'll be far more effective if the two of us are on the same line." In addition, the closing might also leave the door open for later conversation. Julia might say, "If you have any second thoughts, give me a call."

All five steps of a problem-consideration conversation can be seen in the following brief dialogue.

April: Hi, Yolanda. How are you doing?

OBSERVE AND ANALYZE

Problem-Consideration Conversations

Identify two problem-consideration conversations that you have had recently—one that was satisfying and one that was not. Try to recall exactly what was said. Write the scripts for these conversations. Then try to identify each of the five parts of a problem-consideration conversation. Were there any parts missing? Retain these scripts for further use later in the chapter.

Yolanda: Oh, can't complain too much.

April: I'm glad I ran into you—I need to check something out with you.

Yolanda: Can we do this quickly? I've really got to get cracking on the speech I'm doing for class.

April: Oh, this will just take a minute. If I remember right, you said that you'd been to the Dells for dinner with Scot. I'd like to take Rob there to celebrate his birthday, but I wanted to know whether we'd really feel comfortable there.

Yolanda: Sure. It's pretty elegant, but the prices aren't bad, and the atmosphere is really nice.

April: So you think we can really do dinner on fifty or sixty dollars?

Yolanda: Oh, yeah. We had a salad, dinner, and dessert, and our bill was under sixty including the tip.

April: Thanks, Yolanda. I wanted to ask you 'cause I know you like to eat out when you can.

Yolanda: No problem. Gotta run. Talk with you later—and let me know how Rob liked it.

Of course, not all problem-solving or decision-making conversations have all five steps. Sometimes after a greeting, a person might say what she's been thinking and ask the other person how that sounds. Or perhaps people will greet each other, set forth the topic, hash it out for a while, but not be able to come to any agreement at that time. Still, if you listen closely to your conversations of this type, you are likely to be able to identify some if not all of the five stages. Moreover, if you skip a conversational stage, you may notice less satisfaction with the outcome than if you had completed all the stages.

Conversations Are Rules Based

Although our social conversations may seem to be random activities with little form or structure, they are actually based on rules. **Rules** are "unwritten prescriptions that indicate what behavior is obligated, preferred, or prohibited in certain contexts" (Shimanoff 1980, p. 57).

Communication rules give us clues as to what kinds of messages and behavior are proper in a given physical or social context or with a particular person or group of people. They also provide us a framework in which to interpret the behavior of others.

When we communicate with people of a different race, sex, nationality, religion, political affiliation, class, organization, or group, effective communication is likely to be more difficult than when we communicate with people from our

Unwritten rules for conversations guide the kind of messages and appropriate behavior for different physical and social contexts.

own culture because their communication rules may well be different from those with which we are familiar.

Characteristics of Rules

Let's first consider the characteristics of rules and how they are best phrased. As an example, we will use a conversational rule that you've heard in a variety of forms for as long as you can remember: "If one person is talking, another person should not interrupt."

1. **Rules must allow for choice.** This means that rules must give you a choice to follow them or not. In our example, when a person is speaking, you can hear the person out, or you can break the rule and interrupt the person.

2. **Rules are prescriptive.** This means that your failure to follow a rule can be criticized or punished. If you choose to interrupt, the speaker might glare at you or verbally upbraid you.

3. **Rules are contextual.** This means that rules apply in similar communication situations, but may not be applicable under different conditions. For instance, if you are in a group meeting where people are engaging in free-wheeling brainstorming of ideas, the "don't interrupt" rule may not apply.

4. **Rules specify appropriate human behavior.** This means that rules focus on what to do or not do.

Phrasing Rules

Although we phrase rules in many ways, Shimanoff (1980, p. 76) suggests that we are best able to understand a communication rule if it is stated in an "if-then" format. She goes on to state that a rule should begin with *if* to introduce the clause that specifies in what context the rule is operable; the *if* clause should be followed by *then*, which introduces the clause that specifies the nature of the prescription and the behavior that is prescribed. *If* X is the situation or context, *then* Y is required (preferred, prohibited).

Following are some common conversational rules with which you are likely to be familiar. Notice that in some cases the word *then* has been omitted, but it is still implied.

> If your mouth is full of food, then you must not talk.
>
> If you are spoken to, you must reply.
>
> If another does not hear a question you ask, then you must repeat it.
>
> If you are being spoken to, you should direct your gaze to the speaker.
>
> If more than two people are conversing, then you should ensure each has time to speak.
>
> If your conversational partners are significantly older than you, then you should refrain from using profanities and obscenities.
>
> If you can't say something nice, then you don't say anything at all.
>
> If you are going to say something that you don't want overheard, then drop the volume of your voice.

Effective Conversations Follow the Cooperative Principle

The **cooperative principle** states that conversations will be satisfying when the contributions made by conversationalists are in line with the purpose of the conversation (Grice 1975, pp. 44–46). Based on this principle, H. Paul Grice describes four conversational maxims, or truths. Whether maxims are really rules (Shimanoff 1980, p. 61), or assumptions one makes about how to proceed (McLaughlin 1984, p. 31), we believe you will agree with Grice that participants can use these maxims to create an effective conversation.

1. The **quality maxim** calls for us to provide information that is truthful. When we purposely lie, distort, or misrepresent, we are not acting cooperatively in the conversation. Being truthful means not only avoiding deliberate lies or distortions but also taking care to avoid any kind of

misrepresentation. Thus, if a classmate asks you what the prerequisites for BIO 205 are, you share them if you know them, but you don't speculate or offer your opinion as though it were fact. If you don't know or if you have only a vague recollection, say so.

2. The **quantity maxim** calls for us to provide an amount of information that is sufficient to satisfy others' information needs and keep the conversation going, but not so lengthy and detailed that we undermine the informal give-and-take that is characteristic of good conversations. Thus, if Sam asks Randy how he liked his visit to St. Louis, Randy's answering "fine" is too brief; his answering with a twenty-minute monologue on all the activities on his trip is likely to be far too long.

3. The **relevancy maxim** calls for us to provide information that is related to the topic being discussed. Comments that are tangential to the subject, or outright subject changes when other conversational partners are still actively engaged with the current topic, are uncooperative. For example, if Hal, Corey, and Li-sung are chatting about benefits that will accrue for the local homeless shelter from the upcoming 5K walk/run, if Corey asks whether either of them has taken Speech 101, he will be acting uncooperatively. His comments don't relate to the subject.

4. The **manner maxim** calls for us to be specific and organized when communicating our thoughts. We cooperate by organizing our thoughts and using specific language that clarifies our meanings. When we give information that listeners find obscure, ambiguous, or disorganized, we are not cooperating in sharing meaning. Thus, if a person asked you to explain how to use the new photocopier, you would "walk the person through" the steps of using it rather than rambling on about the machine's features in a confusing order.

Bach and Harnish (1979, p. 64) have proposed two additions to Grice's maxims.

5. The **morality maxim** calls for us to speak in ways that meet moral/ethical guidelines. For example, in the United States, violations of the morality maxim would include someone's repeating information that has been disclosed confidentially or persuading someone else to do something that the speaker knows is wrong or against the other's personal interests.

6. The **politeness maxim** calls for us to be courteous to other participants. In our conversations, we should attempt to observe the social norms of politeness in the dominant culture and not purposefully embarrass ourselves or others during the interaction.

Skills of Effective Conversationalists

Although some people have what appears to be a natural gift for effective conversation, almost all of us can learn to be more effective participants. In the remainder of this chapter, we want to describe several basic skills that you can develop that will increase your conversational effectiveness.

Present Quality Information

Although you don't have to be an expert on every subject, the more you know about a range of subjects, the greater the chances are that you will be an interesting conversationalist. What are your information sources? Do you read a newspaper every day (not just the comics or the sports)? Do you read at least one news or special-interest magazine regularly? Do you sometimes watch television documentaries and news specials as well as entertainment and sports programs? (Of course, sports and entertainment are favorite topics of conversation, too—but not with everyone.) Do you make a point of going to the theater, to concerts, to museums or historical sites? If you answered yes to most of these questions, you are likely to have a fountain of information you can call on in social conversations. If you answered no to most of these questions, you may find yourself at a loss when you are trying to join in on social conversations. Exposing yourself to a broad array of information and experiences and learning from them allows you to develop ideas and share information that others will find interesting and provides grist for the conversation mill.

Credit Sources

Crediting sources means verbally footnoting the source from which you have drawn your information and ideas. In a term paper, you give credit to authors you have quoted or paraphrased by footnoting the sources. Similarly, when you use other people's words or ideas in your oral communication, you can credit the source verbally.

By crediting, you enable the other participants to evaluate the quality of the information you are sharing. Moreover, by crediting ideas from people who are acquaintances, you make people feel better about themselves and avoid hard feelings. For instance, if a friend presents a creative idea and verbally acknowledges you as the source, you probably feel flattered. If, however, the person acts as though the idea were his own, you are probably hurt or angry. So, when you repeat ideas that you've gotten from others, make sure that you give proper credit.

Crediting is easy enough. To give credit where it is due and avoid possible hard feelings, just include the name of the person you got the idea from. For example, in a discussion about course offerings, you might say, "I like the list of courses we have to choose from, but you know, we should really have a course

---

OBSERVE AND ANALYZE

Conversational Maxims

Refer back to the two conversation scripts you prepared in the exercise on problem-consideration conversations (p. 166). Which of the conversational maxims were followed? If there were violations, what were they, and how did they affect the conversation? Can you identify specific communication rules that were used? Which of these were complied with, and which were violated? How does this analysis help you understand your degree of satisfaction with the conversation?

OBSERVE AND ANALYZE

Conversational Variety

During the next three days, deliberately try to introduce greater variety in your conversations with others. How well are you able to develop and maintain such conversations? Are they more or less satisfying than conversations on weather, sports, and daily happenings? Why?

in attitude change. Laura was the one who put me onto the idea, and I can see why it's a good idea."

✳ Balance Speaking and Listening

People seldom enjoy conversations when they can't get a word in edgewise and no one seems to care about their opinions. Whether the conversation includes two, three, or even five people, we feel most comfortable when we get our fair share of speaking time. We balance speaking and listening in a conversation by practicing turn-taking techniques.

1. **Effective conversationalists take the appropriate number of turns**. In any conversation, the ideal is for all to have approximately the same number of turns. If you discover that you are speaking more than your fair share, try to restrain yourself by mentally checking whether everyone else has had a chance to talk once before you talk a second time. Similarly, if you find yourself being inactive in a conversation, try to increase your participation level. Remember, if you have information to contribute, you're cheating yourself and the group when you do not share it.

2. **Effective conversationalists speak an appropriate length of time on each turn**. People are likely to tune out or become annoyed with those conversational partners who make speeches, filibuster, or perform monologues rather than engaging in the ordinary give-and-take of conversation. Similarly, it is difficult to carry on a conversation with someone who gives one- or two-word replies to questions that are designed to elicit meaningful information. Turns do vary in length, of course, depending on what is being said. However, if your average statements are much longer or much shorter than those of your conversational partners, you need to adjust.

3. **Effective conversationalists recognize and heed turn-exchanging cues**. Patterns of vocal tone, such as a decrease in loudness or a lowering of pitch, and gestures that seem to show completion of a point are the most obvious turn-taking cues (Duncan and Fiske 1977). When you are trying to get into a conversation, look for these cues.

   By the same token, be careful of giving inadvertent turn-exchanging cues. For instance, if you tend to lower your voice when you are not really done speaking or take long pauses for emphasis when you expect to continue, you are likely to be interrupted because these are cues that others are likely to act on. If you find yourself getting interrupted frequently, you might ask people whether you tend to give false cues. If you come to recognize that another person has a habit of giving these kinds of cues inadvertently, try not to interrupt when speaking with that person.

4. **Effective conversationalists use conversation-directing behavior and comply with the conversation-directing behavior of others**. In general, a person who relinquishes his or her turn may define who speaks next. For instance,

PRACTICE IN CLASS

Informed Conversation

Form groups of five. During one class period, the group should choose a topic that all of you are interested in and would enjoy talking about. Have a fifteen-minute conversation about this topic. Then, agree that between now and the next class meeting, each of you will do some individual research on the topic you have been discussing. Feel free to read books, magazines, newspapers, to cruise the Internet, to interview knowledgeable others. Then, at the beginning of the next class, hold another fifteen-minute discussion on the same topic. When you have finished, discuss which of the two conversations was more enjoyable. How did the knowledge that participants brought to the conversation affect the overall quality of the discussion? Were people careful to credit their sources?

when Paul concludes his turn by saying, "Susan, did you understand what he meant?" Susan has the right to the floor. Skillful turn-takers use conversation-directing behavior to balance turns between those who speak freely and those who may be more reluctant to speak. Similarly, effective turn-takers remain silent and listen politely when the conversation is directed to someone else.

If the person who has just finished speaking does not verbally or nonverbally direct the conversation to a preferred next speaker, then the turn is up for grabs and goes to the first person to speak.

5. **Effective conversationalists rarely interrupt.** Although interruptions are generally considered inappropriate, interrupting for "clarification" and "agreement" (confirming) are interpersonally acceptable (Kennedy and Camden 1983, p. 55). Interruptions that are likely to be accepted include relevant questions or paraphrases intended to clarify, such as "What do you mean by 'presumptuous'?" or "I get the sense that you think presumptuous behavior is especially bad," and reinforcing statements such as "Good point, Max" or "I see what you mean, Suzie." Interruptions that are likely to be viewed as disruptive or impolite include those that change the subject or that seem to minimize the contribution of the interrupted person.

Practice Politeness

Politeness—relating to others in ways that meet their need to be appreciated and protected—is universal to all cultures (Brown and Levinson 1987). Although levels of politeness and ways of being polite vary, all people have what Brown and Levinson call positive and negative **face needs**.

Positive face is the desire to be appreciated and approved, liked and honored. To meet people's positive face needs, we engage in **positive politeness** by making statements that show concern, compliment, or use respectful forms of address. It is polite and meets positive face needs to greet your instructor as "Professor Reynolds" (using a respectful form of address), to say "Did you get enough to eat, or may I offer you dessert?" (showing concern), or to say "Thanks for the tip on how to work that problem, it really helped" (complimenting).

Negative face is the desire to be free from imposition or intrusion. To meet people's negative face needs, we engage in **negative politeness** by making statements that recognize that we are imposing or intruding upon the time of another. It is polite and meets negative face needs to say "I can see you're busy, but I wonder whether you could take a minute to . . ." (recognizing that you are imposing), or to say "I know you don't have time to talk with me now, but I wanted to see whether there was a time we could meet later today or tomorrow" (recognizing that you are intruding).

Sometimes one behavior can meet both needs. For example, knocking on the door and waiting for permission to enter is polite because it both shows respect and recognizes that you are about to impose on someone's solitude or privacy.

Although politeness is always important, it is especially so whenever the central content of our conversation might threaten another person's face. When we say something to a person that might cause the person to "lose face," we commit what Brown and Levinson call **face-threatening acts (FTAs)**. We are committing FTAs when our behavior *fails* to meet positive or negative face needs. The goal of politeness theory is not to avoid face threatening—it is normal. Rather, the goal is to lessen or eliminate potential conversational or relationship problems that could result from FTAs.

Suppose your professor has returned a set of papers, and you believe that your grade does not reflect the quality of the paper. To suggest that the professor may have been wrong or may have overlooked something might well cause that professor to lose face. So, what might you say to your professor if you want her to reconsider? If you were in such a situation (one where an FTA is possible), you have five choices.

1. **You can deliver the FTA openly, without consideration for politeness.** You might say, "I don't think you graded my paper fairly, and I want you to reconsider the grade you gave me." Notice how aggressive this sounds; it is not very polite—in effect, it may be interpreted as "a slap in the face." It places a demand, a direct imposition, on the professor, and it suggests that the grade was "given" arbitrarily and not "earned," either of which is likely to cause the professor to "lose face" and to behave defensively.

2. **You can deliver the FTA, but do it in a way that includes some form of positive politeness.** "I would appreciate it if you could look at my paper again. I've marked the places that I'd like you to consider. My roommate said that you were fair and usually willing to reconsider if there seemed to be a good reason." Although the request still contains a direct imposition on the professor, "I would appreciate it" is much softer than "I want you to." The effort to include a positive politeness statement—that the professor is known to be fair and open-minded—is helpful as well.

3. **You can deliver the FTA with negative politeness.** "I'm sure you're very busy and don't have time to reread and remark every paper, but I'm hoping you'll be willing to look at my paper again. To try to minimize the time it might take, I've marked the places I'd like you to consider. I've also written comments to show why I phrased those sections as I did." Although the request is still a direct imposition, it makes the statement that you recognize you are imposing. It also suggests that you wouldn't do it if there weren't at least potentially good reasons. Moreover, you've taken the time not only to limit how much the professor needs to look at, but also to show why you thought the sections were in keeping with the assignment.

4. **You can deliver the FTA indirectly or off the record.** "Please don't take this the wrong way, but I was surprised by a few of your comments." By saying this in a casual way, you hope your professor might be curious enough to

ask what caused you to be surprised. With this opening, you can move to one of the more direct but face-saving approaches.

5.   **You can choose not to say anything.**

How do we choose whether to be polite or which strategy to use? Brown and Levinson believe that this decision is affected by a combination of three factors:

1.   *How well people know each other and their relative status.* The less familiar we are with someone and the higher the person's social status, the more effort we will put into being polite.

2.   *The power that the hearer has over the speaker.* Most of us will work harder to be polite to those who are powerful than to those who are powerless.

3.   *The risk of hurting the other person.* Most of us do not like to intentionally hurt others.

To show how you might apply this theory, let's consider two examples. First, suppose you want to impose on your roommate to take a look at your paper before you turn it in to your professor. Your roommate is your friend, and you get along quite well. The imposition is relatively minor and only mildly threatening—in the past, both of you have looked at work the other has done. Moreover, your roommate has no special power over you. In light of these considerations, you might not put much effort into trying to be polite. You might make this request without much regard to your roommate's negative face needs and say, "Danny, take a look at this paper. I need to hand it in tomorrow."

Now suppose you want to ask your professor to preread the same paper before you submitted it for a grade. First, your professor is not your friend; you are socially more distant. Second, and even more important, he has considerable power over you—he controls your grade. So, how hard should you work to be polite? If you're smart, you'll work a lot harder than you will to be polite to your friend. Whereas your request to your roommate will very likely be made without consideration for politeness, your request to your professor requires you to make face-saving gestures if you expect to have a positive outcome.

As you come to understand face needs better, you will become better able to diagnose situations in which you should take particular care to engage in polite behavior. More generally, each of us can make the world a bit more humane by working at being polite.

✈ Engage in Ethical Dialogue

The final skill set used by effective conversationalists is the ability to engage in ethical dialogue. According to Johannesen (1996), ethical conversations are characterized by authenticity, empathy, confirmation, presentness, a spirit of mutual equality, and a supportive climate.

Authenticity. Authenticity is the direct, honest, straightforward communication of all information and feelings that are legitimately relevant to the subject at hand. To sit in a discussion, disagreeing with what is being said but saying nothing, is not being authentic. It is also inauthentic to agree verbally with something that you really do not believe in.

Empathy. Empathy is imagining an event or feelings from the other person's point of view without giving up your own position or sense of self. Comments such as "I see your point" or "I'm not sure I agree with you, but I'm beginning to understand why you feel that way" demonstrate empathy.

Confirmation. Confirmation is expressing nonpossessive warmth for others that affirms them as unique persons without necessarily approving of their behaviors or views. Examples of confirmation might include "Well, Keith, you certainly have an interesting way of looking at things, and I must say, you really make me think through my own views on things" or "Well, I guess I'd still prefer that you didn't get a tattoo, but you really have thought this through."

Presentness. Presentness is demonstrating a willingness to become fully involved with the other person by taking time, avoiding distraction, being responsive, and risking attachment. The most obvious way to exhibit presentness is by listening actively to the person with whom you are conversing. During a conversation you can also demonstrate presentness by asking questions that are directly related to what has been said.

OBSERVE AND ANALYZE

Using Politeness

Think about the last time you committed a face-threatening act (FTA). Try to reconstruct the situation. What did you say? Try to recall as specifically as possible the exact words you used. Analyze your FTA in terms of familiarity, status, power, and risk. Did you have greater or lesser status? Did you have greater or lesser social power? Was the risk of hurting the other person large or small? In light of your analysis, write three different ways you could have made your request. Try to write one that uses positive face statements, one that uses negative face statements, and one that combines both positive and negative.

SKILL BUILDERS   Politeness

Skill	Use	Procedure	Example
Relating to others in ways that meet their need to be appreciated and protected.	To determine the degree of politeness necessary to achieve your objective.	1. Recognize when what you are planning to say is likely to be seen as a face-threatening act. 2. Consider how well you know each other, whether one person holds power over the other, and the risk of hurting the other person. 3. Construct the wording of a positive politeness or negative politeness statement based on the issues of relationship, power, and risk.	Chris thinks her boss did not consider all that he should have in determining her year's bonus. She might construct the following positive politeness statement: "Mr. Seward, I know that you take bonus decisions very seriously, and I know that you've been willing to talk about your decisions, so I was hoping you'd be willing to take a few minutes to discuss your decision on my bonus with me."

UNDERSTAND YOURSELF

Ethical Self-Evaluation

Reflect on Johannesen's characteristics of ethical dialogue. If you were to give yourself a report card in which you received a letter grade for your consistency in demonstrating each of the six characteristics, what grades would you receive? Write yourself a letter explaining each grade and making specific suggestions for how you might improve your "marks."

Equality. Regardless of the status differences that separate them from other participants, those who are effective in conversations view their conversational partners as equals. To lord one's accomplishments, one's power roles, or one's social status over another during conversation is unethical because conversations are informal and casual interactions.

Supportive climate. Supportive communication climates encourage the other participants to communicate by praising their worthwhile efforts.

When we engage in ethical dialogue, we improve the odds that the conversations we will have will meet our needs and the needs of those with whom we interact.

✳ Be Aware of Cultural Variations in Effective Conversation

Throughout this chapter, we have been considering rules and maxims that hold for the majority of the people in United States culture. But just as high- and low-context cultures differ in various verbal and nonverbal rules, so too do they differ in guidelines for conversation. You'll recall that the United States, Canada, and most Western European nations are low-context cultures and that Mexico and most countries in Asia, Africa, and South America are high-context cultures. Let's consider just a few of the differences in conversation between

How might culture or gender differences affect the conversation between the people in this photo?

these two cultures that are discussed by Gudykunst, Ting-Toomey, and Nishida (1996, pp. 30–32).

Low-context cultures are likely to be more individualistic, and high-context cultures are likely to be more collectivistic. This difference shows itself in word choice. In conversations, low-context cultures are more likely to use categorical words such as *certainly*, *absolutely*, and *positively*. High-context cultures express ideas through the use of qualifiers such as *maybe*, *perhaps*, and *probably* in their conversations.

Low-context cultures follow the relevancy maxim, using relevant comments that are perceived by listeners to be directly to the point. In high-context cultures, individuals' responses are likely to be more indirect, ambiguous, and apparently less relevant; listeners must infer more about a speaker's intentions in order to understand the relevancy. Thus, people in high-context cultures depend on receivers' sensitivity to nonverbal cues to help them understand.

In response to the quality maxim, low-context cultures are characterized by speaking one's mind and telling the truth. People are expected to communicate their actual feelings about things. People using high-context communication try to communicate in ways that maintain harmony; thus, they may well send

REFLECT ON ETHICS

Sarah, John, Louisa, Naima, and Richard all met at a rave that the university sponsored during First-Year Orientation. During a break, they began sharing where they were from, where they were working, what classes they were taking, and their potential majors. John was having fun talking with Louisa—he thought she was cute and wanted to impress her. When she mentioned that she had been involved in theater during high school and was considering majoring in drama, he began to share his own theater experiences. Everyone listened politely, interested at first, but he kept talking and talking. Finally, Naima interrupted John and changed the subject, for which the rest of the group was quite grateful.

Throughout their twenty-minute conversation, whenever someone brought up a new subject, John would immediately take center stage and expound on some wild story that remotely applied. Not only was he long-winded, but his stories seemed to be fabricated. He was the hero in every one—either through his intellect or his strength. Besides all this, as he talked he included completely inappropriate side comments that were turnoffs to all of the listeners. One by one, each person found a reason to excuse him- or herself. Soon John was standing alone.

Several minutes later, John heard the other four around the corner talking. Before he could round the corner and come into their sight, he heard one of them say, "Do you guys want to go down to the coffeehouse so we can talk in peace? That John was really too much—but I think we can avoid seeing him if we zip out the side door. That way the rest of us can have a chance to talk."

1. Have you ever talked with someone like John? Where did John go wrong in his conversational skills? What should he have done differently?
2. Was it ethical for Louisa and the rest of the group to sneak out the side door without saying anything to John? Defend your position.

Conversation

Working with another student, prepare to hold either a social or a problem-consideration conversation before the entire class (maximum time: 5 minutes). To prepare for the in-class conversation, you will want to meet with the other person to select a topic and even to practice holding the conversation to get ideas in mind.

Criteria for evaluation will include how well you follow conversational rules and maxims. Feel free to use such skills as questioning, paraphrasing, supporting, interpreting, and describing feelings—skills that are relevant for any conversation.

messages that vary from their true feelings. Similarly, whereas low-context communication is expected to be open, high-context communication reveals very little personal information about the speaker.

Finally, in low-context cultures, silence is seldom considered good. People get uncomfortable when three or four people sit together and no one talks. In high-context communication, silence is used to indicate truthfulness, disapproval, embarrassment, or disagreement.

Sample Conversation and Analysis

In the accompanying conversation, Sheila and Susan are talking about the advantages and disadvantages of dating exclusively within one's own religion. As you read the conversation, try to think about what each of the participants is doing that helps to keep the conversation going smoothly and productively. Consider how well they follow conversational rules and maxims; also notice when and how they use such skills as questioning, paraphrasing, supporting, interpreting, and describing feelings—skills that are relevant for any conversation. After you have read through the conversation and made your own analysis, consider the analysis in the right-hand column.

Conversation	Analysis
Susan: How are you and Bill getting along these days?	Susan opens the social conversation with a question.
Sheila: Not too well. I think you could say our relationship is coming to an end. The feelings just aren't there, and so many problems have been building up.	Sheila replies, but her response is neither as specific nor as concrete as it could have been.

Conversation

Analysis

Susan: I get the impression from the expression on your face that you're having problems. Is there one specific problem?

Susan tries to check her perception of what the look on Sheila's face means. It probably would have been better to use a feelings paraphrase such as "From the way you're talking, I get the impression that you're very sad about the outcome of the relationship."

Sheila: Well, there are a lot, but one that I didn't think would make such a difference at the beginning of the relationship that's made a difference now is the fact that we're from different religions. I'm Jewish and he isn't, and at first I never thought it would affect me, but it does make a difference.

Susan: I think I was kind of lucky—well, lucky in the long run. When I was in high school, my parents wouldn't allow me to go out with anybody who wasn't Jewish. I really resented that at first, but now I'm kind of glad because I'm thinking about the future now. And as my parents said, you don't know what could come out of a high-school relationship.

Note that both participants follow turn-taking rules quite well. Moreover, conversation is relevant.

Sheila: It seems like you were a little upset at first, but now you're pretty happy with the whole situation.

Here Sheila uses a paraphrase, but it would be more specific if she had phrased it, "It seems like you were a little upset at first, but now that you're older you have a better understanding of your parents' position."

Susan: Yes, now that I look around, I'm not in the predicament that you are of having to get out of a relationship for something that's not what you want.

Sheila: I can see what you mean, but I'm also happy that my parents didn't restrict me because I think I would have felt a lot of pressure just to always . . . I wouldn't have had a choice of whom to go out with, and I wouldn't have felt very independent. But I feel I have to make my own choices. As long as I know what I want, I feel it's all right.

Although Sheila uses the word "feel," she isn't really describing her feelings.

Conversation

Susan: That was my problem—having to pick and choose. My parents would say, "Oh, is he Jewish?" "I don't know, should I ask him?" They wanted me to say, "Are you Jewish? Oh, you're not? Well, you can't go out with me then."

Sheila: I can see how you feel—that's a tough situation. But I see now that I feel pretty frustrated because I want to date people who are Jewish, but I'm not going to go around picking on them saying this one is and this one isn't. It's too hard to do that. You can't turn your feelings on and off. You have to be interested in someone. So I get pretty frustrated a lot of times.

Susan: Are you saying that you are kind of glad that your parents didn't restrict you in that manner, or are you saying that you're glad they didn't but wish they had?

Sheila: I guess I'm glad they didn't, but maybe it would have been better if they had. I would have been more conscious about it.

Susan: In the long run, I feel it's best to start early to get an idea in your mind of what you really want to do. I never thought a relationship in high school would go anywhere, but the man I'm dating, it's been four years already. That's a long time.

Sheila: You seem happy together. I saw you the other day, and that's really nice. I wish I could find somebody that . . .

Susan: I saw you start shrugging Bill off and just ignoring him.

Analysis

Sheila's acknowledgment of Susan's statement is in the right direction, but her effort appears half-hearted. She needs a good paraphrase of Susan's feelings before going on to describing her own feelings.

This is probably one of the best responses in the dialogue. Although it is cast in question form, it is still a good attempt at seeking clarification of Sheila's feelings.

Both Susan and Sheila continue to make relevant replies that also meet quality and quantity maxims.

Conversation	Analysis
Sheila: Yes, that's a hard situation. I get pretty depressed about it, too. I just never thought religion could make such a big difference. But it means a lot to me, and that's why it makes such a difference.	
Susan: What are you planning on telling him?	Here's one of the few times when Susan focuses her attention on Sheila. Good question.
Sheila: Well, I guess I'll just say that it won't work out. It depresses me to think about that, too.	Sheila states her plans and describes her feelings.
Susan: You should really try to go easy—don't let it upset you too much. It's what you want, right?	Susan gives advice that is meant to be supportive of Sheila's predicament.
Sheila: I guess so. I'll have to try to do the best I can.	This dialogue is a good example of a cooperative conversation.

Summary

Conversation is an informal interchange of thoughts and feelings that usually occurs in a face-to-face setting. There are two types of conversations—social conversations and problem-consideration conversations—each of which has a general structure.

Conversations are guided by unwritten prescriptions that indicate what behavior is required, preferred, or prohibited. Four characteristics of conversational rules are that they allow for choice, they are prescriptive, they are contextual, and they specify appropriate behavior.

Effective conversations are governed by the cooperative principle, which suggests that conversations "work" when participants join together to accomplish conversational goals and make the conversation pleasant for each participant. The cooperative principle is characterized by six maxims: quality, quantity, relevancy, manner, morality, and politeness.

Effective conversationalists demonstrate skills in presenting information honestly (including crediting their sources), balancing speaking and listening (through effective turn-taking behavior), maintaining conversational coherence, practicing politeness (through engaging in positive and negative face-saving strategies), and engaging in ethical dialogue.

OBJECTIVES

After you have read this chapter, you should be able to answer the following questions:

■ What are the major types of relationships?

■ What are some effective ways of starting a relationship?

■ How are descriptiveness, openness, provisionalism, and equality used in maintaining relationships?

■ What is interpersonal needs theory?

■ What is exchange theory?

■ What is the definition of conflict?

■ What are the key features of withdrawal, accommodation, forcing, compromise, and collaboration?

■ What skills are used in initiating conflict?

■ What skills are used in responding to conflict?

8

Communicating in Relationships

"**J**aneen, you're spending a lot of time with Angie. What is Liam going to think about that?"

"Come on, Mom, I know you're just teasing me. Yeah, Liam's my boyfriend, and we get along really well, but there are things I just can't talk about with him."

"And you can with Angie?"

"Right. I can tell her what's going on with my writing, for example, and she really understands. And I do the same for her. We enjoy a lot of the same activities, so Angie is good company for me."

Janeen is lucky because she has two good relationships. Because so many of the interpersonal skills we use are for the purpose of starting, building, and maintaining relationships, we conclude this part with an analysis of relationships. A **good relationship** is any mutually satisfying interaction with another person, whether at the level of acquaintanceship, friendship, or intimacy.

In this chapter, we consider the nature of relationships, explain the role of communication in the stages of relationships, and explore means of managing conflict, one of the main factors that determine whether relationships will grow or deteriorate.

The Nature of Relationships

We behave differently depending on whether our relationships are personal or impersonal (LaFollette 1996, p. 4). A relationship is **impersonal** if either party relates merely because the other fills a role, such as waitress or clerk. A relationship is **personal** when each person relates to the other as a unique individual.

Moving along this continuum from impersonal to personal, we generally classify the people with whom we have relationships as acquaintances, friends, and close friends or intimates.

Acquaintances

Acquaintances are people we know by name and talk with when the opportunity arises, but with whom our interactions are largely impersonal. We become acquainted with those who live in our apartment building or dorm or in the house next door, who sit next to us in class, who go to our church or belong to our club. Many acquaintance relationships grow out of a particular context. Thus Melinda and Paige, who meet in biology class, may strike up an acquaintanceship, but they may make no effort to see each other outside of class; if they do meet in some other context, it is by chance.

Friends

Friends are people with whom we have negotiated more personal relationships voluntarily (Patterson, Bettini, and Nussbaum 1993, p. 145). In early stages of friendships, people move toward interactions that are less role-bound. Thus Melinda and Paige, who are acquaintances in biology class, may voluntarily decide to get together after school one afternoon just to talk and may eventually begin to speak of each other as friends.

Friendships are marked by high degrees of enjoyment, trust, self-disclosure, commitment, and expectation that the relationship will grow and endure (Prisbell and Andersen 1980, pp. 22–33).

- Friends spend time with each other because they enjoy each other's company, they enjoy talking with each other, and they enjoy sharing experiences.

- Friends *trust* each other. They risk putting their well-being in the hands of another because they believe a friend will not intentionally harm their interests (LaFollette 1996, p. 116).

- Friends share personal feelings with each other.

- Friends show a high level of commitment. They are likely to sacrifice their time and energy to help when the other is in need.

- Friends believe that their relationship is enduring—that neither a change of job nor a move to another city is likely to break that friendship.

✳ Close Friends or Intimates

Close friends or **intimates** are those with whom we share our deepest feelings. People may have countless acquaintances and many friends, but they are likely to have only a few truly intimate friends.

Close friends or intimates differ from "regular" friends mostly in degree of enjoyment, trust, disclosure, and commitment in their relationship. For

OBSERVE AND ANALYZE

Types of Relationships

Make a list of the people you have spoken with in the past day or two. Now categorize each. Which are strangers? acquaintances? friends? intimates?

Friendships are marked by enjoyment, trust, self-disclosure, and commitment.

instance, although friends engage in levels of self-disclosure, they are not likely to share every aspect of their lives; intimate friends, on the other hand, often gain knowledge of the innermost being of their partner. Many same-sex friends feel more comfortable sharing their deepest secrets with their close friend than with their lover or spouse.

Communication in the Stages of Relationships

Even though no two relationships develop in exactly the same manner, they tend to move through stages following a "life cycle" that includes starting or building, stability, and deterioration stages (Knapp 1984; Taylor and Altman 1987; Duck 1987). Whether a relationship develops depends on the partners' interacting in ways each finds satisfying.

Starting or Building Relationships

Fundamental to starting or building a relationship is the need for information. We *give* information about ourselves to others so that they will have more accurate perceptions of who we are, and we *seek* information about others so that we can determine whether we wish to develop a relationship with them. Charles Berger and his colleagues called this need for sharing information **uncertainty reduction** (Berger and Brada 1982).

We get information about others *passively* by observing their behavior, *actively* by asking others for information, and *interactively* by conversing with them directly. Gathering information to reduce uncertainty seems to be important in all cultures in the early stages of relationship development. People from some cultures may rely on passive methods of getting the information, whereas people from other cultures may rely on more active or interactive strategies.

Keep in mind that most people seek this information in order to predict the potential outcome of any communication. We are interested in whether continued communication is likely to produce positive or negative outcomes. So, it isn't just how much a person knows about another person, but how much that person wants to know that is significant (Kellermann and Reynolds 1990).

The three communication activities we engage in to start and build relationships are striking up a conversation, keeping the conversation going, and moving toward intimacy.

Striking up a conversation. What happens in the first few minutes of a conversation will have a profound effect on the nature of the relationship that develops. As the old saying goes, you seldom get a second chance to create a first impression. Although thinking up "getting to know you" lines is easy for some, many people become nearly tongue-tied when they want to meet someone and, as a result, make a bad first impression. For those of us who find starting conversations with strangers difficult, the following four strategies may be useful. Notice that each of these strategies is developed in question form designed to invite the other person to respond. A cheerful answer to your question suggests interest in continuing. Refusal to answer or a curt reply may mean that the person isn't really interested in talking at this time.

1. **Formally or informally introduce yourself.** "Hi, my name is Gordon. What's yours?"

2. **Refer to the physical context.** "This is awful weather for a game, isn't it?" "I wonder how they are able to keep such a beautiful garden in this climate?"

3. **Refer to your thoughts or feelings.** "I really like parties, don't you?" "I live on this floor too—do these steps bother you as much as they do me?"

4. **Refer to the other person.** "Marge seems to be an excellent hostess—have you known her long?" "I don't believe I've had the pleasure of seeing you before—do you work in marketing?"

Keeping the conversation going.   Once two people have begun an interaction, they are likely to engage in such **small talk** as information exchange and gossip—conversation that meets social needs with relatively low amounts of risk.

In **idea-exchange communication**, people share information that includes facts, opinions, and beliefs and occasionally reflects values. At the office, Maria may ask Walt about last night's sports scores and Dan may discuss the plot of a sitcom with Teresa. Or, on a more serious level, Jan may talk with Gloria about the merits of funding a new sports stadium or Bonita may talk with Ken about the upcoming election. Although the discussions of elections and community priorities are "deeper" than the conversations about sports or TV, both sets of conversations represent idea exchanges. This type of communication is important to early stages of relationships because through it you learn what the other person is thinking, reassess your attraction level, and decide whether or not you want the relationship to grow.

Gossip is relating information whose accuracy may be unknown about people you both know. Statements such as "Do you know Bill? I hear he has a really great job," "Would you believe that Mary Simmons and Tom Johnson are going together?" and "My sister Eileen is really working hard at losing weight" are all examples of gossip. Gossip may be a pleasant way to pass time with people you know but with whom you have no desire or need for a deeper relationship. It also provides a safe way to explore the potential for the relationship to grow, because it allows each person to see whether the other reacts similarly to the views expressed about the object of the gossip.

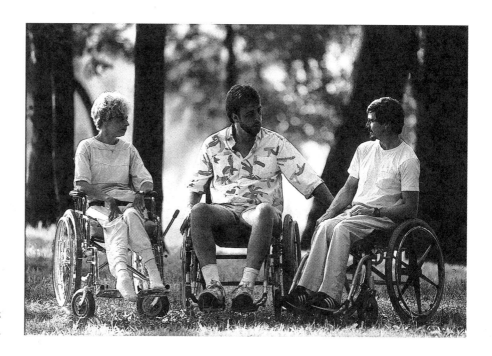

Self-disclosure and feedback help promote friendship.

Gossip can, of course, be malicious. If the information exchanged is found to be inaccurate, the gossip may damage not only the relationship in which it was exchanged, but other relationships as well. More often than not, however, gossip represents a means of interacting amicably with others without becoming personally involved. This is why conversations at parties are comprised largely of gossip.

Moving to deep friendship and intimacy levels. In addition to engaging in small talk, people who are exploring moving to more intimate levels will also begin to talk about more serious ideas and to share their feelings about important matters. Through the sharing of feelings and the process of self-disclosure, you really come to know and to understand another person. And when people find that they get satisfaction out of being together and are able to share ideas and feelings, their friendship grows.

Examining Disclosure and Feedback Ratios in Relationships

A healthy interpersonal relationship, especially one on a friendship or intimate level, is marked by a balance of **self-disclosure** (sharing biographical data, personal ideas, and feelings that are unknown to another person) and **feedback** (the mental and physical responses to people and/or their messages) within the relationship.

How can you tell whether you and another are sharing enough to keep the relationship growing? The best method is to discuss it. As the basis for a worthwhile discussion we suggest the use of a Johari window, named after its two originators, Joe Luft and Harry Ingham (Luft 1970).

The window is divided into four sections, or panes, as shown in Figure 8.1. The first quadrant is called the "open" pane of the window, because it represents the information about you that both you and your partner know. It includes information that you have disclosed and the observations about you that your partner has shared with you. It might include mundane information that you share with most people, such as your favorite colors, but it could also include information that you disclose to relatively few people. It could include simple observations that your partner has made, such as how cute you look when you wrinkle your nose, or more serious feedback you have received about your interpersonal style. If you were preparing a Johari window that represented your side of your relationship with another person, you would include in the open pane all the items of information about yourself that you would feel free to share with that other person.

The second quadrant is called the "secret" pane. It contains all those things that you know about yourself but that your partner does not know about you. This information may run the gamut from where you keep your pencils or why you don't eat meat to deep secrets whose revelation threatens you. If you were preparing a Johari window that represented your side of a relationship with another person, you would include in the secret pane all the items of information that you have not shared with that other person. When you choose to disclose the information to your partner, the information moves into the open pane of the window. If, for example, you had been engaged to be married but on the day of the wedding your fiancée had backed out, this information might be in the secret pane of your window. But when you disclose this fact to your friend, it would move into the open part of your Johari window with this person. So through disclosure, the secret pane of a window becomes smaller and the open pane is enlarged.

UNDERSTAND YOURSELF

Personal Guidelines for Self-Disclosure

Think of one secret about yourself. How many people know it? How do you decide whom to tell? What have been some of the consequences (good and bad) that have resulted from sharing that secret? Write a set of guidelines that is appropriate for you in sharing such secrets.

	Known to self	Not known to self
Known to others	Open	Blind
Not known to others	Secret	Unknown

Figure 8.1
The Johari window.

The third quadrant is called the "blind" pane. This is the place for information that the other person knows about you, but about which you are unaware. Most people have blind spots—parts of their behavior of which they are unaware. For example, Charley may not know that he snores when he sleeps or that he frowns when he is concentrating. But both of these behaviors are known by someone who has slept in the same room with him or been with him when he attends class lectures. Information moves from the blind area of the window to the open area through feedback from others. If no one has ever told Charley about these behaviors, or if he has refused to believe it when he has been told about them, this information will be in the blind part of his Johari window. When someone tells him about them and he accepts the feedback, then the information will move into the open pane of Charley's Johari window with this person. Thus, like disclosure, feedback enlarges the open pane of the Johari window, but in this case it is the blind pane that becomes smaller.

The fourth quadrant is called the "unknown" pane. It contains information about you that you don't know and neither does your partner. Obviously, you cannot develop a list of this information. So how do we know that it exists? Well, because periodically we "discover" it. If, for instance, you have never tried hang gliding, then neither you nor anyone else can really know whether you would chicken out or follow through, do it well or crash, love every minute of it or be paralyzed by fear.

So you can see that in a relationship, as you disclose and receive feedback, the sizes of the various window panes change. As a relationship becomes more intimate, the open pane of both partners' windows become larger, while the secret and hidden parts become smaller.

In Figure 8.2a, we see an example of a relationship in which there is little disclosure or feedback occurring. This person has not shared much information with the other and has received little feedback from the other. We would expect to see this pattern in a new relationship or one between casual acquaintances.

Figure 8.2b shows a relationship in which a person is disclosing to a partner, but the partner is providing little feedback. As you can see, the secret pane is smaller, but the blind pane is unchanged. A window like this indicates that the individual is able to disclose information but the partner is unable or unwilling to give feedback (or perhaps that the individual refuses to accept the feedback that is being given). Since part of the way that we learn about who we

Figure 8.2
Sample Johari windows:
(a) low disclosure, low feedback;
(b) high disclosure, low feedback;
(c) low disclosure, high feedback;
(d) high disclosure, high feedback.

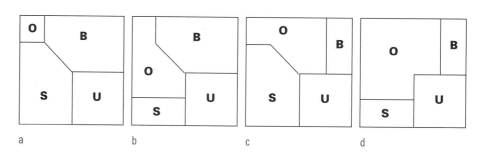

a   b   c   d

are comes from the feedback we receive from others, relationships in which one partner does not provide feedback can become very unsatisfying to the other individual.

Figure 8.2c shows a relationship in which a partner is good at providing feedback, but the individual is not disclosing. Since most of us disclose only when we trust our partners, this pattern may be an indication that the individual does not have confidence in the relational partner.

Figure 8.2d shows a relationship in which the individual has disclosed information and received feedback. As a result of both processes, the open pane of the window has enlarged. Windows that look like this indicate that there is sufficient trust and interest in the relationship that both partners are willing to risk by disclosing and giving feedback.

Obviously, to get a complete "picture" of a relationship, each partner's Johari window would need to be examined. As stated at the beginning of this discussion, the window is a useful tool for helping partners examine and discuss the levels of intimacy and trust in their relationship.

Stabilizing Relationships

When two people have a satisfactory relationship, whether as acquaintances, as friends, or as intimates, they look for **stabilization**—a means of maintaining the relationship at that level for some time. Stabilization occurs when two people agree on what they want from their relationship and are satisfied that they are achieving it.

An important way of making ongoing communication within the relationship successful is to see that partners communicate descriptively, openly, provisionally, and in a climate of equality. Research by Daniel Canary and Laura Stafford (1992, p. 259) supports the idea that maintenance strategies seem to operate in conjunction with equity.

Speaking descriptively. **Speaking descriptively** simply means stating what you see or hear in objective language. In earlier chapters, we spoke of describing feelings and describing behavior, both of which are necessities in maintaining a stable relationship.

Speaking openly. **Speaking openly** means sharing true thoughts and feelings without resorting to manipulation. Relationships grow best in a climate where the subject or the purpose of the communication is readily apparent. For instance, if Shelby wants to find out whether her friend Brent, who is working on the Social Committee with her, has scheduled the band yet, speaking openly would call for Shelby to ask him directly.

Sometimes we think that it is less threatening to approach subjects indirectly. For instance, saying to Brent "That party date is sneaking up and we still have *so much* to do" in hopes that he might say something about scheduling the band may sound tactful, but when the real subject is revealed, her deviousness in trying to find out about what he's doing without asking may actually harm

UNDERSTAND YOURSELF

Johari Windows

Working with a friend, each of you should draw a window that represents your perception of your relationship with the other. Then each of you should draw a window that represents what you perceive to be the other's relationship with you. Share the windows. How do they compare? If there are differences in the representations, talk with your friend about them.

INFOTRAC COLLEGE EDITION

Using InfoTrac College Edition, under the subject "interpersonal relations," click on periodical references. You'll find many articles that consider elements of relationship development. Look for articles that discuss starting relationships and keeping relationships going. What interpersonal skills that we have discussed in this book are emphasized in these articles?

their relationship. Not only will he be angry at her failure to be direct, but he's also likely to be hurt by her lack of trust.

Speaking provisionally. Speaking **provisionally** suggests that the ideas expressed are believed to be correct but may not be. Consider the following examples:

> "If I remember correctly, Dalton was the sales leader last month."
> "I'm telling you, Dalton had the most sales last month."

> "I think you should consider talking with Glenna before doing anything on your own."
> "You'd be an idiot not to talk with Glenna before doing anything on this."

Why is the first sentence of each pair more likely to result in better interpersonal communication? First, the tentativeness of the phrasing is likely to be less antagonizing than the dogmatic statements that use words or vocal tones of certainty. Second, the tentative statements acknowledge that the words come from the speaker—who may have it wrong. "I'm telling you" leaves no room for possible error; "If I remember correctly" not only leaves room for error but also shows that it is the speaker's recollection and not a statement of universal certainty.

Speaking to others as equals. Relationships grow in climates where the people treat each other as equals rather than in climates where one person is perceived as superior to another. **Equality** in communication is usually shown

Mutual respect and equality create a solid foundation for enduring relationships.

by the exclusion of any words or nonverbal signs that might indicate the oppo-site. One way to alter statements that project personal superiority is to give the rationale for any statement that is designed to gain compliance from the other person. For instance, in a work setting, a boss is a superior to a secretary. But line superiority does not mean that the boss is a better person, nor does it mean that the position alone gives the boss the right to treat the subordinate as an inferior whose feelings and needs are less important. So, instead of saying "Bethany, get on this letter right away—I want it on my desk in twenty min-utes," the boss could say, "Bethany, I got behind on framing this letter, and it really should be in the 3:00 mail. Do you think you could get it typed by 2:30 for me?" Even though the person is "the boss," the second phrasing provides a reason for the request and shows sensitivity to the fact that the boss is responsi-ble for the lateness.

In addition to choosing language carefully, we can be conscious of the effects of our tone of voice, facial expressions, dress, and manners. Through both words and actions showing that we are human beings—no better and no worse than others—we can create a positive climate for communication. By lis-tening to others' ideas, by pitching in and working, and by respecting what oth-ers say, you can demonstrate an attitude of equality.

So, in order to maintain a positive communication climate, consider what you are about to say to determine whether it contains a wording that shows an attitude of evaluating, deviousness, certainty, or superiority. If your tentative wording does, think of how you can alter what you were about to say to change the tone. Many times the things we say that hurt the climate come because we are just not thinking. It's a good idea to follow the old advice of "engaging your brain before putting your mouth in action." Take a second to remind yourself that a single thoughtless sentence can take minutes, hours, or days to repair—if it is repairable.

Relationship Disintegration

Regardless of how much one party would like the relationship to remain stable or become more intense, there are times when a relationship comes to an end. Sometimes when a relationship ends we are sad; at other times it is a relief. Regardless of our feelings, it is helpful to know how to end a relationship in an interpersonally competent manner. Even the effects of a wrenching breakup can be somewhat improved by a conscious effort to use good interpersonal commu-nication skills.

Unfortunately, when people decide to end a relationship, they sometimes use strategies that are detrimental to the relationship. Even when relationships have fallen apart, people should still try to use the constructive skills of describ-ing feelings, owning feelings, and disclosing in order to make parting as amica-ble as possible.

OBSERVE AND ANALYZE

Positive and Negative Climates

Think of two recent interactions you have had—one that was characterized by a positive communication climate and one that was characterized by a negative climate. Recall as best you can some of the specific conversation from each interaction, and write each one down like a script. Now, analyze each script. Count specific instances of being descriptive or evaluative. Recall whether hidden agendas were evidenced. Count instances of provisional wordings and of dogmatic wordings. Look for instances where equality was present and instances where one person spoke in a way that conveyed an attitude of superiority. Discuss your results. How much did using or failing to use the four skills presented in this section contribute to the climate you experienced?

Theoretical Perspectives on Relationships

What determines whether or not we will try to build a relationship with another person? Why do some relationships never move beyond a certain level or begin to deteriorate? Two helpful theories—interpersonal needs theory and exchange theory—offer insights into these questions.

Interpersonal Needs Theory

Interpersonal needs theory proposes that whether or not a relationship is started, built, or maintained depends on how well people meet each other's interpersonal needs for affection, inclusion, and control (Schutz 1966, pp. 18–20).

The need for **affection** reflects a desire to express and to receive love. The people you know probably run the gamut of showing and expressing affection

---

TEST YOUR COMPETENCE

Descriptive, Open, Provisional, Equal

Label the following statements as E (evaluative), D (dogmatic), S (superior), or M (manipulative or portraying a hidden agenda). In each case, rephrase the statement so that it is descriptive, provisional, equal, or open. The first one is completed for you. When you are done, share your revisions with other members of the class.

__D__ a. "Shana—turn that off! No one can study with the radio on!"
Suggested rephrasing: "Shana—I'd suggest turning the radio down or off. You may find that you can study better without the distraction."

_____ b. "Did you ever hear of such a tacky idea as having a formal wedding and using paper plates?"

_____ c. "That advertising program will never sell."

_____ d. "Oh, Jack, you're so funny wearing plaids with stripes. Well, I guess that's a man for you!"

_____ e. "Paul, you're acting like a baby. You've got to learn to use your head."

_____ f. Noticing that she has only a short time before she intends to meet Gavin, Tori says, "Yvonne, I don't see anything that looks right for you here—let's plan to try Northgate Mall sometime next week."

_____ g. "You may think you know how to handle the situation, but you are just not mature enough. I know when something's right for you."

Answers: b.E c.D d.S e.E f.M g.S

both verbally and nonverbally. At one end of the spectrum are those who avoid close ties, seldom show strong feelings toward others, and shy away from people who show or want to show affection. At the other end of the spectrum are those who thrive on establishing "close" relationships with everyone. They think of all others as intimates, immediately confide in persons they have met, and want everyone to consider them close friends. Somewhere in between these two extremes are "personal" people—those who can express and receive affection easily and who derive pleasure from many kinds of relationships with others.

The need for **inclusion** reflects a desire to be in the company of other people. Although everyone has some need to be social, at one end of the continuum are those who prefer to be left alone. Occasionally, they seek company or enjoy being included with others, but they do not require a great deal of social interaction to feel satisfied. At the other end of the continuum are those who need constant companionship and feel tense when they must be alone. Their doors are always open—everyone is welcome, and they expect others to welcome them. Of course, most of us do not belong to either of these extreme types. Rather, we are sometimes comfortable being alone and at other times need and enjoy interacting with others.

The need for **control** reflects a desire to influence the events and people around us. As with the other two interpersonal needs, people vary in how much control they require. At one extreme are persons who seem to shun responsibility and do not want to be in charge of anything. At the other extreme are persons who need to dominate others at all times and become anxious if they cannot. Again, most people fall somewhere between these two extremes, needing to lead at certain times, but at other times content to follow the lead of others.

How can this analysis help us understand communication in relationships? Relationships develop and deteriorate in part because of the compatibility or incompatibility of individuals' interpersonal needs. As you interact with others, you can detect whether their needs for affection, inclusion, and control seem compatible with yours. Suppose that Emily and Dan have been seeing each other regularly, and both see their relationship as close. If in response to Dan's attempt to put his arm around her while they are watching television, Emily stiffens slightly, it might suggest that Emily doesn't have quite the same need for affection as Dan. It should be emphasized that people's needs do differ; moreover, people's needs change over time. When other people's needs at any given time differ significantly from ours and we fail to understand that, we can misunderstand what's going wrong in our communication.

Schutz's theory of interpersonal needs is useful because it helps explain a great deal of interpersonal behavior (Trenholm 1991, p. 191). In addition, research on this model has been generally supportive of its major themes (Shaw 1981, pp. 228–231). Interpersonal needs theory does not, however, explain *how* people adjust to one another in their ongoing relationships. The next theory we discuss will help us develop this understanding.

OBSERVE AND ANALYZE

Life Cycle of Relationships

1. Identify five people you consider to be your friends. In what kind of context did you first meet? What attracted you to them? List the aspects of attraction that have proved to be most important as the relationships developed.

2. Identify five people you consider to be acquaintances. List the ways in which communication with your acquaintances differs from communication with your friends.

3. Consider a recent relationship that has deteriorated. When did you notice that deterioration was taking place? List the kinds of communication behavior that have marked the stages of deterioration.

Exchange Theory

John W. Thibaut and Harold H. Kelley, who originated **exchange theory**, believe that relationships can be understood in terms of the exchange of rewards and costs that takes place during the interaction (Thibaut and Kelley 1986, pp. 9–30). **Rewards** are outcomes such as good feelings, prestige, economic gain, and fulfillment of emotional needs that are valued by the receiver. **Costs** are outcomes such as time, energy, and anxiety that the receiver does not wish to incur. For instance, Sharon may be eager to spend time talking with Jan if she anticipates feeling good as a result; she may be reluctant to spend that time if she expects to be depressed at the end of the conversation.

According to Thibaut and Kelley, people seek interaction situations in which their behaviors will yield an outcome of high reward and low cost. For example, if Jill runs into Sarah on campus, she can ignore Sarah, she can smile, she can say "Hi" in passing, or she can try to start a conversation, depending in part on her cost–reward analysis of the outcome of the interaction. For instance, Jill is likely to stop and talk if she wants to arrange a tennis match with Sarah—it's worth a few minutes now to get the match set.

This analysis can be extended from single interactions to relationships. If the net reward is higher than the level viewed as satisfactory, the person will regard the relationship or interaction as pleasant and satisfying. But if, over an extended period, a person's net rewards (rewards minus costs) in a relationship fall below a certain level, that person will come to view the relationship itself as unsatisfactory or unpleasant. Of course, the most desirable ratio between cost and reward varies from person to person and within one person from time to time.

If people have a number of relationships they perceive as giving them a good cost–reward ratio, they will set a high satisfaction level and will probably not be satisfied with low-outcome relationships. By contrast, people who have few positive interactions will be satisfied with relationships and interactions that people who enjoy high-outcome relationships would find unattractive. For instance, Calvin may continue to go with Erica even if she treats him very poorly because based on experiences he has in his other relationships, the rewards he gets from the relationship are on par. In fact, Thibaut and Kelley point out, some people will stay in a relationship that is plainly unsatisfactory because they do not see themselves as having alternatives. Thus, if Joan believes that Chuck is the only man who can provide the companionship she is seeking, she will be more inclined to tolerate his irritating habits.

Thibaut and Kelley's exchange theory is based on the assumption that people consciously and deliberately weigh the costs and rewards associated with any relationship or interaction, seeking out relationships that benefit them and avoid those that are costly (Trenholm 1991, p. 72). In fact, although people may behave rationally in most situations, Thibaut and Kelley's theory cannot always explain complex human behavior. Nevertheless, it can be useful to examine your relationships from a cost–reward perspective. Especially if your relationship is stagnating, you may recognize areas where costs are greater than rewards either for you or for the other person. If so, you may be able to change some aspects of the relationship before it deteriorates completely.

Conflict

THINK CRITICALLY

Needs Theory and Exchange Theory

Think of one specific intimate relationship you have. Explain the development and maintenance of this relationship in terms of needs theory. Choose and use one specific interactional episode as evidence to support your explanation. Then explain the development and maintenance of this relationship using exchange theory. Again, focus on a single interactional episode. What insights into the relationship have you gained from these analyses? How might these insights affect your future interactions?

This final section confronts one of the primary causes leading to the deterioration of relationships: failure to manage conflict successfully. For our purposes, we will define **interpersonal conflict** as a situation in which the needs or ideas of one person are perceived to be at odds or in opposition to the needs or ideas of another. In these conflict situations, participants have choices about how they act and how they communicate with the other person.

Conflicts include clashes over facts ("Conrad was the first one to talk." "No, it was Mark." or "Your mother is a battle-ax." "What do you mean, a 'battle-ax'?"); over values ("Bringing home pencils and pens from work is not stealing." "Of course it is." or "The idea that you have to be married to have sex is completely outdated." "No, it isn't."); and, perhaps the most difficult to deal with, over ego involvement ("Listen, I've been a football fan for thirty years, I ought to know what good defense is." "Well, you may be a fan, but that doesn't make you an expert.").

Although many people view conflict as bad (and, to be sure, conflict situations are likely to make us anxious and uneasy), it is inevitable in any significant relationship. Moreover, conflict is often useful in that it forces us to make choices; to resolve honest differences; and to test the relative merits of our attitudes, behaviors, needs, and goals. In this section, we will look at styles of managing conflict and then suggest some specific communication strategies that can be used to initiate and respond to conflict.

Styles of Managing Conflict

When faced with conflict, people are likely to withdraw, accommodate, force, compromise, or collaborate (Filley 1975; Cahn 1990; Cupach and Canary 1997). These styles differ in outcomes for each of the participants. So we will also look at each in terms of individual and relational satisfaction and relational effects. Finally, we'll show if and when each of these seems appropriate.

Withdrawal. When people **withdraw**, they physically or psychologically remove themselves from the conflict. People may physically withdraw by leaving the site. For instance, when Justina says, "Eduardo, I thought we agreed that you'd pay my folks back the $60 you owe them," Eduardo may walk downstairs to watch television. Eduardo would be withdrawing psychologically if he just ignores Justina and continues to read the paper.

Withdrawal during conflict usually just postpones—and worsens—the confrontation.

Considered from an individual satisfaction standpoint, withdrawal creates a lose/lose situation because neither party to the conflict really accomplishes what he or she wants. Although Eduardo temporarily escapes from the conflict, he knows it will come up again.

Considered from a relational satisfaction standpoint, both kinds of withdrawal usually have negative consequences. When used repeatedly, withdrawal leads to relationship decline. Why? Because the participants neither eliminate nor attempt to manage the nature of the conflict.

Another consequence of withdrawal is that it results in what Cloven and Roloff (1991, p. 136) call "mulling behavior." By *mulling* they mean thinking about or stewing over an actual or perceived problem until the participants perceive the conflict as more severe and begin engaging in blaming behavior. Thus, in many cases, not confronting the problem when it occurs only makes it more difficult to deal with in the long run.

Nevertheless, withdrawal may be effective as a temporary means of creating time to think. For instance, Eduardo might say, "Hold it a minute; let me think about this while I get a cup of coffee, and then we'll talk about it some more." A few minutes later, having calmed down, Eduardo can return, ready to deal with the conflict.

Withdrawal may actually be an appropriate way of dealing with situations in which neither the relationship nor the issue is really important. If Josh runs into Mario, a man with whom he has gotten into several arguments about management, at a party, Josh might just quickly change the subject when Mario begins the argument anew or politely excuse himself to go talk with other people. In this case, Josh judges that it simply isn't worth trying to resolve the disagreement with Mario—neither the issue nor the relationship is that important. So while withdrawal is limited in its usefulness, understanding when to use it can help us in particular situations.

Accommodation. **Accommodating** means giving in to the other's needs while neglecting your own. People who are insecure in their relationships may accommodate because they are so upset by the prospect of conflict that they will do anything to avoid it. For instance, Juan would like to travel alone with Mariana on their vacation, but when Mariana says, "I think it would be fun to go with another couple, don't you?" Juan replies, "OK, whatever you want."

Considered from an individual satisfaction standpoint, accommodation is a win/lose situation for the individuals. The one side gets what it wants, and the other side gives up what it wants.

From a relational satisfaction standpoint, habitual accommodation has two problems. First, conflicts resolved through accommodation may lead to poor decision making because important facts, arguments, and positions are not voiced. Second, habitual accommodation results in one person's taking advantage of the other. This onesidedness can damage self-concept and lead to feelings of resentment that undermine relationships.

While habitual accommodation is a problem, when the issue really isn't important—for instance, whether to have chicken or fish for dinner—it may be appropriate and effective to accommodate.

Moreover, it should be noted that accommodating is a preferred style of dealing with conflict in some cultures. In Japanese culture, for instance, it is thought to be more humble and face-saving to accommodate than to risk losing respect through conflict (Argyle 1991, p. 40).

 Force. **Forcing,** or aggression, is attempting to satisfy your own needs or advance your own ideas through physical threats, verbal attacks, coercion, or manipulation. The saying "Might makes right" captures the forcing style.

Considered from an individual satisfaction standpoint, forcing is win/lose. The side with enough power to get its way can claim victory. The other side loses.

From a relational satisfaction standpoint, forcing seldom improves and usually hurts a relationship, at least in the short term. However, in emergencies, when quick and decisive action must be taken to ensure safety or minimize harm, forcing can be useful.

 Compromise. **Compromising** is attempting to resolve the conflict by providing at least some satisfaction for both parties. Under this approach, both people have to give up part of what they really want or believe, or have to trade one thing they want in order to get something else.

From a personal satisfaction standpoint, compromising creates a lose/lose situation, because both parties in a sense "lose" even as they "win." While compromising is a popular style, there are significant problems associated with it. One of special concern is that the quality of a decision is affected if one of the parties "trades away a better solution" in order to effect the compromise.

From a relational satisfaction standpoint, compromise may be seen as neutral to positive, because both parties gain some satisfaction.

Collaboration. **Collaborating** through problem solving involves trying to fully address the needs and issues of each party and to arrive at a solution that is mutually satisfying. During collaboration, people discuss the issues and their feelings about the issues, and identify the characteristics that are important for them to find in a solution.

Thus, from an individual satisfaction standpoint, discussion is win/win, because both sides feel that they have gained from the method.

From a relational satisfaction standpoint, collaboration is positive because both sides feel that they have been heard. They get to share ideas and weigh and consider information. Whatever the solution, it is a truly collaborative effort. In effect, collaboration proves to be the most appropriate and the most effective means of managing conflict. In the Spotlight on Scholarship that follows, we can see how the research of Daniel Canary has validated the importance of both appropriateness and effectiveness in conflict management.

SPOTLIGHT ON SCHOLARSHIP

Daniel J. Canary, Professor of Speech Communication, College of Liberal Arts at Pennsylvania State University, on Conflict Management

Dan Canary cites the personal benefit in studying conflict: "I learned how to become more effective in my personal relationships." Canary's initial curiosity about effective conflict management behaviors was piqued when he was in graduate school at the University of Southern California. At the time he was a classmate of Brian Spitzberg (see Spotlight on Scholarship, pp. 19–20), who formulated the theory that relational competence is a product of behaviors that are both appropriate and effective, and Bill Cupach, who was studying conflict in relationships. Although Canary saw the connection between their work, it was several years later—after he witnessed several interpersonal conflicts

between people he loved that led to dramatic changes in their relationships—that he began to study in earnest how the way people behave during conflict episodes affects their relationships.

Scholars can become well known by developing a new theory that more clearly describes what really happens when we interact; by carrying out a series of research studies that test and elaborate on the theories developed by others; or by organizing, integrating, and synthesizing the theories and research work that has been done in an area so that people who are not specialists in that particular area can better understand what is known. Dan Canary's reputation has been made in both of the latter types of scholarship.

His research studies are helping to identify the behaviors that lead to perceiving a person as a competent conflict manager. Canary argues that although people will view some of the communication behaviors to manage conflict as appropriate and some behaviors as effective, both are necessary to be perceived as competent. Drawing on Spitzberg's competence theory, Canary's research studies are designed to identify conflict behaviors that accomplish both of the goals of appropriateness and effectiveness.

The results of his studies consistently show that integrative conflict strategies—problem-solving, collaborative, and compromising approaches that display a desire to work with the other person—are perceived to be both appropriate and effective (hence competent). Furthermore, his studies have shown that when one partner in a relationship is thought to be a competent conflict manager, the other one trusts him or her more, is more satisfied with the relationship, and perceives the relationship to be more intimate.

Canary's most recent research studies identify specific conflict-management behaviors that are viewed as appropriate and/or effective. In a soon to be published study, Canary found that when a person acknowledges the arguments of others (saying, for example, "Uh huh, I can see how you would think that") or agrees with the arguments that others makes to support their points (as in "Gee, that's a good point that I hadn't really thought about"), the person is viewed as having handled the conflict appropriately. To be viewed as effective, however, requires a different set of behaviors. According to Canary's findings, conflict-handling behaviors that are seen as effective include stating complete arguments, elaborating and justifying one's point of view, and clearly developing one's ideas. Canary notes that what is viewed as appropriate alone has the potential to be ineffective, because appropriate behaviors seem to involve some sort of agreement with the other person.

Canary reasoned that there must be ways to be both appropriate and effective in conflict situations. This led him to consider methods of sequencing or ordering messages in a conflict episode. His preliminary results suggest that competent communicators (those perceived to be both appropriate and effective) will begin by acknowledging the other's viewpoint, or agreeing with part of the other's argument, before going on to explain, justify, and argue for their own viewpoint. Canary believes that in using this sequence, competent communicators help "frame" the interaction as one of cooperative problem solving rather than framing it as a situation of competing interests in which only one party can "win."

Many of Canary's major contributions to the study of conflict in personal relationships are included in two books: *Relationship Conflict* (coauthored with William Cupach and Susan Messman) is a synthesis of the diverse conflict literature, written for graduate students and other scholars. *Competence in Interpersonal Conflict* (also coauthored with Cupach) focuses on how readers can increase their competence at managing interpersonal conflict in a variety of settings. For complete citations of these and others of Canary's publications, see the References at the end of this book.

Canary teaches undergraduate courses in interpersonal communication, conflict management, and persuasion and graduate courses in interpersonal communication, research methods, and persuasion. In addition, he is Director of Graduate Studies and serves on several editorial boards for scholarly journals.

Resolving conflict through collaborative discussion requires many of the communication skills we have discussed previously. Participants must use accurate and precise language to describe their ideas and feelings. They must empathically listen to the ideas and feelings of the other person. Using the problem-solving approach, they must define and analyze the problem, develop mutually acceptable criteria for judging alternative solutions, suggest possible solutions, select the solution that best meets the criteria, and work to implement the decision.

Collaboration through Problem-Solving Discussion

1. Define the problem.   What's the issue being considered?

2. Analyze the problem.   What are causes and symptoms?

3. Develop mutually agreeable criteria for judging alternative solutions.   What goals will a good solution reach?

4. Generate alternative solutions.   What could we do? List before discussing each.

5. Select the solution that best fits the criteria identified.   Select one or a combination from those listed.

Let's consider a conflict example mentioned earlier: Justina is upset because Eduardo has not paid her folks the money he owes. To collaborate, both parties must honestly want to satisfy the other's concerns as well as his or her own. If they agree to collaborate, each may begin by describing the situation from his or her perspective while the other listens with empathy and understanding.

Approach	Characteristics	Goal	Outlook
Withdrawal	Uncooperative, unassertive	To keep from dealing with conflict	I don't want to talk about it.
Accommodation	Cooperative, unassertive	To keep from upsetting the other person	Getting my way isn't as important as keeping the peace.
Force	Uncooperative, assertive	To get my way	I'll get my way regardless of what I have to do.
Compromise	Partially cooperative, partially assertive	To get partial satisfaction	I'll get partial satisfaction by letting the other person get partial satisfaction as well.
Collaboration	Cooperative, assertive	To solve the problem together.	Let's talk this out and find the best solution possible for both of us.

Justina may describe for Eduardo her folks' need for the money. Eduardo may disclose that he also owes some money to a friend at work and he can't cover both now. From this base, they can work together to establish a solution that would be acceptable to both of them. Justina might say a good solution would be one in which he gives her folks ten dollars now and tries to give them a little each month for the next few months. Eduardo might say a good solution would be his paying a little to both for as long as it takes until the debts are paid.

Does this process sound too idealized? Or impractical? Collaboration is difficult, but when two people commit themselves to trying, chances are they will discover that through discussion they can arrive at solutions that meet both of their needs and do so in a way that maintains their relationship. The five different styles of conflict management, with their characteristics, outcomes, and appropriate usage, are summarized in Figure 8.3.

Interpersonally, one person usually initiates a conflict, and the other person responds to it. In both the initiation and the response role, you can practice collaboration by using specific communication skills and verbal strategies to help resolve the conflict. The remainder of this chapter focuses on guidelines for accomplishing good collaborative discussion.

UNDERSTAND YOURSELF

Conflict Style

What is your preferred conflict style? Which style is most difficult for you to use?

Individual Satisfaction	Relational Satisfaction	Relational Effects	When Appropriate
Lose/lose: neither party gets satisfaction	Negative: no resolution	Drives wedge into relationship: results in mulling and blaming	Either as temporary disengagement or when issue is unimportant
Lose/win: the other party gets satisfaction	Negative: neither party feels good about the process	Hurts relationship because one person takes advantage	To build social credits or when the issue is unimportant
Win/lose: one party, the forcer, gets satisfaction	Negative: physical and psychological pain for the loser	Hurts relationship because one person feels intimidated	In emergencies; when it is critical to one's or others' welfare; if someone is taking advantage of you
Lose/lose or win/win: neither party is fully satisfied	Neutral to positive: at least partial satisfaction for both	May help or hurt because satisfaction is compromised	When issue is moderately important, when time is short, or when other attempts don't work
Win/win: both parties feel satisfied with the process	Positive: relationship strengthened because mutual benefits	Helps the relationship because both sides are heard	Anytime

Figure 8.3
Styles of conflict management.

Initiating Conflict Appropriately

There will be times in any relationship when you will need to initiate conflict. The following guidelines (as well as those for responding to conflict) are based on work from several fields of study (Gordon 1970; Adler 1977; Whetten and Cameron 1995).

1. **State ownership of the apparent problem.** If you are trying to study for a test in your most difficult course and the person next door is playing her stereo so loud that your walls are shaking and you can't concentrate, it is important to acknowledge that *you* are the one who is angry, hurt, or frustrated. Thus, to resolve *your* problem, you decide to confront your neighbor.

    Your initial impulse might be to bang on your neighbor's door and, when she opens it, shout, "Your radio's too loud, turn it down—I'm trying to study!" A more appropriate way of beginning, however, is to own your problem: "Hi, I'm having a problem that I need your help with. I'm trying to study for a midterm in my most difficult class . . ."

2. **Describe the potential conflict in terms of the behavior you observe, the consequences, and your feelings about it.** The behavior-consequences-feelings (b-c-f) framework means, when a *b*ehavior happens, *c*onsequences result, and I *f*eel a certain way (Gordon 1971). It's important to include all three of these in order for the other person to fully understand what is happening. In each of these instances, you are *describing* for the other person what you see or hear, what happens to you as a result, and what feeling you experience. This b-c-f approach is an extension of the owning feelings, describing behavior, and describing feelings skills we discussed earlier.

    So, in the example of the loud stereo, you might follow up on the opening by saying, "When I hear your stereo (b), I get distracted and can't concentrate, which makes it even harder for me to study (c), and then I get

SKILL BUILDERS   Describing Behavior, Consequences, and Feelings

Skill	Use	Procedure	Example
Describing the basis of a conflict in terms of behavior, consequences, and feelings (b-c-f).	To help the other person understand the problem completely.	1. Own the message. 2. Describe the behavior that you see or hear. 3. Describe the consequences that result. 4. Describe your feelings.	Jason says, "I have a problem that I need your help with. When I tell you what I'm thinking and you don't respond (b), I start to think you don't care about me or what I think (c), and this causes me to get very angry with you (f)."

frustrated and annoyed (f)." The loudness of the stereo is the behavior (b) you observe; getting distracted, being unable to concentrate, and finding it hard to study are the consequences (c) that result from this behavior; frustration and annoyance are the feelings (f) you experience.

3. **Avoid letting the other person change the subject.** Suppose when you approach your neighbor about the stereo she says, "Oh come on, everyone plays their stereos loudly in this neighborhood." Don't let yourself get sidetracked into talking about "everybody." Get back to the point by saying, "Yes, I understand it's a noisy neighborhood and loud music normally doesn't bother me. But I'm still having a problem right now, and I was hoping you could help me."

    Notice that you haven't said the person wasn't listening, or is continuing to be insensitive. You are merely attempting to get the focus back on the problem that you are having.

4. **Phrase your solution in a way that focuses on common ground.** Once you have been understood, suggest your solution. Your solution is more likely to be accepted if you can tie it to a shared value, common interest, or shared constraint. In our example, you might say, "I think we both have had times when even little things get in the way of our being able to study. So even though I realize I'm asking you for a special favor, I hope you can help me out by turning down your stereo while I'm grinding through this material." The better you are at initiating conflict appropriately, the more likely you are to achieve a beneficial outcome.

5. **Think through what you will say before you confront the other person, so that your request will be brief and precise.** Perhaps the greatest problem most of us have with initiating conflict is that even though we have good intentions of keeping on track, our emotions get the better of us. Either we say things we shouldn't, or we go on and on and annoy the other person.

    Before you go charging over to your neighbor's room, think to yourself, "What am I going to say?" Take a minute to practice. Say to yourself. "I need to own the problem and then follow the b-c-f formula." Then practice a few statements until you think you can do it when your neighbor comes to the door.

Responding to Conflict Effectively

It is more difficult to respond effectively to a potential conflict than to initiate one because of the tendency to become defensive. For instance, you could respond, "Well, tough rocks, I'll play my stereo any damn way I feel like it! If you can't study, go to the library." But where does this get you? It may make you feel better for the moment, but it certainly doesn't lay the groundwork for a collaborative relationship at any time.

More likely, however, your role will be more difficult because the person may not initiate the conflict effectively. If the initiator phrases the problem appropriately ("I'm having a problem that I need your help with . . ."), most likely you would say something like, "I'm sorry, I know what you mean. I didn't even think that my stereo might be bothering anyone. Here, I'll turn it down." With this second response, the conflict is immediately resolved. But since not all initiators will understand the problem-behavior-consequences-feelings approach to initiating conflict, you may well face a situation that will require great skill.

1. **Listen to nonverbal cues as well as to the verbal message.** Just as in every other kind of interpersonal communication, the use and reading of nonverbal behavior is essential to recognizing and coping with conflict. As Berger puts it (1994, p. 493), failure to account for the nonverbal communication is to "doom oneself to study the tip of a very large iceberg."

   Infante, Rancer, and Jordan (1996, p. 322), found that the people they studied recognized that behaviors such as smiling, pleasant facial expression, wide bright eyes, relaxed body posture, nodding, gesturing, appearing calm/relaxed, a peppy and upbeat voice or a warm and sincere voice, and vocal expressiveness are nonverbal behaviors that may keep conflict from occurring or from escalating. Tense/frowning face or blank facial expression, grinding teeth, stern/staring eyes, rigid/jittery body, clenched fists, crossed arms, shaky or stuttering voice, and loud voice are nonverbal behaviors that are likely to escalate tension.

   Let's say, however, that you are faced with the conflict initiator who says to you, "Turn down that damn radio! Even an idiot would realize that playing it at the top of the volume is likely to tee off someone who's trying to study." In addition to the harsh words, you're also likely to see and hear several of the unaffirming nonverbal behaviors cited above. So, how do you start?

2. **Put your "shields up."** We "Star Trek" buffs know that when the *Enterprise* is about to be attacked or has just been fired upon, the Captain shouts, "Shields up!" With its shields in place, the ship is somewhat protected from the enemy's fire, and the captain and crew are able to continue to function normally while they consider their strategy.

   We also need to learn to mentally put our shields up when someone becomes overly aggressive in initiating a conflict, to give us time to think of an appropriate strategy rather than becoming defensive and blindly counterattacking. So, put those shields up, and while you're "counting to ten," think of your options for turning this conflict into a problem-solving opportunity.

3. **Respond empathically with genuine interest and concern.** When someone initiates a potential conflict inappropriately, they are still watching you closely to see how *you* react. Even if you disagree with the complaint, you should show respect to the person by being attentive and empathizing. Sometimes you can do this by allowing the initiator to vent emotions while you listen. Only when someone has calmed down can you begin to problem-solve. In this case, however, you might well start by saying, "I'm sorry,

I can see why you are angry with me—I wasn't even thinking about anyone else. Here, I'll turn it down."

4. **Paraphrase your understanding of the problem and ask questions to clarify issues.** Since most people are unaware of the b-c-f framework, you may need to paraphrase to make sure that you are understanding. For instance, let's suppose the person says, "What in the world are you thinking?" If information is missing (as with this initiating statement), then you can ask questions that reflect the b-c-f framework. "Can you tell me what it was that I said or did?" "When that happened, did something else result that I don't realize?" "How did you feel about that?"

It can also be helpful to ask the person if there is anything else that has not been mentioned. Sometimes people will initiate a conflict episode on minor issues when what really needs to be considered has not been mentioned.

5. **Seek common ground by finding some aspect of the complaint to agree with.** Seeking common ground does not mean giving in to the other person. Nor does it mean that you should feign agreement on a point that you do not agree with. However, using your skills of supportiveness, you can look for points with which you can agree. Adler (1977) suggests that you can agree with a message without accepting all of its implications. For example, you can agree with part of it, you can agree with it in principle, you can agree with the initiator's perception of the situation, and/or you can agree with the person's feelings.

Let's take our ongoing example: "Turn down that damn radio! Even an idiot would realize that playing it at the top of the volume is likely to tee off someone whose trying to study." In response, you could agree in part: "If the volume is bothering you, I can see why you'd get upset." You could agree in principle: "I agree it's best to study in a quiet place." You could agree with the initiator's perception: "I can see that you are finding it difficult to study with music in the background." Or you could agree with the person's feelings: "It's obvious that you're frustrated and annoyed."

You do not need to agree with the initiator's conclusions or evaluations. You need not concede. But by agreeing with some aspect of the complaint, you create common ground on which a problem-solving discussion can take place.

6. **Ask the person to suggest alternatives.** As soon as you are sure you have agreed on a definition of the problem, ask the person what he or she thinks will best solve the problem. Since the initiator has probably spent time thinking about what needs to be done, your asking for suggested solutions signals your willingness to listen and cooperate. You may be surprised to find that what is suggested seems reasonable to you. If not, you may be able to craft an alternative that builds on one of the ideas presented. In either case, by asking for suggestions you communicate your trust in the other person, thus strengthening the problem-solving climate.

OBSERVE AND ANALYZE

Conflict Failures

Think of a recent conflict you experienced in which the conflict was not successfully resolved. Analyze what happened, using the concepts from this chapter. What type of conflict was it? What style did you adopt? What was the other person's style? How did styles contribute to what happened? How well did your behavior match the guidelines recommended for initiating and responding to the conflict? How might you change what you did if you could "redo" this conflict episode?

PRACTICE IN CLASS

Dealing with Conflict

Working in groups of three, have one person practice initiating a conflict with a second person, who will practice the responding skills. The third person should observe. The practicing pair should decide on a conflict situation (for example, parent discovers that teen has been smoking, or girl discovers sister has borrowed her skirt without asking). They should role-play this situation *twice.* The first time through, the initiator should try to be ineffective while responder uses skills. In the second case, responder need not "buy in" initially and initiator should concentrate on using skills. Once the observer has given feedback, repeat the exercise twice more, switching roles so that each person has an opportunity to initiate, respond, and observe.

Learning from Conflict-Management Failures

Ideally, you want to resolve conflicts as they occur. The biblical admonishment "Never let the sun set on your anger" is sage advice. Nevertheless, there will be times when no matter how hard both persons try, they will not be able to resolve the conflict. Sillars and Weisberg (1987, p. 143) have pointed out that conflict can be an extremely complex process and that some conflicts may not be resolvable even with improved communication.

Especially when the relationship is important to you, take time to analyze your inability to resolve the conflict. Ask yourself such questions as "Where did things go wrong?" "Did one or more of us become evaluative?" "Did I use a style that was inappropriate to the situation?" "Did we fail to implement the problem-solving method adequately?" "Were the vested interests in the outcome too great?" "Am I failing to use such basic communication skills as paraphrasing, describing feelings, and perception checking?" By taking time to analyze your behavior, you put yourself in a better position to act more successfully in the next conflict episode you experience. And because conflict is inevitable, you can count on using this knowledge again.

Summary

One of the main purposes of interpersonal communication is developing and maintaining good relationships. A good relationship is any mutually satisfying interaction, on any level, with another person.

People have three types of relationships. Acquaintances are people we know by name and talk with, but with whom our interactions are limited. Friends are people we spend time with voluntarily because we enjoy their company. Close or intimate friends are those with whom we share our deepest feelings.

Relationships go through a life cycle that includes starting or building, stabilizing, and ending. In the starting or building stage, people strike up a conversation, keep conversations going, and move to more intimate levels. People nurture good relationships through the skills of describing, openness, provisionalism, and equality. The Johari window can be used as a tool for examining the ratio of openness to closedness in a relationship. Many of our relationships end. We may terminate them in interpersonally sound ways or in ways that destroy chances for our being able to continue the relationship on any meaningful level.

Two theories about how relationships work are especially useful for explaining the dynamics of relationships. Schutz sees relationships in terms of the ability to meet the interpersonal needs of affection, inclusion, and control. Thibaut and Kelley see relationships as exchanges: People evaluate relationships through a cost–reward analysis, weighing the energy, time, and money invested against the satisfaction gained.

A primary factor leading to termination of a relationship is failure to manage conflict successfully. Interpersonal conflict occurs when the needs or ideas of one person are perceived to be at odds or in opposition to the needs or ideas of another.

We cope with conflicts in a variety of ways—withdrawal, accommodation, force, compromise, and collaboration—each of which has definable characteristics. In most settings, when we are concerned about the long-term relationship, collaboration will be most appropriate. We can also affect the conflict episode by using specific communication skills and verbal strategies.

When you have a problem with another person or the person's behavior, initiate the conflict using basic communication skills. Own the problem; describe the basis of the potential conflict in terms of behavior, consequences, and feelings; plan what you will say before you confront the other person; avoid evaluating the other person's motives; and phrase your request so that it focuses on common ground.

When you are responding to another person's problem, attend to the non-verbal cues to get a sense of the strength of the person's feelings, put your shields up, respond empathically with genuine interest and concern, paraphrase your understanding of the problem, seek common ground, and ask the person to suggest alternatives.

Finally, learn from conflict-management failures.

REFLECT ON ETHICS

Sally and Ed had been seeing each other for more than three years when Ed moved 150 miles away to attend college. When he left, they promised to continue to see each other and agreed that should either of them want to start seeing someone else, he/she would tell the other person before doing so.

During the first five months that he was away, Sally became friendly with Jamie, a coworker at the child care center on the campus of the local junior college. As time went on, it became apparent to Sally that Jamie's interest in her was going beyond the point of just being friends. Because she didn't want to risk losing his companionship, Sally had never mentioned Ed.

On Friday, just as Sally and Jamie were about to leave the child care center and head for a movie, the door swung open and in walked Ed. Sally hadn't been expecting him, but she took one look at him, broke into a big smile, and ran over and gave him a warm embrace. Too absorbed with her own excitement, Sally didn't even notice Jamie's shock and disappointment. She quickly introduced Ed to him and then casually said to Jamie, "See you Monday!" and left with Ed.

That weekend, Ed confessed that he wanted to end their relationship. He was involved with a woman on campus. Sally was outraged. She accused him of acting dishonestly by violating their agreement about seeing other people. Their conversation went downhill, and eventually Ed left.

On Monday, when Sally saw Jamie at work, he was very aloof and curt. She asked him if he wanted to get a bite to eat before class and was genuinely surprised when he answered with an abrupt "no." As she ate alone, she pondered her behavior and wondered if and how she could ever rectify her relationship with Jamie.

1. Were any of Sally's, Ed's, and Jamie's actions unethical?
2. How could each of their behaviors be changed in ways that would improve the communication ethics and outcome of the situation?

OBJECTIVES

After you have read this chapter, you should be able to answer the following questions:

■ What should you do to prepare for a job interview?

■ What are the important elements of a written résumé?

■ What are the characteristics of open and closed, primary and secondary, and neutral and leading questions?

■ How do you conduct a job interview?

■ What are some typical questions used by job interviewers?

9

Job Interviewing

At 3:30 sharp Chet arrived at the door of the human resources director of Grover Industries for his interview. The secretary led him into the office and introduced him to Miles Beddington.

"Sit down," Beddington said, "and we'll get started. Well, I've looked over your résumé, and now I have just a few questions. How did you get interested in Grover Industries?"

"Our Student Placement Office said you were hiring."

"And for what kind of position do you think you would be most suited?"

"One where I could use my skills."

"What skills do you have to offer our company that would make you a good hire for us?"

"Well, I'm a hard worker."

"Are you familiar with our major products?"

"Not really. I haven't had time yet to look you up."

"What kinds of experience have you had in business?"

"Um, my sister-in-law owns her own business, and I hear her talking about it a lot."

"OK, what do you see as some of your major skills?"

"I told you, I can work really hard!"

"Well, Chet, companies are impressed by hard workers. We're talking to other applicants, of course. So, I'll be in touch."

When Chet got home, Tanya asked, "How did the interview go?"

"Great," Chet replied. "Mr. Beddington was impressed by the fact that I'm a hard worker."

What do you think Chet's chances are for the job?

Although interviewing for a job is often a traumatic experience, especially for those who are going through it for the first time, applicants for nearly every position in nearly any field will go through at least one interview, and possibly several. At its worst, an interview can be a waste of time for everyone; at its best, an interview can reveal vital information about an applicant as well as allow the applicant to judge the suitability of the position, the company, and tasks to be performed.

A skillfully conducted interview can help interviewers determine the applicant's specific abilities, ambitions, energy, ability to communicate, knowledge, intelligence, and integrity. Moreover, it can help the interviewee show his or her strengths in these same areas.

The job interview is a special type of interpersonal situation with specific demands. Let's consider some of the procedures and methods you can use when being interviewed, as well as in interviewing others.

Responsibilities of the Job Applicant

Interviews are an important part of the process of seeking employment. Even for part-time and temporary jobs, you will benefit if you approach the interviewing process seriously and systematically. There is no point in applying for positions that are obviously outside your area of expertise. It may seem a good idea to get interviewing experience, but you are wasting your time and the interviewer's if you apply for a position you have no intention of taking or for which you are not qualified.

When you are granted an employment interview, remember that all you have to sell is yourself and your qualifications. Recall from our discussion of self-presentation in Chapter 4 how much your nonverbal behavior contributes to the impression you make. You want to show yourself in the best possible light. Take care with your appearance; if you want a particular job, dress in a way that is acceptable to the person or organization that may—or may not—hire you.

Preparing for the Interview

Of course you'll want to be fully prepared for the interview. Two important tasks you must complete before the interview itself are writing a cover letter and preparing a résumé. These two documents "advertise you for interviews" (Krannich and Banis 1990, p. 21).

Write a cover letter. The **cover letter** is a short, well-written letter expressing your interest in a particular position. Always address the letter to the person with the authority to hire you (not, for example, to the personnel or human resources department). If you do not already have the appropriate person's name, you can probably get it by telephoning the company. Because you are trying to stimulate the reader's interest in *you*, make sure that your cover letter does not read like a form letter. The cover letter should include the following elements: where and how you found out about the position, your reason for being interested in this company, your main skills and accomplishments (summary of a few key points), how you fit the requirements for the job, items of special interest about you that would relate to your potential for the job, and a request for an interview. The letter should be one page or less. You should always include a résumé with the letter.

Include a résumé. The **résumé** is a summary of your skills and accomplishments. Although there is no universal format for résumé writing, there is some agreement on what should be included and excluded. In writing your résumé, you should include the following information, as appropriate, cast in a form that increases the likelihood of your being asked to interview:

1. **Contact information:** Your name, address, and telephone number(s) at which you can be reached. (Always.)
2. **Job objective:** A one-sentence objective focusing on your specific area(s) of expertise. (Important for full-time career positions.)
3. **Employment history:** Paid and nonpaid experiences beginning with the most recent. Be sure to give employment dates and briefly list important duties and accomplishments.
4. **Education:** Schools attended, degree completed or expected, date of completion, with focus on courses that are most directly related to the job.
5. **Military experience:** Include rank and service and achievements, skills, abilities, and discharge status.
6. **Relevant professional certifications and affiliations:** Memberships, offices held.
7. **Community activities:** Community service organizations, clubs, and the like, including offices and dates.
8. **Special skills:** Fluency in foreign languages, computer expertise.
9. **Interests and activities:** Only those that are related to your objective.
10. **References:** People who know your work, your capabilities, and your character, who will vouch for you. Include only a statement that references are available on request.

Notice that the list does not include such personal information as height, weight, age, sex, marital status, health, race, religion, or political affiliation, nor does it include any reference to salary. Also notice that although you need not include references, you should already have the permission of people whom you will use as references.

Once you've spotted some good job opportunities, refine your résumé and cover letter to address each job.

In addition, you should consider what format your résumé will follow—how wide your margins will be, how elements will be spaced and indented, and so on. The résumé should be no more than three pages; for traditional college students, one or two pages should be your goal. The résumé must be neat, carefully proofread to be error free, and reproduced on a good quality paper. Try to look at your résumé from the employer's point of view. What do you have to present that can help the employer solve problems? Think in terms of what the company needs, and present only your skills and accomplishments that show you can do the job. Most important, be tactful but truthful in what you present. While you want to emphasize your strengths, you want to avoid exaggerating facts, a procedure that is both deceptive and unethical. Figure 9.1 shows a sample cover letter and Figure 9.2 shows a sample résumé of a person who has just graduated from college.

2326 Tower Place
Cincinnati, Ohio 45220
April 8, 1998

Mr. Kyle Jones
Acme Marketing Research Associates
P.O. Box 482
Cincinnati, OH 45201

Dear Mr. Jones:

I am applying for the position of first-year associate at Acme
Marketing Research Associates, which I learned about through the
Office of Career Counseling at the University of Cincinnati. I am
a senior mathematics major at the University of Cincinnati who is
interested in pursuing a career in marketing research. I am highly
motivated, eager to learn, and I enjoy working with all types of
people. I am excited by the prospect of working for a firm like
Axon Group where I can apply my leadership and problem-solving
skills in a professional setting.

As a mathematics major, I have developed the analytical
proficiency that is necessary for working through complex
problems. My courses in statistics have especially prepared me for
data analysis, while my more theoretical courses have taught me
how to construct an effective argument. My leadership training and
opportunities have given me the ability to work effectively in
groups and have taught me the benefits of both individual and
group problem solving. My work on the Strategic Planning Committee
has given me an introduction to market analysis by teaching me
skills associated with strategic planning. Finally, from my
theatrical experience, I have gained the poise to make
presentations in front of small and large groups alike. I believe
that these experiences and others have shaped who I am and have
helped me to develop many of the skills necessary to be
successful. I am interested in learning more and continuing to
grow.

I look forward to having the opportunity to interview with you in
the future. I have enclosed my résumé with my school address and
phone number. Thank you for your consideration. I hope to hear
from you soon.

Sincerely,

Elisa C. Vardin

Figure 9.1

Sample cover letter.

Elisa C. Vardin   2326 Tower Avenue
                                                       Cincinnati, Ohio 45220
                                                       Phone: (513) 861-2497
                                                       E-mail: Elisa Vardin@UC.edu

Professional Objective

To use my intellectual abilities, quantitative knowledge, communication skills, and proven
leadership ability creatively to further the organizational mission of a high-integrity marketing
research organization.

EDUCATIONAL BACKGROUND

UNIVERSITY OF CINCINNATI, Cincinnati, OH. B.A. in Mathematics, June 1998. GPA 3.36. Dean's List.

NATIONAL THEATER INSTITUTE at the Eugene O'Neill Theater Center, Waterford, CT. Fall 1995.
       Acting, Voice, Movement, Directing, and Playwriting.

WORK AND OTHER BUSINESS-RELATED EXPERIENCE

REYNOLDS & DEWITT, SENA WELLER ROHS WILLIAMS, Cincinnati, OH. Summer 1996.
       Intern at Brokerage/Investment Management Firm. Provided administrative support. Created
       new databases, performance comparisons, and fact sheets in Excel and Word files.

MUMMERS GUILD, University of Cincinnati, Spring 1995–Spring 1996.
       As treasurer, responsible for all financial/accounting functions for this undergraduate theater
       community.

SUMMERBRIDGE CINCINNATI, Cincinnati Country Day School, Cincinnati, OH. Summer 1995.
       Full-time teacher in a program dedicated to helping "at risk" junior high students develop an
       interest in learning. Taught two courses in 7th grade mathematics, 6th and 7th grade speech
       communication class, sign language course; Academic adviser; Club leader. Organized five-
       hour diversity workshop and three-hour tension-reduction workshop for staff.

STRATEGIC PLANNING COMMITTEE, Summit Country Day School, Cincinnati, OH. Fall 1993–1994.
       Worked with the Board of Directors (one of two students) to develop the first Strategic Plan
       for this 1000-student independent school (Pre-K through 12).

AYF INTERNATIONAL LEADERSHIP CONFERENCE, Camp Miniwanca, Shelby, MI. Summers 1992–1994.
       Leadership conference sponsored by American Youth Foundation bringing campers from 50
       states and 26 countries. Skills learned: visioning, vision-based goal setting, forming action
       steps, and re-visioning.

PERSONAL

UNIVERSITY OF CINCINNATI: Musical Theater: Lifetime involvement, including leads and
       choreography for several shows. A cappella singing group: 1995–1998, Director 1997–1998.
       Swing Club: 1995–1998, President and Teacher of student-run dance club. Junior High
       Youth Group Leader: 1997. Math Tutor: 1998. Aerobics Instructor: 1997–1998. University
       of Cincinnati Choral Society: 1995, 1996, 1997. American Sign Language Instructor: Winter
       1995, 1996. Six years voice lessons. 12 years off and on training in ballet, tap, jazz, modern,
       and acrobatics. Macintosh and IBM proficient.

REFERENCES

       On request.

Figure 9.2
Sample résumé.

Researching the company before your job interview will show your interest and impress the interviewer.

The Interview

Employers use interviews to decide who will be hired. During the interview, they assess candidates to determine whether the candidate has the skills and abilities needed for the job; more important, they make judgments about the candidate's personality and motivation. The following guidelines will help you prepare for the interview.

1. **Do your homework.** Learn about the company's services, products, ownership, and financial health. Knowing about a company shows your interest in that company and will usually impress the interviewer. Moreover, you'll be in a better position to discuss how you can contribute to the company's mission.

2. **Rehearse the interview.** For most of us, job interviews are at least somewhat stressful. To help prepare yourself so that you can perform at your best, it is a good idea to practice interviewing. First, try to anticipate some of the questions you will be asked and craft thoughtful answers. You might even try writing out or saying answers aloud. Give careful thought to such subjects as your salary expectations, your possible contributions to the

INFOTRAC COLLEGE EDITION

Is self-presentation really important in an employment interview? Using InfoTrac College Edition, under the subject "employment interviews," click on periodical references. Select two articles that talk about self-presentational issues to help you answer the question.

School:
How did you select the school you attended?
How did you determine your major?
What extracurricular activities did you engage in at school?
In what ways does your transcript reflect your ability?
How were you able to help with your college expenses?

Personal:
What are your hobbies? How did you become interested in them?
Give an example of how you work under pressure.
At what age did you begin supporting yourself?
What causes you to lose your temper?
What are your major strengths? weaknesses?
Give an example of when you were a leader and what happened?
What do you do to stay in good physical condition?
What was the last non-school-assigned book that you read? Tell me about it.
Who has had the greatest influence on your life?
What have you done that shows your creativity?

Position:
What kind of position are you looking for?
What do you know about the company?
Under what conditions would you be willing to relocate?
Why do you think you would like to work for us?
What do you hope to accomplish?
What qualifications do you have that make you feel you would be beneficial to us?
How do you feel about traveling?
What part of the country would you like to settle in?
With what kind of people do you enjoy interacting?
What do you regard as an equitable salary for a person with your qualifications?
What new skills would you like to learn?
What are your career goals?
How would you proceed if you were in charge of hiring?
What are your most important criteria for determining whether you will accept a position?

Figure 9.3
Frequently asked interview questions.

company, and your special skills. Figure 9.3 represents some common questions that are frequently asked in interviews.

3. **Dress conservatively.** Because you want to make a good impression, it is important that you look neat, clean, and appropriate. Men should wear a collared shirt, dress slacks, and a tie and jacket. Women should wear conservative dresses or suits.

4. **Arrive promptly.** The interview is the company's first exposure to your work behavior. If you are late for such an important event, the interviewer will conclude that you are likely to be late for work. So, give yourself extra travel time to cover any possible traffic problems. Plan to arrive fifteen to twenty minutes before your appointment.

5. **Be alert, look at the interviewer, and listen actively.** Remember that your nonverbal communication tells a lot about you. Company representatives are likely to consider eye contact and posture as clues to your self-confidence.

TEST YOUR COMPETENCE

Preparing a Résumé

Prepare a résumé that you might use in the foreseeable future.
What is missing? Is there some experience, skill, or accomplishment that would make it look better? What kinds of activities can you engage in that will strengthen your résumé?

6. **Give yourself time to think before answering a question.** If the interviewer asks you a question that you had not anticipated, give yourself time to think before you answer. It is better to pause and appear thoughtful than to give a hasty answer that may cost you the job. If you do not understand the question, paraphrase it before you attempt to answer.

7. **Ask questions about the type of work you will be doing.** The interview is your chance to find out if you would enjoy working for this company. You might ask the interviewer to describe a typical work day for the person who will get the job. If the interview is conducted at the company offices, you might ask to see where you would be working. In this way, you prepare yourself to know how you will respond to a job offer.

8. **Show enthusiasm for the job.** The interviewer is likely to reason that if you are not enthusiastic during an interview, then you may not be the person for the job. Employers expect applicants to look and sound interested.

9. **Do not engage in long discussions on salary.** The time to discuss salary is when the job is offered. If the company representative tries to pin you down, ask, "What do you normally pay someone with my experience and education for this level position?" Such a question allows you to get an idea of what the salary will be without committing yourself to a figure first.

10. **Do not harp on benefits.** Again, detailed discussions about benefits are more appropriate after the company has made you an offer.

THINK CRITICALLY

Job Interview

Think of a job interview that you have had. What parts of the interview were most difficult for you? Why? If you were to engage in that same interview again, what would you do differently?

If you have never had a job interview, talk with others who have. Find out what parts of the interview were most difficult for them and why.

In light of this information, where are you likely to put your greatest emphasis in preparation for your next job interview?

Interpersonal Skills in Interviewing Others

In your work relationships, you will experience interviewing from both sides of the desk—you will need experience in both interviewing and being interviewed. Once on the job, you may be called on to interview customers about complaints, interview coworkers to get information relevant to your work, or interview prospective employees. So you need to know how to plan and conduct interviews.

As an interviewer, you represent the link between a job applicant and the company. Much of the applicant's impression of the company will depend on his or her impression of you, and you will want to be able to provide answers to questions applicants may have about your company. Besides the obvious desire for salary information, applicants may seek information about opportunities for advancement, influences of personal ideas on company policy, company attitudes toward personal life and lifestyle, working conditions, and so forth. Moreover, you are primarily responsible for determining whether this person will be considered for the position available or for possible future employment with the company.

Determining the Procedure

The most satisfactory employment interview is probably a highly to moderately structured one. In the unstructured interview, the interviewer tends to talk more and to make decisions based on less valid data than in the structured interview (Arvey and Campion 1982). Especially if you are screening a large number of applicants, you want to make sure that all have been asked the same questions and that the questions cover subjects that will be most revealing of the kinds of information you need in order to make a reasonable decision.

Before the time scheduled for the interview, become familiar with all available data about the applicant: application form, résumé, letters of recommendation, test scores if available. Such written data will help determine some of the questions you will want to ask.

DILBERT reprinted by permission of United Features Syndicate, Inc.

Conducting an Interview

An **interview** is a structured conversation with the goal of exchanging information that is needed for decision making. So, a well-planned interview comprises a list of questions designed to get the needed information. Interviews, like speeches and essays, have an appropriate opening, body, and conclusion.

Opening the interview. Open the interview by stating its purpose and introducing yourself if you have not previously met.

Sometimes interviewers begin with "warm-up" or easy questions to help establish rapport. A good interviewer senses the nature of the situation and tries to use a method that is most likely to encourage the other person to talk and provide adequate answers. Although warm-up questions may be helpful, most participants are ready to get down to business immediately, in which case warm-up questions may be counterproductive (Cogger, 1982).

Questions used in the body of the interview. The body of the interview consists of the primary questions to which you need answers. Since the quality of information depends on how the questions are phrased, let's consider the types of questions you will ask. Interview questions may be phrased as open or closed, neutral or leading, primary or secondary.

Open questions are broad-based questions that ask the interviewee to provide whatever information he or she wishes. **Closed questions** are narrow-focus questions that require very brief answers. **Neutral questions** are those that allow a person to give an answer without direction from the interviewer. **Leading questions** are phrased in a way that suggests the interviewer has a preferred answer. **Primary questions** are those open or closed questions that the interviewer plans ahead of time. **Follow-up** or **secondary questions** can be planned or spontaneous, but are designed to pursue the answers given to primary questions.

Refer back to Figure 9.3 for a set of questions that you are likely to draw from for your interviews. This list was compiled from a variety of sources and is only representative, not exhaustive. It sets no limitations on your own creativity, but is intended to suggest the kinds of questions you may wish to ask. Notice that it focuses questions on educational background, personal interests, and job-related attitudes, goals, and skills—three areas of information that are relevant to making a decision on a candidate. You might use this as a starter list or as a checklist for your own wording of questions. Notice that some questions are open-ended and some are closed, but none is a yes-or-no question.

Closing the interview. Toward the end of the interview, you should always explain to the interviewee what will happen next and how the information you gathered will be used. Explain the procedures for making decisions based on the information. Also let the interviewee know whether and how he or she will receive feedback on the decision. Then close the interview in a courteous, neutral manner, thanking the interviewee for his or her time and interest.

PRACTICE IN CLASS

Interviewing for a Job

Select a partner in class, and interview each other for a particular job. Try to follow the guidelines for employment interviewing provided in this chapter.

Throughout the interview, be careful of your own presentation. Try not to waste time, and give the applicant time to ask questions.

Summary

At work we use our interpersonal skills to get a job, to relate to colleagues and clients, and to interview job candidates.

Before you interview for a job, you need to take the time to learn about the company and prepare an appropriate cover letter and résumé designed to motivate an employer to interview you. For the interview itself, you should be prompt, be alert and look directly at the interviewer, give yourself time to think before answering difficult questions, ask intelligent questions about the company and the job, and show enthusiasm for the position.

To interview others, you need to learn to ask primary and secondary, open and closed, neutrally worded questions effectively. When you are interviewing prospective applicants for a job, structure your interview carefully to elicit maximal information about the candidate. Before the interview starts, become familiar with the data contained in the interviewee's application form, résumé, letters of recommendation, and test scores if available. Be careful how you present yourself, do not waste time, and give the applicant an opportunity to ask questions. At the end of the interview, explain to the applicant what will happen next in the process.

OBSERVE AND ANALYZE

What Interviewers Look For

Call a large local company and make an appointment to interview a person in the human resources department whose job it is to interview candidates for employment. Develop a set of interview questions and follow-ups. Focus your interview on obtaining information about the person's experiences that will help you. For example, you might ask, "How do you decide whom to interview?" and "What are the characteristics you like to see an interviewee demonstrate?" After you have conducted the interview, be prepared to discuss your findings in class.

REFLECT ON ETHICS

After three years of working at Everyday Products as a clerk, Mark decided to look for another job. As he thought about preparing a résumé, he was struck by how little experience he had for the kind of job he wanted.

When he talked with his friend Ken about the problem, Ken said, "Exactly what have you been doing at Everyday?"

"Well, for the most part I've been helping others look for information. I've also done some editing of reports."

"Hm," Ken thought for a while. "Why not retitle your job 'editorial assistant'—it's more descriptive."

"But my official title is clerk."

"Sure, but it doesn't really describe what you do. This way you show major editorial experience. Don't worry, everybody makes these kinds of changes—you're not really lying."

"Yeah, I see what you mean. Good idea!"

1. Is it interpersonally ethical for Mark to follow Ken's advice? Why?
2. How should we deal with statements like "Everybody does it"?

S E L F - R E V I E W

Interpersonal Communication from Chapters 5 to 9

What kind of an interpersonal communicator are you? The following analysis looks at specific behaviors that are characteristic of effective interpersonal communicators. On the line provided for each statement, indicate the response that best captures your behavior: 1, never; 2, rarely; 3, occasionally; 4, often; 5, almost always.

_____ I describe objectively to others my negative feelings about their behavior toward me without withholding or blowing up. (Ch. 5)

_____ I am quick to praise people for doing things well. (Ch. 5)

_____ I criticize people for their mistakes only when they ask for criticism. (Ch. 5)

_____ I change the way I listen depending on the purpose of my listening. (Ch. 6)

_____ I listen attentively, regardless of my interest in the person or the ideas. (Ch. 6)

_____ I am able to remember names, telephone numbers, and other specific information that I have heard only once. (Ch. 6)

_____ When I'm not sure whether I understand, I seek clarification. (Ch. 7)

_____ In conversation, I am able to make relevant contributions without interrupting others. (Ch. 7)

_____ I am able to maintain a positive communication climate by speaking in ways that others perceive as descriptive, provisional, and nonmanipulative. (Ch. 8)

_____ When I find myself in conflict with another person, I am able to discuss the issue openly without withdrawing or appearing competitive or aggressive. (Ch. 8)

Based on your responses, select the interpersonal communication behavior that you would most like to change. Write a communication improvement goal statement similar to the sample goal statement in Chapter 1 (page 24). If you would like verification of your self-analysis before you write a contract, have a friend or coworker complete this same analysis for you.

three

Ours is a government by committee—small groups of people working together to reach decisions. Indeed, reliance on the group process as an instrument of decision making extends into nearly every facet of our lives. But as informal conversation moves to the structure of small-group communication, the group itself presents a new set of variables we need to consider.

This two-chapter unit begins with an analysis of the nature of an effective work group, focusing on the necessary roles of participants. It concludes with a discussion of the most important role in effective group communication: leadership.

GROUP COMMUNICATION

OBJECTIVES

After you have read this chapter, you should be able to answer the following questions:

- What are the key characteristics of effective group communication?

- How does a group achieve cohesiveness?

- How do task roles differ from maintenance roles?

- What differentiates questions of fact, value, and policy?

- What are the steps of the problem-solving method?

10

Participating in Small Groups

Members of the advertising division of Meyer Foods were gathered to review their hiring policies. At the beginning of the first meeting, Kareem, head of the division, began, "You know why I called you together. Each department has to review its hiring practices. So, let's get started. Drew, what have you been thinking?"

"Well, I don't know," Drew replied, "I haven't really given it much thought."

"I'd like to contribute," Dawn said. "I just don't have much information."

"But I sent around questions for discussion," Kareem said.

"Oh," Byron said. "I guess I didn't pay much attention to the material."

"Why don't we just say we wish to keep them the way they are?" Dawn asked.

"But," replied Kareem, "I think the CEO is looking for some specific recommendations. They'd like us to comment on how we process minority and female applicants."

"Anything you think would be important would be OK with me," Byron replied.

"Well, how about if we each try to come up with some ideas for next time?" Kareem suggested. "Meeting's adjourned."

As the group dispersed, Kareem overhead Drew say, "These meetings sure are a waste of time, aren't they?"

Perhaps you belong to a fraternal, business, governmental, or religious group. Or perhaps you have worked on a committee. Does this opening dialogue reflect the way your group meetings have gone? When group work is ineffective, it is easy to point the finger at the leader, but often, as is the case with this group, the responsibility for the "waste of time" lies squarely on the shoulders of the individuals involved. Because most of us spend some of our communication time in groups, we need to know how to participate in ways that maximize group effectiveness.

In this chapter, we consider characteristics of effective **work groups**— groups of two or more people using logical means, in public or in private, to solve a problem or arrive at a decision. Then we consider the specific roles group members play and a method for group problem solving. In the next chapter, we consider one of the most important group roles: leadership.

Characteristics of Effective Work Groups

Because work groups seek to achieve specific goals, it is relevant to ask what makes work groups effective. Research shows that effective groups generally have a good working environment, have an optimum number of members, show cohesiveness, are committed to the task, respect rules, find ways to achieve consensus, are well prepared, and meet key role requirements (Shaw 1981).

Good Working Environment

A good working environment begins with seating arrangements that encourage full participation. Seating can be too formal when it approximates a board of directors seating style, as illustrated in Figure 10.1a, in which seating location is an indication of status. In this style, a boss-and-subordinate pattern emerges that can inhibit group interaction. Seating that is excessively informal can also inhibit interaction. For instance, in Figure 10.1b, the three people sitting on the couch form their own little group, the two people seated next to each other form another group, and two members have placed themselves out of the main flow. As a result, it is unlikely that all the people in such an informal arrangement will interact as one group.

The circle, the ideal arrangement depicted in Figure 10.1c, increases participant motivation to speak because sight lines are better for everyone and everyone appears to have equal status. If the meeting place does not have a round table, the group may be better off without a table or with tables arranged to form a square, as in Figure 10.1d.

Figure 10.1
Which group members do you think will be able to arrive at a decision easily? Why or why not?

As a group deliberates, certain individuals may earn higher status than others as a result of having better information, greater insight, or a more logical perspective. But an effective group provides a climate in which everyone has an equal opportunity to earn such status.

Optimum Number of Members

Effective groups contain enough members to ensure good interaction, but not so many members that discussion is stifled.

Although optimum size depends on the nature of the task, groups consisting of five members are most desirable (Hare 1976, p. 214). Why five? Groups with fewer than five members almost universally complain that they are too small and that there are not enough people for specialization. To be effective, a group needs certain skills. When the group contains only three or four members, chances are that not all these skills will be present. Moreover, if one member of a group of three does not feel like contributing, you no longer have much of a group. Nevertheless, for small tasks the three-person group often works well. It's easier to get three people together than five or more. And if the task is relatively simple or within the expertise of the individuals, the three-person group may be a good choice.

When a group numbers more than seven or eight people, reticent members are even less likely to contribute. As the group grows larger, two, three, or four people may become the active participants, with others playing more passive roles (Shaw 1981, p. 202). In larger groups, many people cannot or will not contribute, cohesiveness is nearly impossible to develop, and the decision is seldom a product of the group's collective thought (Beebe and Masterson 1997, p. 125; Mullen et al. 1994).

In a group of any size, an odd number is better than an even number. Why? Although voting is not the best way of reaching a decision, if a group finds it necessary to resolve an issue on which it cannot achieve consensus, the odd number will prevent tie votes.

The optimum group size is five to seven people.

✳ Cohesiveness

Cohesiveness means sticking together, pulling for one another, and being caught up in the task. Remember the Three Musketeers, who were all for one and one for all? They are the prototype of a cohesive group.

One of the qualities that seems particularly important in developing cohesiveness is the attractiveness of the group's purpose. Social or fraternal groups, for example, build cohesiveness out of devotion to service or brotherhood. In a decision-making group, attractiveness is likely to be related to how important the task is to members. Suppose a church congregation forms a committee to consider how its outreach program can be made more responsive to community needs. The cohesiveness of the members of that committee will depend, at least in part, on the importance they attribute to this issue.

A second important quality is similarity of the needs and interests of group members. Groups can be characterized as homogeneous or heterogeneous. A **homogeneous** group is one in which members have a great deal in common. For example, a group of five women of the same age who are all strong feminists would be homogeneous. By contrast, a **heterogeneous** group is one in which various ages, levels of knowledge, attitudes, and interests are represented. A homogeneous group will generally achieve cohesiveness more quickly than a heterogeneous group because the members are more likely to identify with one another's needs and interests from the start.

A third important quality is reinforcement of the interpersonal needs of affection, inclusion, and control. As people decide that they like one another, that they want to be around one another, and that their opinions will be respected, they begin to work more effectively as a unit.

Cohesiveness is difficult to develop in a one-meeting group, but it should be characteristic of ongoing groups. Because of the importance of cohesiveness, many groups engage in **team building**—activities that are designed to help groups work together better (Clark 1994). Often this means having the group meet someplace outside of its normal setting, where members can engage in activities designed to help them recognize one another's strengths, share in group successes, and develop rituals.

⨁ Commitment to the Task

Whether the group is assigned a task or the group determines its task, members must be sufficiently committed to the group for it to succeed. When the task is deemed important and when the group believes that what it is doing will matter, members are much more inclined to devote their full energies to the task.

When someone appoints you to a committee or asks you to serve on one, you have to decide whether you really want to be a part of that work group. If you aren't fully committed to the task described, you are better off declining. When people aren't committed, they miss meetings, avoid work, and fail to do what is expected of them.

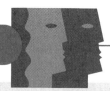

DIVERSE VOICES

The Group: A Japanese Context

by Delores Cathcart and Robert Cathcart

One of Japan's most prominent national characteristics is the individual's sense of the group. Loyalty to the group and willingness to submit to its demands are thus key virtues in Japanese society.

This dependency and the interdependency of all members of a group is reinforced by the concept of *on*. A Japanese is expected to feel an indebtedness to those others in the group who provide security, care, and support. This indebtedness creates obligation and when combined with dependency is called *on*. *On* functions as a means of linking all persons in the group in an unending chain because obligation is never satisfied, but continues throughout life. *On* is fostered by a system known as the *oyabun-kobun* relationship. Traditionally the *oyabun* is a father, boss, or patron who protects and provides for a son, employee, or student in return for his or her service and loyalty. This is not a one-way dependency. Each boss or group leader recognizes his own dependency on those below. Without their undivided loyalty he or she could not function. Oyabun are also acutely aware of this double dimension because of having had to serve a long period of *kobun* on the way up the hierarchy to the position at the top. All had oyabun who protected and assisted them, much like a father, and now each must do the same for their kobun. Oyabun have one or more kobun whom they look after much as if they were children. The more loyal and devoted the "children" the more successful the "father."

This relationship is useful in modern life where large companies assume the role of super-family and become involved in every aspect of their workers' lives. Bosses are oyabun and employees are kobun. . . .

This uniquely Japanese way of viewing relationships creates a distinctive style of decision making known as *consensus decision*. The Japanese devotion to consensus building seems diffi-

cult for most Westerners to grasp but loses some of its mystery when looked at as a solution to representing every member of the group. In a system that operates on oyabun-kobun relationships nothing is decided without concern for how the outcome will affect all. Ideas and plans are circulated up and down the company hierarchy until everyone has had a chance to react. This reactive process is not to exert pressure but to make certain that all matters affecting the particular groups and the company are taken into consideration. Much time is spent assessing the mood of everyone involved and only after all the ramifications of how the decision will affect each group can there be a quiet assent. A group within the company may approve a decision that is not directly in its interest (or even causes it difficulties) because its members know they are not ignored, their feelings have been expressed and they can be assured that what is good for the company will ultimately be good for them. For this reason consensus decisions cannot be hurried along without chancing a slight or oversight that will cause future problems.

The process of consensus building in order to make decisions is a time-consuming one, not only because everyone must be considered, but also because the Japanese avoid verbalizing objections or doubts in order to preserve group harmony. The advice, often found in American group literature, that group communication should be characterized by open and candid statements expressing individual personal feelings, wishes, and dislikes, is the antithesis of the Japanese consensus process. No opposing speeches are made to argue alternate ideas; no conferences are held to debate issues. Instead, the process of assessing the feelings and mood of each work group proceeds slowly until there exists a climate of agreement. This process is possible because of the tight relationships that allow bosses and workers to know each other intimately and to know the group so well that needs and desires are easy to assess.

Excerpted from Delores Cathcart and Robert Cathcart, "The Group: A Japanese Context," From Intercultural Communication: A Reader, *8th ed., eds. Larry A. Samovar and Richard E. Porter (Belmont, CA: Wadsworth, 1997), pp. 329–339. Reprinted by permission of the authors.*

Group Rules

Rules are the guidelines for behavior that are established, or are perceived to be established, for conducting group business. They are the most powerful determiners of behavior in groups. Groups begin to establish rules at the outset of their deliberations; these rules grow, change, and solidify as people get to know one another better.

Rules for a group may be formally spelled out in a group's operating guidelines (as in parliamentary procedures for organizational meetings), they may be adapted from proven social guidelines (such as "Don't talk about yourself in a decision-making group meeting"), or they may simply develop within a particular context. For instance, without any conscious decision, group members may avoid using common four-letter words during the meeting. When business has ended, conversation may become more earthy.

Although formally stated rules may be known to group members from the beginning, most group rules are learned through experience with a specific group. Because rules thus vary from one group to the next, we have to constantly relearn them. Two particularly important areas of rule development are group interaction and group procedure. In one group, it may be acceptable to interrupt any speaker at any time; in another group, it may be forbidden for anyone to speak until he or she is recognized. Thus, Martha, who is used to raising her hand to be recognized at the business meetings of her social organization, may find herself unable to speak in a group meeting where the participants break in whenever they have a chance. In one group, it may be all right

DILBERT reprinted by permission of United Features Syndicate, Inc.

OBSERVE AND ANALYZE

Group Rules

Divide the class into A groups and B groups of five each. While the A groups discuss what kinds of activities groups can engage in to strengthen cohesiveness, the B groups should observe and make note of what communication rules seem to be in operation. At the end of ten minutes, the B groups should take up the discussion of coherence-building activities and the A groups should observe apparent communication rules. At the end of that ten-minute period, the entire class should discuss the communication rules they observed to see which ones seemed to be shared by all and which ones were not.

for someone to openly express anger or hostility toward a person or an idea; in another group, such displays may be frowned on. In one group, members' relative status may determine who speaks first, longest, or most often; in another group, the status of members may have no effect on interaction.

Rules help a group develop cohesiveness. As members conform to stated or implied guidelines for behavior, they find themselves relating to one another more effectively. One of the initial hurdles group members must surmount is **primary tension**—the anxieties of getting to know one another. As group members test out verbal and nonverbal behavior to see what will be accepted, they begin to become more comfortable with one another, primary tension is lessened, and the group is able to concentrate on its task.

Although rules are essential, some rules can be detrimental or destructive. Suppose that at the beginning of the first meeting, a few members of the group tell jokes and generally have a good time. If such behavior is allowed or encouraged, cutting up, making light of the task, and joke telling become a group norm. As a result, the group may become so involved in these behaviors that the task is delayed, set aside, or perhaps even forgotten. Participants may describe their experience by saying, "We don't do much, but it's fun." Even if some group members are concerned about such behavior, once it goes on for several meetings, it will be very difficult to change. As you participate in a group, you can try to be conscious of what rules seem to be in operation and whether or not those rules are helping the group's work. If you believe that certain rules are detrimental or destructive, make your position and the reasons for it known so that those rules do not become established and reinforced.

Groups must also recognize that rules are culturally based, and behavior that is normal for one culture may not be for another. For instance, in some cultures people have learned that it is impolite to interrupt another under any circumstances, but a person who never seems to be a part of freewheeling group deliberation might be perceived to be uncooperative by other members of the group who are used to breaking in and being interrupted. To avoid **ethnocentric** behavior—interpreting others' behavior from our own cultural perspective—before a mixed-culture group gets very far along, the group needs to discuss the rules that will guide group participation so that people will fully understand what is permissible and expected and what is not.

 ## Consensus

If a decision is not a product of group thought and group interaction, the advantages of group decision making are lost. In addition, group members often feel more pleased about the process and more committed to the resulting decisions when such decisions are reached democratically, through group interaction.

Democratic decision making may be achieved through **consensus,** or total group agreement. After the group has discussed a point for a while, one member might pose a question that is phrased to capture the essence of the group's position. For example, someone might ask, "Are we in agreement that lack of direction is frustrating the efforts of department members?" If everyone agrees, the decision is reached by consensus. If the group does not agree, the group can continue to discuss the point until a statement can be made that incorporates differing viewpoints without compromising the principles behind them. But it takes the participation of most group members to arrive at a statement that represents the group position.

If consensus still cannot be reached, the group usually takes a vote. Suppose that after considerable discussion on the policy question "What measures should be taken to open lines of communication between the director and department employees?" it becomes obvious that the group cannot agree on whether to install a "gripe box" as one of the measures. The group should then take a vote. If in a seven-person group, the vote is six to one or five to two, the decision has been given solid support. If it is a four-to-three vote, there may be some questions about later group support of that decision; nevertheless, the principle of majority rule is the only choice open.

Preparation

In most group deliberations, the better the quality of the information shared, the better will be the quality of the group's decisions. And the quality of information is largely a function of how well prepared group members are when discussion begins. The kind of preparation necessary for informed participation varies from group to group, depending on the topic being discussed. But regardless of topic, you will want to make sure that your preparation includes the following:

1. **Read circulated information carefully before the meeting.** The whole point of starting a meeting with well-prepared members is short-circuited if you and other members of the group don't do the reading beforehand.

2. **Think about relevant personal experience.** For many of the topics you will discuss, you will have had some relevant personal experience. For instance, if your group will be considering how to arrange available parking space so that it is distributed equitably among administrators, faculty, and students, your own parking experiences may be useful to the group.

Some topics may require library research, surveys, and interviews. These three methods of research will be discussed in Chapter 13.

OBSERVE AND ANALYZE

Group Interaction

Select for analysis one of the most recent work groups in which you have participated. Which of the following had the greatest effect on group interaction or the quality of the group decision: environment, group size, presence or lack of cohesiveness, commitment to task, adherence to rules, methods of decision making, or group preparation? On what do you base your analysis?

Major Group Roles

Effective groups contain people who meet key role requirements. A role is a pattern of behavior that characterizes an individual's place in a group. Students of group dynamics have identified two key types of roles that are filled in productive groups: task roles and maintenance roles. **Task roles** pertain to the work a group must do to accomplish its goal; **maintenance roles** pertain to the group behaviors that keep the group working together smoothly.

In this section, we examine the major task and maintenance roles that are necessary for a group to function effectively; we also look at those negative roles that need to be kept to a minimum. The role of leadership is discussed in Chapter 11.

Task Roles

Information or opinion givers provide content for the discussion. The more material you have studied, the more valuable your contributions will be. Information: "According to statistics gathered by the campus police, theft has increased by at least 10 percent each of the last three years." Opinion: "According to Leonard Eron and Rowell Huesman, two Chicago doctors who have studied children's viewing habits for 22 years, watching television violence is the single best indicator of violent behavior in later life."

Information seekers probe for information from others. "Before going further, do we have information about how raising fees is likely to affect membership?" or "Do we need this information before we can move to the next point?"

Analyzers probe the content and the reasoning involved in the discussion. Suppose a group member reports that the number of new cable TV subscriptions dropped last month. An analyzer might ask, "How many new subscriptions has the company been averaging each month over the past year? In how many months were new subscriptions below the average for this year? For last year? Has this drop been consistent?" If data are partly true, questionable, or relevant only to certain aspects of the issue, a different conclusion or set of conclusions might be appropriate.

Analyzers also examine the reasoning of various participants. They make such statements as "Enrique, you're generalizing from only one instance. Can you give us some others?"

Expediters keep the group on track. When the group has strayed, expediters will make statements like "I'm enjoying this, but I can't quite see what it has to do with resolving the issue" or "Let's see, aren't we still trying to find out whether these are the only criteria that we should be considering?"

Recorders take careful notes in order to have a record of the group's procedure and decisions. They then distribute **minutes**—major motions, key debates, and conclusions agreed on by the group—to group members prior to the next meeting. The minutes then become a public record of the group's activities.

Maintenance Roles

Whereas task roles help the group deal with the content of discussion, maintenance roles help the group work together smoothly as a unit.

Supporters respond nonverbally or verbally when good points are made, giving such nonverbal cues as a smile, a nod, or a vigorous head shake and make statements like "Good point, Ming," "I really like that idea, Nikki," "It's obvious you've really done your homework, Janelle," and "That's one of the best ideas we've had today, Drew."

Tension relievers recognize when the group process is stagnating or when the group is tiring. They have a sixth sense for when to tell a joke, when to take off on a digression, and when to get the group to loosen up a little before returning to the task. In some situations, a single well-placed one-liner will get a laugh, break the tension or the monotony, and jolt the group out of its lethargy. Tension relieving adds nothing to the content of the discussion, but it does improve immeasurably the spirits of the participants.

Harmonizers bring the group together. Even when people get along well, they are likely to become angry over some inconsequential point in a heated discussion. Norbert Kerr (1992) shows that when an issue is especially important, group members are likely to experience greater polarization and thus greater conflict. Harmonizers are responsible for reducing tensions and for straightening out misunderstandings, disagreements, and conflicts. Harmonizers are likely to make such statements as "Brandon, I don't think you're giving Jana a chance to make her point," "Tom, Jack, hold it a second. I know you're on opposite sides of this, but let's see where you might have some agreement," "Lynne, I get the feeling that something Todd said really bugged you. Is that right?" or "Hold it, everybody, we're really coming up with some good stuff; let's not lose our momentum by getting into name-calling."

Gatekeepers help keep communication channels open. The gatekeeper is the one who helps keep balance in discussion by encouraging those who are having difficulty getting the floor and making sure that no one in the group dominates. We show how a leader can implement this role effectively in the next chapter.

Gatekeepers can also be sensitive to social, cultural, and gender factors that may affect group members' participation. For example, even within the same culture, group members may bring very different backgrounds, vocabularies, and stores of information to the discussion. Thus, some members may not understand some of the terms, historical allusions, or other information that other speakers take for granted—and they may be too embarrassed to ask for clarification. The same point applies, only more so, when a group consists of people from different cultures (Jensen and Chilberg 1991).

Negative Roles

Just as the work group prospers when members fill the various task and maintenance roles, the group suffers when members play certain negative roles.

Aggressors seek to enhance their own status by criticizing almost everything or blaming others when things get rough and by deflating the ego or status of others. One way of dealing with aggressors is to confront them. Ask them whether they are aware of what they are doing and of the effect their behavior is having on the group.

Jokers' behavior is characterized by clowning, mimicking, or generally disrupting by making a joke of everything and calling attention to themselves. One way to proceed is to encourage them when tensions need to be released but ignore them when serious work needs to be done.

Withdrawers refuse to be a part of the group. Sometimes they are withdrawing from something that was said; sometimes they are just showing their indifference. To get them involved in the group, try to draw them out with questions. Find out what they are especially good at, and rely on them when their skill is required. Compliments will sometimes bring them out of their shell.

Monopolizers need to talk all the time to give the impression that they are well read, knowledgeable, and of value to the group. They should be encouraged when their comments are helpful, of course, but held in check when they are talking too much or when their comments are not helpful.

Normal Group Behavior

You may be wondering about the proportion of time devoted in a "normal" group to the various functions described in this section. According to Robert Bales (1971), one of the leading researchers in group interaction processes, 40 to 60 percent of discussion time is spent giving and asking for information and opinion; 8 to 15 percent of discussion time is spent on disagreement, tension, or unfriendliness; and 16 to 26 percent of discussion time is characterized by agreement or friendliness (positive maintenance functions). Two norms we can apply as guidelines for effective group functioning, therefore, are (1) that approximately half of all discussion time is devoted to information sharing and (2) that group agreement far outweighs group disagreement.

Problem Solving in Groups

Research shows that groups follow many different approaches to problem solving. Some groups move linearly through a series of steps to reach consensus, and some move in a spiral pattern in which they refine, accept, reject, modify, and combine ideas as they go along. Whether groups move in something approximating an orderly pattern or go in fits and starts, those groups that arrive at high-quality decisions are likely to accomplish certain tasks during their deliberations—namely, identifying a specific problem, arriving at some criteria that a solution must meet, identifying possible solutions to the problem, and determining the best solution or combination of solutions.

Defining the Problem

Work groups are formed either to consider all issues that relate to a specific topic (a social committee, a personnel committee, or a public relations committee would be formed for this reason) or to consider a specific issue (such as the year's social calendar, criteria for granting promotions, or a long-range plan for university growth). Since much of the wheel-spinning that takes place during the early stages of group discussion results from members' not understanding their specific goal, it is the duty of the person, agency, or parent group that forms a particular work group to give the group a clear goal such as "determining the criteria for merit pay increases" or "preparing guidelines for hiring at a new plant." If the goal is not stated clearly or if the group is free to determine its goal, it should move immediately to get the goal down on paper; until everyone in the group agrees on the goal, they will never agree on how to achieve it.

For successful deliberation, the group needs to make sure that the charge or problem meets certain criteria.

It is appropriate for group consideration. Unfortunately, groups often waste time on tasks best dealt with by individuals. How can you tell whether your group should be discussing a particular question? Among the most important considerations are whether a high-quality decision is required and whether acceptance by members of the group is necessary to put the decision into practice (Vroom and Yetton 1973). A high-quality decision is one that is well documented. Often high-quality decisions are too much for one person to handle; gathering the data alone may require hours of work by several people. Moreover, because vigorous testing is necessary at every stage of the decision-making process, a group is more likely to ask the right questions. Likewise, individuals within the organization are the ones who must carry out the decision. If group members are involved in the decision, they will be motivated to see that the decision is implemented.

Other conditions can indicate that an individual decision is more appropriate than group discussion. If one person has the necessary information and authority to make a good decision, if a solution that has worked well in the past

---

TEST YOUR COMPETENCE

Roles

Identify the role that is represented in each of the following examples as (A) information or opinion giver, (B) information seeker, (C) analyzer, (D) recorder, (E) expediter, (F) supporter, (G) tension reliever, (H) harmonizer, or (I) gatekeeper.

_____ 1. "Shelby, I get the feeling that you have something you wanted to say here."

_____ 2. "The last couple of comments have been on potential causes of the problem, but I don't think we've fully addressed the scope of the problem. If we've really identified the scope, perhaps we could draw a conclusion and then move on to causes."

_____ 3. "Antoine, that was a good point. I think you've really put the problem in perspective."

_____ 4. "Paul and Gwen, I know you see this issue from totally different positions. I wonder whether we might not profit by seeing whether there are any points of agreement; then we can consider the differences."

_____ 5. "Well, according to the latest statistics cited in the *Enquirer*, unemployment in the state has gone back up from 7.2 to 7.9 percent."

_____ 6. "Sarah, you've given us some good statistics. Can we determine whether or not this is really an upward trend or just a seasonal factor?"

Answers: 1.I 2.E 3.F 4.H 5.A 6.C

INFOTRAC COLLEGE EDITION

Using InfoTrac College Edition, under the subject "problem solving discussion," click on periodical references. Select two articles that talk about guidelines for effective group problem solving. In what ways does the information support material in this chapter?

can be applied to this situation, or if time is limited and immediate action is necessary, group discussion is less appropriate.

It is stated as a question. Since groups begin from the assumption that answers are not yet known, phrasing the group's problem as a question furthers the spirit of inquiry.

It contains only one central idea. If the charge includes two questions ("Should the college abolish its foreign language and social studies requirements?"), it needs to be broken down into two separate deliberations. Either one would make a good topic for discussion, but they cannot both be discussed at once.

It contains wording that is clear to all group members. For instance, the question "What should the department do about courses that aren't getting the job done?" may be well intentioned and participants may have at least some idea about their goal, but such vague wording as "getting the job done" can lead to trouble in the discussion. Notice how this revision of the preceding question makes its intent much clearer: "What should the department do about courses that receive low scores on student evaluations?"

It encourages objective discussion. Subjective phrasing colors group discussion and may drastically affect a group's decisions. For instance, if the problem is phrased "How should our sexist guidelines for promotion be revised?" objective discussion is unlikely to occur, because right from the start the group has agreed that the guidelines are sexist. With such wording, not only are the scales tilted before the group even gets into the issues, but the group's thinking is pointed in a single direction. The phrasing of the question should neither prejudice the group's thinking nor indicate which direction the group will go in even before discussion begins.

It can be identified as one of fact, value, or policy. How you organize your discussion will depend on the kind of question. Later, we discuss organization; for now, let's consider the three types of questions.

1. **Fact.** Questions of fact concern truth or falsity. Implied in such questions is the possibility of determining the facts by way of directly observed, spoken, or recorded evidence. For instance, "Is Smith guilty of stealing equipment from the warehouse?" is a question of fact. Either Smith committed the crime, or he did not.

2. **Value.** Questions of **value** concern subjective judgments of quality and are characterized by the inclusion of some evaluative word such as *good, reliable, effective,* or *worthy.* For instance, advertisers may discuss the question "Is the proposed series of ads too sexually provocative?" In this case, "too sexually provocative" stands as the evaluative phrase. Another group may discuss the question "Is the sales force meeting the goals effectively?"

Although we can establish criteria for "too sexually provocative" and "effectively" and measure material against those criteria, there is no way to verify our findings objectively. The answer is still a matter of judgment, not fact.

3. **Policy.** Questions of **policy** ask whether or not a future action should be taken. "What should we do to lower the crime rate?" seeks a solution that would best address the problem of increased crime. "Should the university give equal amounts of money to men's and women's athletics?" seeks a tentative solution to the problem of how to achieve equity in the financial support of athletics. The inclusion of the word *should* in questions of policy makes them the easiest to recognize and the easiest to phrase of all discussion questions. Most issues facing work groups are questions of policy.

If you are discussing either a question of fact or a question of value, the remaining steps of problem solving (analyzing the problem, determining possible solutions, and selecting the best solution) are not relevant to your discussions. What kind of structure, then, is appropriate for discussing questions of fact and value?

Discussions of questions of fact focus primarily on finding the facts and drawing conclusions from them. For instance, in discussing the question "Is Smith guilty of stealing equipment from the warehouse?" the group would decide (1) whether facts can be assembled to show that Smith did take equipment from the warehouse and (2) whether his taking the equipment constituted stealing (as opposed to, say, borrowing or filling an order for equipment).

Discussions of questions of value follow a similar format. The difference is that with questions of value, the conclusions drawn from the facts depend on the criteria or measures used to weigh the facts. For instance, in discussing the question "Who is the most effective teacher in the department?" the group would decide (1) what the criteria for an "effective teacher" are and (2) which teacher meets those criteria better than other teachers in the department.

Analyzing the Problem

Analysis of a problem entails finding out as much as possible about the problem and determining the criteria that must be met to find an acceptable solution. If you were discussing the question "What should be done to equalize athletic opportunities for women on campus?", these two aspects of your analysis might be phrased as follows:

1. What has happened on campus that signifies the presence of a problem for women? (Nature of the problem)
    A. Have significant numbers of women been affected?
    B. Do women have less opportunity to compete in athletics than men?
    C. Has the university behaved in ways that have adversely affected women's opportunities?

2. By what means should we test whether a proposed solution solves the problem? (Criteria)
   A. Does the proposed solution cope with each of the problems uncovered?
   B. Can the proposed solution be implemented without creating new and perhaps worse problems?

Determining Possible Solutions

For most problems, many possible solutions can be found. At this stage of discussion, the goal is not to worry about whether a particular solution is a good one or not but to come up with a list of potential answers.

One way to identify potential solutions is to brainstorm for ideas. Brainstorming is a free-association procedure; that is, it involves stating ideas as they come to mind, without stopping to evaluate their merits, until you have compiled a long list. In a good ten- or fifteen-minute brainstorming session, you may think of several solutions by yourself. Depending on the nature of the topic, a group may come up with a list of ten, twenty, or more possible solutions in a relatively short time.

Brainstorming works best when the group postpones evaluating solutions until the list is complete. If people feel free to make suggestions—however bizarre they may sound—they will be much more inclined to think creatively

Brainstorming can be an effective method of problem solving in a group. Each person is encouraged to state ideas as they come to mind.

than if they fear that each idea will be evaluated on the spot. Later, each solution can be measured against the criteria. For the question on equalizing athletic opportunites for women, a framework for determining possible solutions might be outlined as follows:

3. What can be done to equalize opportunities? (Possible solutions)
   A. Can more scholarships be allocated to women?
   B. Can the time allocated to women's use of university facilities be increased to a level comparable with men's use?

Selecting the Best Solution

At this stage in the discussion, the group evaluates each prospective solution on the basis of how well it meets the criteria agreed on earlier. For the question on equalizing athletic opportunities for women, each solution would have to pass the following tests:

4. Which proposal (or combination) would work the best? (Best solution)
   A. How well would increasing women's scholarships solve each of the problems that have been identified? Would it create worse problems?
   B. How well would increasing women's time for use of facilities solve each of the problems that have been identified? Would it create worse problems?
   C. Based on this analysis, which solution is best?

In this section we've considered the steps for ensuring a thorough discussion of problems and solutions. These guidelines also result in an ethical discussion. The purpose of group problem solving is to reach a good decision based on a more thorough understanding of complex issues than could be developed by a single individual working alone. Therefore, when someone intentionally violates a guidelines for good discussion or manipulates the discussion so that some issues are not given full consideration, that person is behaving unethically. For example, if one person presented important but perhaps controversial information and then tried to get the group to accept the information without discussing it, that person would be behaving unethically.

TEST YOUR COMPETENCE

Group Decision Making

Divide into groups of about four to six. Each group has ten to fifteen minutes to arrive at a solution to one of the following: (1) What should professors do to discourage cheating on tests? (2) What should the college or university do to increase attendance at special events? (3) What should be the role of students in evaluating their curriculum? After discussion, each group should determine (1) what roles were operating in the group during the discussion; (2) who was filling those roles; (3) whether the group considered the nature of the problem, criteria, and possible solutions before arriving at a solution; and (4) what factors helped or hurt the problem-solving process.

Summary

Effective groups meet several criteria: They work in a physical and psychological setting that facilitates good interactions, they are of an optimum size, they

SKILL BUILDERS   Problem Solving: Fact/Value Questions

Skill
Arriving at a conclusion about a fact or value question.

Use
A guide for groups to follow in arriving at conclusions to fact or value questions.

Procedure
1. Clarify the specific fact or value question.

2. Analyze the question by determining the criteria that must be met to establish the fact or value.

3. Examine the facts to determine whether the subject meets those criteria.

Example
Question: "Did Branson behave ethically in firing Peters?" The group then discusses and arrives at the criteria for determining whether a firing procedure is ethical. Then the group considers whether Branson's procedure met those criteria.

SKILL BUILDERS   Problem Solving: Policy Questions

Skill
Arriving at a solution to a policy question by following four steps.

Use
A guide for groups to follow in finding solutions to policy questions.

Procedure
1. Clarify the specific policy question.

2. Analyze the question by finding out the nature of the problem and determining the criteria that must be met to find an acceptable solution.

3. Brainstorm potential solutions.

4. Select the solution that best meets the criteria.

Example
Question: "What should we do to increase alumni donations to the Department Scholarship Fund?" The group begins by discussing "Why are alumni not donating to the fund?" and asking "What criteria must be met to find an acceptable solution?" After brainstorming potential solutions, the group discusses each and selects the one or ones that best meet the criteria.

work as a cohesive unit, they show a commitment to the task, they develop and adhere to rules that help the group work, their members interact freely to reach consensus, their members are well prepared, and they contain people who have enough expertise and aggregate skills to meet key role requirements.

Group members may perform one or more of the task roles of giving information, seeking information, analyzing, expediting, and recording. They may also perform one or more of the maintenance roles of supporting, tension relieving, harmonizing, and gatekeeping. They should try to avoid the negative roles of aggressor, joker, withdrawer, and monopolizer.

Questions for group discussion may be questions of fact, value, or policy.

Effective work groups discussing questions of policy define the problem, analyze the problem, determine possible solutions, and then select the best solution.

REFLECT ON ETHICS

The Community Service and Outreach committee of Students in Communication was meeting to determine what cause should benefit from the annual fund-raising Talent Contest that SIC held each year.

"So," said Mark, "does anyone have any ideas about whose cause we should sponsor?"

"Well," replied Glenna, "I think we should give it to a group that's doing literacy work."

"Sounds good to me," replied Mark.

"My aunt works at the Boardman Center as the literacy coordinator, so why don't we just adopt them?" asked Glenna.

"Gee, I don't know much about the group," said Reed.

"Come on, you know, they help people learn how to read," replied Glenna sarcastically.

"Well, I was kind of hoping we'd take a look at sponsoring the local Teen Runaway Center," offered Kareem.

"Listen, if your aunt works at the Boardman Center," commented Laticia, "let's go with it."

"Right," said Pablo, "that's good enough for me."

"Yeah," replied Heather, "let's do it and get out of here."

"I hear what you're saying, Heather," Mark responded. "I've got plenty of other stuff to do."

"No disrespect meant to Glenna, but wasn't the Boardman Center in the news because of questionable use of funds?" countered Kareem. "Do we really know enough about them?"

"OK," said Mark, "enough discussion. I've got to get to class. All in favor of the literacy program at the Boardman Center indicate by saying 'aye.' I think we've got a majority. Sorry, Kareem, you can't win them all."

"I wish all meetings went this smoothly," Heather said to Glenna as they left the room. "I mean that was really a good meeting."

1. What did the group really know about the Boardman Center? Is it good group discussion practice to rely on a passing comment of one member?

2. Regardless of whether the meeting went smoothly, is there any ethical problem with the process? Explain.

OBJECTIVES

After you have read this chapter, you should be able to answer the following questions:

■ What are the two major characteristics of leadership?

■ What differentiates task-oriented and person-oriented leadership styles?

■ How do you prepare to lead groups?

■ What are the four most important specialized skills necessary for effective leadership?

Leadership
in Groups

"**C**hapman, as you know, I'm concerned with the basic skill levels of the people we've been interviewing for jobs in manufacturing. The more I think about it, the more I believe we need to play a more active role in providing adult education that would not only be good for the community, but I think would benefit us in the long run. The reason I called you in here was to see whether you would take leadership in setting up a group whose goal it is to establish an adult literacy program that our company could sponsor. You can select the people you'd like to work with, and I'll give you full support."

Like Norm Chapman, you are likely to be called on to take a leadership role. As much as we may believe that we're up to the task, we are often uncertain exactly how we should go about exercising leadership in group decision making.

Our goal in this chapter is to show what it means to be the leader of a work group, how to proceed if you want to try for leadership, and what you are responsible for doing in the group after you get the job. Although much of this discussion is applicable to all leadership situations, we focus on the question of leadership in the decision-making or work group context.

What Is Leadership?

The definition of leadership varies from source to source, yet common to most definitions are the ideas of exerting influence and reaching goals (Bass 1990, pp. 19–20). Let's explore these two ideas.

1. **Leadership means exerting influence.** Influence is the ability to bring about changes in the beliefs and actions of others. Although as a leader you can influence members indirectly by serving as a role model, in this chapter, we look at what you can do consciously to help guide your group through the decision-making process.

    The exercise of influence is different from the exercise of raw power. When you exercise raw power, you force the group to submit, perhaps against its will; when you influence others, you show them why an idea, a decision, or a means of achieving a goal is superior in such a way that they will follow your lead of their own free will. Members will continue to be influenced as long as they are convinced that what they have agreed to is right or is in their best interest as individuals or as a group.

2. **Leadership results in reaching a goal.** Reaching the goal means accomplishing the task or arriving at the best solution available at that time.

Becoming a Leader

Although one person is likely to be appointed or elected to lead a group, in actuality one or more of the other members of the group are likely to provide leadership at various times or under various circumstances. What determines effectiveness of leadership? Researchers have considered traits, styles, and situations, as well as possible gender differences.

Leadership Traits

In the past, researchers believed that there were certain traits that predict an individual's success as a leader (Bass 1990). For instance, Marvin Shaw (1981, p. 325) looked specifically at traits related to ability, sociability, motivation, and communication skills. He concluded that in the area of ability, leaders exceed average group members in intelligence, scholarship, insight, and verbal facility; in sociability, leaders exceed group members in dependability, activeness, cooperativeness, and popularity; in motivation, leaders exceed group members in initiative, persistence, and enthusiasm; and in communication, leaders exceed average group members in several skills discussed in the chapters on interpersonal communication. These general findings do not mean that the person with the highest intelligence, who is most liked, has the greatest enthusiasm, or communicates best will necessarily be the leader of any given group. However, it probably does mean that people are unlikely to be leaders if they do not exhibit at least some of these traits to a greater degree than do those they are attempting to lead.

Leadership means exerting influence and reaching a goal.

Do you perceive yourself as having many of these traits? If so, you are a potential leader. However, because several individuals in almost any grouping of people have the potential for leadership, which one ends up actually leading others depends on factors other than having these traits. One of the most important of these other factors is a person's style.

Leadership Styles

Although there is no one "right" way to lead, it is possible to identify the most common styles of leadership and how they affect the way groups work in various circumstances.

Most leaders tend to be either task-oriented (sometimes called authoritarian) or person-oriented (sometimes called democratic). As you read about these two major styles, notice that they correspond to the task and maintenance functions of groups described in Chapter 10.

The task-oriented leader exercises more direct control over the group. Task leaders will determine the statement of the question. They will make the analysis of procedure and state how the group is to proceed to arrive at the decision. They are likely to outline specific tasks for each group member and suggest the roles they want members to play.

The person-oriented or democratic leader may propose phrasings of the question, suggest procedure, and offer tasks or roles for individuals. But in every facet of the discussion, the person-oriented leader encourages group participation to determine what will actually be done. Everyone feels free to offer suggestions to modify the leader's proposals. What the group eventually does is determined by the group itself. Person-oriented leaders will listen, encourage, facilitate, clarify, and support. In the final analysis, however, it is the group that decides.

Pioneer work by Ralph White and Ronald Lippitt (1968) suggests the following advantages and disadvantages of each style: (1) More work is done under a task-oriented leader than under a person-oriented leader. (2) The least amount of work is done when no leadership exists. (3) Motivation and originality are greater under a person-oriented leader. (4) Task-oriented leadership may create discontent or result in less individual creativity. (5) More friendliness is shown in person-oriented groups.

Situational Leadership

So which style is to be preferred? Research by Fred Fiedler (1967) suggests that whether a particular leadership style is successful depends on the situation: (1) how good the leader's interpersonal relations are with the group, (2) how clearly defined the goals and tasks of the group are, and (3) to what degree the group accepts the leader as having legitimate authority to lead. Some situations will be favorable to the leader on all dimensions: The leader has good interpersonal relations with the group, the goal is clear, and the group accepts the leader's authority. Some situations will be unfavorable to the leader on all dimensions: The leader has poor interpersonal relations with the group, the goal is unclear, and the group fails to accept the leader's authority. Then, of course, there are situations that are partly favorable or partly unfavorable to the leader on the various dimensions.

Fiedler proposes that task leaders are most effective in favorable or extremely unfavorable situations. In positive situations, where the leader has good interpersonal relations, a clear goal, and group acceptance, the leader can focus entirely on the task. In very negative situations, there will be little that the leader can do to improve member perceptions, so the leader may as well storm forward on the task. Where people-oriented leadership is likely to be most effective is in those moderately good or bad situations in which the leader has the most to gain by improving interpersonal relations, clarifying the goal, and building credibility with the group.

Let's take an example. Suppose you are leading a group of employees who are meeting to determine the recipient of a merit award. If you have good interpersonal relations with the group, if the criteria for determining the award are clearly spelled out, and if the group accepts your authority, you are likely to be highly effective by adopting a task-oriented style of leadership. The group will understand what it is supposed to do and will accept your directions in proceeding to accomplish the task. If, on the other hand, your interpersonal relations with two of the group's four other members has been shaky, the group is not sure how it is supposed to go about making the decision, and at least two members of the group are undecided about your ability to lead, a person-oriented style of leadership is necessary. Before the group can really begin to function with the task, you will need to build your interpersonal relations with at least two members of the group, work with them to clarify the goal, and engage in behaviors that will help build your credibility. So, it isn't a matter of which style is always best; it is a matter of what kinds of circumstances are present.

Are leaders likely to be equally adept at task- and person-oriented styles? Although it is possible, many people show more skill at one or the other style. Thus in many groups, even those with a designated leader, more than one person is needed to fulfill all the leadership roles within the group. Throughout this book, we have discussed those kinds of skills that may be used to enable you to be skilled at either a task- or a people-oriented style.

Gender Differences in Leader Acceptability

A question that has generated considerable research is whether the gender of a leader has any effect on a group's acceptance of leadership. Research suggests that gender does affect group acceptance, but not because women lack the necessary traits or abilities. Negative perceptions are largely a result of sex-role stereotypes and devaluing.

Sex-role stereotypes influence how leaders' behaviors are perceived. A persistent research finding is that the same messages are evaluated differently

Sex-role stereotyping can influence how women leaders are perceived by the group.

depending on the source of message (Butler and Geis 1990, p. 54). Thus, women exhibiting certain behaviors will be considered bossy, dominating, and emotional, whereas men exhibiting essentially the same behaviors will be judged as responsible, as offering high-quality contributions, and as showing leadership. So the problem that women face is not that they don't possess or exhibit leadership characteristics, but that their efforts to show leadership are misperceived.

Moreover, sex-role stereotypes lead to devaluing cooperative and supportive behaviors that many women use quite skillfully. As Sally Helgesen (1990) points out, many female leaders are successful *because* they respond to people and their problems with flexibility and *because* they are able to break down barriers between people at all levels of the organization.

As a result of male bias and devaluing of female skills, some women get discouraged in seeking leadership roles. But changes in perception are occurring as the notion of "effective" leadership changes. Thus, as women continue to show their competence, they will be selected as leaders more often. As Jurma and Wright (1990, p. 110) have pointed out, research studies have shown that men and women are equally capable of leading task-oriented groups. Patricia

Andrews (1992, p. 90) supports this conclusion, noting that it is more important to consider the unique character of a group and the skills of the person
serving as leader than the sex of the leader. She goes on to show that a complex
interplay of factors (including how much power the leader has) influences effectiveness more than gender does.

By the mid 1990s, studies were showing that task-relevant communication
was the only significant predictor of who would emerge as a leader, regardless
of gender. Katherine Hawkins' (1995) study noted no significant gender differences in production of task-relevant communication. Such communication, it
seems, is the key to emergent leadership in task-oriented group interaction, for
either gender.

**OBSERVE AND
ANALYZE**

Leadership Preparation

Identify a group that you would like
to lead (such as a college or social
group committee). Write what you
would have to do to show (1) that
you are knowledgable about the
subject; (2) that you have worked
hard to be prepared; (3) that you can
be decisive; and (4) that you have
both people and task skills.

Preparing for Leadership

Suppose you want to have more opportunities to show your leadership abilities.
What can you do to encourage people and groups to support your leadership
efforts?

1. **Be knowledgeable about the particular tasks.** People are more willing to
   follow when the leader appears to be well informed. The more knowledgeable you are, the better you will be able to analyze individual contributions.

2. **Develop mental models for managing meaning.** Effective leaders make sure
   that people share meaning. But because their job requires them to behave
   spontaneously, they need to anticipate what might happen and have mental
   models available to deal with various contingencies. Gail T. Fairhurst—subject of this chapter's Spotlight on Scholarship—has done research on one
   such model called **framing.**

3. **Work harder than anyone else.** Leadership is often a question of setting an
   example. When members of a group see a person who is willing to do more
   than his or her fair share for the good of the group, they are likely to support that person. Of course, such hard work often takes a lot of personal
   sacrifice, but the person seeking to lead must be willing to pay the price.

4. **Be personally committed to the group's goals and needs.** To gain and maintain leadership takes great commitment to the particular task. The greater
   your commitment, the greater the chances are that group members will support you.

5. **Be willing to be decisive.** When leaders fail to act decisively, their groups
   can become frustrated and short-tempered. Sometimes leaders must make
   decisions that will be resented; sometimes they must decide between com-

SPOTLIGHT ON SCHOLARSHIP

Gail T. Fairhurst, Professor of Communication, University of Cincinnati, on Leadership in Work Organizations

According to Gail T. Fairhurst, who has studied organizational communication throughout her career, leadership is not a trait possessed only by some people, nor is it a simple set of behaviors that can be learned and then used in any situation. Rather, Fairhurst's research has convinced her that leadership is the process of creating social reality by managing the meanings that are assigned to certain behaviors, activities, programs, and events. Further, she believes that leadership is best understood as a relational process.

Fairhurst's current work is focused on how organizational leaders "frame" issues for their members. Framing is the process of managing meaning by selecting and highlighting some aspects of a subject, while excluding others. When we communicate our frames to others, we manage meaning because we are asserting that our interpretation of the subject—as opposed to other possible interpretations—should be taken as "real." How leaders choose to verbally frame events at work is one way that these leaders influence workers' and others' perceptions.

Framing is especially important when the organization experiences change, such as downsizing. To reduce their uncertainty during times of change, members of the organization seek to understand what the change "means" to them personally and to the way they work in the organization. Leaders are expected to help members understand what is happening and what it means. By framing the change, they select and highlight some features of the change while downplaying

others, providing a "lens" through which organizational members can understand what the change means.

In *The Art of Framing* (with Robert A. Sarr 1996), Fairhurst observes that leaders use five language forms or devices to frame information: metaphors, jargon or catch phrases, contrast, spin, and stories. Metaphors show how the change is similar to something that is already familiar. For instance, leaders may frame downsizing using weight and prizefighting metaphors, suggesting that the organization is "flabby and needs to get down to a better fighting weight so it can compete effectively." Jargon or catch phrases are similar to metaphors in that they help us understand the change in language with which we are already familiar, as in the phrase "lean and mean." Contrast frames help us understand what the change is by first seeing what it is not. Thus, a leader may say that downsizing "is not an attempt to undermine the union, it is simply an attempt to remain competitive." Spin frames cast the change in either a positive or a negative light. Using a positive spin frame, leaders may point out that the company will not use forced layoffs, but only early retirement and natural attrition, to reduce the size of the work force. Story frames make the change seem more "real" by providing examples, as when a leader recounts the success achieved by another well-known company that has used the same strategy.

Fairhurst has also studied how the meaning of a change is continually reframed as members of the organization work out the specifics of how to implement the change. She analyzed the transcripts of tape-recorded conversations between managers and their subordinates during times when the company was undergoing a significant change in the way that it worked. Her analysis revealed that employees' reactions to change are often framed as "predicaments" or "problems," showing that they are confused or unclear about the change, or they feel that what they are being asked to do is in conflict with the goals of the change. In response, the leader might counter the employee predicament by using one of several reframes—for example, "personalization." Using personalization, a leader might point out the specific behaviors that the employee needs to adopt in order to be in line with change. Fairhurst suggests that such reframing techniques help people understand what to do next to bring about the change.

Fairhurst's experience in analyzing the real conversations of managers and subordinates indicates that many of those in organizational leadership roles are not very good at framing and may need to be trained to develop mental models that they can draw on to be more effective during their day-to-day interactions with workers. For complete citations of many of Fairhurst's publications, see the references list at the end of this book.

Now that Fairhurst has completed a term as head of the Department of Communication Arts at the University of Cincinnati, she will resume her role as an active member of the faculty. In addition to teaching courses in organizational communication at both the graduate and undergraduate levels, Fairhurst works with the Center for Environmental Communication Studies, a research and consulting organization which she helped found.

peting ideas about courses of action. Any decisions leaders make may cause conflict. People who are unwilling or unable to be decisive are not going to maintain leadership for long.

6. **Develop people skills as well as task skills.** Most effective leaders have both person-oriented and task-oriented skills. Effective leaders make others in their groups feel good by supporting valuable statements, seeing to it that everyone gets a chance to contribute, and handling conflicts in ways that don't lead to hard feelings.

Leadership Functions

Three of the functions that leaders must be adept at are meeting management, coaching, and counseling.

Leading Group Discussion and Decision Making: Meeting Management

Within an organization, leadership often occurs in work groups. Entire books are devoted to leadership skills, but a few of the important skills necessary to leading work groups are planning the agenda, giving everyone an equal opportunity to speak, asking appropriate questions, dealing with cultural diversity, and summarizing discussion and crystallizing consensus.

Planning the agenda. An **agenda** is an outline of the topics that need to be covered at a meeting. When possible, the agenda should be in the hands of the group several days before the meeting. Unless group members get an agenda ahead of time, they won't be able to prepare for the meeting.

The agenda usually includes a sketch of the things that need to be accomplished. In a problem-solving discussion, the agenda comprises an outline of the steps of problem solving. Suppose you are leading a group concerned with integrating the campus commuter into the social, political, and extracurricular aspects of student life. Figure 11.1 shows a satisfactory agenda for a group discussing the question "What should be done to integrate the campus commuter into the social, political, and extracurricular aspects of student life?"

Although the meeting is unlikely to follow the exact sequence of the agenda, group members understand that the agenda questions will need to be answered before the group has finished its work.

Giving everyone an equal opportunity to speak (gatekeeping). Without leader direction, some people are likely to talk more than their fair share. For instance, in an eight-person group, left to its own devices, two or three people may tend to speak as much as the other five or six together, and one or two members may contribute little or nothing. As leader, you must assume that every member of the group has something to contribute. As a result, you may have to hold some members in check, and you may have to draw reluctant members into the discussion.

UNDERSTAND YOURSELF

Self-Monitoring

When you are a member of a group, are you inclined to keep mental track of your participation? If you have not talked as much as others, what strategies do you use to be heard? How effective are they? When you are really involved in the discussion question, do you tend to want to have more speaking opportunities than others? What do you do, if anything, to self-monitor?

March 1, 1997

To: Campus commuter discussion group
From: Janelle Smith
Re: Agenda for discussion group meeting

Date: March 8, 1997
Place: Student Union, Conference Room A
Time: 3:00 p.m. (Please be prompt.)

Please come prepared to discuss the following questions. Be sure to bring specific information you can contribute to the discussion of questions 1 through 4. We will consider question 5 on the basis of our resolution of the other questions.

Agenda for Group Discussion
Question: What should be done to integrate the campus commuter into the social, political, and extracurricular aspects of student life?

1. What percentage of the student body commute?
2. Why aren't commuters involved in social, political, and extracurricular activities? What specific factors hinder their involvement?
3. What criteria should be used to test possible solutions to the problem?
4. What are some possible solutions to the problem?
5. What one solution or combination of solutions will work best to solve the problem?

Figure 11.1
Agenda for discussion group meeting.

How to accomplish balance is a real test of leadership. If you want to clear the road for shy speakers who give clues that they want to speak, you might say something like, "Just a second, Lonnie, I think Dominique has something she wants to say here." Then instead of "Dominique, do you have anything to say here?" you may be able to phrase a question that requires more than a yes-or-no answer such as "Dominique, what do you think of the validity of this approach to combating crime?" When people contribute a few times, it builds up their confidence, which makes it easier for them to respond later when they have more to say.

Similar tact is called for in controlling overzealous speakers. You don't want to prevent talkative members from speaking. For example, Lonnie, the most talkative member, may be talkative because he has done his homework—if you turn him off, the group's work will suffer. After he has finished a turn but seems to want to speak again, you might try statements such as "Lonnie, you've made some excellent contributions; let's see whether we can get some reactions from other members of the group on this issue." Notice that a statement of this kind does not stop him; it suggests that he should hold off for a while.

Look at Figure 11.2. You will have achieved your goal of maintaining balance if the group's communication pattern is more like Figure 11.2c than either Figure 11.2a or 11.2b. Figure 11.2a shows a leader-dominated group. The lack of interaction often leads to a rigid, formal, and usually poor discussion. Figure

SKILL BUILDERS   Gatekeeping

Skill

A leader intrusion that is designed to achieve balance in group participation.

Use

To stimulate hesitant or reluctant members to contribute and to control overzealous members.

Procedure

1. Listen carefully to the discussion.

2. Note when some members are reluctant to share information or are unable to get the floor; also note when some members are dominating the discussion.

3. Phrase specific questions to reluctant members that require more than a yes-or-no answer; phrase statements that get talkative members to yield the floor without making them defensive.

Example

When Della notices that Maria seems to have something to say but can't get the floor, she might say, "Maria, I get the sense that you have something you've wanted to say here—tell us what you're thinking"; or when Della notices that Greg has talked three times in the last six turns even though there are five people in the group, she might say, "Greg, we want to hear what you have to say, but let's hear from those folks who haven't had a chance to be heard, and then we'll be sure to get back to you."

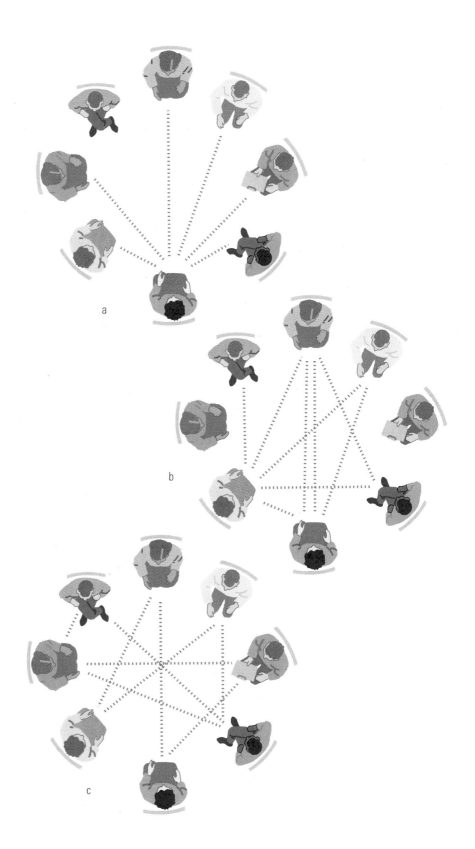

Figure 11.2
Three common patterns of group communication.

11.2b shows a more spontaneous group. Because three people dominate and two are not heard from, however, conclusions will not represent group thinking. Figure 11.2c shows something close to the ideal pattern. It illustrates a great deal of spontaneity, total group representation, and—theoretically, at least—the greatest likelihood for reliable conclusions.

Asking appropriate questions. Although people bring a variety of skills, information, and degrees of motivation to meetings, they do not always operate at peak efficiency without help from the leader. Perhaps one of the most effective tools of leadership is the ability to question appropriately. This skill requires knowing what kinds of questions to ask, and when to ask them.

The two most effective types of questions are those that call for supporting information and those that are completely open-ended and give members complete freedom of response. Try to avoid asking questions that can be answered yes or no, for after the yes-or-no answer you must either ask another question to draw people out or change the subject. For instance, rather than asking John whether he has had any professors who were particularly good lecturers, you could inquire, "John, what are some of the characteristics that made your favorite lecturers especially effective?"

Knowing when to ask questions is equally important. You will want to ask questions to initiate, to focus, to probe, and to deal with interpersonal problems.

1. **To initiate discussion.** When discussion of one point is drying up, you'll want to move discussion to a different point. For instance, "OK, we seem to have a pretty good grasp of the nature of the problem, but we haven't looked at any causes yet. What are some of the causes?"

2. **To focus discussion.** Sometimes people talk around points; at these times you'll want to ask questions to focus discussion. For instance, to relate

SKILL BUILDERS   Questioning

Skill	Use	Procedure	Example
A sentence phrased to get additional information.	To initiate discussion, to focus discussion, to probe for information, or to deal with interpersonal problems.	1. Listen carefully to the discussion. 2. Note the kind of information you want to get into the discussion. 3. Phrase specific questions that focus on achieving that particular goal. 4. Deliver them in a sincere tone of voice.	When Connie says, "Well, it would be better if she weren't so sedentary." Jeff, seeing a need to probe for additional information, replies, "I'm not sure that we all understand what you mean by 'sedentary'—would you explain?"

a statement to the larger topic in a discussion of marijuana use, you might ask, "Are you saying that the instances of marijuana's leading to hard-drug use don't indicate a direct causal relationship?" Or, in response to what has just been said, "How does that information relate to the point that Mary just made?" Or, to ask about an issue or an agenda item, "In what way does this information relate to whether or not marijuana is a health hazard?"

3. **To probe for information.** When comments are made and apparently accepted without discussion, you'll want to ask questions to probe for additional information. For example, to test the support for an assertion, you can say, "Where did you get that information, Miles?" or "That seems pretty important; what do we have that corroborates the point?" To test the strength of a point, you might ask, "Does that statement represent the thinking of the group?"

4. **To deal with interpersonal problems that develop.** Sometimes the leader can use questions to help members ventilate personal feelings. For example, "Ted, I've heard you make some strong statements on this point. Would you care to share them with us?" At times, a group may attack a person instead of the information that is being presented. Here you can say, "Juan isn't the issue here. Let's look at the merits of the information presented. Do we have any information that runs counter to this point?"

Keep in mind that too frequent use of questions can hurt the discussion that is taking place. The effective leader uses questions sparingly but incisively.

Dealing with cultural diversity. As John Brilhart and Gloria J. Galanes (1995) point out, every group discussion is "intercultural to some extent" (p. 107). Thus, it is important for a leader to recognize and accept differences within the group.

Most of us will see our group as comprised of individuals who, working hard enough together, can make changes. Thus, we see things from an individualistic rather than a collectivist worldview. According to Gudykunst and Kim (1992, pp. 42–43), individualistic cultures promote self-realization for their members; collectivist cultures require that individuals fit into the group. How might such differences in outlook affect a group and its work? From a collectivist point of view, the group is comprised of members that sacrifice for the good of the group. When a group does well, all members are praised. Likewise, if a member stands out from the group, the group may feel an obligation to force the individual to conform. Such a view differs from the individualistic point of view, which says that although the group is a group, it is comprised of individuals and it is all right to praise an individual for his or her contribution to the group effort. Moreover, from an individualistic perspective, it is important to stand out.

To deal with these sorts of differences, Brilhart and Galanes (1995) suggest that before drawing inferences about group members when their behavior appears to be generally different, ask yourself whether you could be observing a cultural difference, and if so, try to adapt to different cultural practices (p. 107). Because this book is written from an individualist perspective, your task may prove to be even more difficult when you as a leader hold a collectivist perspective. Before a group with major cultural differences can work effectively, it is important for all members to recognize such differences and be willing to try to work through them.

Summarizing and crystallizing consensus. Often, when a group talks for a considerable time around a topic, the members become uncertain as to what has been said and agreed to. During the discussion, individuals might draw six, eight, ten, or even fifteen conclusions that relate to agenda items. Some will be compatible; others will be contradictory.

It is up to the leader to point out intermediate conclusions by summarizing what has been said and pointing out areas of agreement and disagreement before seeking consensus. Following are some phrases that can be used to summarize and assess consensus:

> "I think most of us are stating the same points. Are we really in agreement that . . ." (State the conclusion.)

> "We've been discussing this for a while, and I think I sense an agreement. Let me state it, and then we'll see whether it does summarize the group's feeling." (State the conclusion.)

> "Now we're getting into another area. Let's make sure that we are really agreed on the point we've just finished." (State the conclusion.)

> "Are we ready to summarize our feelings on this point?" (State the conclusion.)

Coaching Others at Work

Coaching "is a day-to-day, hands-on process of helping others recognize opportunities to improve their work performance" (Robbins and Hunsaker 1996, p. 151). A good coach observes what people are doing, shows them the problems or inefficiencies with their methods, offers suggestions for improving their methods, and helps use the methods effectively. Of course, effective coaching requires a supportive climate and using the active listening skills of paraphrasing, questioning, and supporting.

1. **An effective coach is a technically adept and keen observer.** You cannot coach effectively if you do not understand the correct or more efficient way to perform the particular behavior. In addition, as a coach your technical expertise is of little value unless you carefully watch people perform and note their deficiencies. For example, Sandy's task force on reducing crime on campus is to present its recommendations at a meeting of the President's Cabinet. If Sandy is an accomplished public speaker who has done premier presentations, she is technically competent to coach team members on their

THINK CRITICALLY

Effective Coaching

Think about two situations in which someone else has coached you. Pick one that was effective and one that was ineffective. What was similar and what was different between what the coaches did?

INFOTRAC COLLEGE EDITION

Using InfoTrac College Edition, under the subject "executive coaching" click on periodical references. Look for articles that discuss (1) how coaching is done and (2) what kinds of services outside companies offer organizations to improve their leadership effectiveness. For variety, change the subject to just "coaching." Look for information related to athletic coaching that can be used by business leaders.

PRACTICE IN CLASS

Coaching Skills

Working in groups of three, have each person think of a communication problem they experience. Then have one person describe a problem while a second person serves as the coach. The third person observes. When the two have finished, the observer "coaches the coach" by providing feedback on the coaching behavior. Change roles and repeat the process until each person has had an opportunity to coach.

presentations. When they rehearse the presentation, Sandy may carefully observe their trial run and take notes on what she sees.

2. **An effective coach both analyzes and supplies specific suggestions for improvement.** Some people are good observers, but they don't really know what the employee needs to do to improve. For instance, a new sales associate may be weak on closing deals because he or she misses cues that people give to show that they're receptive to what the sales associate is saying. An effective coach not only spots the negative—the failure to close—but also uses her or his expertise to help the young sales associate identify the cues that indicate the right time for moving into the close.

3. **An effective coach creates a supportive problem-solving environment.** Some people are excellent observers, and know exactly what needs to be done, but end up antagonizing the other by being "preachy." An effective coach helps people improve their performance by creating a positive problem-solving environment.

An effective coach will often begin by acknowledging an area of strength that suggests the other has undeveloped potential. For instance, in our example, the coach may praise the young sales associate's product knowledge by saying, "Lydell, I've watched you work, and you have really developed a lot of product knowledge. I think you're really going to be good at this job. Would you like to know what you might be able to do to increase your percentage of sales?" This approach helps Lydell see that they have shared goals. When a person makes a mistake, rather than jumping all over the person, the effective coach might say something like, "Lydell, I think you lost a sale you might have gotten. Can you think of what you might have done differently that will help you close sales like this in the future?" Finally, when the person does succeed, effective coaches praise them but also ask them to reflect on why they were successful. "Lydell, wow, a $300 sale! What did you do this time to close such a big sale?"

Counseling

Whereas coaching deals primarily with work performance, counseling involves helping others deal with their personal problems. Specifically, **counseling** is the discussion of an emotional problem with another in order to resolve the problem or help the other cope better (Robbins and Hunsaker 1996, p. 153). Under the pressures of work and in some cases living in general, people experience a variety of problems that affect their lives in general and their performance at work in particular. These problems include coping with the death of a loved one, lingering illness, divorce and its aftermath, and financial problems. They also include the effects of chemical dependence, depression, and overwhelming anxiety. At work, then, we will sometimes need to demonstrate our leadership through counseling. Effective counselors maintain confidentiality, listen empathically to others' feelings and circumstances, and help others determine what to do, including seeking professional help.

1. **Effective counselors assure confidentiality.** Personal problems are just that—personal. Colleagues at work often avoid discussing such issues with their supervisors, but talk freely to coworkers. Under most circumstances, effective counselors do not tell anyone else another's personal problems. Just because a coworker prefaces a remark with "Don't tell anyone," however, doesn't relieve us from the ethical responsibility to let the other know the limits to which we will go to maintain his or her confidentiality. There are some circumstances under which maintaining confidentiality would be wrong—for example, keeping confidential information that could jeopardize the health or well-being of others. Under these circumstances, ethical counselors first advise the person to disclose the information to an appropriate authority and, second, inform the other that the leader is ethically bound to disclose.

2. **Effective counselors are good listeners.** Good counseling begins with empathic listening. Empathic listening results in appropriate responses. So, a good counselor will ask questions for clarification, paraphrase to make sure they understand, and most of all provide comforting replies. Supportiveness and at times interpreting responses are keys to effective counseling. When people are emotionally distraught, they need to talk out their feelings. Only after they have vented these powerful emotions can they begin the logical problem-solving process. So, effective counselors need to listen and ask questions, sometimes for long periods of time.

3. **Effective counselors help colleagues find help.** At times the best thing a good lay counselor-leader can do next is to suggest that people could benefit from professional help with their particular problems. Many of the kinds of problems we face do not call for professional treatment. But when peer counselors see that the problems are long-term or severe, they are ethically bound to try to use their leadership—their influence—to help others seek appropriate professional guidance. By way of preparation, it is useful to be familiar with the kinds of services available within your business or organization. Some large companies have employee assistance programs, various services are available in the community, and some religious organizations also have professional counselors on staff.

Leaders cannot be expected to and should not act as professional counselors, but because some problems are of short duration and not overly intense, leaders can use their influence to help others sort through and triumph over personal problems.

THINK CRITICALLY

Counseling Guidelines

How will you know when another person needs more help than you can provide by peer counseling? Develop a list of ten guidelines to help you identify when you need to counsel another to seek professional help. Be ready to share your list in class.

PRACTICE IN CLASS

Exercising Leadership Responsibilities

In groups of five, discuss a topic such as "What can be done to increase student motivation to keep classrooms free of litter?" Each person leads the group for approximately five minutes. After everyone has had a chance to lead, discuss efforts at giving people equal opportunity to speak, asking questions, and summarizing. Focus on behaviors that characterized successful efforts.

DILBERT reprinted by permission of United Features Syndicate, Inc.

Evaluating Group Communication

You are likely to learn to increase your effectiveness in groups as you get feedback about individual and group performance. Groups can be evaluated on the quality of the decision, the quality of individual participation, and the quality of leadership.

The Decision

The questionnaire in Figure 11.3 gives you a framework for evaluating the quality of a group's decision. This questionnaire calls for you to consider the following three major questions:

1. **Did the group arrive at a decision?** That a group meets to discuss does not necessarily mean that it will arrive at a decision. As foolish as it may seem, some groups thrash away for hours only to adjourn without having come to a conclusion. Of course, some groups discuss such serious problems that a decision cannot be reached without several meetings. In such cases, it is important to ensure that the group adjourns with a clear understanding of what the next step will be. When a group "finishes" its work without arriving at some decision, however, the result is likely to be frustration and disillusionment.

2. **What action will be taken as a result of the decision?** Problem-solving decisions imply implementation. If the group has "finished" without considering means for putting the decision into action, there is reason to question the practicality of the decision.

3. **Was the group decision a good one?** This may be the most difficult question to answer. Of course, whether a decision is good or bad is a value judgment. I suggest applying six criteria for such an evaluation:

   a. Was quality information presented to provide a basis for the decision?

   b. Were the data discussed fully?

   c. Did interim conclusions relate to information presented, or were they stated as opinions that had no relation to content?

   d. Did a given conclusion seem to be the product of consensus, or was it determined by the persuasive or authoritarian power of the leader?

   e. Was the final decision measured against some set of criteria or objectives?

   f. Did the group agree to support the decision?

Individual Participation

Although a group will struggle without good leadership, it may not be able to function at all without members who are willing and able to meet the task and maintenance functions of the group. The questionnaire in Figure 11.4 incorporates each of the elements considered in Chapter 10 on group participation and provides a simple checklist that can be kept for each individual.

Leadership

Although some group discussions are leaderless, no discussion should be without leadership. If there is an appointed leader—and most groups have one—evaluation can focus on that individual. If the group is truly leaderless, the evaluation should consider attempts at leadership by the various members or focus on the apparent leader who emerges from the group. Figure 11.5 contains a simple checklist for evaluating group leadership.

Group Decision Analysis

Analysis of group characteristics: _____

_____

Did the group arrive at a decision? Explain. _____

_____

What action was taken as a result of that decision? Explain. _____

_____

Was the group decision a good one? Explain. _____

_____

Was quality information presented? _____

_____

Were the data fully discussed? _____

_____

Did interim conclusions reflect group discussion? _____

_____

Were conclusions measured against some set criteria? _____

_____

Did the group arrive at the decision by consensus? _____

_____

Did the group agree to support the decision? _____

_____

Figure 11.3

Form for evaluating group decisions.

Individual's Group Participation Checklist

For each of the following questions, rate the participant on a scale of 1 to 5:
1 = high; 2 = good; 3 = average; 4 = fair; 5 = poor.

Preparation	1	2	3	4	5
Seems to be well prepared	❑	❑	❑	❑	❑
Is aware of the problem	❑	❑	❑	❑	❑
Analyzes the problem	❑	❑	❑	❑	❑
Suggests possible solutions	❑	❑	❑	❑	❑
Tests each solution	❑	❑	❑	❑	❑

Carrying Out Roles					
As information or opinion giver	❑	❑	❑	❑	❑
As information seeker	❑	❑	❑	❑	❑
As analyzer	❑	❑	❑	❑	❑
As expediter	❑	❑	❑	❑	❑
As recorder	❑	❑	❑	❑	❑
As supporter	❑	❑	❑	❑	❑
As tension reliever	❑	❑	❑	❑	❑
As harmonizer	❑	❑	❑	❑	❑
As gatekeeper	❑	❑	❑	❑	❑

Avoiding Negative Roles					
As aggressor	❑	❑	❑	❑	❑
As joker	❑	❑	❑	❑	❑
As withdrawer	❑	❑	❑	❑	❑
As monopolizer	❑	❑	❑	❑	❑

Write an analysis of the person's group participation (two to five paragraphs) based on this checklist.

Figure 11.4

Form for evaluating individual participation.

Group Leadership Checklist

For each of the following questions, rate the participant on a scale of 1 to 5:
1 = high; 2 = good; 3 = average; 4 = fair; 5 = poor

Preparation to Lead	1	2	3	4	5
Understands topic	❏	❏	❏	❏	❏
Works hard	❏	❏	❏	❏	❏
Shows commitment	❏	❏	❏	❏	❏
Interacts freely	❏	❏	❏	❏	❏
Is decisive	❏	❏	❏	❏	❏

Leading the Group					
Has group of optimum size	❏	❏	❏	❏	❏
Creates and maintains a suitable atmosphere	❏	❏	❏	❏	❏
Works to develop a cohesive unit	❏	❏	❏	❏	❏
Helps the group develop appropriate rules	❏	❏	❏	❏	❏
Has an agenda	❏	❏	❏	❏	❏
Promotes systematic problem solving	❏	❏	❏	❏	❏
Asks good questions	❏	❏	❏	❏	❏
Encourages balanced participation	❏	❏	❏	❏	❏
Refrains from dominating group	❏	❏	❏	❏	❏
Deals with conflict	❏	❏	❏	❏	❏
Arrives at decisions by means of consensus or voting	❏	❏	❏	❏	❏
Brings discussion to a satisfactory close	❏	❏	❏	❏	❏

Write an analysis (two to five paragraphs) based on this checklist.

Figure 11.5
Form for evaluating group leadership.

REFLECT ON ETHICS

"You know, Sue, we're going to be in deep trouble if the group doesn't support McGowan's resolution about dues reform."

"Well, we'll just have to see to it that all the arguments in favor of that resolution are heard. "But in the end, it's the group's decision."

"That's very democratic of you, Sue, but you know that if it doesn't pass, you're likely to be out on your tail."

"That may be, Heather, but I don't see what I can do about it."

"You don't want to see. First, right now the group respects you. If you would just apply a little pressure on a couple of the members, you'd get what you want."

"What do you mean?"

"Look, this is a good cause. You've got something on just about every member of the group. Take a couple aside and let them know that this is payoff time. I think you'll see that some key folks will see it your way."

Heather may well have a point about how Sue can control the outcome. Should Sue follow Heather's advice? Why?

Summary

Leadership means exerting influence to accomplish a goal. Although leaders may show greater degrees of ability, sociability, motivation, and communication skills than others in the group, the presence of such traits does not guarantee that you will lead effectively.

How well you lead may depend on your style and how you put it into operation. Some leaders adopt the task-oriented style, focusing on what needs to be done and how to do it; others adopt the person-oriented style, focusing on interpersonal relationships of group members. As Fiedler's work has shown, how a leader performs depends on the interaction of task structure, leader–member relations, and position power. If you hope to earn the support of group members for leadership, you will want to be knowledgeable about the task, work harder than others in the group, be personally committed to group goals and needs, be willing to be decisive, interact freely with others in the group, and develop skill in maintenance and task functions.

Leaders have several specific functions. To lead a group well, you must plan an agenda, ensure everyone has an equal opportunity to speak, ask appropriate questions, deal with cultural diversity, and summarize as needed. You may also demonstrate your leadership through coaching and counseling.

You can evaluate a group's performance in terms of the group's decision, the participation of its members, and the quality of its leadership.

S E L F - R E V I E W

Group Communication from Chapters 10 and 11

What kind of a group communicator are you? The following analysis looks at ten specifics that are basic to a group communication profile. On the line provided for each statement, indicate the response that best captures your behavior: 1, never; 2, rarely; 3, occasionally; 4, often; 5, almost always.

_____   I enjoy participating in group discussions like committees. (Ch. 10)

_____   I prepare well beforehand for group discussions. (Ch. 10)

_____   I analyze a problem to determine the questions that need to be asked in order to solve the problem. (Ch. 10)

_____   I contribute freely and openly in groups. (Ch. 10)

_____   My contributions are very helpful in the group's effort to accomplish its task. (Ch. 10)

_____   I help the group consider whether material presented is relevant. (Ch. 10)

_____   I am good at saying things that help the group work well together. (Ch. 10)

_____   I try to provide leadership for the group. (Ch. 11)

_____   When I am a leader, I provide the members of the group with a carefully thought-out suggested procedure. (Ch. 11)

_____   When I am a leader, I ask relevant questions that help the group move forward with its task. (Ch. 11)

Based on your responses, select the group communication behavior that you would most like to change. Write a communication improvement goal statement similar to the sample goal statement in Chapter 1 (page 24). If you would like verification of your self-analysis before you write a goal statement, have a friend or coworker complete this same analysis for you.

Although many people seem to think that public speaking isn't relevant to them, right from the start we want to emphasize that developing your public-speaking skill is important to you. Why? Mostly because skill at public speaking is a form of empowerment.

First, effective public speakers communicate information to people in a way that enables them to use that information to make sound decisions. Many of the most important issues facing us involve information that is not easily understood. In these instances, it is vital to have spokespersons who can explain complex information in a way that *all* members of an audience can understand.

Second, effective public speakers are able to present information in ways that influence people's attitudes and behavior. It's one thing to have good ideas—and quite another to persuade people to believe in their value and act on them. Politicians might have excellent ideas for lowering taxes, dealing with crime, and eliminating poverty, but if they cannot convince voters of the value of their plans, they won't get elected.

Third, effective public-speaking skill is necessary in moving up the organizational ladder. From presenting oral reports and proposals, to responding to questions, to training coworkers, we all spend important time in speaking activities. Now perhaps you see why a course in public speaking is truly a form of empowerment.

Still, many of us think that effective speakers are born not made—nothing can be further from the truth. Even Demosthenes, the great Athenian orator who is often cited as the prototype of brilliant speaking, was highly criticized as a speaker when he first entered public life. In fact, the time and effort he spent improving his speaking stands as a testament to the importance and value of hard work. The lesson to be learned? Effective public speaking is a learned activity.

In order to have the greatest chance of presenting an effective speech in any situation, you need to have a plan—a strategy for achieving your goal. An effective speech plan is a product of five action steps, presented and discussed in Chapters 12 through 16. In the final two chapters, we consider additional skills related specifically to speeches intended to inform and to persuade.

IV

PUBLIC SPEAKING

OBJECTIVES

After you have read this chapter, you should be able to answer the following questions:

- How do you brainstorm for topics?

- How do you compile audience data?

- How do you predict level of audience interest in, knowledge of, and attitude toward your topic?

- What are the key physical and psychological conditions affecting the speech?

- How do you write and test your speech goal?

12

Topic and Goal

As a graduate who has "made good" and is on scholarship at a major university, Ayanna has been invited to speak to an assembly at her old inner-city high school. She's excited by the invitation but also anxious about the speech. She feels vaguely that she might have a lot to say to the students coming up behind her, but she wonders whether they will be interested in her speech and isn't quite sure where to begin her preparation or exactly what her focus should be. She wonders, "Where do I start?"

Many of us find ourselves in situations like Ayanna's. We have a general idea of some of the kinds of things we might like to include in a speech but don't know how to put it all together.

An effective speech plan is a product of five action steps. In this chapter, we consider the first step: **Determine a specific speech goal that is adapted to your audience and occasion.** This step involves selecting a topic from a subject area that is important to you and that you know something about, analyzing your audience and the speaking occasion, and finally, articulating your goal by determining the response that you want from your audience. Although each issue in the process is discussed separately, they do overlap and are sometimes accomplished in a different order.

Selecting a Topic from a Subject Area

In real-life settings, people are invited to give speeches because of their expertise on a particular subject. But even when an organization requests a speech on a particular subject, selecting the topic is often in the hands of the speaker. What is the difference between subject and topic? A **subject** is a broad area of knowl-

You will be a more forceful speaker if you plan your speech carefully so that your goal or purpose is clear to your audience.

© Cable News Network, Inc.

edge, such as the stock market, cognitive psychology, baseball, or the Middle East. A **topic** is some specific aspect of a subject. Thus, an authority on the subject of the stock market might be prepared to speak on such diverse topics as the nature of the New York Stock Exchange, NASDAQ, investment strategies, or bull versus bear markets.

The goal of this section is to help you identify some suitable subject areas and then select potential specific topics from those subject areas.

Identifying Subjects

When you are asked (or required) to give a speech, use the same criteria for identifying subjects as those used by professional speakers. Start by identifying subject areas that (1) are important to you and (2) you know something about, and then select suitable topics within those areas.

Subjects that meet these criteria probably include such things as your vocation (major, prospective profession, or current job), your hobbies or leisure activities, and your special interests (social, economic, educational, or political concerns). Thus, if retailing is your actual or prospective vocation, tennis is your favorite activity, and problems of illiteracy, substance abuse, and toxic and nontoxic waste are your special concerns, then these are subject areas from which you could draw topics.

At this point it is tempting to think, "Why not just talk on something I know an audience wants to hear?" The reason for avoiding this temptation is that an audience chooses to listen to a speaker *because* of perceived expertise or insight in a particular subject. When even professional speakers believe that they can talk about anything, they find it very easy to get in "over their heads."

Of course, over time you can become an expert in a particular subject area, and occasionally you may be asked to speak on subjects that are less familiar to you, but to begin with it's a good idea to speak about those subject areas in which you already have spent months or years developing expertise and insight.

Obviously, speakers do need to be sensitive to the needs of audience and occasion. As we will see, information about audience and occasion helps shape the speech goal and determine the kinds of information to use in a speech.

Brainstorming for Topics

To generate a list of specific topics from the subject areas you have identified, you can use **brainstorming**—an uncritical, nonevaluative process of generating associated ideas. Under the subject of tennis, for example, you might list players (Pete Sampras, Martina Hinges), equipment (rackets, balls, shoes), strokes (serves, volleys, forehands, backhands, lobs), strategy (net play, baseline shots), tournaments (Wimbledon, U.S. Open), and surfaces (grass, clay, concrete). When you start with a subject area of expertise and interest, you can often list twenty, thirty, fifty, or even more related topics.

Hobby: Computers

games	software	graphics	printers
spreadsheets	windows	hard disk	floppy disk
hardware	hacking	programming	memory
mouse	word processing	keyboards	color monitors
uses	networks	costs	CD-ROM
capabilities	viruses	databases	ethics

Figure 12.1
Brainstorming.

Brainstorming allows you to take advantage of a basic commonsense principle: Just as it is easier to select a correct answer to a multiple-choice question than to think of the answer to the same question without the choices, so too it is easier to select a topic from a list than to come up with a topic out of the blue. Instead of asking "What should I talk about?" ask yourself, "What is the topic under each subject heading that is most compelling to me?" Figure 12.1 depicts a brainstorming list for the subject "Computers" under the heading "Hobby."

Audience Analysis

Speeches are given for a particular audience. No matter what your specific topic, how you go about discussing that topic depends to a large extent on the nature of your audience. Consequently, early in your preparation process you need to analyze your prospective audience.

Audience analysis is the study of the specific audience for your speech. It includes (1) gathering essential audience demographic data in order to determine in what ways a majority of audience members are alike and (2) making predictions of audience level of interest in, knowledge of, and attitudes toward

---

PRACTICE IN SPEECH PREPARATION

Brainstorming for Topics

The goal of this practice is to help you identify three prospective topics for your first speech.

Divide a sheet of paper into three columns. Label column 1 with your major or vocation, such as Art History; label column 2 with a hobby or an activity, such as Chess; and label column 3 with a concern or an issue, such as Water Pollution.

Working on one column at a time, brainstorm a list of at least twenty related topics for each column (see Figure 12.1).

Check one topic in each column that has special meaning to you or that seems particularly appropriate for your classroom audience. Then select the one topic out of these three that you will consider for your first speech.

SKILL BUILDERS Brainstorming

Skill	Use	Procedure	Example
An uncritical, nonevaluative process of generating associated ideas.	To generate a list of specific topics from the subject areas you have identified.	1. Label a column with your major or vocation, a hobby or activity, or a concern or issue. 2. Without trying to evaluate them, list at least twenty one- or two-word related ideas or topics. 3. Check the one topic that has special meaning to you or that seems particularly appropriate for your classroom audience.	Under the column marked Tennis (a hobby), you might list rackets, balls, strokes, net play, tournaments, serving, stars, leagues, footwear, racket stringing, lobs, strategy, singles, doubles, forehand, backhand, overhead, surfaces, clay, grass. Then, from the list, you might select racket stringing.

you and your topic. The results of this analysis can guide you in determining your goal, selecting supporting material, and organizing and presenting your speech. And of course, audience analysis serves as a prelude to determining strategies for audience adaptation.

Effective speakers make awareness of their audience a central focus of their speech preparation process.

Gathering Audience Data

Let's first consider what kinds of audience data you need for your speech; then we'll consider ways in which you can get that information.

Since all audiences are different, sometimes in subtle ways, the goal of audience analysis is to find out how the members of a particular audience are alike so that later you'll have a basis for selecting information that will resonate with large segments of the audience.

The specific categories in which you need accurate audience data are age, education, gender, occupation, income, culture, geographic uniqueness, and group affiliation.

Age. You will want data to confirm both the average age and the age range.

Education. You want data to confirm whether audience members have high school, college, or postcollege education or whether their education levels are mixed.

Gender. You will want data to confirm whether your audience will be primarily male, primarily female, or fairly well balanced.

Occupation. You want data to confirm whether the majority of your audience have a single occupation, such as nursing, banking, drill-press operating, teaching, or sales.

Income. You will want data to confirm that the average income level of the audience is high, low, or average.

Culture. You want data to confirm whether your audience is alike ethnically, including race, religion, and nationality.

Geographic uniqueness. You want data to confirm whether audience members are from the same state, city, or neighborhood.

Group affiliation. You want data to confirm whether the majority of audience members belong to the same social or fraternal group.

Now that we have considered the kinds of audience data you need to help you predict how an audience will receive your speech, let's consider the three ways you can gather that information.

1. **Assemble data you have observed.** If you are in some way associated with your audience (as you are with your classroom audience), you can get much of the significant data about them from personal observation. For instance, from being in class for even a couple of sessions, you will have a good idea of class members' approximate age, the ratio of men to women, and their racial makeup. As you listen to them talk, you will learn more about their interest in, knowledge of, and attitudes about many issues.

2. **Question the person who scheduled your speech.** When you are invited to speak, ask your contact person to supply as much of the relevant data as

possible. Even if the information is not as specific as you would like, it will still be useful.

3. **Make intelligent guesses about audience demographics.** If you can't get information in any other way, you will have to make informed guesses based on such indirect information as the general makeup of the people who live in a specific community or the kinds of people who are likely to attend a speech on your topic.

Predicting Audience Reactions

The next step in audience analysis is to use the data you've collected to predict the audience's potential interest in, knowledge of, and attitudes toward you and your topic. These predictions form a basis for the development of your speech strategy, which we will consider in greater detail in Chapter 15, Adapting to Audiences Verbally and Visually.

Audience interest. Your first goal is to predict how interested the audience is likely to be in your topic. For instance, suppose you are planning to give a speech on cholesterol to your classroom audience. You can predict that you will have to build audience interest. Why? Because the cholesterol–heart attack connection is not meaningful to most college-age students.

Audience understanding. Your second goal is to predict whether the audience has sufficient background to understand your information. For instance, for a speech on big band music or folk music, an older audience is likely to have better background knowledge than a younger audience. On the other hand, for a speech on rap music, a younger audience is likely to have better background knowledge than an older audience.

Audience attitude toward you as speaker. Your third goal is to predict your audience's attitude toward you. Your success in informing or persuading an audience is likely to depend on whether it perceives you as a *credible* source of information. Although speech experts differ in listing the characteristics of credibility, most include knowledge and expertise, trustworthiness, and personality.

1. **Knowledge and expertise** include your qualifications, capability, or what is referred to as your "track record." Is there any information to suggest that your audience will accept you as an authority on your topic? If you answer yes, what makes you think so? For instance, an audience is likely to believe that a professor of economics is knowledgeable about the stock market, but not necessarily about hockey, the Pyramids, or weather patterns.

2. **Trustworthiness** refers both to a person's character (honesty, dependability, moral strength) and apparent motives (reasons for giving a speech on this topic). Is there any information to suggest that your audience will see you as having character or good motives? If you answer yes, what makes you

think so? For instance, an audience for a speech about the effects of smoking tobacco is more likely to consider a physiologist trustworthy than an executive of a tobacco company.

3. **Personality** refers to a person's likability, often based on first impressions. Is there any information to suggest that your audience will find you likable? If you answer yes, what makes you think so? For instance, audiences often look favorably on speakers who show enthusiasm, who seem to be warm and friendly, have a ready smile, and seem to really care about the audience. Because perception of personality weighs so much in determining a person's credibility, we'll focus on the elements of effective delivery in Chapter 16.

Audience attitude toward your topic. Your final goal is to predict your audience's attitude toward your topic. Audience attitudes are usually expressed by opinions that may be distributed along a continuum from highly favorable to hostile. Even though any given audience may have one or a few individuals with opinions at nearly every point of the distribution, in most audiences opinions will tend to cluster at a particular point on the continuum. Except for polling the audience, there is no way to be sure about your assessment, but you can make reasonably accurate estimates based on demographic knowledge. Is there any information to suggest that your audience will have a favorable attitude toward listening to a speech on your topic? If you answer yes, what makes you think so? For instance, unskilled workers are likely to look at minimum-wage proposals differently than are business executives; many men will look at women's rights proposals differently than will most women; a meeting of the local Right-to-Life chapter will look at abortion differently than will a meeting of NOW (National Organization for Women). The more data you have about your audience and the more experience you have in analyzing audiences, the better are your chances of accurately predicting audience attitudes.

PRACTICE IN SPEECH PREPARATION

Analyzing Your Audience

The goal of this exercise is to help you determine the nature of your speech audience and record your predictions about their response to your prospective speech topic.

1. Copy or duplicate the audience analysis checklist (Figure 12.2). Next to the second heading, Predictions, write the topic you plan to use for your first speech.

2. Fill in the checklist, including both data about your classroom audience and predictions about their reaction to your topic.

3. Save the results. You will use the data from this checklist to help you determine a strategy for adapting to your audience.

Checklist: Audience Analysis

Data

1. The audience education level is ____ high school ____ college ____ post-college.

2. The age range is from ____ to ____ . The average age is about ____ .

3. The audience is approximately ____ percent male and ____ percent female.

4. My estimate of the income level of the audience is ____ below average ____ average ____ above average.

5. The audience is basically ____ the same race ____ a mixture of races.

6. The audience is basically ____ the same religion ____ a mixture of religions.

7. The audience is basically ____ the same nationality ____ a mixture of nationalities.

8. The audience is basically from ____ the same state ____ the same city ____ the same neighborhood ____ different areas.

Predictions

1. Audience interest in this topic is likely to be ____ high ____ moderate ____ low.

2. Audience understanding of the topic will be ____ great ____ moderate ____ little.

3. Audience attitude toward me as speaker is likely to be ____ positive ____ neutral ____ negative.

4. Audience attitude toward my topic will be ____ positive ____ neutral ____ negative.

Figure 12.2
Audience analysis checklist.

Analyzing the Occasion and Setting

Analysis of the occasion and setting provides a speaker with guidelines for both meeting audience expectations and determining the tone of the speech.

1. **How large will the audience be?** If you are anticipating a small audience (perhaps up to 50 people or so), you can gear yourself for an informal setting in which you are close to all listeners. With a small audience, you can talk in a normal voice and feel free to move about. In contrast, if you anticipate a large audience, in addition to needing a microphone, you will probably want to make your presentation more formal.

2. **When will the speech be given?** The time of day can affect how the speech is received. If a speech is scheduled after a meal, for instance, the audience may be lethargic, mellow, or even on the verge of sleep. As a result, it helps

to insert more "attention getters"—examples, illustrations, and stories—to counter potential lapses of attention.

3. **Where in the program does the speech occur?** If you are the featured speaker, you have an obvious advantage: You are the focal point of audience attention. In the classroom, however, and at some rallies, hearings, and other events, there are many speeches, and your place on the schedule may affect how you are received. For example, speaking first or last can make a difference. If you go first, you may need to "warm up" the listeners and be prepared to meet the distraction of a few audience members strolling in late; if you speak last, you must counter the tendency of the audience to be weary from listening to several speeches.

4. **What is the time limit for the speech?** The amount of time you have to speak greatly affects the scope of your speech and how you develop it. Keep in mind that the time limit for classroom speeches is quite short. People often get overly ambitious as to what they can accomplish in a short

In planning your speech, use the setting and the occasion to guide you in selecting your content and tone.

speech. "Three Major Causes of Environmental Degradation" can be presented in five minutes, but "A History of Human Impact on the Environment" cannot.

Problems with time limits are not peculiar to classroom speeches. Any speech setting includes actual or implied time limits. For example, a Sunday sermon is usually limited to about twenty minutes; a keynote speech for a convention may be limited to thirty minutes; a political campaign speech may be limited to forty-five minutes or an hour.

5. **What are the expectations for the speech?** Every occasion provides some special expectations. For classroom speeches, one of the major expectations is meeting the assignment. Whether the speech assignment is defined by purpose (to inform or to persuade), by type (expository or descriptive), or by subject (book analysis or current event), your goal should reflect the nature of that assignment.

Meeting expectations is equally important for speeches outside the classroom. At an Episcopalian Sunday service, for example, the congregation expects the minister's sermon to have a religious theme; at a campaign rally, listeners expect a speech on political issues; at a social dinner event, the audience often expects a lighthearted and entertaining talk.

6. **Where will the speech be given?** The room in which you are scheduled to speak also affects your presentation. If you are fortunate, your classroom will be large enough to seat the class comfortably. But classrooms vary in size, lighting, seating arrangements, and the like. A room that is long and narrow creates different problems for a speaker than one that is short and wide. In a long, narrow room, for instance, the speaker's voice must be louder to reach the back row, but eye contact can be limited to a narrower range. Likewise, in a dimly lit room, try to get the lights turned up, especially if you are planning to use visual aids. Investigating the environment for the speech helps you to meet the demands of the situation.

PRACTICE IN SPEECH PREPARATION

Analyzing the Occasion and Setting

The goal of this exercise is to help you determine the nature of your speech occasion.

1. Copy or duplicate the occasion and setting checklist (Figure 12.3).

2. Answer the questions about the occasion and setting for your first speech.

3. Save the results. You will use the data from this checklist to help you determine strategies for adapting to your audience.

Checklist: Occasion and Setting

1. How large will the audience be? _____
2. When will the speech be given? _____
3. Where in the program does the speech occur? _____
4. What is the time limit for the speech? _____
5. What are the expectations for the speech? _____
6. Where will the speech be given? _____
7. What facilities are necessary to give the speech? _____

Figure 12.3
Occasion and setting checklist.

Outside the school setting, speakers often encounter even greater variations in rooms. You will want to have specific information about seating capacity, shape, number of rows, nature of lighting, existence of a speaking stage or platform, distance between speaker and first row, and so on, before you make final speech plans. If possible, visit the place and see it for yourself.

7. **What facilities are necessary to give the speech?** For some speeches, you may need a microphone, a chalkboard, or an overhead or slide projector and screen. In most instances, speakers have some kind of speaking stand, but it's wise not to count on it. If the person who has contacted you to speak has any control over the setting, be sure to explain what you need. But always have alternative plans in case what you have asked for is unavailable. It's frustrating to plan a slide presentation, for example, and then discover that there's no place to plug in the projector!

INFOTRAC COLLEGE EDITION

Using InfoTrac College Edition, click on Power Trac. Press on Key Word and drag down to Journal Name. Enter "Vital Speeches." View Vital Speeches and find a speech on a topic that interests you. Then read that speech. Identify the speaker's goal. Was the goal clearly stated in the introduction? Was it implied but clear? Was it unclear? Note how this analysis can help you clarify your own speech goal.

Writing the Speech Goal

Once you have chosen your topic and analyzed the audience and setting for your speech, you continue the preparation process by identifying the general goal you are hoping to achieve and then writing a specific speech goal.

General Goal

Most speeches can be classified under the three major headings of entertaining, informing, and persuading. Because speech is a complex act that may affect an audience in different ways, these headings are useful only to show that in any public speaking act one overriding general goal is likely to predominate. Consider the following examples.

Jay Leno's opening monologue on "The Tonight Show" is a speech that may give some information and may even contain some intended or unintended persuasive message, but his general goal is to entertain his audience.

A history professor's lecture on the events leading to the Gulf War may use humor to gain and hold attention, and the discussion of the events may affect the class's attitudes about war, but the professor's primary goal is to explain those events so that the class understands them.

Political candidates may amuse us with their anecdotes about life in politics and may give us some information that clarifies aspects of key political issues, but their general goal is to persuade us to vote for them.

Although some public speakers give speeches solely for the purpose of entertaining, in this text we focus attention on informative and persuasive speeches—the kinds of speeches most of us give in our daily lives.

Specific Goal

The specific goal, or specific purpose, is a single statement that specifies the exact response the speaker wants from the audience. For a speech on the topic "Evaluating Diamonds," the goal could be stated as "I would like the audience to understand the four major criteria for evaluating a diamond." For a speech on "Supporting the United Way," the goal could be stated as "I would like the audience to donate money to the United Way." In the first example, the goal is informative: The speaker wants the audience to understand the criteria. In the second example, the goal is persuasive: The speaker wants the audience to donate money. Figure 12.4 gives further examples of specific goals that clearly state how each speaker wants the audience to react to a specific topic.

Entertainment Goals

I would like my audience to be amused by my portrayal of an over-the-hill football player.

I would like my audience to laugh at my experience as a waiter.

Informative Goals

I would like my audience to understand the characteristics of the five common types of coastlines.

I would like my audience to understand the three basic forms of mystery stories.

Persuasive Goals

I would like my audience to believe that drug testing by business and industry should be prohibited.

I would like my audience to join Amnesty International.

Figure 12.4
Specific speech goals.

Now let us consider a step-by-step procedure for completing the specific speech goal.

1. **Write a first draft of your speech goal.** Suppose for Julia's first draft on the topic of Illiteracy she writes "Problems of Illiteracy." This first draft indicates an aspect of her topic, but it is not very specific. Or suppose she writes "Three Aspects of the Problem of Illiteracy." This wording limits what she will talk about to a specific number, but she does not yet have a clearly written speech goal.

2. **Revise your first draft until you have written a complete sentence that states the specific response or behavior you want from your audience.** As Julia reviews the wording, she amends it to read "I would like the audience to understand three aspects of the problem of illiteracy in the workplace." This draft is a complete-sentence statement of her speech goal. Notice that it includes an infinitive ("to understand") indicating the desired response.

3. **Make sure that the goal contains only one idea.** Suppose Julia had written "I would like the audience to understand three aspects of the problem of illiteracy in the workplace and to prove how it is detrimental to both industry and the individual." This draft includes two distinct ideas; either one can be used, but not both, because together they blur the focus of the

---

SKILL BUILDERS   Writing Speech Goals

Skill	Use	Procedure	Example
A single statement that specifies the exact response the speaker wants from the audience.	To give direction to the speech.	1. Write a first draft. 2. Revise the draft until you have a complete sentence that states the specific response or behavior you want from your audience. 3. Make sure that the goal contains only one idea. 4. Revise the infinitive or infinitive phrase until it indicates the specific audience reaction desired. 5. Write at least three different versions of the goal.	Ken first writes, "I want my audience to know what to look for in buying a canine companion." As he revises, he arrives at the wording "I want my audience to understand four considerations in purchasing the perfect canine companion." Once Ken assures himself that the goal has a single focus and that the infinitive "to understand" indicates the preferred audience reaction desired, he then writes two differently worded goals to make sure that his first one is the best.

PRACTICE IN SPEECH PREPARATION

Writing Speech Goals

The goal of this exercise is to help you arrive at a well-worded speech goal.

Following the five-step procedure outlined in the text, write a speech goal for the topic you have selected for your first speech.

speech. She would have to make a decision: Does she want to focus her talk on aspects of the problem? Then the goal "I would like the audience to understand three major aspects of illiteracy in the workplace" is the better statement. Does she want to focus on how harmful it is? Then the goal "I would like to prove that illiteracy is detrimental to the individual and to industry" is preferable.

4. **Revise the infinitive or infinitive phrase until it indicates the specific audience reaction desired.** If you regard your ideas as useful but noncontroversial, then your intent is primarily informative, and the infinitive that expresses your desired audience reaction should take the form "to understand" or "to appreciate." If, however, the main idea of your speech is controversial, a statement of belief, or a call to action, then your intent is persuasive and will be reflected in such infinitives as "to believe" or "to change."

5. **Write at least three different versions of the goal.** The clearer your specific goal, the more purposeful and effective your speech is likely to be. Even if Julia likes her first sentence, she should write at least two additional versions. The second or third version may prove to be an even clearer statement. For instance, on a second try, she might write "I would like the audience to understand three major effects of the problem of illiteracy in the workplace." Changing "three aspects" to "three major effects" gives the goal a different emphasis. She may decide she likes that emphasis better.

Summary

The first step in effective speech preparation is to determine your speech goal. You begin by selecting a subject that you know something about and are interested in, such as a job, a hobby, or a contemporary issue of concern to you. To

REFLECT ON ETHICS

Although Glen and Adam were taking the same speech course, they were in different sections. One evening when Adam was telling Glen about his trouble finding a topic, Glen mentioned that he was planning to speak about affirmative action. Since the number of different speech goals from this topic seemed unlimited, he didn't see any harm in showing Adam his bibliography, so he brought it up on his computer screen.

As Adam was looking at it, Glen went down the hall to get a book he had lent to a friend earlier that morning. While Glen was away, Adam thought he'd take a look at what else Glen had in the file. He was soon excited to see that Glen had a complete outline on the goal "I want the class to understand the steps in designing a home page." Figuring he could save himself some time, Adam printed the outline—justifying his action on the basis that it represented a good start that would give him ideas. As time ran short, however, Adam decided to just use Glen's outline for his own speech.

Later in the week, Glen's instructor happened to be talking to Adam's about speeches she had heard that week. When she mentioned that Glen had given a really interesting speech on home pages, Adam's teacher said, "That's interesting. I heard a good one on the same topic just this morning. Now what did you say the goal of the speech you heard was?" When the goals turned out to be the same, Glen's instructor went back to her office to get the outline that she would be returning the next day. As the two instructors went over the outlines, they saw that the two speeches were exactly the same. The next day, they left messages for both Adam and Glen to meet with them and the department head that afternoon.

1. What is the ethical issue at stake?
2. Was there anything about Glen's behavior that was unethical? Anything about Adam's?
3. What should be the penalty, if any, for Glen? for Adam?

arrive at a specific topic, brainstorm a list of related words under each subject heading. When you have brainstormed at least twenty topics, you can check the specific topic under each heading that is most meaningful to you.

Next you analyze the audience and occasion to decide how to shape and direct your speech. Audience analysis is the study of your audience's knowledge, interests, and attitudes. Gather specific data about your audience to determine how its members are alike and how they differ. Use this information to predict audience interest in your topic, level of understanding of your topic, and attitude toward you and your topic. Also, consider how the occasion of the speech and its physical setting will affect your overall speech plan.

Once you have a speech topic and have accounted for your audience and setting, you can determine your speech goal and write a thesis statement. The general goal of a speech is to entertain, to inform, or to persuade. The specific goal is a complete sentence that specifies the exact response the speaker wants from the audience. Writing a specific speech goal involves the following five-step procedure: (1) Write a first draft of your speech goal. (2) Revise your first draft until you have written a complete sentence that states the specific response or behavior you want from your audience. (3) Make sure that the goal contains only one idea. (4) Revise the infinitive or infinitive phrase until it indicates the specific audience reaction desired. (5) Write out at least three different versions of the goal before deciding on one.

OBJECTIVES

After you have read this chapter, you should be able to answer the following questions:

- What are the key sources of information for speeches?

- What is the difference between factual and opinion statements?

- How can you determine whether a source will be useful?

- What should be included on note cards?

- What is the best way to cite sources in your speeches?

Research

Tasha was upset. The Student Senate was beginning hearings on complaints about course registration, and since she was representing an important segment of the student body she felt a need to speak. What was bothering her was that although she had some strong opinions, she felt that she didn't have any specific information to communicate.

Tasha's experience is not unlike that of many of us. We believe that our views on subjects are worth being heard, but we just don't know how to go about explaining or supporting what we want to say.

Your search for information has two goals. The first is to find high-quality information that will explain or prove your specific speech goal. The second is to find information that will relate to your audience.

You'll recall that an effective speech plan is a product of five action steps. In this chapter, we consider the second step: **Gather and evaluate material that you can use in the speech.** This step involves surveying sources that are most likely to yield quality information, recording information that is relevant to your specific speech goal on note cards, and being prepared to cite that information in your speech.

Where to Look: Sources of Information

Where do you look for the best material available on your topic? Effective speakers build on their own knowledge and experiences with information from observation, interviews, surveys, and written sources.

Personal Knowledge

If you have chosen to speak on a topic you know something about, you may already have some material that you can use in your speech. For instance, athletes have special knowledge about their sports, coin collectors about coins, detective-fiction buffs about mystery novels, "do-it-yourselfers" about home repairs and gardening, musicians about music and instruments, farmers about animals or crops and equipment, and camp counselors about camping. For many of your speeches, then, you are likely to have information that may be usable in your speech—especially examples drawn from your personal experiences. This firsthand knowledge will contribute to the development of imaginative and original speeches. Nevertheless, for most real-life speeches, you'll need information that goes beyond your own experience.

Observation

For many topics, you can get good, specific information through careful observation. If, for instance, you are planning to talk about how newspapers are printed, you can learn about printing operations by touring your local newspaper printing plant and observing the process in action. Observation adds a personal dimension to your speeches that can make them more informative as well as more interesting.

Good observers focus their attention. Suppose you wanted to learn more about the duties of partners in a mixed-doubles tennis match. Instead of just watching the match, which for most people means trying to follow the ball, you might focus on the server's partner's net play during the set. If you take notes, you will have a record of specifics that you can use in your speech.

Interviewing

Like media reporters, you may get some of your best information from **interviewing**—the skillful asking and answering of questions. Students interview outside sources to obtain information for papers; people wanting to learn about career and job possibilities interview individuals working in a given field; lawyers interview witnesses to establish facts on which to build their cases; doctors interview patients to obtain medical histories before making diagnoses; and reporters interview sources to get facts for their stories. Interviewing is a valuable skill by which you can get information for interpersonal, group, or public-speaking purposes. To be effective, you'll want to select the best person to interview and have a list of good questions to ask.

Selecting the best person.   Somewhere on campus or in the larger community there are people who have information you can use in your speech. Usually a few telephone calls will lead you to the person who would be best to talk with about your topic. For instance, for the goal "I want the audience to understand the major elements a dietitian must take into account in order to plan dormitory meals," you could phone your student center and inquire about who is in

Interviews allow you to add details, anecdotes, observations, and expert opinion to enhance your speech.

charge of food service. When you have decided whom you should interview, make an appointment—you cannot walk into an office and expect the prospective interviewee to drop everything just to talk to you. Be forthright in your reasons for scheduling the interview. Whether your interview is for a class speech or for a different audience, say so.

Before going into the interview, make sure that you have done some research on the topic. Interviewees are more likely to talk with you if you appear informed; moreover, familiarity with the subject will enable you to ask better questions.

Writing good questions.   The heart of an effective interviewing plan is a list of good questions. To generate your list, begin by writing down all the questions you can think of. Then revise them until you have worded them clearly and concisely and put them in the order that seems most appropriate. Make your questions a mix of open and closed primary or follow-up questions, and phrase them to be neutral rather than leading.

Primary questions—questions the interviewer plans ahead of time—serve as the main points for the interview outline. Depending on the kind of information you want, primary questions may be open or closed and leading or neutral.

Open questions are broad-based questions that ask the interviewee to provide whatever information he or she wishes ("What can you tell me about yourself?" "What do you believe has prepared you for this job?"). Through open questions, the interviewer finds out about the person's perspectives, values, and goals, but these questions do take time to answer (Tengler and Jablin 1983, p. 261).

Closed questions are narrow-focus questions, ranging from those that require only yes or no ("Have you had a course in marketing?") to those that require only a short answer ("How many restaurants have you worked in?"). By asking closed questions, interviewers can control the interview and obtain large amounts of information in a short time. On the other hand, the closed question seldom enables the interviewer to know *why* a person gave a certain response, nor is the closed question likely to yield much voluntary information (Biagi 1992, p. 94).

Leading questions are questions phrased in a way that suggests the interviewer has a preferred answer ("You don't like the new job, do you?").

Neutral questions (which are preferred) are phrased without direction from the interviewer ("How do you like your new job?").

Follow-up questions are designed to pursue the answers given to primary questions. Although some follow-ups are planned ahead by anticipating possible answers, more often than not they are composed as the interview goes along. Some like "And then?" and "Is there more?" encourage further comments; some like "What does 'frequently' mean?" and "What were you thinking at that time?" probe; and some like "How did it feel to get the prize?" and

"Were you worried when you didn't find her?" plumb the person's feelings. All are designed to motivate a person to enlarge on an answer.

The topics of good questions are determined by the purpose of the interview. For instance, if you decide to interview the cafeteria dietitian to find out how dormitory meals are planned, you'll want information about the dietitian, his or her responsibilities, and how he or she plans. How many questions you plan to ask depends on how much time you have for the interview. Keep in mind that you never know how a person will respond. Some people are so talkative and informative that in response to your first question they answer every question you were planning to ask in great detail; other people will answer each question with just a few words.

In the opening stage of the interview, plan to ask some questions that can be answered easily and that will show your respect for the person you are interviewing. In an interview with the head dietitian, you might start with background questions such as "How did you get interested in nutrition?" The goal is to get the interviewee to feel at ease and to talk freely.

The body of the interview includes the major questions you have prepared. You may not ask all the questions you planned to, but you don't want to end the interview until you have the important information you intended to get. The questions are designed to get the information necessary to achieve your goal.

Figure 13.1 shows appropriate sample questions for an interview with the cafeteria dietitian.

Background Information
How did you get interested in nutrition?
What kind of background and training do you need for the job?

Responsibilities
What are the responsibilities of your job besides meal planning?
How far in advance are meals planned?
What factors are taken into account when you are planning the meals for a given period?
Do you have a free hand, or are there constraints placed on you?

Planning
Is there any set ratio for the number of times you put a particular item on the menu?
Do you take individual preferences into account?
How do you determine whether you will give choices for the entree?
What do you do to try to answer student complaints?
How do your prices compare with meals at a commercial cafeteria?

Figure 13.1
Sample interview questions.

Conducting the interview. By applying the interpersonal skills we have discussed in this book, you'll find that you can turn your careful planning into an excellent interview.

1. **Be courteous during the interview.** Start by thanking the person for taking the time to talk to you. Throughout the interview, respect what the person says regardless of what you may think of the answers.

2. **Listen carefully.** You will want to incorporate those skills relating to attending, understanding, and remembering, with special emphasis on asking questions, paying attention to nonverbal cues, and paraphrasing.

3. **Keep the interview moving.** Although some people will get so involved that they will not be concerned with the amount of time spent, most people will have other important business to attend to.

4. **Make sure that your nonverbal reactions—facial expressions and gestures—are in keeping with the tone you want to communicate.** Maintain good eye contact with the person. Nod to show understanding. And smile occasionally to maintain the friendliness of the interview.

Surveys

A **survey,** often in the form of a questionnaire, is a means of gathering information directly from people. Surveys may be conducted orally or in writing. For speeches on such diverse topics as student reaction to dormitory food, the local volleyball team's chances in an upcoming match, banning automatic weapons, increasing property taxes, or how well the council is governing the city, you can obtain useful information through a survey.

For instance, suppose you wanted to continue your research on food at the campus cafeteria. In the previous section, we saw how you might interview the dietitian who determines the menus and orders the food. Now that you have his or her insight into the way the cafeteria is run, you might decide that you want to survey student opinion about the cafeteria.

Samples. To begin, consider who is to be surveyed. Suppose you want the opinion of the student body on the cafeteria. Although you could attempt to survey the entire student body (say, 12,000 students), it is far more likely that you would select a sample. At first, it would seem that the more people you sample, the smaller the chances are of error. And although that is true, most samples that are used for polls are rather small. For instance, to get the opinion of a population of 100 million, a poll of 1,000 to 1,500 will reveal as much as a poll of 10,000 to 50,000 (Hennessy 1985, p. 73). Thus, for a population of 12,000, you might want to survey 50 to 100 students.

Since the size of a poll is less significant than the type of sample, make sure that your sample is representative of the entire group in question. For instance, for a poll concerning whether a course on Fundamentals of Effective Speaking should be required for all students, you must sample freshmen, sophomores, juniors, and seniors; an equal number of males and females; fraternity/sorority members and independents; and people of all races.

A survey of those students who eat at the student union cafeteria would be a **stratified survey**—one that surveys only a part of the total population. If you gave your questionnaire to every student as he or she entered the cafeteria on one day and collected it from as many students as possible as they left, you would have a good sample of the students who eat at the cafeteria. For other situations you may wish to stratify by race, age, sex, education, or any other variable. If you are doing a stratified survey, then you must make sure that each person surveyed is within the survey group.

Types of surveys. A well-designed survey focuses on the information you need to achieve your goal. If your goal for a survey of students who eat at the student union cafeteria is to get their answers to questions about food quality, atmosphere, and prices, then you need to phrase your questions accordingly. The four kinds of questions most likely to be used in a survey are called two-sided, multiple-choice, scaled, and open-ended.

1. **Two-sided questions** call for a yes-no or true-false response. These questions are used most frequently to get easily sorted answers. For a cafeteria survey, you might consider a two-sided phrasing such as "Do you approve of the quality of the food at the student union cafeteria—Yes or No?"

   Despite their popularity, two-sided questions do not offer people the opportunity to express their degree of agreement or disagreement.

2. **Multiple-choice questions** give respondents alternatives. This type features such variations as checklists and rank ordering.

   For a cafeteria survey you might phrase the following question:

   I eat at the student union cafeteria
   ____ nearly every day
   ____ at least three times a week
   ____ at least once a week
   ____ at least once a month
   ____ rarely (less than once a month)

3. **Scaled questions** allow a range of responses to a statement. Scaled responses are particularly good for measuring the strength of a person's attitudes toward a subject. If you had decided to use scaled questions for your cafeteria survey, to the statement "I like the food at the university cafeteria," each person would be allowed a range of choices, such as

PRACTICE IN CLASS

Creating Survey Questions

Working in groups, select a topic such as campus parking, registration, or computer access. Groups should then make a list of questions that they might use on a survey to sample student opinion about these topics. Practice with at least two different types of survey questions.

strongly agree, agree somewhat, don't know (or not sure), disagree somewhat, and strongly disagree. For a survey for the student union cafeteria's clientele, you might use the following questions.

> **For each of the following three statements, circle the answer that best represents your opinion:**
>
> **1. I like the food at the university cafeteria.**
>
> Strongly agree | Agree somewhat | Don't know | Disagree somewhat | Strongly disagree
>
> **2. I believe the food at the university cafeteria is fairly priced.**
>
> Strongly agree | Agree somewhat | Don't know | Disagree somewhat | Strongly disagree
>
> **3. I believe the atmosphere at the university cafeteria is pleasant.**
>
> Strongly agree | Agree somewhat | Don't know | Disagree somewhat | Strongly disagree

4. **Open-ended questions** encourage statements of opinion. These questions produce the greatest amount of depth, but because of the likelihood of a wide variety of responses, they are the most difficult to process. For your cafeteria survey, you might ask this open-ended question:

> **Assuming that any cafeteria can be improved, what changes would you make in the student union cafeteria?**

Analysis of statistics. After you have taken the survey, analyze your data. If the survey indicates a clear-cut trend, then use the results of the poll to help make a point in your speech. If the poll is inconclusive, then it's wise to avoid making too much of the results. No matter how you do your survey, it is open to some percentage of statistical error. The only poll without error would be one in which everyone in the population was surveyed and everyone completed the survey. Even then, people's opinions may change somewhat from day to day.

Written Sources

Since for many speeches, the best material will come from what you read, you'll want to be able to access and draw information from your library's books, periodicals, and other specialized sources.

Books. In the past, libraries featured a card catalog for accessing books the library held. And although some libraries may still have a card catalog, most of them have transferred records of their holdings to a computer system. Whether you are looking for books in a card catalog or on a computer, books are listed by title, author, and subject.

You may need to exercise some creativity in discovering the categories and subject listings under which useful books are catalogued. Suppose you are researching the topic Illiteracy. You may find little or nothing under that heading in the card catalog or computer file. With a few minutes of creative thinking, however, you should be able to come up with such additional headings as Literacy, Education—comparative, Reading, Reading comprehension, Reading disabilities, and so forth. Regardless of topic, you may have to turn to alternative headings to discover the extent of your library's listings.

Periodicals. Periodicals are magazines and journals that appear at fixed periods: weekly, biweekly, monthly, quarterly, or yearly. Since material from weekly, biweekly, and monthly magazines is more current than that which you find in books, a periodical is likely to be your best source when your topic is one that's "in the news." A periodical is also your best source when the topic is so limited in scope that it is unlikely to provide enough material for a book or when you are looking for a very specific aspect of a particular topic.

The following four sources index the types of periodicals that are likely to produce relevant information for your speeches. *The Readers' Guide to Periodical Literature* is an index of articles in some 150 popular magazines and journals, such as *Business Week, Ebony, Newsweek, Reader's Digest*, and *Vital Speeches. The Humanities Index* and *The Social Sciences Index* will lead you to articles in more than 300 scholarly journals, such as *The American Journal of Sociology, The Economist, Modern Language Quarterly*, and *Philosophical Review. The Education Index* will lead you to articles in 350 English-language periodicals, yearbooks, and monographs.

Although you can do manual searches through these indexes, most university and public libraries subscribe to services that use a CD-ROM system to provide computerized versions of all the bound-volume indexes. For instance, the University of Cincinnati library subscribes to *Wilson Databases*, which gives access to all the indexes mentioned here.

Periodical indexes are published each year and in monthly and quarterly supplements for the current year. If you are doing a manual search, in order to find appropriate articles about your topic, you need to determine when the events occurred or when the topic was actively discussed. If you are preparing a speech on the effects of political infomercials like those used by Ross Perot during the 1992 presidential campaign, begin your research in the index for 1992, election year, and work forward and backward from there until the supply of articles dries up. Similarly, if you are preparing a speech on what it was like to be a television writer during the McCarthy era and you want material published during that time period, begin your research in the index for 1953, the height of the McCarthy era.

Encyclopedias. Most libraries have a recent edition of *Encyclopaedia Britannica, Encyclopedia Americana*, or *World Book Encyclopedia*. An encyclopedia can be a good starting point for research. There are also specialized encyclopedias in such areas as religion, philosophy, and science. Encyclopedias give an excellent overview of many subjects, but you certainly should never limit your research to encyclopedias.

Statistical sources. Statistical sources present numerical information on a wide variety of subjects. When you need facts about demography, continents, heads of state, weather, or similar subjects, refer to one of the many single-volume sources that report such data. Two of the most popular sources in this category are *The World Almanac and Book of Facts* and *Statistical Abstract of the United States*.

Biographical sources. When you need accounts of a person's life, from thumbnail sketches to reasonably complete essays, you can turn to one of the many biographical sources available. In addition to full-length books and encyclopedia entries, consult such books as *Who's Who in America* and *International Who's Who*.

Newspapers. Newspaper articles are excellent sources of facts about and interpretations of contemporary issues. Approach newspaper research in much the same way as magazine research, to gather information on subjects from a particular time in history. Your library probably holds both an index of your nearest major daily and the *New York Times Index*.

U.S. government publications. Two government publications are especially useful for locating primary sources. The *Federal Register* publishes daily regulations and legal notices issued by the executive branch and all federal agencies. It is divided into sections such as rules and regulations and Sunshine Act meetings. Of special interest are announcements of hearings and investigations, committee meetings, and agency decisions and rulings. The *Monthly Catalog of United States Government Publications* covers publications of all branches of the federal government. It has semiannual and annual cumulative indexes by title, author/agency, and subject.

Electronic Databases and Networking

An **electronic database** is information stored so that it can be retrieved from a computer terminal. Rubin, Rubin, and Piele (1996), compilers of research sources, point out, "A researcher who is reluctant to use computers to find information or who does not know how to do so effectively will be severely handicapped" (p. 42). The advantages of college library electronic databases are that they can be searched much more quickly than their print counterparts, results can be printed or downloaded onto a floppy disk, and at most schools the use of databases is free of charge.

Depending on the size of your library, you may have access to such self-service databases as ERIC (700 educational journals and thousands of research reports collected by the U.S. Department of Education), INFOTRAC Expanded Academic Index (more than 1,000 journals and newspapers emphasizing communication, history, humanities, law, political science, psychology, religion, sciences, social sciences, and sociology), MEDLINE (some 3,600 journals in biomedicine, health sciences, and medicine), PSYCLIT (more than 1,400 English and foreign-language journals in education, psychology, and sociology), SOCIOFILE (communication, criminal justice, demography, geography,

INFOTRAC COLLEGE EDITION

Using InfoTrac College Edition, under the subject you've selected for your speech, click on periodical references. Look for articles that seem to include information that would be useful to you in preparing your speech. Be sure to cite information you use.

Electronic databases are excellent sources of information and can be researched more quickly than most print sources.

political science, sociology, and speech), and LEXIS/NEXIS (accounting, business, government, law, and medicine) to name just a few.

You can use these databases to compile bibliographies and view abstracts, or even full articles, on the computer screen. Reference librarians should know which databases your library subscribes to and can help you learn to access them.

Today, anyone with access to a personal computer also has access to national and international electronic networks. Most colleges and universities are now connected to the **Internet**—an international electronic network of networks. This superhighway of information provides access to an ever-increasing number of information resources. Students and faculty use the Internet to give them access to databases and bulletin boards, scholarly and professional electronic discussion groups, library holdings at colleges and universities across the United States and abroad, and exchange of e-mail (electronic mail).

Regardless of what you look for, don't hesitate to ask library staff for help; helping library patrons is a major professional responsibility, and with very few exceptions, librarians will gladly offer their assistance.

Skimming to Determine Source Value

Since you are likely to uncover far more articles and books than you can use, you will want to skim sources to determine whether or not to read them in full.

Skimming is a method of going rapidly through a work to determine what is covered and how.

If you are evaluating a magazine article, spend a minute or two finding out whether it really presents information on the exact area of the topic you are exploring and whether it contains any documented statistics, examples, or quotable opinions. (We'll examine the kind of information to look for in the next section.)

If you are evaluating a book, read the table of contents carefully, look at the index, and skim pertinent chapters, asking the same questions as you would for a magazine article.

Skimming helps you decide which sources should be read in full, which should be read in part, and which should be abandoned. Minutes spent in such evaluation will save hours of reading.

If you are compiling a periodical bibliography on computer, you will discover that the services your library subscribes to are likely to include short abstracts for each article that comes up on the computer screen. A look at these abstracts will help you determine which sources you want to read in their entirety. Once you have the sources in hand, however, you'll still need to follow a skimming procedure.

What Information to Look For

Whatever the source, you'll be looking for both factual statements and expert opinions.

PRACTICE IN SPEECH PREPARATION

Listing Sources

The goal of this exercise is to help you compile a list of potential sources for your first speech.
  For the topic you have selected for your first speech, fill in the following information:

1. Name a person, an event, or a process that you could observe to broaden your personal knowledge base.

2. Name a person you could interview for additional information on this topic.

3. Write survey questions—if a survey is appropriate.

4. Working with manual or computerized versions of your library's card catalog or periodical indexes discussed in this chapter, list a total of six specific books and/or magazine articles that appear to provide information on your topic.

Factual Statements

Factual statements are those that can be verified. "A recent study confirms that preschoolers watch an average of 28 hours of television a week," "The Macintosh Performa comes with a CD-ROM port," and "Johannes Gutenberg invented printing from movable type in the 1400s" are all statements of fact that can be verified.

When you find what appears to be factual information, you need to be concerned with the degree of confidence you can have in the information (Nickerson 1986). One way to verify whether information is factual is to check it against material from another source on the same subject.

You'll want to be especially skeptical of "facts" that are asserted on the Internet. Since anyone can say virtually anything on-line, you should never use any information that is not carefully documented unless you have corroborating sources.

Expert Opinions

Expert opinions are interpretations and judgments made by authorities in a particular subject area. "Watching 28 hours of television a week is far too much for young children," "Having a CD-ROM port on your computer is a necessity," and "The invention of printing from movable type was for all intents and purposes the start of mass communication" are all *opinions* based on the previous factual statements. Whether they are *expert opinions* or not depends on who made the statements.

The quality of opinion depends on whether its source is an expert on the matter at hand. How do you tell an expert from a "quack"? First, the expert is recognized by others in his or her field. Second, the expert must be a student of the matter at hand. For instance, if a pediatrician who has gained a reputation specializing in the care of at-risk newborns has studied the relationship between drug use and birth defects and asserts that such defects occur in higher numbers when the mothers are drug users, then her opinion is expert, because it meets both criteria.

Of course, opinions are most trustworthy when they are accompanied by factual data. If the pediatrician can cite data from reputable scientific studies, her opinion is worth even more.

If you plan to use expert opinions in your speech, identify them as opinions and indicate to your audience the level of confidence that should be attached to the statement. For instance, an informative speaker might say, "The temperatures throughout the last half of the 1980s were much higher than average. Paul Jorgenson, a space biologist, believes that these higher-than-average temperatures represent the first stages of the greenhouse effect, but the significance of these temperatures is not completely accepted as fact."

Although opinions cannot entirely take the place of documented facts, expert opinion can be used to interpret and give weight to facts that you have

UNDERSTAND YOURSELF

Asking for an Example

Recall a time when you didn't understand what a person was telling you and you asked for an example. How did you expect to profit from the example?

discovered. Moreover, in situations where you cannot get facts, where the facts are inconclusive, or where they need to be supplemented, you will have to further support your claims with expert opinion.

Verbal Forms of Information

Factual information and expert opinions may be presented in the form of examples and illustrations, statistics, anecdotes and narratives, comparisons and contrasts, and quotable explanations and opinions.

Examples and illustrations. **Examples** are specific instances that illustrate or explain a general factual statement. The generalization "American cars are beginning to rival the quality of Japanese cars," for instance, may be illustrated or explained with the following specific example: "The frequency-of-repair records for Dodge Intrepid and Buick Regal in the past year are much closer than in previous years to those of the Nissan Maxima and Toyota Camry." Examples are useful because they provide concrete detail that makes a general statement more meaningful to the audience.

You will find examples used individually or in series. In the following passage, notice how Mario Cuomo (1980, p. 268), then the governor of New York, uses a series of examples to support his point about the importance of family education.

> **I learned to do all the basic things from my family before I ever went to school. . . . The real tough teaching jobs were left up to my mom and pop: things like tying my shoes, not playing with fire, learning my way to the potty, picking up my own toys and socks, not hitting my brother or sister, standing up to the bully down the block. In short, I learned to be a worker, a citizen, a neighbor, a friend, a husband and I hope a civilized human being all under the tutelage of this marvelous university called the family and all before I set foot in a school.**

Although most of the examples you find will be real, you may find hypothetical examples you can use. **Hypothetical examples** are drawn from reflections about future events; they develop the idea "What if . . . ?" In the following excerpt, John A. Ahladas (1989, p. 382) presents hypothetical examples of what it will be like in the year A.D. 2039 if global warming continues.

> **In New York, workers are building levees to hold back the rising tidal waters of the Hudson River, now lined with palm trees. In Louisiana, 100,000 acres of wetland are steadily being claimed by the sea. In Kansas, farmers learn to live with drought as a way of life and struggle to eke out an existence in the increasingly dry and dusty heartland. . . . And reports arrive from Siberia of bumper crops of corn and wheat from a longer and warmer growing season.**

You may also find a good example cast in illustration form. An **illustration** is an example that has been developed with added detail. The following segment shows the difference between casting the same information in example form and in illustration form.

Generalization: Most people want to accomplish an objective with the least amount of effort.

Example: When entering a building, people will wait for an open door rather than use the energy to open a closed door.

Illustration: "I remember watching the entrance of a large office building. There were five doors. The one on the far left was open, the rest closed. Most everybody used the open door, even waiting for people to come out before they could enter just because the door was easier than the effort of pushing another door open. This is true of much of life" (G. Jones 1987, p. 493).

Now let us consider guidelines for selecting and using examples. First, the examples should be specific enough to create a clear picture for the audience. If you exemplified the generalization "American cars are beginning to rival the quality of Japanese cars," with the statement "Some American cars are quite reliable," the audience would still not have a clear idea of the degree of reliability. But if you gave the example "The 1997 Dodge Intrepid reliability record, as shown in the April 1998 issue of *Consumer Report*s, is virtually the same as that of the 1997 Toyota Camry," the point would be clear and specific.

Second, the examples you use should not be misleading. For instance, if Ford Taurus was the *only* American car whose frequency-of-repair record was anything like the records of Japanese cars, it would be unethical to start with the generalization "American cars are beginning to rival the quality of Japanese cars."

Third, examples should relate to the generalization. If you say "American cars are beginning to rival the quality of Japanese cars" and then give the example "Chrysler Corporation has run a series of commercials showing the beauty of their leather interiors," the example may concern quality, but it does not show how Chrysler Corporation cars compare to Japanese cars.

Because specifics both clarify and substantiate, it's a good idea to follow this rule of thumb in preparing your speeches: Never let a generalization stand without at least one example.

Statistics. Statistics are numerical facts. Statistical statements, such as "Seven out of every ten local citizens voted in the last election" or "The cost of living rose 2.5 percent in 1997," enable you to pack a great deal of information into a small package. Statistics can provide impressive support for a point, but when they are poorly used in the speech, they may be boring and, in some instances, downright deceiving. Following are some guidelines on using statistics effectively.

1. **Record only statistics whose reliability you can verify.** Taking statistics from only the most reliable sources and double-checking any startling

Use statistics from only the most reliable sources and double-check any startling statistics with another source.

statistics with another source will guard against the use of faulty statistics. For example, it is important to double-check statistics that you find in such sources as paid advertisements or publications distributed by special-interest groups. Be especially wary if your source does not itself provide documentation for the statistics it reports.

2. **Record only recent statistics so that your audience will not be misled.** For example, if you find the statistic that only 2 of 100 members of the Senate, or 2 percent, are women (true in 1992), you would be misleading your audience if you used that statistic in a speech. If you want to make a point about the number of women in the Senate, find the most recent statistics. Check for both the year and/or the range of years to which the statistics apply.

3. **Look for statistics that are used comparatively.** By themselves, statistics are hard to interpret, but when used comparatively, they have much greater impact.

In a speech on chemical waste, Donald Baeder (1980, p. 497) points out that whereas in the past chemicals were measured in parts per million, today they are measured in parts per billion or even parts per trillion. Had he stopped at that point, the audience would have had little sense of the immensity of the figures. Notice how he goes on to use comparisons to put the meaning of the statistics in perspective:

One part per billion is the equivalent of one drop—one drop!—of vermouth in two 36,000-gallon tanks of gin, and that would be a very dry

martini even by San Francisco standards! One part per trillion is the equivalent of one drop in two thousand tank cars.

In your comparisons, be careful not to present a misleading picture. If you say that during the past six months Company A doubled its sales while its nearest competitor, Company B, improved by only 40 percent, the implication would be misleading if you did not indicate the size of the base; Company B, with a larger base of sales, could have more sales and proportionately more impressive sales growth than Company A.

4. **Do not overuse statistics.** Although statistics may be an excellent way to present a great deal of material quickly, be careful not to overuse them. A few pertinent numbers are far more effective than a battery of statistics. When you believe you must use many statistics, try preparing a visual aid, perhaps a chart, to help your audience visualize them.

Anecdotes and narratives. Anecdotes are brief, often amusing stories; narratives are tales, accounts, personal experiences, or lengthier stories. Each presents material in story form. Because holding audience interest is so important in a speech and because audience attention is likely to be captured by a story, anecdotes and narratives are worth looking for, creating, and using. For a two-minute speech, you have little time to tell a detailed story, so one or two anecdotes or a very short narrative would be preferable.

The key to using stories is to make sure that the point of the story states or reinforces the point you make in your speech. In his speech about telecommunication, Randall Tobias (1993, p. 273), vice chairman of AT&T, uses a story to make a point about the promise and the threat of technology:

> **A lighthearted story I heard from a scientist-colleague illustrates the point.**
>
> **A theologian asked the most powerful supercomputer, "Is there a God?" The computer said it lacked the processing power to know. It asked to be connected to all the other supercomputers in the world. Still, it was not enough power. So the computer was hooked up to all the mainframes in the world, and then all the minicomputers, and then all the personal computers. The theologian asked for the final time, "Is there a God?" And the computer replied: "There is now."**

Neither the anecdote nor the narrative needs to be humorous to be effective. In her speech on the subject of blacks and women in universities, Patti Gillespie (1988, p. 237) tells the following story to show the inaccuracy of perceptions even among university faculty:

> **I recently heard a male senior professor say with considerable pride that on his faculty there were now an equal number of men and women. His observation was quickly affirmed by one of the junior men in the department. Because I knew the department and could not get the figures**

to tally, I asked that we go through the faculty list together. Both men
were surprised when we discovered that, by actual count, the current
faculty consisted of nine men and five women—that is, almost two men
for each woman.

Comparisons and contrasts. One of the best ways to give meaning to new
ideas is through comparison and contrast. Comparisons illuminate a point by
showing similarities. Although you can easily create comparisons using information you have found, you should still keep your eye open for creative comparisons developed by the authors of the books and articles you have found.

Comparisons may be literal or figurative. Literal comparisons show similarities of real things: "The walk from the lighthouse back up the hill to the
parking lot is equal to walking up the stairs of a thirty-story building." Figurative comparisons express one thing in terms normally denoting another: "I
always envisioned myself as a four-door sedan. I didn't know she was looking
for a sports car!"

Comparisons make ideas not only clearer but also more vivid. Notice how
Stephen Joel Trachtenberg (1986, p. 653), in a speech to the Newington High
School Scholars' Breakfast, uses figurative comparison to demonstrate the
importance of being willing to take risks, even in the face of danger.

> The eagle flying high always risks being shot at by some harebrained
> human with a rifle. But eagles and young eagles like you still prefer the
> view from that risky height to what is available flying with the turkeys far,
> far below.

Whereas comparisons show similarities, contrasts show differences. Notice
how this humorous contrast dramatizes the difference between "participation"
and "commitment":

> If this morning you had bacon and eggs for breakfast, I think it
> illustrates the difference. The eggs represented "participation" on the part
> of the chicken. The bacon represented "total commitment" on the part of
> the pig! (Durst 1989, pp. 309–310)

Quotations. When you find an explanation, an opinion, or a brief anecdote
that seems to be exactly what you are looking for, you may quote it directly in
your speech. Because audiences want to listen to your ideas and arguments,
they do not want to hear a string of long quotations. However, a well-selected
quotation might be perfect in one or two key places.

Quotations can both explain and vivify. Look for quotations that make a
point in a particularly clear or vivid way. For example, in her speech "The
Dynamics of Discovery," Catherine Ahles (1993, p. 352), vice president for
College Relations at Macomb Community College, used the following quote
from Helen Keller to show the detrimental effects of pessimism: "No pessimist
ever discovered the secrets of the stars . . . or sailed to an uncharted land . . . or
opened a new heaven to the human spirit."

Frequently, historical or literary quotations can reinforce a point vividly. In his introduction to a speech on "Integrity," for example, Ronald W. Roskens (1989, p. 511) quoted Sir Harold Macmillan, the former British prime minister, as saying, "If you want to know the meaning of life . . . don't ask a politician." C. Charles Bahr (1988, p. 685), chairman of Bahr International, in his speech on telling the truth to sick companies, quoted Mark Twain on the importance of telling the truth: "Always do right. It will amaze some people and astonish the rest."

To take advantage of such opportunities, you need access to one or more of the many available books of quotations. One is *The International Thesaurus of Quotations*, compiled by Rhoda Thomas Tripp (1987). Another is *Bartlett's Familiar Quotations*, which came out in a new edition in 1992 (Kaplan 1992). Library reference sections carry several books of quotations. These books are often organized by topic, which helps in finding a particularly appropriate quote to use in your speech.

Keep in mind that when you use a direct quotation, it is necessary to credit the person who formulated it. Using any quotation or close paraphrase without crediting its source is plagiarism.

Recording Data and Citing Sources

Whether the research materials you find are factual statements or opinions, you need to record the data accurately and keep a careful account of your sources so that they can be cited appropriately.

Recording Data

It is important to record data so that you can provide the information and its source in a speech or report the documentation to anyone who might question the information's accuracy. When question periods are provided at the end of a speech, members of an audience will often ask for sources of information. Whether or not there is a question period, however, listeners need the assurance that they can find the material used in your speech if they should decide to look for it.

How should you record the materials you uncover in your research (including not only research into printed sources but also personal knowledge, observations, interviews, and surveys)? Because most speakers use only some of their research material and are never sure of the final order in which it will be used, it's best to record the material so that it can be easily selected and moved around. The note-card method is probably the best.

In the note-card method, each factual statement or expert opinion, along with bibliographical documentation, is recorded on a separate four-by-six-inch or larger index card. Although it may seem easier to record all material from one source on a single sheet of paper (or to photocopy source material), sorting and arranging material is much easier when each item is recorded separately. On each card, indicate the topic of the recorded information, the information, and the publication data. Any part of the information that is quoted directly should be enclosed in quotation marks. Publication data differs depending on whether the information is from a book or from a periodical or newspaper. For a book, write the name of the author, the title, the publisher, the date, and the page number from which the information was taken. For a periodical or newspaper, write the name of the author if one is given, the title of the article, the name of the periodical or newspaper, the date, and the page number from which the information was taken. List bibliographical information in enough detail so that the information can be found later if needed. Figure 13.2 illustrates a useful note-card form.

As your stack of information grows, you can then sort the material. Each item goes under a heading to which it is related. For instance, for a speech on Ebola, the deadly disease that has broken out in Africa, you might have note

SKILL BUILDERS   Recording Data

Skill

Having a written record of information drawn from a source with complete documentation.

Use

To provide information and its source in a speech or to report the documentation to anyone who might question the information's accuracy.

Procedure

1. Indicate the topic in the upper-left-hand corner.

2. Record each factual statement or expert opinion on a separate four-by-six-inch or larger index card. Any part of the information that is quoted directly should be enclosed in quotation marks.

3. For a book, write the name of the author, the title, the publisher, the date, and the page number from which the information was taken.

4. For a periodical or newspaper, write the name of the author if one is given, the title of the article, the name of the periodical or newspaper, the date, and the page number from which the information was taken.

Example

While gathering material for a speech on effects of electronic delivery services on mail delivery, Tamika found an article with relevant information. In the upper-left-hand corner of one four-by-six card, she wrote: U.S. Postal Service Record. Then she wrote the data she had discovered: In 1997, the U.S. Postal Service delivered 630 million pieces of mail a day and "raised its on-time rate for first-class letters to a remarkable 92%." Under the information, she wrote: John Greenwald, "Zapping the Post Office," *Time*, January 19, 1998, p. 40.

Topic: Ebola
Heading: Means of transmission

Scientists now believe that the Ebola virus that killed 13 people in a remote village in Gabon last week "was transmitted to humans from chimpanzees or other forest creatures."

"Where Does Ebola Hide?" <u>Time</u>, March 4, 1996, p. 59.

Figure 13.2
Example of a note card recording information.

cards related to causes, symptoms, and means of transmission. The card in Figure 13.2 would be indexed under the heading Means of Transmission.

The number of sources that you should use depends in part on the type of speech. For a narrative of a personal experience, you obviously will be the main, if not the only, source. For reports and persuasive speeches, however, speakers ordinarily use several sources. For a speech on Ebola in which you plan to talk about causes, symptoms, and means of transmission, you should probably have two or more note cards under each heading.

Moreover, the note cards should come from at least three different sources. One-source speeches often lead to plagiarism. Furthermore, a one- or two-source speech simply does not provide sufficient breadth of material. Selecting and using information from several sources will enable you to develop an original approach to your topic.

Citing Sources in Speeches

In your speeches, as in any communication in which you use ideas that are not your own, try to work the source of your material into your presentation. Such efforts to include sources not only help the audience evaluate the content but also add to your credibility. In addition, citing sources will give concrete evidence of the depth of your research. Failure to cite sources, especially when you are presenting information that is meant to substantiate a controversial point, is unethical.

In a written report, ideas taken from other sources are designated by footnotes; in a speech, these notations must be included within the context of your statement of the material. Your citation need not be a complete representation of all the bibliographical information. Figure 13.3 gives examples of several appropriate source citations.

Although you do not want to clutter your speech with bibliographical citations, make sure to mention the sources of your most important information.

"According to an article about Japanese workers in last week's _Time_ magazine . . . "

"In the latest Gallup poll cited in the February 10 issue of _Newsweek_ . . . "

"But to get a complete picture we have to look at the statistics. According to the 1992 _Statistical Abstract_, the level of production for the European Ecnomic Community rose from . . . "

"In a speech on business ethics delivered to the Public Relations Society of America last November, Preston Townly, CEO of the Conference Board, said . . . "

Figure 13.3
Appropriate source citations.

PRACTICE IN SPEECH PREPARATION

Preparing Note Cards

The goal of this exercise is to help you prepare note cards that you can use as you complete the outline for your first speech.

From the sources that you identified in "Listing Sources," p. 302, complete at least six note-cards that provide information related to your specific speech goal. Include (1) a specific factual statement, (2) an expert opinion, and three others from among the following types: examples and illustrations, statistics, anecdotes and narratives, comparisons and contrasts, and quotations.

On your note-cards from magazine articles, cite (1) the name of the author if one is given, (2) the title of the article, (3) the title of the magazine, (4) the publication data, and (5) the page number on which this information appears.

On your note-cards from books, cite (1) the name of the author if one is given, (2) the title of the book, (3) the publication data including the name of the publisher and the year the book was published, and (4) the page number on which this information appears.

Summary

Effective speaking requires high-quality information. You need to know where to look for information, what kind of information to look for, how to record it, and how to cite your sources in your speeches.

To find material, begin by exploring your own knowledge and work outward through observation, interviewing, surveying, and written and electronic sources. You can look for material in books, periodicals, encyclopedias, statistical sources, biographical sources, newspapers, government publications, computer databases, and on-line. By skimming material, you can quickly evaluate sources to determine whether or not to read them in full.

"Dan, I was wondering whether you'd listen to the speech I'm giving in class tomorrow. It will only take about five minutes."

"Sure."

Tom and Dan find an empty classroom, and Tom goes through his speech. "What did you think?"

"Sounded pretty good to me. I could follow the speech—I knew what you wanted to do. But I was wondering about that section where you had the statistics. You didn't give any source."

"Well, the fact is I can't remember the source."

"You remember the statistics that specifically, but you don't remember the source?"

"Well, I don't remember the statistics all that well, but I think I've got them about right."

"Well, you can check it, can't you?"

"Check it? Where? That would take me hours. And after all, I told you I think I have them about right."

"But Tom, the accuracy of the statistics seems pretty important to what you said."

"Listen, trust me on this—no one is going to say anything about it. You've already said that my goal was clear, my main points were clear, and I sounded as if I know what I'm talking about. I really think that's all Goodwin is interested in."

"Well, whatever you say, Tom. I just thought I'd ask."

"No problem, thanks for listening. I thought I had it in pretty good shape, but I wanted someone to hear my last practice."

"Well, good luck!"

1. What do you think of Tom's assessment of his use of statistics—that "no one is going to say anything about it?"
2. Does Tom have any further ethical obligation? If so, what is it?

Two major types of supporting material for speeches are factual statements and expert opinions. Factual statements report verifiable occurrences. Expert opinions are interpretations of facts made by qualified authorities. Although you will use some of your material as you find it, you may want to present the information in a different form. Depending on your topic and speech goal, you may use facts and opinions orally as examples, illustrations, anecdotes, narratives, statistics, comparisons, contrasts, and quotations.

A good method for recording material that you may want to use in your speech is to record each item of information, along with necessary bibliographical documentation, on a separate note-card. As your stack of information grows, sort the material under common headings. During the speech, cite the sources for the information.

OBJECTIVES

After you have read this chapter, you should be able to answer the following questions:

■ How do you use semantic mapping to construct a thesis statement?

■ How do you determine the main points for your speech?

■ How do you determine the best order for your speech?

■ What is the goal of transitions?

■ What are the goals of an effective speech introduction?

■ What are the most common types of speech introductions?

■ What are the essentials of an effective speech conclusion?

■ What are the major elements of a well-written speech outline?

14

Organization

"Troy, that was a terrific speech. I haven't heard so many good stories in a long time."

"You're right, Brett, the stories were interesting, but, you know, I had a hard time following it."

"Well, he was talking about ways that we can help save the environment—but, you're right, I can't seem to remember anything but that one point about recycling. Let's see, what were the other key points?"

Amazingly enough, Troy and Brett's experience is not unusual, for many speakers don't seem to take the time to work out a basic structure. Plato, the classical Greek philosopher, was one of the first people to recognize the organic nature of a speech. He wrote, "Every discourse, like a living creature, should be put together so that it has its own body and lacks neither head nor feet, middle nor extremities, all composed in such a way that suit both each other and the whole." Or, to put it in a way that follows the old military guideline: First you tell them what you're going to tell them, then you tell them, then you tell them what you told them.

You'll recall that an effective speech plan is a product of five action steps. In this chapter, we consider the third step: **Organize and develop your material in a way that is best suited to your particular audience.** This step involves choosing an organizational pattern that clearly communicates the material, developing an introduction that both gets attention and leads into the body of the speech, developing a conclusion that both summarizes the material and leaves the speech on a high note, and refining the speech outline.

Preparing the Body of the Speech

Many speakers assume that because the introduction is the first part of the speech to be heard by the audience, they should begin outlining with the introduction. When you think about it, however, you realize that it is difficult to work on an introduction until you have considered the material to be introduced. To prepare the body of your speech, you need to write a thesis statement, select and state the main points, determine the best order, and finally, select and develop the examples, quotations, and other elements that explain or support the main points.

Writing a Thesis Statement

Now that you have gathered information in support of your speech goal, you can turn your speech goal into a thesis statement. Whereas the specific goal is a statement of how you want your audience to respond, the **thesis statement** is a sentence that outlines the specific elements of the speech supporting the goal statement. For instance, the speech goal "I would like the audience to understand the major criteria for evaluating a diamond" can be turned into the thesis statement "The major criteria for evaluating diamonds are carat (weight), color, clarity, and cutting."

Let's consider an example of the process of arriving at a meaningful thesis statement. Suppose Joanne has written the specific goal "I want the audience to understand the major roles of the president of the United States." She then uses her research on presidential roles to brainstorm a **semantic map**—a visual diagram of all the roles she's discovered.

The semantic-mapping process allows you to list relevant ideas without initial regard to whether they are really the main ideas you want to discuss. Once you get a number of specific ideas down on paper, you can begin to evaluate them to select the most relevant ones for your thesis statement. For the presidential roles speech goal, Joanne could list roles she has identified in her research to form the semantic map shown in Figure 14.1.

Joanne's map includes six potential major roles. Depending on the breadth of the subject area, you might brainstorm six, eight, or even a dozen potential main points that you have discovered in your research.

Mapping gives Joanne a chance to put her thoughts on paper without being concerned about weight, order, or appropriateness. Then she can analyze the ideas to see which have the most promise. As she examines these six, she may decide that "greeter of foreign dignitaries" is a role that is not important enough to talk about in a short speech. Likewise, she may see "example for the people" as too vague to work with. Now she's left with "head of executive branch," "chief of a political party," "boss of armed forces," and "responsible for foreign relations." Thus, she could write the following tentative thesis statement: "The four major roles of the president are head of executive branch, chief of a political party, boss of armed forces, and responsible for foreign relations." As she considers various revisions of these main points, she will arrive at the final wording of her thesis statement.

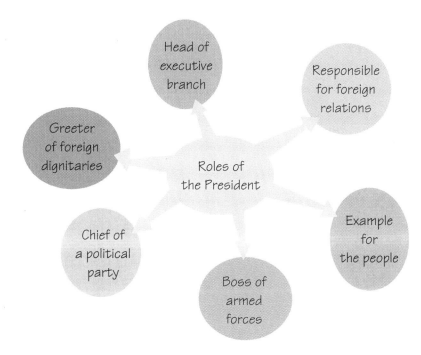

Figure 14.1
Brainstorming for main ideas.

Begin to organize your research materials by first turning your speech goal into a thesis statement.

✳ Selecting and Stating Main Points

Main points are the key building blocks of a speech—the ideas you want your audience to remember if they remember nothing else. Assuming that you really have completed your thesis statement, then you already have the basis for your main point topics. For instance, Joanne has written, "The four major roles of the president are head of executive branch, chief of a political party, boss of armed forces, and responsible for foreign relations." Written in outline form, a first draft of the main points for her speech would thus be as follows:

    I. Responsible for things related to foreign countries

   II. Commander-in-chief of the armed forces

PRACTICE IN SPEECH PREPARATION

Writing Thesis Statements

The goal of this exercise is to help you arrive at a well-worded thesis statement for your speech.

1. Map the elements of your speech goal—elements that might become the main points of your speech (see Figure 14.1).

2. After selecting the specific elements that best reflect your speech goal, combine them into a complete sentence that is your thesis statement.

SKILL BUILDERS   Writing a Thesis Statement

Skill	Use	Procedure	Example
A sentence that outlines the specific elements of the speech supporting the speech goal statement.	To specify the main points of the speech.	1. Write the specific speech goal. 2. Brainstorm potential parts or elements of that goal. 3. Select those elements that best develop the goal. 4. Write a complete sentence that best incorporates those elements.	Sally writes her speech goal: "I want the audience to understand the three steps involved in shooting a jump shot." She then thinks of balance, holding the ball steady, squaring shoulders to the basket, bending knees, and delivering the ball smoothly. She selects squaring shoulders, balance, and smooth delivery. She then writes her thesis statement: "The three steps required to shoot a jump shot are to square yourself to the basket, balance yourself properly, and deliver the shot smoothly."

   III. Head of a political party

   IV. Head of the executive branch

Once you have selected the topics for the main points, the next step is to analyze them to make sure that you have (1) complete sentences that are (2) clear, (3) parallel in structure, (4) meaningful, and (5) limited to five or less in number.

Main points are complete sentences when they have a subject and a verb. Joanne could quickly revise her main points to meet this test by prefacing each of them with "One (Another) role of the president is. . . ."

   I. One role of the president is being responsible for things related to foreign countries.

   II. Another role of the president is commander-in-chief of the armed forces.

   III. Another role of the president is the head of a political party.

   IV. Another role of the president is the head of the executive branch.

Main points are clear when their wording is likely to call up the same images in the minds of all audience members. For her speech, Joanne has written the first main point as follows:

    I. One role of the president is being responsible for things related to foreign countries.

"One role of the president is being" is both awkward and wordy. Joanne could make the phrase clearer by changing the wording to "The president is responsible for." Likewise, "things related to foreign countries" is so general that the audience is unlikely to understand what she means. Thus, Joanne could further revise the main point for clarity by substituting "foreign relations" for "things related to foreign countries," with the following result:

    I. The president is responsible for foreign relations.

Main points are parallel when their wording follows the same structural pattern, often using the same introductory words. Parallel structure helps the audience recognize main points by recalling a pattern in the wording. For example, each of the main points in Joanne's speech about the roles of the president could begin with the words "The president is. . . ." With this change, Joanne's main points would be as follows:

    I. The president is responsible for foreign relations.

   II. The president is commander-in-chief of the armed forces.

 III. The president is the head of a political party.

 IV. The president is the head of the executive branch.

Based on this wording of her main points, Joanne could then refine her thesis statement to read: "The president is responsible for foreign relations, commander-in-chief of the armed forces, head of a political party, and head of the executive branch."

Sometimes parallelism is achieved by less obvious means. One method is to start each sentence with an active verb. For instance, suppose Kenneth wished to have his audience understand the steps involved in antiquing a table. He might write the following first draft of his outline:

FIRST DRAFT

    I. Clean the table thoroughly.

   II. The base coat can be painted over the old surface.

 III. A stiff brush, sponge, or piece of textured material can be used to apply the antique finish.

 IV. Then you will want to apply two coats of shellac to harden the finish.

Note that the wording of this first draft does not present a clear, parallel structure. The first point is stated as an imperative; the next two use passive verbs; the last one refers to "you." With careful revision, Kenneth might construct a final draft in which the main points are parallel (parallel active verbs are italicized):

FINAL DRAFT

    I.   *Clean* the table thoroughly.

   II.   *Paint* the base coat over the old surface.

 III.   *Apply* the antique finish with a stiff brush.

 IV.   *Harden* the surface with two coats of shellac.

Notice how the similarity of structure clarifies and strengthens the message. The audience can immediately identify the key steps in the process. In addition to being clear and parallel in structure, main points should be meaningful.

Main points are meaningful when they are informative complete sentences. If the main points are not really meaningful, even if the audience remembers them, what they will remember may not be significant. For instance, let's contrast the wording of the four steps in antiquing a table as shown in Figure 14.2.

The items in the first column indicate the topics only. Although the words *clean*, *paint*, *apply*, and *harden* indicate the steps, they are only labels. They may be useful as keywords on note cards, but they will not work at this stage of preparation because the ideas they represent, and the relationship among them, need to be clarified and sharpened.

Notice the improvement in the second column. Now the steps are beginning to be meaningful. But even though the wording is better, the sentences are not as meaningful as they could be—that is, they do not give as much information as is necessary.

In the third column, the main points are not only complete sentences, but they maximize the information without making the sentences too long to remember. If the listeners remember only the main points of this sentence out-

Topics	Short Sentences	More Informative Sentences
I. Clean	I. Clean the table.	I. Clean the table thoroughly.
II. Paint	II. Paint on the base coat.	II. Paint the base coat over the old surface.
III. Apply	III. Apply the antique finish.	III. Apply the antique finish with a stiff brush.
IV. Harden	IV. Harden the surface.	IV. Harden the surface with two coats of shellac.

Figure 14.2

Contrasting wording of main points.

line, they will still know exactly what is to be accomplished in each of the four steps. Moreover, after writing the main points as meaningful sentences, the speaker is more likely to think of them as sentences and present complete-sentence main points during speech practice.

Main points should be limited to a maximum of five in number. As you begin to phrase prospective main points, you may find your list growing to five, seven, or even ten points that seem to be main ideas. A list that long is usually a clue that some points are really "subpoints" or repeat other points. Because every main point must be developed in some detail, it is usually impractical to have more than two to five main points. If you have more than five, rework your speech goal to limit the number of main points, group similar points under a single heading, or determine whether some points are subpoints that can be included under main points.

Determining the Best Order

A speech can be organized in many different ways. Although your thesis statement will often control the type of organization, there are times when you may decide to revise the thesis statement (or even the goal) to achieve a different

The time and thought you put into finding an effective speech organization will pay off in audience interest and understanding.

organization. Your objective is to find or *create* the structure that will help the audience make the most sense of the material and so achieve your speech goal. Although "real speeches" come with many types of organization, three basic orders that are useful for the beginning speaker to master are topic, time, and logical reasons.

Topic order. An extremely common way of ordering main points is to organize them by topic. Nearly any subject can be subdivided or categorized in many different ways. The order of topics may go from general to specific, least important to most important, or in some other logical sequence. Joanne's speech on roles of the presidency is one example of topic order.

If topics vary in weight and importance to the audience or to the goal of the speech, how you order them may influence your audience's understanding or acceptance of them. Following is an example of ordering topics from *least* important to *most* important.

Specific Goal: I want the audience to understand the insights our clothes give us into our society.

Thesis Statement: Our clothing gives insight into our society's casual approach, its youthful look, the similarity in men's and women's roles, and the lack of visual distinction between rich and poor in our society.

    I.   Our clothes indicate our casual approach.

    II.   Our clothes indicate our emphasis on youthfulness.

    III.   Our clothes indicate the similarity in men's and women's roles.

    IV.   Our clothes indicate the lack of visual distinction between rich and poor.

Time or chronological order. When you select a chronological arrangement of main points, you focus on what comes first, second, third, and so on. The audience understands that there is a particular importance to the sequence as well as the content of those main points. Time order is most appropriate when you are explaining how to do something, how to make something, how something works, or how something happened. Kenneth's speech on steps in antiquing a table is one example of time order.

In the following example, notice how the order of main points is as important to the logic of the speech as the wording.

Specific Goal: I want the audience to understand the four steps involved in preparing an effective résumé.

Thesis Statement: The steps in preparing a résumé include gathering relevant information, deciding on an appropriate format, planning the layout, and polishing the statements of information.

    I.   First, gather relevant information.

    II.   Second, decide on an appropriate format.

III. Third, plan the layout.

IV. Fourth, polish the statements of information.

Although the designations first, second, and so on are not necessary to the pattern, their inclusion helps the audience to understand that the sequence is important. In Chapter 17, Informative Speaking, we consider other informative speaking orders.

Logical reasons order. Unlike the other two arrangements of main points, the logical reasons order is most appropriate for a persuasive speech. This order emphasizes *why* the audience should believe something or behave in a particular way. In Chapter 18, we consider additional ways of phrasing and ordering reasons for persuasive speeches.

> **Specific Goal:** I want the audience to donate money to the United Way.
>
> **Thesis Statement:** Donating to the United Way is appropriate because your one donation covers many charities, you can stipulate which specific charities you wish to support, and a high percentage of your donation goes to charities.
>
> I. You should donate to the United Way because one donation covers many charities.
>
> II. You should donate to the United Way because you can stipulate which charities you wish to support.
>
> III. You should donate to the United Way because a high percentage of your donation goes directly to the charities.

These three organizational patterns—topic, time, and logical reasons—are the ones most commonly used. As you develop your public-speaking skill, you may find that you will need to revise an existing pattern or create a totally different one to meet the needs of your particular subject matter or audience.

In summary, then, to organize the body of your speech, (1) turn your speech goal into a thesis statement that forecasts main points; (2) state main points in complete sentences that are clear, parallel, meaningful, and limited to five in number; and (3) organize the main points in the pattern best suited to your material and the needs of your specific audience.

Selecting and Outlining Supporting Material

The main points outline the structure of your speech. Whether your audience understands, believes, or appreciates what you have to say usually depends on how well those main points are explained and supported.

As we saw in Chapter 13, factual statements and expert opinions are the principal types of research information used in speeches. Once the main points are in place, you can select the most relevant of those materials and decide how to build each main point.

1. **List supporting material.** First, using the semantic-mapping technique, write down each main point and under it state the information that you have found that develops that main point. Don't worry if ideas don't seem to relate to each other as you write them down. For example, for the first main point of a speech with the goal "I want the audience to understand the four C's that determine the value of a diamond," your semantic map might resemble Figure 14.3.

2. **Subordinate the material.** Once you have listed the items of information that make the point, look for relationships between and among ideas, and draw lines that connect information logically. Sometimes you'll find you have stated the same point two different ways ("How much a diamond costs depends on its size" and "Price of high-quality diamonds may multiply as they get larger"). Often items can be grouped under a more general heading. Occasionally you will have listed some information that you decide not to include in the outline ("Price is determined by the amount of rock that is mined"). In outline form, then, a main point will have two or more subdivisions and each subdivision may have two or more sub-subdivisions. The items of information mapped in Figure 14.3 might be grouped and subordinated as follows:

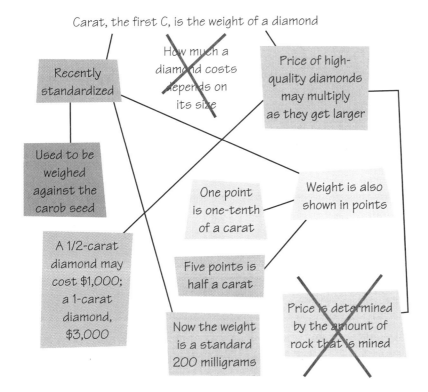

Figure 14.3
Semantic mapping of supporting material.

    I. Carat, the first C, is the weight of the diamond.
      A. Diamond weight has been standardized only recently.
        1. Originally, merchants measured the carat of diamonds against the carob seed.
        2. Now the carat has been standardized as 200 milligrams.
        3. Partial weight of a carat is shown in points.
          a. One point is one-tenth of a carat.
          b. Five points is half of a carat.
      B. As diamond weights increase, the costs multiply.
        1. A high-quality ½-carat stone may cost $1,000.
        2. A high-quality 1-carat stone may cost $3,000.

In this speech, each subpoint might be developed with additional examples, illustrations, anecdotes, and other supporting material. The outline only needs to include enough supporting information to ensure that you can explain and clarify the point you are making.

Determining Section Transitions

Section transitions are complete sentences that link major sections of a speech. They summarize what has gone before and/or show movement to the next main idea. These transitions act like a tour guide leading the audience through the speech and are helpful when you do not want to take a chance that the audience might miss something.

Section transitions work best at breaks from one part of the speech to another or from one main point to another. For example, suppose Kenneth has just finished the part of the introduction of his speech on antiquing tables. Before stating his first main point, he might say, "Antiquing a table is a process that has four steps." When his listeners hear this transition, they are likely to think, "Now we're ready to move to the first of those main points." Then, when he finishes talking about the first main point, he might use another transition: "Now that we see what is involved in cleaning the table, let's move on to the second step."

Section transitions are important for several reasons. First, they help the audience follow the flow of the speech. If every member of the audience were able to pay 100-percent attention to every word, then perhaps section transitions wouldn't be needed. But as people's attention rises and falls during a speech, they often find themselves wondering where they are. Section transitions show them.

Second, section transitions are important in helping us retain information. We may well remember something that was said once in a speech. But our retention is likely to increase markedly if we hear something more than once. So, if we forecast main points, then state each main point, and have transitions

PRACTICE IN SPEECH PREPARATION

Outlining the Speech Body

The goal of this exercise is to help you outline the body of your first speech.

1. Select the headings from the thesis statement that you wrote earlier in this chapter.

   a. Write the prospective main points in outline form.

   b. Revise the wording of the main points so that each is written in a complete sentence that is clear, parallel, and meaningful.

   c. Based on the nature of the material and the nature of your audience, determine what order to use for your main points: topic order, time order, or logical reasons order. If need be, rewrite the main points in this order.

2. Map the factual statements, expert opinions, and other information that you have found to develop each main point.

   a. Group the points of information that relate to each other (see Figure 14.3, p. 325).

   b. Subordinate material so that each subpoint contains only one idea.

3. Write transition statements that summarize the previous main point and/or forecast the next main point before each main point in the body of the outline.

between each point, not only are audiences more likely to follow, they are also more likely to remember the organization.

In the sample speech outline at the end of this chapter, section transitions are written in parentheses at the junctures of the speech. Later in the book, we'll discuss other kinds of transitions.

Preparing the Introduction

At this stage of preparation, the body of the speech is sufficiently well developed that you can concentrate on how to begin your speech. Here we consider what a speech introduction should accomplish and how to craft effective ones.

Goals of the Introduction

A good introduction is likely to (1) get attention, (2) set the tone for a speech, (3) create a bond of goodwill between speaker and audience, and (4) lead into the content of the speech.

1. **Getting attention.** Since an audience's physical presence does not guarantee that they will listen to your speech, your first goal is to create an opening

An effective introduction will get attention and lead into the body of your speech; it will also build goodwill and set the tone for your speech.

that will win the listeners' attention by arousing their interest and providing them a need to know the information that will be presented. In the following section, we discuss several types of attention-getting devices you can use.

2. **Setting a tone.** A humorous opening will signal a lighthearted tone; a serious opening signals a more thoughtful or somber tone. A speaker who starts with a rib-tickling ribald story is putting the audience in a lighthearted, devil-may-care mood; if that speaker then says, "Now let's turn to the subject of abortion (or nuclear war, or drug abuse)," the audience will be confused, and the speech may be doomed.

3. **Creating a bond of goodwill.** In the first few words you often establish how an audience will feel about you as a person. If you're enthusiastic, warm, and friendly and give a sense that what you're going to talk about is in the audience's best interest, it will make them feel more comfortable about spending time listening to you.

4. **Leading into content.** Since audiences want to know what the speech is going to be about, it's useful to forecast your organization in the introduction. For instance, in a speech on campaigning, after your attention-getter you might say, "In this speech, I'll explain the four stages of a political campaign." A clear forecast of the main points is appropriate unless you have some special reason for not revealing the organization.

Types of Introduction

Ways to begin a speech are limited only by your imagination. To find the most effective opening, try two or three different introductions in practice and pick the one that seems best suited to your purpose and meets the needs you have identified in your analyses of the audience and the occasion. In very short speeches—the kinds you will be giving this term—you will want to focus on getting attention and leading into the content of the speech. Startling statement, rhetorical question, story, personal reference, quotation, and suspense openings are types that you can adapt to both short and longer speeches.

Startling statement. One excellent way to grab your listeners' attention and focus on the topic quickly is to open with a startling statement that will override the various competing thoughts in your listeners' minds. The following example illustrates the attention-getting effect of a startling statement:

> **If I pointed a pistol at you, you would be justifiably scared. But at least you would know the danger to your life. Yet every day we let people fire away at us with messages that are dangerous to our pocketbooks and our minds, and we seldom say a word. I'm talking about television advertisers.**

Rhetorical question. Asking a rhetorical question—a question seeking a mental rather than a vocal response—is another appropriate opening for a short speech. Notice how a student began her speech on counterfeiting with three short questions:

> **What would you do with this ten-dollar bill if I gave it to you? Take your friend to a movie? Treat yourself to a pizza and drinks? Well, if you did either of these things, you could get in big trouble—this bill is counterfeit!**

Story. If you have a good story that gets an audience's attention and is really related to the goal of the speech, you probably have an unbeatable opening. Because many good stories take time to tell, they are more appropriate for longer speeches; however, you will occasionally find or think of a story that is just right for your speech, as was this one on balancing stakeholder interests (Deavenport 1995, p. 49):

> **A tightrope walker announced that he was going to walk across Niagara Falls. To everyone's amazement, he made it safely across and everybody cheered. Who believes I can ride a bicycle across? And they all said, "Don't do it, you'll fall!" But he got on his bicycle and made it safely across. "Who believes I can push a full wheelbarrow across?" Well by this time the crowd had seen enough to make real believers of them, and they all shouted, "We do! We do!" At that he said, "OK . . . Who wants to be the first to get in?"**
>
> **Well, that's how many investors feel about companies who have adopted the philosophy that balancing the interests of all stakeholders is the true route to maximum value. They go from skeptics to believers, but are very reluctant to get in that wheelbarrow.**

Personal reference. Although any good opening should engage the audience, the personal reference is directed solely to that end. In addition to getting attention, a personal reference can be especially effective at engaging listeners as active participants in a speech. A personal-reference opening like this one on exercise may be suitable for a speech of any length:

> Say, were you panting when you got to the top of those four flights of stairs this morning? I'll bet there were a few of you who vowed you're never going to take a class on the top floor of this building again. But did you ever stop to think that maybe the problem isn't that this class is on the top floor? It just might be that you are not getting enough exercise.

Quotation. A particularly vivid or thought-provoking quotation makes an excellent introduction to a speech of any length. You will need to use your imagination to relate the quotation to your topic so that it yields maximum benefits. In the following introduction, notice how William McCormick (1986, p. 267) uses a familiar Shaw quote as a preface to material that would be less attention-getting without the quotation:

> George Bernard Shaw once wrote, "The road to hell is paved with good intentions." Probably no statement better describes the state of our tort system in this country. With the best of intentions, the scales of a system designed to render justice have been tipped. The balance has moved so far toward the desire to compensate all injuries and all losses that the overall cost to society has become too high. We have reached a point where exposure to liability is becoming almost limitless and incalculable, making everyone—governments, businesses, and individuals—a victim.

Suspense. If you can start your speech in a way that gets the audience to ask, "What is she leading up to?" you may well get them hooked for the entire speech. The suspense opening is especially valuable when the topic is one that the audience might not ordinarily be willing to listen to if the speech were opened less dramatically. Consider the attention-getting value of the following introduction:

> It costs the United States more than $116 billion per year, it has cost the loss of more jobs than a recession. It accounts for nearly 100,000 deaths a year. I'm not talking about cocaine abuse—the problem is alcoholism.

Notice that by putting the problem "alcoholism" at the end, the speaker encourages the audience to try to anticipate the answer. And since the audience may well be thinking "narcotics," the revelation that the answer is alcoholism is likely to be that much more effective.

Selecting an Introduction

Because the introduction is critical in establishing your relationship with your audience, it's worth investing the time to compare different openings. Try working on two or three different introductions; then pick the one you believe will work best for your specific audience and speech goal.

OBSERVE AND ANALYZE

Analyzing Introductions

Of the six examples of introduction given, which one or ones would have most motivated you to listen to the speech? Why?

How long should the introduction be? Most introductions range from 5 to 10 percent of the speech. Thus, for a five-minute speech (approximately 750 words), an introduction of 35 to 75 words is appropriate; for a thirty-minute speech, an introduction of two to four minutes is appropriate. Whether your speech introduction meets all four of the goals directly, it should be long enough to put listeners in the frame of mind that will encourage them to hear you out without being so long that it leaves too little time to develop the substance of the speech. Of course, the shorter the speech, the shorter the introduction must be.

The introduction will not make your speech an instant success, but it can get an audience to look at and listen to you and to focus on your topic. That is about as much as a speaker can ask of an audience during the first minute or two of a speech.

Preparing the Conclusion

Shakespeare said, "All's well that ends well," and nothing could be truer of a good speech. The conclusion offers you one last chance to hit home with your point. Too many speakers either end their speeches so abruptly that the audience is startled or ramble on aimlessly until they exhaust both the topic and the audience. A weak conclusion—or no conclusion at all—can destroy much of the impact of an otherwise effective speech. Even the best conclusion cannot save a poor speech, but it can heighten the impact of a good speech.

Goals of the Conclusion

A conclusion has two major goals: (1) to wrap up the speech so that it reminds the audience of what you have said and (2) to hit home so that the audience will

---

PRACTICE IN SPEECH PREPARATION

Writing Speech Introductions

The goal of this practice is to help you create choices for how you will begin your first speech.

1. For the speech body you outlined earlier, prepare three separate introductions that you believe would be appropriate for your speech, and present them aloud.

2. Which do you believe is the best? Why?

remember your words or consider your appeal. Even though the conclusion will be a relatively small part of the speech—seldom more than 5 percent (35 to 40 words for a five-minute speech)—it is worth the time and effort to make it effective.

⚘ Types of Conclusions

The following are four basic types of conclusions that you will want to master.

Summary. By far the easiest way to end a speech is to summarize the main points. Thus, the shortest appropriate ending for a speech on the warning signs of cancer would be, "So remember, if you experience a sudden weight loss, lack of energy, or blood in your urine or bowels, then you should see a doctor immediately." Such an ending restates the key ideas the speaker wants the audience to remember. Summaries are appropriate for either informative or persuasive speeches.

Although effective speakers often summarize to achieve the first goal, wrapping up the speech so that it reminds the audience of what they have said, they are likely to supplement their summaries with material designed to achieve the second goal: hitting home so that the audience will remember their words or consider their appeal. The following represent several ways to supplement or replace the summary.

Story. Storylike, or anecdotal, material that reinforces the message of the speech works just as well for the conclusion as for the introduction. In his speech on banking, Edward Crutchfield (1980, p. 537) ends with a personal experience showing that bankers must be ready to meet competition coming from any direction:

> **I played a little football once for Davidson—a small college about 20 miles north of Charlotte. One particularly memorable game for me was one in which I was blindsided on an off-tackle trap. Even though that was seventeen years ago, I can still recall the sound of cracking bones ringing in my ears. Well, seventeen years and three operations later my back is fine. But I learned something important about competition that day. Don't always assume that your competition is straight in front of you. It's easy enough to be blindsided by a competitor who comes at you from a very different direction.**

Storylike conclusions will work for either informative or persuasive speeches.

Appeal to action. The appeal to action is a common way to end a persuasive speech. The appeal describes the behavior that you want your listeners to follow after they have heard the arguments. Notice how Marion Ross (1989, p. 284), professor of economics at Mills College, concludes her speech on living a full and creative life with a memorable figure of speech that captures the appeal she is making to her students:

OBSERVE AND ANALYZE

Analyzing Conclusions

If you want to supplement a summary of main points, which of the three examples given here of types of conclusions would you be most inclined to use? Why?

> **We, the faculty, want you to grow wings that won't melt in the sun as did those of Icarus. We want to give you the materials to make your own wings, and we are bold enough to say the thoughts of great thinkers, works of great art and, in some cases, musings of tinkerers of the past are wrought of gold. They won't melt. Use them. It is you who must take these materials, forge them with your own energy and burnish them with your own imagination to make your own wings.**

By their nature, appeals are most relevant for persuasive speeches, especially when the goal is to motivate an audience to act.

Emotional impact. No conclusion is more impressive than one that drives home the most important points with real emotional impact. Consider the powerful way in which General Douglas MacArthur (1951/1968, p. 344) used plain, strong language to conclude his speech when he ended his military career:

> **But I still remember the refrain of one of the most popular barrack ballads of that day, which proclaimed most proudly that "Old soldiers never die; they just fade away."**
>
> **And like the old soldier of that ballad, I now close my military career and just fade away—an old soldier who tried to do his duty as God gave him the light to see that duty.**
>
> **Good-bye.**

Like the appeal, the emotional conclusion is likely to be used for a persuasive speech where the goal is to reinforce belief, change belief, or motivate an audience to act.

Selecting a Conclusion

Speakers select the type of conclusion for their speeches on the basis of the speech goal and the likely appeal to the audience. To determine how you will conclude your speech, try out two or three conclusions, then choose the one that you believe will best reinforce your speech goal with your audience.

INFOTRAC COLLEGE EDITION

Using InfoTrac College Edition, click on Power Trac. Press on Key Word and drag down to Journal Name. Enter "Vital Speeches." View Vital Speeches and find speeches related to your topic. Then view those speeches. Read the introductions and conclusions to those speeches. What qualities did you find helpful in preparing your introduction and conclusion?

PRACTICE IN SPEECH PREPARATION

Writing Speech Conclusions

The goal of this exercise is to help you create choices for how you will conclude your first speech.

1. For the body of the speech you have outlined, prepare three separate conclusions that you believe would be appropriate, and present each aloud.

2. Which one works best? Why?

Cathy copyright 1983 Cathy Guisewite. Reprinted with permission
of Universal Press Syndicate. All rights reserved.

Completing the Outline

From the moment you begin organizing your material, the goal is to create a complete outline for your speech—a short representation of the speech with key points expressed in complete sentences. Think of an outline not as an entire speech written in outline form, but as a blueprint to follow as you consider ways to present the speech. The value of working with an outline is that you can test the logic, development, and overall strength of the structure of your speech before you prepare the wording or begin practicing its delivery.

Although some professional speakers have learned alternate means of planning speeches and testing structure that work for them, over the years I have seen ample proof that for student speeches there is a direct relationship between the quality of the outline and the effectiveness of the speech.

As you read the following five guidelines for constructing outlines, notice how they are incorporated in the sample speech outline on pp. 336–337.

1. **Use a standard set of symbols to indicate structure.** Main points are usually indicated by roman numerals, major subdivisions by capital letters, minor subheadings by Arabic numerals, and further subdivisions by lowercase letters.

2. **Use complete sentences for main points and major subdivisions.** Complete sentences help you to see (1) whether each main point actually develops your speech goal and (2) whether the wording makes your intended point. Unless the key ideas are written out in full, it will be difficult to follow the next guidelines.

3. **Check to make sure that each main point and major subdivision contains a single idea.** This guideline ensures that the development of each part of the speech will be relevant to the point. Thus, rather than

    I. The park is beautiful and easy to get to.

divide the sentence so that both parts are separate:

    I. The park is beautiful.

   II. The park is easy to get to.

The two-point example sorts out distinct ideas so that the speaker can line up supporting material with confidence that the audience will see and understand its relationship to the main points.

4. **Check to make sure that each major subdivision relates to or supports a major point.** This principle is called **subordination.** Consider the following example:

    I. Proper equipment is necessary for successful play.
       A. Good gym shoes are needed for maneuverability.
       B. Padded gloves will help protect your hands.
       C. A lively ball provides sufficient bounce.
       D. And a good attitude doesn't hurt.

Notice that the main point deals with equipment. A, B, and C (shoes, gloves, and ball) relate to the main point. But D, attitude, is not equipment and should appear somewhere else, if at all.

5. **Limit the total words in the outline to no more than one-third the total number anticipated in the speech.** An outline is only a skeleton of the speech—not a manuscript with letters and numbers. The outline should be short enough to allow you to experiment with methods of development during practice periods and to adapt to audience needs during the speech itself. An easy way to judge whether your outline is about the right length is to make sure that it is around one-third the number of words of the speech or less. Because approximate figures are all that are needed, to compute the approximate maximum words for your outline, start by assuming a speaking rate of 150 words per minute. Thus, for a three- to five-minute speech, which would include roughly 450 to 750 words, the outline should be approximately 150 to 250 words. The outline for an eight- to ten-minute speech, which would include roughly 1,200 to 1,500 words, should be approximately 400 to 500 words.

Now that we have considered the various parts of an outline, let us put them together for a final look. The outline in Figure 14.4 illustrates the principles in practice. The analysis in the margin focuses on each guideline we have considered.

ANALYSIS

Writing the specific goal at the top of the page before the outline of the speech reminds the speaker of the goal. The speaker should refer to the specific goal to test whether everything in the outline is relevant.

The heading *Introduction* sets this section apart as a separate unit. Whether every aspect is stated or not, the introduction (1) gets attention, (2) sets the tone, (3) gains goodwill, and (4) leads into the body.

The thesis statement outlines the elements that were forecast in the specific goal. In the speech, the thesis serves as a transition from the introduction to the body. In an informative speech, the thesis statement will probably be presented as a forecast of the body of the speech; in a persuasive speech presentation, the thesis statement may be withheld if there is some strategic reason for so doing.

The heading *Body* sets this section apart as a separate unit. Main point I reflects a topical relationship of main ideas. It is stated as a complete, substantive sentence. The main point could be developed in many ways. These two subdivisions, shown by consistent symbols (A and B) and indicating the equal weight of the points, consider the origin and the restrictions.

This transition reminds listeners of the first distinction and forecasts the nature of the second one.

Main point II continues the topical relationship. The sentence is a complete, substantive statement paralleling the wording of main point I. Furthermore, notice that each main point considers one major idea. The degree of subordination is at the discretion of the speaker. After the first two stages of subordination, words and phrases may be used in place of complete sentences in further subdivisions.

OUTLINE

Specific Goal: I want my audience to understand why Roquefort cheese is unique.

Introduction

I. For millions of Americans, the answer to the question "What kind of dressing would you like on your salad?" is "Roquefort, please."

II. Yet very few of us realize how truly unique this delectable product is.

Thesis Statement: The three distinct elements of Roquefort cheese are that it's trademarked, it's made from ewe's milk, and its distinct flavor comes from a mold grown in only one place in the world.

Body

I. Roquefort cheese is trademarked.
   A. Cheesemakers still follow legislation of the Parliament of Toulouse that dates from 1666.
   B. All salad dressings claiming to be Roquefort must contain at least 1.5 percent legislated Roquefort.
   (In addition to being trademarked, a second distinct element of Roquefort cheese relates to the kind of milk that is used.)

II. Roquefort cheese is made exclusively from ewe's milk, instead of from cow's or goat's milk.
   A. This particular type of sheep dates back to Neolithic times.
   B. Ewe's milk is quite precious.
      1. It takes thirty ewes to produce the amount of milk that could be gotten from one cow.
      2. It takes 800,000 ewes to keep the cheesemakers in business.

OUTLINE

(The final distinction of Roquefort relates to the source of the molds that give it its taste.)

III. Roquefort cheese is made from molds grown only in caves located in Roquefort-sur-Soulzon.
    A. The mold is grown in caves that were discovered four to six thousand years ago.
        1. The caves are $1\frac{1}{4}$-miles long and 300 yards deep.
        2. The caves are made up of blocks that resemble sugar cubes.
    B. The specific mold, Penicillum roquefortii, grows in cracks and fissures in these caves.
    C. The mold is cultivated in bread, ground, and injected into the cheese to give the distinctive color and flavor.

Conclusion

I. We see, then, that Roquefort cheese is truly unique because it is trademarked, made from ewe's milk, and flavored with a mold grown in only one place in the world.
II. The next time you ask for Roquefort on your salad, you'll have a better appreciation of what you are getting.

Bibliography

"Cheese," *Encyclopedia Americana* 6 (1992): 354–358.
Marquis, Vivienne, and Patricia Haskell, *The Cheese Book.* New York: Simon & Schuster, 1985.
Sahatjian, E., "Growing Mold Gracefully," *Esquire* (October 1990): 48.
Wernick, Robert, "From Ewe's Milk and a Bit of Mold: A Fromage Fit for a Charlemagne," *Smithsonian* (February 1983): 57–63.

ANALYSIS

This transition lays the foundation for the statement of the third and final distinction.

Main point III continues the topical relationship, is parallel to the other two in phrasing, and is a complete, substantive sentence.

Throughout the outline, notice that each statement is an explanation, definition, or development of the statement to which it is subordinate.

The heading *Conclusion* sets this section apart as a separate unit. The content of the conclusion is a form of summary tying the key ideas together. Although there are many types of conclusions, a summary is always acceptable for an informative speech.

In any speech where research has been done, a bibliography of sources should be included.

Figure 14.4
Sample complete outline for a four- to six-minute speech.

Completing the Speech Outline

The goal of this practice is to help you complete the outline for your first speech.

1. Using information from the three previous Practices in Speech Preparation (pp. 327, 331, and 333), complete the sentence outline for your first speech. Include your bibliography at the end of the outline.

2. Compare what you have written to the sample outline on pp. 336 and 337 to make sure that it conforms to the guidelines discussed in this chapter. Check to see whether you have included your speech goal, the thesis statement (to be placed at the end of the introduction), clearly written main points, and transitions between main points.

Summary

A speech is organized with an introduction, a body, and a conclusion.

First, organize the body of the speech. Begin by writing a thesis statement based on the speech goal. When you have the potential main points, select the ones you will use and write them as complete sentences that are specific, vivid, and written in parallel language.

A speech can be organized in many different ways depending on the type of speech and the nature of the material. The most common organizational patterns are topic, time, and logical reasons.

Main points are embellished with supporting material. A useful process is to begin by mapping the potential material, then subordinating the material in a way that clarifies the relationship between and among subpoints and main points.

Prepare transitions to be used between points. Transitions are complete sentences that link major sections of a speech.

After you have outlined the body of the speech, outline the introduction. The introduction is used to gain attention, set the tone for the speech, create goodwill, and lead into the body of the speech. Types of introductions include startling statements, rhetorical questions, stories, personal references, quotations, and suspense.

Finally, outline the conclusion. A well-designed speech conclusion ties the speech together and ends it on a high note. Types of conclusions include summaries, stories, appeals to action, and emotional impact.

As Marna and Gloria were eating lunch together, Marna happened to ask Gloria, "How are you doing in Woodward's speech class?"

"Not bad," Gloria replied. "I'm working on this speech about product development. I think it will be really informative, but I'm having a little trouble with the opening. I just can't seem to get a good idea for getting started."

"Why not start with a story? That always worked for me in class."

"Thanks, Marna, I'll think on it."

The next day, when Marna ran into Gloria again, she asked, "How's that introduction going?"

"Great. I've prepared a great story about Mary Kay—you know, the cosmetics woman? I'm going to tell about how she was terrible in school and no one thought she'd amount to anything. But she loved dabbling with cosmetics so much that she decided to start her own business—and the rest is history."

"That's a great story. I really like that part about being terrible in school. Was she really that bad?"

"I really don't know—the material I read didn't really focus on that part of her life. But I thought that angle would get people listening right away. And after all, I did it that way because you suggested starting with a story."

"Yes, but . . ."

"Listen, she did start the business. So what if the story isn't quite right? It makes the point I want to make: If people are creative and have a strong work ethic, they can make it big."

1. What are the ethical issues?
2. Is anyone really hurt by Gloria's opening her speech with this story?

To refine the outline, check to be sure that you have followed all of the guidelines: Use a standard set of symbols, use complete sentences for main points and major subdivisions, limit each point to a single idea, relate minor points to major points, use no more than five main points, and make sure the outline length is no more than one-third the number of words of the final speech.

OBJECTIVES

After you have read this chapter, you should be able to answer the following questions:

- How can you develop common ground with your audience?

- What can you do to create or build audience interest?

- What can you do to adapt to your audience's level of understanding?

- What can you do to build the audience's perception of you as a speaker?

- What can you do to reinforce or change an audience's attitude toward your topic?

- What do you include in an audience adaptation strategy?

- What criteria do you use to select and construct visual aids?

Adapting to Audiences Verbally and Visually

Dan had gathered a wide variety of information for his speech. As he was pondering which information he should use and how he should use it, he began to get frustrated. As he was sharing his frustrations with his friend Gloria, she looked at him and asked, "Well, Dan, doesn't what you include and how you use it depend on who you're going to be talking with?" Dan slowly shook his head and said, "Of course—I forgot all about the audience!"

Dan had forgotten what has been recognized as long as speeches have been given—that a speech is intended for an audience.

Audience adaptation is the active process of verbally and/or visually relating material directly to the specific audience. You'll recall that an effective speech plan is a product of five action steps. In this chapter, we consider the fourth step: **Develop a strategy for adapting material to your specific speech audience.** This step involves developing common ground, building and maintaining audience interest, relating to your audience's level of understanding, reinforcing or changing your audience's attitude toward you or your topic, and relating information visually. In the next chapter, we continue to emphasize means of adapting to your audience through speech presentation.

Developing Common Ground

The effective speaker recognizes that listeners have expectations that speakers will recognize their presence. The first and perhaps most important way that speakers show awareness of their audiences' presence is to develop **common ground**—an awareness that the speaker and audience share the same or similar information, feelings, and experiences.

When you develop common ground with your audience, they will relate better to what you're saying.

© Cable News Network, Inc.

Let's look at five specific means of developing common ground, many if not all of which you should use in any speech.

Use Personal Pronouns

A sign of common ground is the use of personal pronouns. Merely by speaking in terms of "you," "us," "we," and "our," you give listeners verbal signs that you are talking with them. Compare the following two wordings from a speech on restaurants:

Impersonal: "When *people* go to a restaurant, *they* often wonder why servers are seldom responsible for tables that are next to each other."

Personal: "When *you* go to a restaurant, *you* may wonder why servers are seldom responsible for tables that are next to each other."

The difference between these two sentences may not seem like much, but it can mean the difference between audience attention and audience indifference to you and your speech.

Ask Rhetorical Questions

Although public speaking is not direct conversation with your audience, you can create the impression of conversation by asking rhetorical questions. **Rhetorical questions** are questions that are phrased to stimulate a mental response on the part of the audience rather than an actual spoken response. Thus, in the preceding restaurant example, one more change in the sample sentence would increase the sense of audience participation even more:

> **When you eat at a restaurant, have you ever said to yourself, "I wonder why our waiter has a table at the other side of the restaurant rather than next to ours?" or "I wonder why the waitress who has the table next to ours doesn't have ours as well?"**

Rhetorical questions generate audience participation; once the audience participates, it becomes more involved in the content. Since rhetorical questions must be sincere to be effective, practice them until you can ask questions naturally and sincerely.

Share Common Experiences

Another way of developing common ground is to share common experiences. Talking about common experiences allows your audience to identify with you. If you are talking to a group of scouts, for example, you might drive home the point that important tasks require hours of hard work by saying, "Remember the hours you put in working on your first merit badge? Remember wondering whether you'd ever get the darned thing finished? And do you remember how good it felt to know that the time you put in really paid off?" In this case, the members of the audience are led to think, "Yes, I remember—I worked hard

OBSERVE AND ANALYZE

Gaining Audience Attention

Think back to instances when people have used personal pronouns or rhetorical questions when they were addressing an audience. What effect did their efforts have on your attention to what they were saying? Why?

because I had a specific goal in mind." In addition to relating the common experience, also notice how this example incorporates personal pronouns and rhetorical questions to heighten the sense of shared experience. When members of an audience identify with you as a speaker, they will pay more attention to what you say.

✴ Personalize Information

Rather than using information in the same *form* as they found it, effective speakers are likely to look for ways to personalize that information. Suppose you are giving a speech on Japanese management techniques to your student chapter of the Society for Advancement of Management at a University in California. You want to begin by helping listeners understand some basic geographic data about Japan. You could just cite the following statistics from this year's *World Almanac*:

> **Japan is small and densely populated. The nation's 124 million people live in a land area of 145,000 square miles that gives them a population density of 844 persons per square mile.**

Although this passage conveys the information, it is not at all related to the specific audience. Notice how you could state the same information in a way that would be both more interesting and more meaningful to your California audience.

> **Japan is a small, densely populated nation of 124 million—about half the population of the United States. Yet the Japanese are crowded into a land area of only 145,000 square miles—roughly the same size as the state of California. Just think of the implications of having half the population of the United States living in California, where 30 million now live. On the average, Japan packs 844 persons into every square mile of land, whereas in the United States we average about 64 persons per square mile. Japan, then, is about thirteen times as crowded as the United States.**

This revision includes an invented comparison of the unknown, Japan, with the familiar, the United States and the state of California. Even though most Americans do not have the total land area of the United States on the tip of their tongue, they do know that the United States covers a great deal of territory. Likewise, a California audience would have a mental picture of the size of their home state compared to the rest of the nation. If you were speaking to an audience from another part of the country, you could make your comparison to a different state, such as Texas, New York, or Florida. Such personalized comparisons allow the audience to visualize just how small and crowded Japan is.

Reworking information so that it creates common ground will take time, but the effort will pay big dividends. Your listeners are always going to be asking, "What does this have to do with me?" And unless the way you present your information answers that question, your speeches are not going to be as

INFOTRAC COLLEGE EDITION

Using InfoTrac College Edition, click on Power Trac. Press on Key Word and drag down to Journal Name. Enter "Vital Speeches." View Vital Speeches and find a speech on or related to your topic. Then read that speech. Look for ways that the speaker attempted to create common ground. Did the speaker use personal pronouns or rhetorical questions? Share common experiences? Personalize information? If you find many examples, how do they help make the speech better? If you found few examples, how would their use have made the speech better?

effective as they should be. Examples, stories, illustrations, and quotations that relate to your audience answers that question.

Joan Gorham, the subject of the accompanying Spotlight on Scholarship, has conducted many research projects that show the effect of adaptation—or what she calls "immediacy"—not only in building attention, but also in ensuring audience retention of information.

SPOTLIGHT ON SCHOLARSHIP

Joan Gorham, Professor of Communication Studies and Associate Dean of Academic Affairs, Eberly College of Arts and Sciences, West Virginia University, on Immediacy

Since Joan Gorham began her professional career as a high school teacher, it is not surprising that her substantial body of research has focused on "immediacy"—the use of communicative behaviors to enhance the physical and psychological closeness between a teacher and student that ultimately affects student learning. Her first major work on the role of implicit communication in teaching was her dissertation at Northern Illinois University, in which she examined how a teacher's "silent messages"—those sent through the nonverbal channels—affected both adult and child learners.

When Gorham accepted a position at West Virginia University, she began building upon research by Jan Andersen, James McCroskey, Virginia Richmond, and others on the specific subject of immediacy. Although at that time she had not really intended to focus her lifetime research on immediacy, Gorham explained, "The research just grew out of itself. As I reported the data from one study, I found myself with many unanswered questions that motivated me to initiate new studies on different facets of the subject."

Taken together, Gorham's studies are helping teachers to understand how their communication behavior affects their relationship with their students and how significantly it is associated with student learning outcomes. Some of the early research on immediacy suggested that the learning outcome was just a perception: Students reported that they learned more from more immediate teachers, but these studies did not document actual learning gains. But as Gorham refined her research methods, she began to see results that supported the hypothesis that immediacy is directly correlated with learning.

Because the learning process consists of arousal, attention, and recall, Gorham believes that not only are teachers who demonstrate appropriate immediacy more likely to stimulate their students to pay attention, but also their lively interaction is more likely to increase the students' interest and motivation. As a result, students more easily understand and ultimately remember the information being presented.

In a practical sense, what specific behaviors must teachers use to increase their immediacy? From Gorham's studies we learn that teachers gain immediacy in part through such nonverbal behaviors as using gestures, looking directly at students, smiling, moving around the classroom, and using variety in their vocal expressions.

Moreover, Gorham's studies have also shown that teachers gain immediacy through such verbal behaviors as using personal examples, relating personal experiences, using humor, using personal pronouns, addressing students by name, conversing with students outside of class, praising students' work, and soliciting students' perceptions about assignments.

Gorham's studies, then, show that teachers can engage in behaviors that increase student motivation and ultimately student learning. Gorham has also probed the other side of the question: Do teachers exhibit behaviors related to immediacy that are "demotivating"—that is, behaviors that cause students to decrease attention and interest? What Gorham found was that although students identify teacher behaviors as a factor in motivating them to do their best in college courses, negative teacher behaviors are perceived by students as more central to their "demotivation" than positive factors are to their motivation. Some of the most demotivating teacher behaviors noted by students are lacking a sense of humor, lacking in dynamic behavior, lacking empathy for the students' perspective, not being available for individual help, using nonimmediate nonverbal behaviors, and using too many stories or examples—engaging in overkill.

Can teachers learn to increase their immediacy and reduce nonimmediate behaviors?

Gorham's research has shown that teachers can accurately monitor their own use of specific immediacy behaviors. Thus, she believes that as teachers are made aware of the critical role that immediacy plays in student motivation and learning, they can modify their own behavior and work toward incorporating the methods that lead to appropriate levels of immediacy. High-immediacy teachers are rated by students as higher in extroversion, composure, competence, and character than are low-immediacy teachers. They are rated as more similar to their students in attitude, but also as more expert, than nonimmediate teachers. Students report being significantly more likely to engage in behaviors recommended by teachers who use immediacy behaviors. Thus, learning the appropriate degree of immediacy between teachers and students becomes an important goal in the teaching/learning process.

In addition to her work as Associate Dean of Academic Affairs, Gorham also teaches courses in media effects, media literacy, and nonverbal and intercultural communication. In the future, not only does she plan to continue with replication and extension of her studies, she is also interested in engaging in longitudinal studies of motivation and immediacy. For titles of several of her research publications, see the References at the end of this book.

Creating and Maintaining Audience Interest

Listeners' interest depends on whether they believe that your information has personal impact ("What does this have to do with me?"). Let's consider four principles that you can use to build and maintain audience interest.

Timeliness

Listeners are more likely to be interested in information they perceive as timely; they want to know how they can use the information *now*. Suppose for your speech on "The criteria for evaluating the quality of diamonds," you determine that the topic is not likely to kindle much immediate audience interest. The following introduction may help motivate your audience to see knowledge of diamonds as timely:

> **In thinking about a gift for your spouse or significant other to celebrate a special occasion, you may have thought briefly about purchasing a diamond ring, earring, or necklace. But if you're like me, you might have shied away from that thought because you really don't know much about diamonds and you thought you couldn't afford it. Well, today I'd like to help you out some by talking about criteria for evaluating the quality of diamonds.**

Proximity

Listeners are more likely to be interested in information that has **proximity**—a relationship to their personal space. Psychologically, we pay more attention to information that affects our "territory" than information that we perceive as remote. You've heard speakers say something like, "Let me bring this closer to home by showing you. . . ." Statements like these work because information becomes important to people when they perceive it as affecting "their own backyard." If, for instance, you were giving a report on the difficulties that the EPA is having with its environmental cleanup campaigns, you would want to focus on examples in the audience's community. If you don't have that kind of information, take time to find it. For the EPA topic, for instance, a well-placed telephone call to the local or regional EPA office or even to your local newspaper will get the information you need to make the connection.

Impact

Listeners are more likely to be interested in information that has a serious physical, economic, or psychological impact on them. To build or maintain interest during a speech on toxic waste, you could show serious *physical* impact by saying "Toxic waste affects the health of all of us"; you could show serious *economic* impact by saying "Toxic waste cleanup and disposal are expensive—they raise our taxes"; or you could show serious *psychological* impact by saying "Toxic waste erodes the quality of our life and the lives of our children."

Think of how classroom attention picks up tremendously when the professor reveals that a particular piece of information is going to "be on the test." The potentially serious economic impact (not paying attention can cost us a lowered grade) is often enough to jolt us into attention. Most of us just don't put our attention into high gear unless we see the seriousness of information.

Vividness

Listeners are more likely to be interested in anecdotes, examples, and other information that is vivid—that arouses the senses. In the middle of a speech on toxic waste, for instance, you may see attention flagging. As you see attention to technical information waning, instead of waiting until you've lost the audience, you might choose this time to say, "Let me share with you a story that illustrates the gravity of toxic waste."

Just because you have a great number of attention-getting stories, examples, and illustrations does not mean that you have to use all of them. The effective speaker is sensitive to audience reaction at all times. When the audience is really with you, there's no need to break the rhythm. But when you sense that the audience is not following your ideas, that's the time to lighten up with material that will pique interest and attention. Keep in mind, however, that such information must pertain directly to the point you are making or it will be counterproductive.

Also remember that there is almost no way to keep audience members on the edge of their seats throughout the entire speech. Some sections of a speech may demand more from an audience. Any speech, regardless of how good, has highs and lows. The difference between an excellent speech and a mediocre one is that the highs are much higher and the lows are at the level of the mediocre speech's highs.

Adapting to Audience Level of Understanding

If you predict that your listeners do not have the necessary background to understand the information you will present in your speech, you will need to orient them. If, however, you predict that your audience has sufficient background, you will need to present the information in a way that will ensure continuous understanding.

Orienting Listeners

Since your listeners are likely to stop paying attention if they are lost at the start of your speech, a good rule of thumb is to err on the side of expecting too little knowledge rather than expecting too much. So, if there is any reason to believe that some people may not have necessary background knowledge, take time to review basic facts. For instance, for a speech about changes in political and economic conditions in Eastern Europe, you can be reasonably sure that everyone in your audience is aware of the breakup of the Soviet Union and Yugoslavia, but they may not remember all the specific countries that have been created. Before launching into changing conditions, remind your listeners of the names of the nations that you are going to be talking about.

Since some of your listeners may be well oriented, a good way to present that information without insulting their intelligence is to give the impression that you are reviewing information that the audience remembers. By saying, "As you will remember," "As we have come to find out," "As we all learned in our high school courses," your orientation will be accepted as review statements and not put-downs. For instance, for the speech on changes in political and economic conditions in Eastern Europe, you might say, "As you will recall, the old Soviet Union now consists of the following separate states." If listeners already know the information, they will see your statements as reminders; if they do not know it, they are getting the information in a way that doesn't call attention to their information gaps—they can act as if they do in fact remember.

How much orientation you can give depends on how much time is available. When you don't have the time to give a complete background, determine where a lack of information will impinge on your ability to get through to your audience and fill in the crucial information that closes those gaps.

Presenting New Information

Even when we predict that our audience has the necessary background information, we still need to work on ways of presenting new information that ensures continued understanding. Speakers can use such devices as defining, describing, exemplifying, and comparing to help clarify information that may be confusing or difficult for some audience members. A speaker must keep in mind that an audience is made up of individuals, and thus an effective speaker anticipates the different comprehension styles of those individuals. As you plan your speech, ask the following questions.

1. **Have you defined all key terms carefully?** For instance, if your speech goal is "I want my audience to understand four major problems faced by those who are functionally illiterate," you might present the following definition: "By 'functionally illiterate,' I mean people who have trouble accomplishing transactions involving reading and writing in which those individuals wish to engage."

2. **Have you supported every generalization with at least one specific example?** For instance, in support of the statement "The functionally illiterate have difficulty reading simple directions," you could use the following example: "For instance, a person who is functionally illiterate might not be able to read or understand a label that says 'take three times a day after eating.'"

3. **Have you compared and/or contrasted new information to information your audience already understands?** For instance, if you want to talk about badminton, a sport that your audience is unlikely to be familiar with, you may decide to compare badminton with tennis, a sport for which most Americans have a reasonably well developed set of procedures. For instance, you could say that the court is about two-thirds the size of a tennis court; that in both sports the players hit an object across a net with their

rackets, but a badminton racket is less than half the size of a tennis racket; that both sports use a net, but for badminton the net is five feet high instead of three feet six inches; and that instead of hitting a ball in the air or on the bounce, badminton players hit a shuttlecock—often called a bird—which must be kept in the air at all times.

In short, at any point in a speech where the audience may have difficulty understanding an idea or a concept, be prepared to define, exemplify, and compare. This advice is based on a sound psychological principle: The more different kinds of explanations a speaker gives, the more listeners will understand.

Now let's see how this works in practice. Suppose that a speaker says, "A significant number of Americans are functionally illiterate." A few audience members may understand the extent of illiteracy in America on the basis of that statement alone. Notice, however, how much clearer the statement becomes after the speaker says, "That is, large numbers of Americans cannot read well enough to understand simple cooking instructions, directions on how to work an appliance, or rules on how to play a game." With just the addition of three examples, many more people are likely to understand completely. Now notice how the extent of the problem is clarified with the addition of statistics: "About 20 percent of the adult population, or around 35 million people, have serious difficulties with common reading tasks."

Moreover, using different methods gives further emphasis to the material. The first statement, "A significant number of Americans are functionally illiterate," consists of eight words that are likely to be uttered in slightly less than five seconds! A listener who coughs, drops her pencil, or happens to remember an appointment she has during those five seconds will miss the entire sentence. The reiteration with examples adds thirty-one words and takes an additional ten or more seconds to utter. Now, even in the face of some distractions, it is likely that most listeners will have heard and registered the information.

Because another way of presenting information is to show it as well as to talk about it, later in this chapter we will consider adapting to audiences visually.

Building a Positive Attitude toward You as the Speaker

If you predict that your audience will have a positive attitude toward you as a speaker, then you need only try to maintain that attitude; if, however, you predict that the audience has no opinion or for some reason has a negative attitude toward you, then you will want to change that attitude.

Your audience will expect you to have a wealth of high-quality examples, illustrations, and personal experiences in your speech.

Audience attitude toward you relates to your **credibility** with the audience—the level of trust that an audience has or will have in you. As you recall from the discussion in Chapter 12, your credibility is based primarily on the listener's perception of your knowledge/expertise on the particular subject and your trustworthiness and personality.

Build Audience Perception of Your Knowledge and Expertise

As you will recall, the dimension of **knowledge and expertise** includes your qualifications or capability, or what is referred to as your "track record."

The first step in building a perception of knowledge and expertise is to go into the speaking situation fully prepared. Audiences have an almost instinctive knowledge of when a speaker is "winging it," and most audiences lose respect for a speaker who hasn't thought enough of them or the situation to have a well-prepared message.

The next step is to show your audience that you have a wealth of high-quality examples, illustrations, and personal experiences. Recall how much more favorably you perceive your professors who have an inexhaustible supply of supporting information as opposed to those professors who present, and seem to have, only the barest minimum of facts.

The third step is to show any direct involvement you have had with the topic area. In addition to increasing the audience's perception of your depth of

knowledge, your personal involvement increases the audience's perception of your practical understanding of the issues and your personal concern for the subject. For example, if you are speaking on toxic waste, your credibility will increase manifold if you share with the audience your personal experiences in petitioning for local environmental controls.

Build Audience Perception of Your Trustworthiness

Trustworthiness, you recall, refers both to your character and your apparent motives for speaking. The more your listeners see you as one of them, the easier it will be for you to establish your trustworthiness; the more your listeners see you as different, the more difficult it will be. Whether people *should* be or not, they are more distrustful of those they see as different. Thus, women are generally more trusting of other women than of men; African Americans are more trusting of other African Americans than of European Americans or Asian Americans; Christians are more trusting of other Christians than of Jews or Muslims. Part of building your credibility, then, depends on your ability to bridge gaps between you and members of your audience.

First, listeners will make value judgments of your character based on their assessment of your moral and ethical traits. What are your character strengths? Are you an honest, industrious, dependable, morally strong person? As you plan your speech, you need to ask yourself what you can do in the speech to demonstrate these moral and ethical traits. For instance, how can you convince your audience that you have presented your information honestly?

In addition, listeners will consider your apparent motives. Early in your speech, it's important to show why listeners need to know your information. Then, throughout the speech, you can emphasize your sincere interest in their well-being. In a speech on toxic waste, for example, you could explain how a local dumpsite affects the community. As you present documented facts and figures showing the extent of danger to individuals, your audience is likely to form the belief that you have a sincere interest in the well-being of the community.

Build Audience Perception of Your Personality

You'll recall that **personality** is the impression you make on your audience based on such traits as enthusiasm, friendliness, warmth, and a ready smile.

Since audience perceptions of your personality are likely to be based on their first impressions of you, try to dress appropriately, groom yourself carefully, and carry yourself in an attractive manner. The old compliment "He/she cleans up real good" is one to remember. It is surprising how much an appropriately professional manner of dress and demeanor will increase audience perception of personality.

In addition, audiences react favorably to a speaker who acts friendly. A smile and a pleasant tone of voice go a long way in showing a warmth that will increase listeners' comfort with you and your ideas.

We will discuss three additional features of personality (enthusiasm, eye contact, and vocal expressiveness) in the next chapter on speech presentation.

In addition to what you can do in the speech, you can also enlist the help of the person who is assigned to introduce you in building your credibility. Although classroom speeches are given without benefit of an introductory speech, in real-life situations there is almost always someone assigned to introduce you and your speech. Well before the day of the speech, provide that person with information about you. If the introducer asks you to write an introduction for him or her to present, by all means take advantage of the opportunity. Include information that shows your experience in the subject area. If, for example, you are speaking about literacy to a Parents and Teachers Association meeting, be sure to mention your experience in tutoring children and adults.

Adapting to Audience Attitude toward Your Speech Goal

Although adapting to listeners' attitudes toward your speech goal is especially important for persuasive speeches, it can be important for informative speeches as well. An audience **attitude** is a predisposition for or against people, places, or things, usually expressed as an opinion. So, for a speech on refinishing wooden furniture, your listeners may hold the opinion that "refinishing furniture is too hard."

At the outset, try to predict whether listeners will view your topic positively, negatively, or have no opinion. If, for instance, you think your listeners view refinishing positively or neutrally, you can move forward with your speech; if, however, you think your listeners view refinishing furniture as too hard or unimportant, then you'll need to take time early in the speech to change their opinion. In Chapter 18, Persuasive Speaking, we will consider strategies for dealing with listeners' attitudes in more detail.

Special Problems of Speakers from Different Cultures

This chapter has been written with the assumption that you have been raised in the United States. But even in the United States, you may have to adapt to cultural differences of your listeners. For instance, Mexican Americans, Japanese

The Need to Be: The Socio-Cultural Significance of Black Language

by Shirley N. Weber

A major aspect of adapting to different groups is understanding their expectations and their reactions to your words. In this excerpt, Shirley Weber describes the African American perspective on audience role in speaking.

To fully understand and appreciate black language and its function in the black community, it is essential to understand that while philosophies that govern the different groups in Africa vary, some general concepts are found throughout African cultures. One of the primary principles is the belief that everything has a reason for being. Nothing simply exists without purpose or consequences. This is the basis of John's explanation of the four basic elements of life, which are Muntu, mankind; Kintu, things; Hantu, place and time; and Kuntu, modality. These four elements do not exist as static objects but as forces that have consequences and influence. For instance in Hantu, the West is not merely a place defined by geographic location, but a force that influences the East, North, and South. Thus, the term "Western world" connotes a way of life that either complements or challenges other ways of life. The Western world is seen as a force and not a place. (This is applicable to the other three elements also.) Muntu, or mankind, is distinguished from the other three elements by his possession of Nommo, the magical power of the word. Without Nommo, nothing exists. Consequently, mankind, the possessor of Nommo, becomes the master of all things. . . .

Nommo is so powerful and respected in the black community that only those who are skillful users of the word become leaders. One of the main qualifications of leaders of black people is that they must be able to articulate the needs of the people in a most eloquent manner. And because Muntu is a force who controls Nommo,

which has power and consequences, the speaker must generate and create movement and power within his listeners. One of the ways this is done is through the use of imaginative and vivid language. Of the five canons of speech, it is said that Inventio or invention is the most utilized in black American. Molefi Asante called it the "coming to be of the novel," or the making of the new. So that while the message might be the same, the analogies, stories, images, and so forth must be fresh, new, and alive.

Because nothing exists without Nommo, it, too is the force that creates a sense of community among communicators, so much so that the speaker and audience become one as senders and receivers of the message. Thus, an audience listening and responding to a message is just as important as the speaker, because without their "amens" and "right-ons" the speaker may not be successful. This interplay between speaker and listeners is called "call and response" and is a part of the African world view, which holds that all elements and forces are interrelated and indistinguishable because they work together to accomplish a common goal and to create a sense of community between the speaker and the listeners.

This difference between blacks and whites was evident, recently, in a class where I lectured on Afro-American history. During the lecture, one of my more vocal black students began to respond to the message with some encouraging remarks like "all right," "make it plain," "that all right," and "teach." She was soon joined by a few more black students who gave similar comments. I noticed that this surprised and confused some of the white students. When questioned later about this, their response was that they were not used to having more than one person talk at a time, and they really could not talk and listen at the same time. They found the comments annoying and disruptive. As the lecturer, I found the comments refreshing and inspiring. The black student who initiated the responses had no difficulty understanding what I was saying while she was reacting to it, and did not consider herself "rude."

In addition to the speaker's verbal creativity and dynamic quality of the communication environment, black speech is very rhythmic. It

flows like African languages in a consonant-vowel-consonant-vowel pattern. To achieve this rhythmic effect, some syllables are held longer and are accented stronger and differently from standard English, such as DE-troit. This rhythmic pattern is learned early by young blacks and is reinforced by the various styles it complements.

Excerpted from Shirley N. Weber, "The Need to Be: The Socio-Cultural Significance of Black Language." From Intercultural Communication: A Reader, *7th ed., eds. Larry A. Samovar and Richard E. Porter (Belmont, CA: Wadsworth, 1994), pp. 220–225. Reprinted by permission of the author.*

Americans, and African Americans raised in the United States may maintain a strong sense of their Mexican, Japanese, or African heritage and, as a result, may see things differently from each other. The accompanying Diverse Voices feature gives you a sense of one of the kinds of differences you may have to adapt to.

In addition, the chances of students in this course coming from foreign cultures has increased dramatically. Suppose, for a minute, that you have recently immigrated to the United States or have come here from abroad for your higher education. Being less familiar with the general United States culture, you will have a more difficult time adapting to your classroom audiences than will other students in the class.

Two of the problems with adaptation for people from foreign backgrounds are difficulty with the English language and lack of a common set of experiences to draw from. Difficulty with the language includes both difficulty with pronunciation and difficulty with vocabulary and idiomatic speech. Both of these could make you feel self-conscious. But the lack of a common set of experiences to draw from may be even more significant. So much of our information is gained through comparison and examples that the lack of common experiences may make drawing comparisons and using appropriate examples much more difficult.

What can you do to help you through the public-speaking experience? Difficulty with language might require you to speak more slowly and articulate as clearly as possible. Also, make sure that you are comfortable with your topic. You might want to consider talking about aspects of your homeland. Since you would be providing new information, your classmates would likely look forward to hearing you speak. It would be useful for you to practice at least once with a person raised in the United States. You can ask the person to help you make sure that you are using language, examples, and comparisons that the audience will be able to relate to.

On the other hand, you'll find that most American students are much more tolerant of mistakes made by people who are speaking in their second or even third language than they are of mistakes made by American-born students. Also keep in mind that the more practice you can get speaking to people from this culture, the more comfortable you will become with the language and with your ability to relate to them.

Adapting to Audiences Visually

At this point in your preparation, you are ready to consider how to adapt to your audience visually. A **visual aid** is a form of speech development that allows the audience to see as well as hear information. You'll want to consider using visual aids because they help both to clarify and to dramatize verbal information. Research findings suggest that people remember features of visual aids well even over long periods (Pavio 1979); that some people retained pictorial information without loss of accuracy for more than four months (Mandler and Ritchey 1977); and that people learn considerably more when ideas appeal to both eye and ear than when they appeal to the ear alone (Gadzella and Whitehead 1975).

In my own classes, a great many students report that for the round of speeches in which I require the use of visual aids they enjoy the speeches more and remember more information from them than from speeches in any other round. You can use one or more of the following types of visual aids for your speeches.

Yourself

On occasion, you can become your own best visual aid. Through descriptive gestures, you can show the size of a soccer ball or the height of a tennis net; through your posture and movement, you can show the motions involved in swimming the butterfly stroke or administering artificial respiration; through your attire, you can illustrate the native dress of a foreign country, the necessary equipment for a cave explorer, or the uniform of a firefighter.

Objects

The objects you are talking about make good visual aids if they are large enough to be seen and small enough to carry around with you. A vase, a basketball, or a braided rug is the kind of object that can be seen by the audience and manipulated by the speaker.

Models

When an object is too large to bring to the speech site or too small to be seen, a three-dimensional model may prove a worthwhile substitute. If you were to talk about a turbine engine, a suspension bridge, an Egyptian pyramid, or the structure of an atom, a model might well be the best visual aid. Working models are especially eye-catching.

Charts

A **chart** is a graphic representation that distills a lot of information and presents it to an audience in an easily interpreted format. The most common are word charts, organizational charts, bar charts, line graphs, and pie charts.

Word charts are often used to preview material that will be covered in a speech, to summarize material, and to remind an audience of speech content. For a speech on the parts of a computer, a speaker might make a word chart that lists key topics, as shown in Figure 15.1. To make the points more eye-catching, the speaker could use a picture or a sketch to portray each word. A variety of computer programs offer "clip art" that you can use.

Organizational charts use symbols and connecting lines to diagram step-by-step progressions through a complicated procedure or system. The chart in Figure 15.2 illustrates the organization of a student union board.

Bar charts—graphs with vertical or horizontal bars—can show relationships between two or more variables at the same time or at various times on one or more dimensions. For instance, if you were giving a speech on gold, you could use the bar graph in Figure 15.3 to show comparative holdings of gold by member nations of the International Monetary Fund (IMF).

Line graphs indicate changes in one or more variables over time. In a speech on the population of the United States, for example, the line graph in Figure 15.4 helps by showing the population increase, in millions, from 1810 to 1990.

COMPUTER ESSENTIALS

1. **Central Processing Unit**

2. **Memory**

3. **Input/Output**

Figure 15.1
A sample word chart.

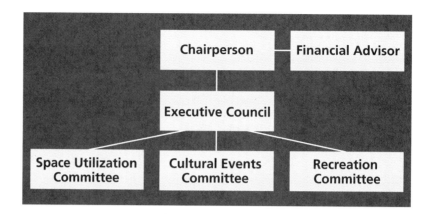

Figure 15.2
A sample organizational chart.

Pie charts help audiences to visualize the relationships among parts of a single unit. The pie chart in Figure 15.5, for example, shows visually how U.S. exports of frozen French fries are distributed among various countries.

A **flipchart**—a large pad of paper mounted on an easel—is a popular method of displaying charts. Flipcharts (and easels) are available in many sizes. For a presentation to four or five people, a small tabletop version works well; for a larger audience, it is wise to use a larger size, such as thirty-by-forty inches.

Pictorial Representations

In addition to charts, other types of graphic visuals include pictorial representations such as diagrams, drawings, maps, and photographs.

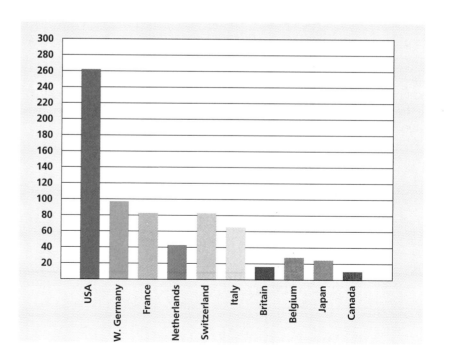

Figure 15.3
A bar graph showing comparative holdings of gold in 1993 by IMF member nations (in millions of fine troy ounces). (Source: *1995 World Almanac.*)

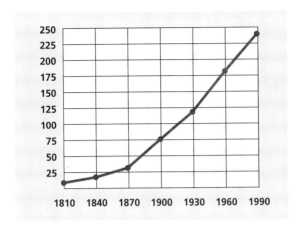

Figure 15.4
A line graph showing U.S. population increase from 1810 to 1990 (in millions).

Diagrams and **drawings** are popular visual aids because they are easy to prepare. If you can use a compass, a straightedge, and a measure, you can draw well enough for most speech purposes. For instance, if you are making the point that water skiers must hold their arms straight, with the back straight and knees bent slightly, a stick figure (see Figure 15.6) will illustrate the point. Stick figures may not be as aesthetically pleasing as professional drawings, but they work just as well. In fact, elaborate, detailed drawings are not worth the time and effort and may actually obscure the point you wish to make. If your prospective drawing is too complicated for you to handle personally, then you may need professional help. A major advantage of drawings is that you can often sketch cartoon figures to help you make a point humorously.

Maps are pictorial representations of a territory. Well-prepared maps allow you to focus on landforms (mountains, rivers, and lakes), states, cities, land routes, or weather systems. The map in Figure 15.7 is a good example of a map that focuses on weather systems.

The major problems that people encounter with drawing visual aids involve size, color, and neatness. First, check your lettering for size. Move as far away from the visual aid you've created as the farthest person in your audience will be sitting. If you can read the lettering and see the details from that distance, then both are large enough; if not, draw another sample and check it for size.

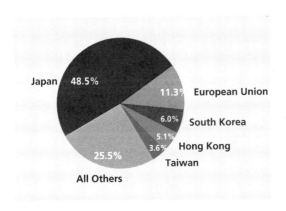

Figure 15.5
A pie chart showing distribution of U.S. frozen French fry exports in 1995. (Source: *USA Today*, February 27, 1996, p. B2.)

Figure 15.6
Sample drawing.

Second, check the colors for contrast. Black or red on white always provides a good contrast, but some color combinations cannot be seen well. Before you commit yourself to colors, draw sample color contrasts and look at them from a distance. Third, make sure that the visual aid is uncluttered and free of smudges.

Photographs are useful visual aids when you need an exact reproduction. To be effective, photographs need to be large enough to be seen from the back of the room and simple enough to make your point at a glance.

Projections

Almost any kind of graphic or pictorial visual aid can be prepared for projection onto a screen. Projection media include overhead transparencies, slides, and films.

Overhead transparencies are projected onto a screen by means of an overhead projector. Overheads can be made easily and inexpensively either by hand (traced or hand-lettered) or by machine (copy machine, thermographic, color lift, or computer). They work well in nearly any setting, and unlike other kinds of projections, they don't require dimming the lights in the room. Overheads

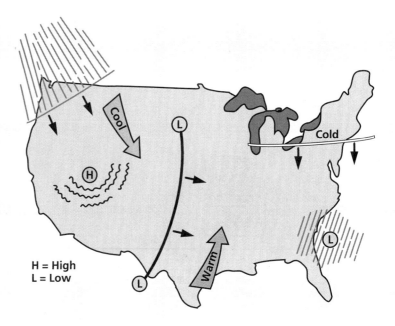

H = High
L = Low

Figure 15.7
A sample map.

Slides and overhead transparencies get and hold attention and can be seen by the entire audience.

are especially useful for showing how formulas work, for illustrating computations, or for analyzing data because you can write, trace, or draw on the transparency while you are talking.

Slides are mounted transparencies that can be projected individually. The advantage of slides over film is that you can control when each image will be shown. The remote-control device allows you to pace your showing of slides and to talk about each one as long as necessary. But because slides require darkening the room while they are projected, novice speakers may lose control of their audience.

Perhaps the single biggest potential problem is that slides are often out of order. When you have finished rehearsing your speech (be sure to rehearse using the slides as you plan to use them in your speech), double-check that the slides are in the right order.

Although **films** may be beautifully done, they are seldom appropriate for speeches, mostly because films so dominate that the speaker loses control. Occasionally during a longer speech you may want to use short clippings of a minute or two each. Still, because projecting film requires a darkening of the room for that portion of time, using film in a speech is often disruptive.

Chalkboard

As a means of displaying simple information, the chalkboard, a staple in every college classroom, is unbeatable. Unfortunately, the chalkboard is also easy to misuse and to overuse. Moreover, it is unlikely that the chalkboard would be your first choice for any major analysis of a process or procedure because of its limitations in displaying complex material. Nevertheless, effective use of the chalkboard should be a part of any professional speaker's repertoire.

One common error in using the chalkboard is to write too much material while you are talking, an error that often results in displays that are either illegible or partly obscured by your body as you write. A second common error is to spend too much time talking to the board instead of to the audience.

The chalkboard is best used for short items of information that can be written in a few seconds. If you plan to draw or write while talking, practice doing it. If you are right-handed, stand to the right of what you are drawing. Try to face at least part of the audience while you work. Although it may seem awkward at first, your effort will allow you to maintain contact with your audience and will allow the audience to see what you are doing while you are doing it.

Handouts

Among the first visual aids that come to mind for many speakers are handouts. On the plus side, you can prepare handouts quickly, and all the people in the audience can have their own professional-quality material to refer to and take with them from the speech. On the minus side is the distraction of distributing handouts and the potential for losing the audience's attention when you want it to be looking at you. Before you decide on handouts, consider each of the other types of visual aids discussed previously. If you do decide on handouts, it is a good idea to distribute them at the end of the speech.

Computer Graphics

The availability of software designed especially for producing "presentation graphics" is rapidly changing how many speakers prepare charts, diagrams, and other visual aids. Software is now available that allows users to display the

---

PRACTICE IN SPEECH PREPARATION

Selecting Visual Aids

The goal of this exercise is to help you determine what, if any, visual aids you will use in your speech.

1. Carefully study the verbal information you are planning to use in the speech. Where do you believe visual aids would be effective in creating audience interest, facilitating understanding, or increasing retention?

2. What kinds of visual aids would be most effective in each of the places you have identified? Yourself? Objects? Models? Charts? Pictorial representations? Projections? Chalkboard? Handouts? Computer graphics?

graphics directly on a monitor as a computer slide show. Graphics prepared on a computer can be projected with special equipment, printed out and enlarged, photographed to make slides, or used to create overhead transparencies or handouts. Except for complex multimedia presentations, then, computer graphics are not so much a new type of visual aid as a new way of producing the kinds of visuals already discussed.

The ever-growing capabilities of personal computers and popular software packages are rapidly making computer graphics a regular part of many speakers' repertoires. Today's computers are so easily accessible and so advanced in capabilities that any professional speaker should experiment with computer graphics, such as *PowerPoint*, to prepare visual material for speeches. If you have not tried a presentation graphics package or if you are unsure of which one to try and what its capabilities might be, investigate computer magazines for reviews of graphics. When you learn to use one of the many computer graphics packages, you will find that with a few computer keystrokes or with the click of a "mouse" you can change lines of facts and figures into a variety of graphic displays.

If you experiment with computer graphics, though, keep in mind that all the guidelines for using visual aids still apply. In particular, be wary of the temptation to produce overly fancy graphics that actually obscure the information you want the audience to assimilate. With the ability the computer gives to manipulate graphics—for example, to easily create complex three-dimensional bar charts or combine several images and typefaces in a single display—it is easy to let the medium overpower the message.

A Plan of Adaptation

Now that you have considered how to adapt speech information to a given audience verbally and visually, it is time to determine a specific plan of adaptation. Adaptation is relatively easy when the majority of the audience members are like you—that is, similar to you in age, race, religion, academic background, and so forth. As you face more diverse audiences, however, problems of adaptation become more complex. As a result, you must think through the basis for your predictions very carefully and speak to each of them completely. Even experienced speakers find that it helps to write out a governing strategy.

Specifics of a Plan

To begin a plan of adaptation, you need to assemble a specific audience analysis for each speech situation (see checklist, p. 281). Analyze your information on audience age, education, occupation, income, race, religion, nationality, group

Once you have analyzed your audience, you need to develop a plan of adaptation to address that audience.

affiliation, and geographic uniqueness to determine the significant characteristics of your audience. Recall that you are predicting whether or not your audience is interested in the topic, likely to understand your material, and likely to have a positive attitude toward you and your topic or speech goal. Direct audience adaptation may be relevant for all three of these assessments. When you have reviewed your predictions, you can consider strategies for adaptation.

1. **What will you do to establish common ground?** Where and how will you use personal pronouns, rhetorical questions, common experiences, and personalized information?

2. **What will you do to build and maintain interest?** Write down what you will do to show timeliness, proximity, and seriousness of impact. Also indicate what attention-getting techniques you plan to use during the speech to rebuild or heighten interest. Indicate where you can use visual aids to gain or heighten interest.

3. **What will you do to increase audience understanding?** Show what you will do to orient your listeners if they have insufficient background to understand your speech. Then, how will you use definition, examples, comparisons, and contrasts to facilitate listener understanding? Indicate where you can use visual aids to increase understanding.

4. **What will you do to build your credibility?** Write how you will attempt to show your knowledge/expertise, trustworthiness, and appealing personality. If you will be introduced by another speaker, list what you hope will be

the result of that introduction. The majority of your analysis should focus on what you will do in the speech.

5. **What will you do to build and maintain a positive attitude toward your topic?** Write about how you will focus on the importance of understanding the information you will present. Even if an audience has a negative attitude toward your goal, you may be able to show them that they still need the information you will present. Since audience attitude toward the speech goal is much more significant in persuasive speeches, we will consider specific strategies in Chapter 18.

Examples of Adaptation Strategies

For practice, let us consider two contrasting cases—one in which audience factors are known and in your favor, and one in which audience factors have to be inferred from the data available and are less favorable to your success.

Case 1: Audience factors are known and in your favor. Lana Jackson, the immediate supervisor for all clerical staff at her company, is speaking to inform them about the installation of a new word-processing program on all computers.

Because Lana is the supervisor, she knows that the audience will be comprised of about twenty-five Cincinnati women and men of mixed race, religion, and nationality, ages from nineteen to forty, whose educational levels range from high school graduate to graduates of two-year college programs.

Based on that information, her analysis could include the following predictions: First, audience interest is likely to be high because they will have to become proficient with the new program in a short period of time. Second, because of their familiarity with the company, the types of computers, and the previous package, audience level of understanding of the information about the new package is likely to be high. Third, while their attitude toward her may be generally positive, her audience may not be sure of her expertise with the new package. And fourth, although audience attitude toward changing programs may vary, they are likely to be open to the information if they can be convinced that the new package provides many improvements allowing them to accomplish their goals more easily. As a result of these predictions, Lana might write the strategy shown in Figure 15.8.

Case 2: Audience factors have to be inferred from the data available and are less favorable to your success. This time Lana Jackson is asked to talk about computer software packages to the monthly meeting of a local community organization. Because members of the speaker committee of this organization wanted to be "up to date," they thought it would be worthwhile to have a speech on this topic so that their members could learn something about how they could make greater use of a computer if they owned or had access to one.

Common ground: Throughout the speech I will use personal pronouns and ask appropriate rhetorical questions. Whenever possible, I will try to personalize information.

Interest: Because interest is likely to be high, I will place my emphasis on maintaining that interest. Since the staff are familiar with word-processing packages, I can focus on several of the features that will enable them to produce better copy more easily; thus, I can emphasize timeliness and economic impact (saving time and money). I will also use visual material to show my listeners what I am talking about.

Understanding: To adapt to their knowledge level, I will use comparisons of the key features of the new package to operations they are familiar with. And where possible, I will share common experiences and personalize information. I will use overhead projections to help clarify difficult ideas.

Attitude toward speaker: Audience attitude toward me may be skeptical. Because I am "management," they may be a little cynical about my intentions. I will have to stress that what is good for the company is also good for them. They may also wonder about my expertise with the new package. I will have to be especially careful to present information smoothly and accurately.

Attitude toward topic or speech goal: Although their attitude toward the speech goal is likely to be favorable, I will still attempt to feature improvements so that they will understand why they need to spend their time and energy learning the new system. I will show them that the improvements are significant.

Figure 15.8
Sample adaptation strategy: audience factors known/favorable.

If the only information Lana has about the audience is that they are adult members of a community organization who have agreed to schedule a speech on computer software, she can still infer data about them that will help her determine a speech strategy.

Because it is an adult organization, Lana can infer that the audience will be comprised of both males and females of mixed race, religion, and nationality, with a mixed educational background, and ages ranging from about twenty-five upward. Moreover, she can infer that many have homes and families, and because they are members of a local community organization, they will have a geographic bond.

Even though her information is inferred, Lana can still make predictions about interests, understanding, and attitude. Based on that information, her analysis could include the following predictions:

First, the audience's interests are likely to vary, because they have no immediate need for information about computer packages other than natural curiosity. Still, they wouldn't come if they didn't have some interest.

Second, because their background knowledge probably ranges widely, it is likely that their level of understanding of the specifics of software packages is relatively low.

Third, their attitude toward the speaker is likely to be neutral because they won't know much about her.

Fourth, their attitude about software packages is likely to range from favorable to neutral or even slightly negative. Some will be very positive about what the software can do for them; others will be fearful and will see the computer as an intrusion into their privacy.

As a result of these predictions, Lana might develop the strategy shown in Figure 15.9.

Common ground: Throughout the speech I will use personal pronouns and ask appropriate rhetorical questions. Whenever possible, I will try to personalize information.

Interest: Because interest levels will vary, I will have to begin the speech with an anecdote or a personal experience that will capture initial interest. Very early in the speech I will also try to develop a need to gain information about computer software packages. I will stress those software packages that would be useful immediately to a general adult audience and would have a real impact on them. I should limit my speech to packages that would help them manage finances—including those providing investment information. And of course, I will develop visual aids to reinforce key points.

Understanding: Because the audience members are unlikely to share the same background information on computers, I will need background information about the usefulness of computers and computer packages in general to all adults. I must keep information on an elementary level, and I must define all terms carefully. I must also take into account the perceptions of people of different races and cultural backgrounds. I will need a variety of examples, illustrations, and anecdotes that relate to a racially and culturally diverse audience. To adapt to their level of understanding, I will compare computer package information to other operator manuals and directions they are familiar with. And of course, wherever possible, I will try to personalize information. I will also try to show visually how packages are used.

Attitude toward speaker: Because they know little about me, I will have to demonstrate my expertise and assure them that my intentions are to help them learn more about technology that could be useful to them. Moreover, since they may perceive themselves as being different from me, I'm going to have to demonstrate my trustworthiness. I will be especially careful with the way I present information so that they will see me as reliable. I will also try to keep the speech light and somewhat humorous.

Attitude toward topic or speech goal: Because their attitudes are also likely to vary, I will use examples and illustrations of "average Americans" who have found interest in computer packages.

Figure 15.9

Sample adaptation strategy: audience factors unknown/unfavorable.

Summary

Speakers adapt to their audiences by speaking directly to them and by planning strategies that create or build audience interest, adapt to audience levels of understanding, and adapt to audience attitudes toward the speaker and the speech goal.

Direct audience adaptation includes using personal pronouns, rhetorical questions, common experiences, and personalized information.

Most people's interest is determined by whether they believe that information relates specifically to them. Strategies include stressing the timeliness of the information, the impact on the audience's personal space, and the seriousness of the personal impact. To deal with lapses in attention, prepare stories, examples, and illustrations that you can use when attention flags.

Strategies for adapting to audience understanding of information depend on the audience's existing knowledge level. If the audience lacks specific topic knowledge, then fill in necessary background information. During the remainder of the speech use definitions, examples, and comparisons.

If the audience has a positive attitude toward you, try to maintain that attitude; if, however, it has no opinion or for some reason is negative, then work to change that attitude. Attitude toward the speaker is based on audience perception of the speaker's credibility, the level of trust that audience members have in the speaker, and their impression of the speaker's personality. Although a positive introduction by another person can help, speakers build positive attitudes by going into the speech fully prepared, by emphasizing sincere interest in the audience's well-being, by dressing, grooming, and presenting themselves attractively, and by smiling and talking in a pleasant tone of voice.

Audience attitudes toward the speech goal can be classified as no opinion, in favor, or opposed. If the audience has no opinion, is in favor, or is only

"Kendra, I heard you telling Jim about the speech you're giving tomorrow. You think it's a winner, huh?"

"You got that right, Omar. I'm going to have Bardston eating out of the palm of my hand."

"You sound confident."

"This time I have reason to be. See, Prof. Bardston's been talking about the importance of audience adaptation. These last two weeks that's all we've heard—adaptation, adaptation."

"What does she mean?"

"Talking about something in a way that really relates to people personally."

"OK, so how are you going to do that?"

"Well, you see, I'm giving this speech on abortion. Now here's the kick. Bardston let it slip that she's a supporter of Right to Life. So what I'm going to do is give this informative speech on the Right to Life movement. But I'm going to discuss the major beliefs of the movement in a way that'll get her to think that I'm a supporter. I'm going to mention aspects of the movement that I know she'll like."

"But I've heard you talk about how you're pro-choice."

"I am—all the way. But by keeping the information positive, I'll let her think I'm a supporter. It isn't as if I'm going to be telling any lies or anything."

1. In a speech, is it ethical to adapt in a way that resonates with your "audience" but isn't in keeping with what you really believe?
2. Could Kendra have achieved her goal by using different methods? How?

slightly opposed to your topic, efforts to create and build attention and relate to the audience's level of understanding will also work to improve attitude. If the audience is opposed to the topic or goal, select another one that is less challenging.

Visual aids include the speaker, objects, models, charts, pictorial representations, projections, chalkboard, handouts, and computer graphics. Visual aids have the greatest impact if they are used in ways that reinforce the points of the speech.

For your first few speeches, it may help to write out a governing strategy that specifies how you plan to adapt your speech to the specific audience.

OBJECTIVES

After you have read this chapter, you should be able to answer the following questions:

■ How does extemporaneous speaking differ from other methods of delivery?

■ What verbal components are most relevant to public speaking?

■ What nonverbal components are most relevant to public speaking?

■ How can you achieve a conversational quality in your speaking?

■ What are the characteristics of effective speech practice?

■ What are some comforting ideas about speaker nervousness?

■ What are some specific behaviors for limiting nervousness?

■ By what criteria is an effective speech measured?

16

Presenting Your Speech

"That was really good," Keisha said to Derek as Mikala finished her speech. "She didn't seem to be giving a speech—she was just talking with us."

"True," Derek replied, "but the way she described the procedure you could tell that she had worked to make sure the steps were clear."

"Maybe, but it just seemed so easy for her—I wish I could be so smooth."

Easy? Maybe, but the fact is that in addition to the hours she spent finding and organizing her material, Mikala also practiced the speech many times until she was sure that her speech was well presented.

You'll recall that an effective speech plan is a product of five action steps. In this chapter, we consider the fifth step: **Practice the presentation of the speech until the wording is clear, vivid, and emphatic and until the delivery represents a conversational style that shows enthusiasm, vocal expressiveness, spontaneity, fluency, and eye contact.**

Although speeches may be presented impromptu (on the spur of the moment without prior preparation), by manuscript (completely written out and then read aloud), or by memory (completely written out and then memorized), the material you have been reading is designed to help you present your speeches extemporaneously. An **extemporaneous** speech is carefully prepared and practiced, but the exact wording is determined at the time of utterance. If you have mastered the action steps of preparing an extemporaneous speech, your impromptu and manuscript speeches will be better as well.

In this chapter, we will consider verbal components of presentation, nonverbal components of presentation, characteristics of conversational style, guidelines for effective practice, coping with nervousness, and criteria for evaluating a speech. Then we will look at a sample speech.

Components to Practice in Your Speech

As you practice your speech, you'll be analyzing the verbal and nonverbal components of your presentation. Let's consider each of these elements.

Verbal Components

Good speaking, unlike good writing, is measured by the ear, not the eye. Since listeners cannot "reread" what you have said, your speech must be clear (using specific/concrete, precise, and, when possible, simple language), vivid, and emphatic.

Clarity. Words that are **specific** and **concrete**, as we saw in Chapter 3, help listeners visualize what you're saying. Try to weed out expressions like "You'll need a lot of things," "They live in a really big place," or "You've got to go for it"; replace them with expressions that we can visualize like "You'll need sharp pencils," "They live in a ten room Victorian mansion," or "You've got to focus your attention on singing on key."

Precise words (also discussed in Chapter 3) create a meaning in the minds of an audience that is as close as possible to the meaning intended. Thus, to convey the idea of a large body of running water precisely, you say "river"; to convey the idea of a small body of running water, you say "stream" or "creek."

Simple words are words that are readily understood by all listeners. When handling complex ideas, speakers sometimes go overboard and use words that seem pompous, affected, or stilted. When you have a choice, select the simplest, most familiar word that expresses your precise meaning. For example, an effective speaker will say

building rather than *edifice*

clothing rather than *apparel*

bury rather than *inter*

begin rather than *commence*

use rather than *utilize*

view rather than *vista*

Vividness. Words that are **vivid** are descriptive, full of life, vigorous, bright, intense. Instead of saying "Jackson made a great catch," it would be more vivid to say "Jackson made a dramatic one-hand catch against the wall." An even more vivid phrasing, however, would be "Jackson, racing with his back to the infield, leaped and made a one-hand stab just as he crashed into the center field wall." The words *racing*, *leaped*, *stab*, and *crashed* paint an intense verbal picture of the action.

Vivid speech begins with vivid thought. You're much more likely to *express* yourself vividly if you can *sense* the bite of the wind, the sting of the freezing rain, or the sizzle of a thick, juicy sirloin steak on the grill.

Vividness is often enhanced through similes and metaphors. A **simile**, usually expressed with the word *like* or *as*, is a direct comparison of dissimilar things. Such clichés as "She runs like a turtle" and "He's thin as a rail" are both similes. A more vivid simile would be "Trucks are like monstrous boxcars that eat highways for breakfast."

A **metaphor** is a comparison that establishes a figurative identity between objects being compared. Instead of saying that one thing is *like* another, a metaphor says that one thing *is* another. Thus, problem cars are "lemons" and a team's porous infield is a "sieve." A more original metaphor might be "The ship plowed its way through the water."

Although similes and metaphors usually add vividness to a speech, stay away from trite clichés and try to develop original similes and metaphors.

Emphasis. Emphasis means gives force or intensity to certain words or ideas. In your speeches, you can emphasize through **proportion**—spending more time on one idea than another. When you spend more time on a point, your listeners will perceive the point that you spent the most time as more important.

Another way of adding emphasis is **repetition** of important words or ideas. Sometimes you will want to repeat the exact word or words: "A ring-shaped coral island almost or completely surrounding a lagoon is called an atoll—the

word is *atoll*." Other times you can restate the same idea in different language: "The test will be made up of four essay questions; that is, all the questions on the test will be the kind that require you to discuss material in some detail."

You can also emphasize by using **transitions.** In Chapter 14, Organization, we talked about using section transitions to summarize, clarify, and forecast. You can also use word transitions to emphasize the relationships between ideas.

- To add material: *also, and, likewise, again, in addition, moreover, similarly, further*
- To add up consequences, summarize, or show results: *therefore, so, finally, all in all, on the whole, in short, thus, as a result*
- To indicate changes in direction or contrasts: *but, however, yet, on the other hand, still, although, whereas*
- To indicate reasons: *because, for*
- To show causal or time relationships: *then, since, as, while*
- To explain, exemplify, or limit: *in other words, in fact, for example, that is, more specifically*

✳ Nonverbal Components

You will recall from our earlier discussion that nonverbal components of speech presentation are voice, articulation, and bodily action.

Voice. Elements of voice include **pitch** (highness or lowness on a scale), **volume** (loudness), **rate** (speed of speech), and **quality** (tone of voice). You'll want to make sure that your listeners perceive your voice as pleasant—neither too high nor too low, neither too loud nor too soft, neither too fast nor too slow.

Articulation. **Articulation** is the shaping of speech sounds into recognizable oral symbols that combine to produce a word. Articulation often is confused with **pronunciation,** the form and accent of various syllables in a word. In the word *statistics*, for instance, articulation refers to the shaping of the ten sounds (s-t-a-t-i-s-t-i-k-s); pronunciation refers to the grouping and accenting of the sounds (sta-tis′-tiks). If you are unsure of how to pronounce a word in a speech, consult a dictionary for the proper pronunciation.

Consider whether you add a sound where none appears (ath*a*lete for athlete), leave out a sound where one occurs (li*b*ary for library), transpose sounds (re*va*lent for re*lev*ant), or distort sounds (tru*f* for tru*th*). Although some of us have consistent articulation problems that require speech therapy (such as substituting *th* for *s* consistently in speech), most of us are guilty of carelessness that can be corrected.

Check to make sure that you are not guilty of two of the most common articulation faults: slurring sounds (running sounds and words together) or leaving off word endings. Spoken English will always contain some running together of sounds. For instance, most people are likely to say "tha-table" for

"LADIES AND GENTLEMEN... IS <u>THAT MY VOICE</u>?.. I
NEVER HEARD IT AMPLIFIED BEFORE. IT SOUNDS SO
WEIRD. HELLO. HELLO. I CAN'T BELIEVE IT'S ME.
WHAT A STRANGE SENSATION. ONE, TWO, THREE...
HELLO. WOW..."

"that table"—it is simply too difficult to make two "t" sounds in a row. But
many of us slur sounds and drop word endings to excess. "Who ya gonna see?"
for "Who are you going to see?" illustrates both of these errors. If you have a
mild case of "sluritis" caused by not taking the time to form sounds clearly, you
can make considerable improvement by taking ten to fifteen minutes three days
a week to read passages aloud, trying to overaccentuate each sound. Some
teachers advocate "chewing" your words—that is, making sure that lips, jaw,
and tongue move carefully for each sound you make. As with most other

problems of delivery, speakers must work conscientiously several days a week for months to improve significantly.

Figure 16.1 lists a number of common words that people are likely to mispronounce or misarticulate.

A major concern of speakers from different cultures and different parts of the country is their **accent**—the inflection, tone, and speech habits typical of the natives of a country, a region, or even a particular state or city. Thus, one doesn't have to be from a foreign culture to have an accent. Natives of a particular city or region—say, Boston or the Mississippi Delta—will speak with inflections and tones that they believe are "normal" North American speech. But to people in a different city or region, they have an "accent," because the people living in that city or region hear inflections and tones that they perceive as *different* from their own speech.

When should people work to lessen or eliminate an accent? An accent becomes a problem only when it is so "heavy" or different from people's expectations that it interferes with effective communication. An accent can also be a problem for people who expect to go into teaching, broadcasting, or other professions in which an accent may have an adverse effect on their performance.

Bodily action. Bodily action includes your facial expression, gestures, posture, and movement. Bodily actions were discussed in some detail in Chapter 4;

Word	Correct	Incorrect
arctic	arc'-tic	ar'-tic
athlete	ath'lete	ath'a-lete
family	fam'-a-ly	fam'-ly
February	Feb'-ru-ary	Feb'-yu-ary
get	get	git
larynx	ler'-inks	lar'-nix
library	ly'brer-y	ly'-ber-y
nuclear	nu'-klee-er	nu'-kyu-ler
particular	par-tik'-yu-ler	par-tik'-ler
picture	pic'-ture	pitch'-er
recognize	rek'-ig-nize	rek'-a-nize
relevant	rel'-e-vant	rev'-e-lant
theater	thee'-a-ter	thee-ay'-ter
truth	truth	truf
with	with	wit or wid

Figure 16.1
Problem words.

here we want to focus on aspects of those nonverbal behaviors that are particularly relevant to public speaking.

Make sure that your **facial expressions** (your eye and mouth movements) are appropriate to what you are saying. Audiences will respond negatively to deadpan expressions and perpetual grins or scowls; they will respond positively to honest and sincere expressions that reflect your thoughts and feelings. Think actively about what you are saying, and your face will probably respond accordingly.

Your **gestures** are the movements of your hands, arms, and fingers that describe and emphasize. If gesturing does not come easily to you, it is probably best not to force yourself to gesture in a speech. To encourage gestures, leave your hands free at all times to help you "do what comes naturally." If you clasp your hands behind you, grip the sides of the speaker's stand, or keep your hands in your pockets, you will not be able to gesture naturally even if you want to.

Your **posture** is the position or bearing of your body. In speeches, an upright stance and squared shoulders communicate a sense of poise to an audience. Speakers who slouch may give an unfavorable impression of themselves, indicating limited self-confidence and an uncaring attitude. If you find yourself in some peculiar posture during the speech, return to the upright position with your weight equally distributed on both feet.

Your **movement** refers to motion of your entire body. Ideally, movement should help focus on transitions, emphasize ideas, or call attention to a particular aspect of the speech. Avoid such unmotivated movement as bobbing and weaving, shifting from foot to foot, or pacing from one side of the room to the other. At the beginning of your speech, stand up straight on both feet.

Poise refers to an assurance of manner. A poised speaker is able to avoid mannerisms that distract the audience, such as taking off or putting on glasses, smacking the tongue, licking the lips, or scratching the nose, hand, or arm. As a general rule, anything that calls attention to itself is negative, and anything that helps reinforce an important idea is positive. Likewise, a poised speaker is able to control speech nervousness, a topic we will discuss later in this chapter.

In this section, we have looked at several elements of delivery that may seem especially difficult for people with handicaps to achieve. The Diverse Voices feature provides an example showing that regardless of apparent handicaps, people can build confidence and succeed in speaking.

PRACTICE IN CLASS

Presentation

Divide into groups of three to six. Each person should have at least two minutes to tell a personal experience. The other members of the group should observe the speaker for any problems in voice, articulation, and bodily action.

TEST YOUR COMPETENCE

Monitoring Voice and Bodily Action

Use one of the following methods to monitor your nonverbal behaviors:

1. Practice a portion of your speech in front of a mirror to see how you look to others when you speak. (Although some speakers swear by this method, others find it a traumatic experience.)

2. Videotape your speech and replay it for analysis.

3. Practice your speech in front of a friend who is willing to give you feedback on your nonverbal behavior. Give specific instructions, such as "Raise your hand every time I begin to rock back and forth." By getting immediate feedback when a specific behavior occurs, you can learn to become aware of it and make immediate adjustments.

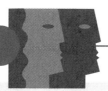

You're Short, Besides!

by Dr. Sucheng Chan

Although nearly everyone shows nervousness at the thought of speaking in public, some people face more difficult situations than others. In this excerpt, Dr. Chan tells us about problems that to many would seem nearly impossible to surmount. She not only overcame these apparent problems, but used them as motivation to succeed.

I was stricken simultaneously with pneumonia and polio at the age of four. Uncertain whether I had polio of the lungs, seven of the eight doctors who attended me—all practitioners of Western medicine—told my parents they should not feel optimistic about my survival. A Chinese fortune teller my mother consulted also gave a grim prognosis. All these pessimistic predictions notwithstanding, I hung onto life, if only by a thread. Being confined to bed was thus a mental agony as great as my physical pain. But I was determined to walk.

We left China as the Communist forces swept across the country in victory. We found an apartment in Hong Kong. After a year and a half in Hong Kong, we moved to Malaysia. The years in Malaysia were the happiest of my childhood even though I was consistently fending off children who ran after me calling, *"Baikah! Baikah!"* ("Cripple! Cripple!" in the Hokkien dialect commonly spoken in Malaysia). The taunts of children mattered little because I was a star pupil. I won one award after another for general scholarship as well as for art and public speaking. Whenever the school had important visitors, my teacher always called on me to recite in front of the class.

A significant event that marked me indelibly occurred when I was twelve. That year my school held a music recital and I was one of the students chosen to play the piano. I managed to get up the steps to the stage without any problem, but as I walked across the stage, I fell. Out of the audience, a voice said loudly and clearly, "Ayah! a *baikah* shouldn't be allowed to perform in public." I got up before anyone could get on stage to

help me and, with tears streaming uncontrollably down my face, I rushed to the piano and began to play. That I managed to do so made me feel really strong. I never again feared ridicule.

Regardless of racial or cultural background, most handicapped people have to learn to find a balance between the desire to attain physical independence and the need to take care of ourselves by not overtaxing our bodies.

I've often wondered if I would have been a different person had I not been physically handicapped. I really don't know, though there is no question that being handicapped has marked me. But at the same time I usually do not *feel* handicapped—and consequently, I do not *act* handicapped. People are therefore less likely to treat me as a handicapped person. There is no doubt, however, that the lives of my parents, sister, husband, other family members, and some close friends have been affected by my physical condition. They have had to learn not to hide me away at home, not to feel embarrassed by how I look or react to people who say silly things to me, and not to resent me for the extra demands my condition makes on them. Perhaps the hardest thing for those who live with handicapped people is to know when and how to offer help.

So, has being physically handicapped been a handicap? It all depends on one's attitude. Some years ago, I told a friend that I had once said to an affirmative action compliance officer (somewhat sardonically since I do not believe in the head count approach to affirmative action) that the institution which employs me is triply lucky because it can count me as nonwhite, female, and handicapped. He responded, "Why don't you tell them to count you four times? . . . Remember, you're short, besides!"

Excerpted from Making Waves *by Asian Women United. © 1989 by Asian Women United. Reprinted by permission of Beacon Press.*

Achieving a Conversational Quality

In your speech practice, as well as in the speech itself, the final measure of your presentation is how well you use your vocal and nonverbal components to develop a **conversational quality**—a style of presentation that sounds like conversation to your listeners. Five components of conversational quality are enthusiasm, vocal expressiveness, spontaneity, fluency, and eye contact.

Enthusiasm

Enthusiasm is the way you convey excitement or passion about the topic.

If sounding enthusiastic does not come naturally to you, make sure that you have a topic that really excites you. Even normally enthusiastic people can have trouble sounding enthusiastic when they choose an uninspiring topic. Then, focus on how your listeners will benefit from what you have to say. If you are convinced that you have something worthwhile to communicate, you are likely to feel and show more enthusiasm.

SKILL BUILDERS   Enthusiasm

Skill	Use	Procedure	Example
Using your voice and bodily action to show the audience that you are excited about the topic and your opportunity to talk with the audience about it.	To ensure audience perception of the importance and relevance of the information to them.	1. Make sure that you are truly excited about your topic. 2. As you speak, re-create your original feelings of excitement. 3. Focus on sharing that feeling of excitement with the audience.	As Trisha was practicing her speech on Alberta, Canada, she refocused on her feelings of awe as she first saw mountain peak after mountain peak. She also reminded herself of how much she wanted her audience to actually "see" what she had experienced.

To validate the importance of enthusiasm, think of how your attitude toward a class differs depending on whether the professor's presentation says "I'm really excited to be talking with you about geology (history, English lit)" or "I'd rather be anywhere than talking to you about this subject." A speaker who looks and sounds enthusiastic will be listened to, and that speaker's ideas will be remembered (Williams and Ware 1976, p. 50).

Vocal Expressiveness

The greatest sign of enthusiasm is **vocal expressiveness**—a result of vocal contrasts in pitch, volume, rate, and quality that affect the meaning audiences get from the sentences you present. Read the following sentence:

I am going to the office to finish the report.

What did the writer intend that sentence to mean? Without a context, who knows? Now, to illustrate how vocal expressiveness affects meaning, read the sentence aloud three times. The first time emphasize *I*, the second time emphasize *office*, and the third time emphasize *report*.

When you emphasize *I*, it answers the question "Who went?"; when you emphasize *office*, it answers the question "Where are you going?"; when you emphasize *report*, it answers the question "Why are you going?" Thus, to ensure audience understanding, your voice must be expressive enough to delineate shades of meaning.

A total lack of vocal expressiveness produces a **monotone**—a voice in which the pitch, volume, and rate remain constant, with no word, idea, or sentence differing significantly from any other. Although few people speak in a true monotone, many severely limit themselves by using only two or three pitch levels and relatively unchanging volume and rate. An actual or near monotone not only lulls an audience to sleep, but more important, diminishes the chances of audience understanding. For instance, if the sentence "Congress should pass laws limiting the sale of pornography" is presented in a monotone, listeners will

A speaker's vocal variety and emphasis help to control the meaning listeners receive.

SKILL BUILDERS   Vocal Expressiveness

Skill	Use	Procedure	Example
Using contrasts in pitch, volume, rate, and quality.	To express the meanings you want audiences to get from the sentences you present.	1. Identify the words you want to stress to best express your intended meaning. 2. Raise your pitch and/or increase your volume on key words.	As Marquez thought about what he wanted to emphasize, he said, "You need to put your *left hand* at the *bottom* of the bat."

be uncertain whether the speaker is concerned with who should be responsible for the laws, what Congress should do with the laws, or what should be the subject of the laws.

☀ Spontaneity

Speakers who are enthusiastic and vocally expressive are also likely to present their speeches in a way that sounds spontaneous. **Spontaneity** means being so responsive to your ideas that the speech seems as fresh as a lively conversation, even though it has been well practiced.

How can you make your outlined and practiced speech sound spontaneous? Learn the *ideas* of the speech—*don't memorize words*. Suppose someone asks you about the route you take on your drive to work. Because you are familiar with the route, you need not write it out or memorize it—you can present it spontaneously because you "know it." You develop spontaneity in your speeches by getting to know the ideas in your speech as well as you know the route you take to work.

☘ Fluency

Effective presentation is also **fluent**—devoid of hesitations and vocal interferences such as "uh," "er," "well," "okay," "you know," and "like" (discussed in Chapter 4). Fluency can be developed through awareness and practice.

Again, train yourself to hear your interferences by getting a friend to listen to practice sessions and call attention to them. As you learn to hear them, you'll find that you can start to eliminate them from your speech practices and eventually from the speech itself.

✳ Eye Contact

Eye contact in public speaking involves looking at various groups of people in *all parts* of an audience throughout a speech. As long as you are looking at

---

PRACTICE IN CLASS

Vocal Expressiveness

1. Prepare a short explanation (such as how to play a game or run a computer program). As you prepare, concentrate on the meaning to determine which words you will try to emphasize.

2. Have a classmate listen to your explanation and make note of which words were higher in pitch, louder, or slower and which words were given special emphasis.

3. Compare the listener's reaction with your plan. If you spoke in such a way that the person selected the words you were trying to emphasize, you are using vocal expressiveness effectively to clarify meaning.

SKILL BUILDERS   Spontaneity

Skill	Use	Procedure	Example
Being responsive to the ideas of your speech.	To ensure that your audience perceives your speech as a lively and fresh interaction even though it has been well practiced.	1. Learn the ideas of your speech. 2. In each practice, allow yourself to express the ideas and their development in slightly different language.	As Connie was talking about day care, she allowed herself to report a personal experience that she hadn't planned on using in the speech.

people (those in front of you, in the left rear portion of the room, in the right center of the room, and so on), and not at your notes or at the ceiling, floor, or window, everyone in the audience will perceive you as having good eye contact.

By maintaining eye contact, you'll help your listeners concentrate on the speech. If you look at your listeners, they are likely to maintain eye contact with you and listen more effectively.

In addition, maintaining eye contact increases listener confidence in what you have to say. Just as you are likely to be skeptical of people who do not look you in the eye as they converse, so too your listeners will be skeptical of you if you do not look at them. Speakers who fail to maintain eye contact with audiences are perceived almost always as ill at ease and often as insincere or dishonest (Burgoon, Coker, and Coker 1986).

Maintaining eye contact also helps you gain insight into your listeners' reaction to the speech. Your listeners are speaking to you nonverbally at the same time you are speaking to them. By keeping good eye contact, you'll notice if listeners begin to yawn, look out the window, and slouch in their chairs. On this basis, you can determine what adjustments, additions, and deletions you should make in your plans. As speakers gain greater skill in monitoring listeners, they make more and better use of the information they get from their listeners.

SKILL BUILDERS Eye Contact

Skill	Use	Procedure	Example
Looking directly at members of the audience while you are talking to them.	To strengthen the sense of interaction.	1. Consciously look at the faces of groups of people in your audience while you are talking. 2. If your eyes drift away, try to bring them back.	As Bill was talking about how people can sign up for tutoring other students, he was talking to people near the back of the room. When he looked down at his notes to make sure he had included all he wanted, he found himself continuing to look at his note card rather than at the audience. As he moved to the next point of his speech, he forced himself to look at people sitting in the front right of the room.

Rehearsal

At this stage of preparation, you are ready to begin **rehearsing**—practicing the presentation of your speech aloud. In this section, we consider a timetable for preparation and practice, use of notes, use of visual aids, and guidelines for effective rehearsals.

I. Determine a specific speech goal that is adapted to your audience and occasion. (Chapter 12)
   A. Select a topic from a subject area you know something about and that is important to you.
   B. Analyze your audience.
   C. Analyze your occasion.
   D. Articulate your goal by determining the response that you want from your audience.

II. Gather and evaluate material that you can use in the speech. (Chapter 13)
   A. Survey sources that are most likely to yield quality information.
   B. Record information that is relevant to your specific speech goal on note cards.

III. Organize and develop your material in a way that is best suited to your particular audience. (Chapter 14)
   A. Write a thesis statement.
   B. Choose an organizational pattern that clearly communicates the material.
   C. Develop an introduction that both gets attention and leads into the body of the speech.
   D. Develop a conclusion that both summarizes the material and leaves the speech on a high note.
   E. Refine the speech outline.

IV. Develop a strategy for adapting material to your specific speech audience. (Chapter 15)
   A. Create common ground with your audience.
   B. Adapt to your audience's level of interest.
   C. Adapt to your audience's level of understanding.
   D. Adapt to your audience's attitude toward you as speaker.
   E. Adapt to your audience's attitude toward your topic.
   F. Create visual aids to clarify, emphasize, and dramatize verbal information.

V. Practice the presentation of the speech until the wording is clear, vivid, and emphatic and until the delivery represents a conversational style that shows enthusiasm, vocal expressiveness, spontaneity, fluency, and eye contact. (Chapter 16)

Figure 16.2
Speech preparation review.

When practicing your speech, try to make the practice session as similar to the speech situation as possible.

Timetable for Preparation and Practice

Too often speakers believe that they are ready to present the speech once they have finished their outline. But, if you are scheduled to speak at 9 A.M. Monday and you do not finish the outline until 8:45, the speech is likely to be far less effective than it would have been had you allowed yourself sufficient practice time. It is only through practicing the speech aloud that you can assure effective presentation.

In general, try to complete the outline at least two days before the speech is due so that you have sufficient practice time to revise, evaluate, and mull over all aspects of the speech. Figure 16.3 provides a useful timetable for preparing a classroom speech.

7 days (or more) before	Select topic; begin research.
6 days before	Continue research.
5 days before	Outline body of speech.
4 days before	Work on introduction and conclusion.
3 days before	Finish outline; find additional material if needed; have all visual aids completed.
2 days before	First rehearsal session.
1 day before	Second rehearsal session.
Due date	Give speech.

Figure 16.3
Timetable for preparing a speech.

Is there really a relationship between practice time and speech effectiveness? A study by Menzel and Carrell (1994) offers tentative confirmation for the general hypothesis that more preparation time leads to better speech performance. They conclude, "The significance of rehearsing out loud probably reflects the fact that verbalization clarifies thought. As a result, oral rehearsal helps lead to success in the actual delivery of a speech" (p. 23).

Using Notes in Your Speech

Appropriate notes are composed of key words or phrases that help trigger your memory. Notes will be most useful to you when they consist of the fewest words possible written in lettering large enough to be seen instantly at a distance. Many speakers condense their written preparatory outline into a brief word or phrase outline.

For a speech in the three- to five-minute category, one or two three-by-five-inch note cards are all you will need; for a speech in the five- to ten-minute category, three or four three-by-five cards should be enough: one card for goal and introduction, one or two cards for the body, and one card for the conclusion. When your speech contains a particularly good quotation or a complicated set of statistics, you may want to write them in detail on separate three-by-five

That detailed manuscript in her hands probably means she's reading her speech—and losing spontaneity and connection with her audience. Brief notes are better.

cards. Two typical sets of notes are made from the body of the preparatory out-line illustrated in Chapter 14 and are shown in Figure 16.4.

During practice sessions, use the notes as you would in the speech. Either set the notes on the speaker's stand or hold them in one hand and refer to them only when needed. Speakers often find that the act of making a note card is so effective in helping cement ideas in the mind that during practice, or later dur-ing the speech itself, they do not need to use the notes at all.

Using Visual Aids in Your Speech

You will also want to make sure that you practice using visual aids in your rehearsals. Many speakers think that once they have prepared good visual aids, they will have no trouble using them in the speech. However, many speeches with good visual aids have become shambles because of the lack of careful prac-tice with them. During practice sessions, indicate on your notes exactly when you will use the visual aid (and when you will remove it). Work on statements for introducing the visual aids, and practice different ways of showing the visual aids until you are satisfied that everyone in the audience will be able to see them. Here are several guidelines for using visual aids effectively in your speech.

1. **Plan carefully when to use visual aids.** As you practice your speech, indicate on your outline when and how you will use each visual aid.

2. **Carefully consider audience needs.** If your audience would find a graphic helpful in understanding and remembering a portion of your speech, then a visual aid at that point is appropriate. On the other hand, regardless of how

BRIEF WORD OUTLINE	PHRASE OUTLINE
Uniqueness of Roquefort	**Uniqueness of Roquefort**
Trademarked	Roquefort is trademarked
Toulouse 1666	Legislation Toulouse, 1666
15% required	15% Roquefort required
Ewe's milk	Made from ewe's milk, not cow's
Neolithic	Type sheep date to Neolithic
30 ewes to 1 cow	Precious: 30 ewes to 1 cow
800,000 ewes	800,000 ewes required
Mold from caves	Mold: caves in Roquefort-sur-Soulzo
4–6,000 yr old	4-6,000 yr old
1 1/4 mile long, 300 yds deep	1 1/4 mile long, 300 yds deep
Penicillum roquefortii	Penicillum roquefortii
in fissures	grows in fissures
cultivated	is cultivated in bread
injected	is injected into cheese

Figure 16.4
Speech notes.

Visual aids can add dramatic interest to your speeches.

exciting a visual may be, if it does not contribute directly to the audience's attention to, understanding of, or retention of information on your topic, then reconsider its use.

3. **Show visual aids only when talking about them.** Visual aids will draw audience attention. So, when the visual aid is no longer the focus of attention, keep it out of sight.

  Often a single visual aid contains several bits of information. In order to keep audience attention where you want it, you can prepare the visual aid with cover-ups. Then, as you move from one portion of the visual aid to another, you can remove covers to expose the portion of the visual aid that you are then discussing.

4. **Talk about the visual aid while showing it.** Since you know what you want your audience to see in the visual aid, tell your audience what to look for, explain the various parts, and interpret figures, symbols, and percentages.

5. **Display visual aids so that everyone in the audience can see them.** If you hold the visual aid, position it away from your body and point it toward the various parts of the audience. If you place your visual aid on a chalk-

board or easel or mount it in some way, stand to one side and point with the arm nearest the visual aid. If it is necessary to roll or fold the visual aid, bring some transparent tape to mount it to the chalkboard or wall so that it does not roll or wrinkle.

6. **Talk to your audience, not to the visual aid.** You may need to look at the visual aid occasionally, but it is important to maintain eye contact with your listeners as much as possible, in part so that you can gauge how they are reacting to your visual material. When speakers become too engrossed in their visual aids, they tend to lose contact with the audience entirely.

7. **Pass objects around the audience with caution.** People look at, read, handle, and think about whatever they hold in their hands; and while they are so occupied, they may not be listening to you. Keep control of people's attention by telling them what they should be looking at and when they should be listening to you.

Rehearsing Your Speech

A good rehearsal period involves practicing the speech, analyzing it, and practicing it again.

First practice. In practicing your speech, try to follow these six steps.

1. Tape-record your practice session. If you do not own a recorder, try to borrow one. You may also want to have a friend sit in on your practice.

2. Read through the outline once or twice to refresh ideas in your mind. Then put the outline out of sight.

3. Make the practice as similar to the speech situation as possible, including using any visual aids you've prepared. Stand up and face your imaginary audience. Pretend that the chairs, lamps, books, and other objects in your practice room are people.

4. Write down the time that you begin.

5. Begin speaking. Keep going until you have presented your entire speech.

6. Write down the time you finish. Compute the length of the speech for this first practice.

Analysis. Replay the tape. Look at your outline again. Did you leave out any key ideas? Did you talk too long on any one point and not long enough on another? Did you clarify each of your points? Did you try to adapt to your anticipated audience? (If you had a friend or relative listen to your practices, then have that person help with your analysis.)

Second practice. Go through the six steps outlined for the first practice. By practicing a second time right after your analysis, you are more likely to make the kind of adjustments that begin to improve the speech.

After you have completed one full rehearsal consisting of two sessions of practices and analysis, put the speech away until that night or the next day. Although you may need to go through the speech one or several more times, there is no value in cramming all the practices into one long rehearsal time. You may find that an individual practice right before you go to bed will be very helpful; while you are sleeping, your subconscious will continue to work on the speech. As a result, you are likely to find significant improvement in your mastery of the speech when you practice again the next day.

How many times you practice depends on many variables, including your experience, your familiarity with the subject, and the length of your speech.

Ensuring spontaneity.   When practicing, try to learn the speech, not memorize it. Memorizing the speech involves saying the speech the same way each time until you can give it word for word without notes. **Learning** the speech involves understanding the ideas of the speech but having the freedom to word the ideas differently during each practice. Let us illustrate the method of learning a speech by using a short portion of the speech outline on pages 336–337 of Chapter 14 as the basis for the practice. That portion of the outline reads as follows:

    I. Roquefort cheese is trademarked.
        A. Cheesemakers still follow legislation of the Parliament of Toulouse that dates from 1666.
        B. All salad dressings claiming to be Roquefort must contain at least 15 percent legislated Roquefort.

Now let us consider three practices that focus on point I. B of the outline: the amount of pure Roquefort that must be included before a salad dressing can be called "Roquefort."

> **First practice:** "So, the point is that all salad dressings claiming to be Roquefort must contain at least 15 percent of legislated Roquefort—that's 15 percent of pure Roquefort."

> **Second practice:** "So, let's say that you order Roquefort for your salad. How do you know what you're getting? According to law, that dressing you order must contain at least 15 percent of legislated Roquefort."

> **Third practice:** "When you order Roquefort dressing for your salad, you may find that the taste varies a little from restaurant to restaurant. Still, according to law, you can be sure that what you are getting has at least 15 percent of the real thing—legislated Roquefort."

Notice that point I. B of the outline is in all three versions. As this example illustrates, the essence of the outline will be a part of all your practices. But because you have made slight variations each time, when you finally give the speech there will still be that sense of spontaneity. In your speech, you may well use a fourth wording, but you will be assured that you are likely to get the key point across.

Coping with Nervousness

By far the most frequently asked question about speaking is, "What can I do about nervousness?" Perhaps the most important things to realize are that (1) nearly everyone reports nervousness about speaking and (2) we can all learn to cope with that nervousness.

Let's begin by identifying what nervousness is all about. Whether we call it stage fright, speech fright, shyness, reticence, communication apprehension, or some other term, the meaning of that feeling is essentially the same: a fear or anxiety about public speaking.

Much of what we know about fear of speaking comes from research conducted by James McCroskey, who has developed the most valid instrument for measuring what he calls communication apprehension. The accompanying Spotlight on Scholarship gives insight into his research program.

Although we may feel some degree of nervousness in any situation, the majority of us notice it most in public speaking. Some of this nervousness is **cognitive** —that is, we think about how nervous we're likely to be. Much of the nervousness is **behavioral**—that is, we display physical reactions. For instance, we may experience stomach cramps, sweaty palms, dry mouth, and the use of such filler expressions as "um," "like," and "you know." Other behavioral reactions may be to avoid speaking in public or to speak for the shortest possible time.

To help cope with this nervousness, keep in mind that fear is not an either-or matter—it is a matter of degree. Most of us fall somewhere between the two

James McCroskey, Professor and Former Chair of the Department of Communication at West Virginia University, on Communication Apprehension

Since Jim McCroskey's academic interest had been in public speaking and debate, it was somewhat by chance that he became involved in the study of what was to become a focus of his  lifelong scholarship. One day McCroskey got a call from a therapist at the university's Psychology Center who was concerned about a student who was suicidal and kept repeating, "I just can't face giving my speech." The thought that some people's fear of speaking in public was so profound that they considered suicide preferable to speaking was so compelling to McCroskey that he began an in-depth study of what he eventually called "communication apprehension."

Although a lot had been written about what was then called "stage fright," McCroskey found that there was no agreement about its causes and no way to go about measuring it. Since that time, McCroskey has made a significant contribution to our understanding of communication apprehension and ways of measuring it. When instruments for measuring a variable are developed, they must be both valid and reliable—*valid* in that the instrument must be proved to measure apprehension and not other related things, and *reliable* so that people with similar amounts of apprehension will score the same and people who are measured more than once will receive a similar score. McCroskey's and his colleagues' work culminated in what is considered the primary measure of communication apprehension, the Personal Report of Communication Apprehension (PRCA).

McCroskey first published this self-report instrument in 1970. Since then, there have been several versions.

Although apprehension can be measured by observation (examining the behaviors exhibited during communication) and physiological response (outfitting people with measuring devices to record physiological information during speech), McCroskey found that the self-report instrument (having people fill out a questionnaire detailing their feelings and opinions) was the most valid and reliable. In everyday terms, he explains, "Many times the people we observe may be terrified, but show no outward signs. Likewise, many times people register tremendous physiological reaction to the thought of public speaking, but when questioned, some of these people don't recognize their reactions as fear. Rather, they report excitement or other feelings that aren't at all debilitating. On the other hand, when people report, 'I'm scared stiff,' you can pretty well believe that they are."

From research using the PRCA, we have learned that 15 to 20 percent of the U.S. population experiences high levels of "trait" communication apprehension. *Trait apprehension* means that some people seem to be predisposed to be apprehensive and will show high levels of nervousness in all forms of speech, including public speaking, interpersonal communication, and group communication. Likewise, we have learned that nearly everyone experiences times of high "state" communication apprehension. *State apprehension* means that under some circumstances people will show high levels of nervousness in a single communication context, such as public speaking.

McCroskey's research has made it possible to identify high communication apprehension students and provide appropriate intervention programs. Through these programs, people with high communication apprehension don't eliminate their fears, but they do learn to reduce their tension so that they can function competently.

Later, McCroskey's interest in communication apprehension led him to related studies in talking frequency (verbal activity, talkativeness, compulsive communicators) and preference to approach or avoid communication (reticence, unwillingness to communicate, and willingness to communicate). During the past twenty years, he has validated scales for measuring both willingness to communicate and talkativeness.

What's next for McCroskey? Recently, he has begun to study genetic causes of apprehension. This move is prompted by the fact that although we can now identify those who suffer from communication apprehension and help them reduce their fears, there seem to be limits to how much reduction can take place for particular individuals. He believes that genetic study is the wave of the future and may ultimately provide answers to dealing completely with communication apprehension.

Over the past forty years, McCroskey has published more than 175 articles, 40 books, and 40 book chapters, and presented more than 250 convention papers. Currently he teaches courses in interpersonal communication, nonverbal communication, communication in instruction, organizational communication, and a graduate seminar.

As we might expect, McCroskey has received many awards for his scholarship, including the prestigious Robert J. Kibler Memorial Award of the National Communication Association and the Distinguished Research Award from the National Association of Teacher Educators. For a partial list of McCroskey's publications in communication apprehension, see the References at the end of this book.

McCroskey's scholarship—from identifying those with communication apprehension to finding ways to help people reduce their apprehension—has helped tremendous numbers of people become more competent communicators.

extremes of no nervousness at all and total fear. The point is that nervousness about speaking in public is *normal*.

Many of us believe that we would be better off if we could be totally free from nervousness. But Gerald Phillips, a speech scholar who has been studying public-speaking nervousness for more than twenty years, says that's not true. Phillips (1977, p. 37) has noted that "learning proceeds best when the organism is in a state of tension." In fact, it helps to be a little nervous to do your best: If you are lackadaisical about giving a speech, you probably will not do a good job.

Because at least some tension is constructive, our goal is not to eliminate nervousness but to learn how to cope with it. Phillips (1977) cites results of studies that followed groups of students with speaker nervousness. He found that nearly all of them still experienced tension, but almost all of them had learned to cope with their nervousness. He concludes that "apparently they had learned to manage the tension; they no longer saw it as an impairment, and they went ahead with what they had to do" (p. 37).

Now let's look at some reassuring information about nervousness.

Speakers can use the secrets of winning athletes: realize that your initial nervousness can prime you for the speech ahead and will decline once you start speaking, and visualize success before you start.

1. **Despite nervousness, you can make it through your speech.** Very few people are so bothered that they are unable to function. You may not enjoy the "flutters" you experience, but you can still deliver an effective speech.

2. **Listeners are not as likely to recognize your fear as you might think.** The thought that audiences will notice an inexperienced speaker's fear often increases that fear. Thoughts that an audience will be quick to laugh at a speaker who is hesitant or that it is just waiting to see how shaky a person appears can have devastating effects. But the fact is that members of an audience, even speech instructors, greatly underrate the amount of stage fright they believe a person has (Clevenger 1959, p. 136).

3. **The better prepared you are, the better you will cope with nervousness.** Many people show extreme nervousness because either they are not well prepared or they think they are not well prepared. According to Gerald Phillips (1991, p. 6), a positive approach to coping with nervousness is "(1) learn how to try, (2) try, and (3) have some success." As you learn to recognize when you are truly prepared, you will find yourself paying less attention to your nervousness. A recent study by Kathleen Ellis (1995) reinforces pervious research findings that "students' self-perceived public

speaking competency is indeed an important predictor of their public speaking anxiety" (p. 73).

4. **The more experience you get in speaking, the better you can cope with nervousness.** Beginners experience some fear because they do not have experience speaking in public. As you give speeches, and see improvement in those speeches, you will gain confidence and worry less about any nervousness you might experience. In a recent study of the impact of basic courses on communication apprehension, experience in a public-speaking course was able to reduce students' communication apprehension scores (Rose, Rancer, and Crannell 1993, p. 58).

5. **Experienced speakers learn to channel their nervousness.** The nervousness you feel is, in controlled amounts, good for you. It takes a certain amount of nervousness to do your best. What you want is for your nervousness to dissipate once you begin your speech. Just as soccer players are likely to report that the nervousness disappears once they engage in play, so too should speakers find nervousness disappearing once they get a reaction to the first few sentences of their introduction.

Specific Behaviors

Now let's consider specific behaviors that are likely to help you control your nervousness.

1. **Pick a topic you are comfortable with.** An unsatisfactory topic lays the groundwork for a psychological mind-set that almost guarantees nervousness at the time of the speech. Having a topic you know about and that is important to you lays the groundwork for a satisfying speech experience.

2. **Take time to prepare fully.** If you back yourself into a corner and must find material, organize it, write an outline, and practice the speech all in an hour or two, you almost guarantee failure and destroy your confidence. On the other hand, if you do a little work each day for a week before the assignment, you will experience considerably less pressure and increased confidence.

    Keep in mind that giving yourself enough time to prepare fully includes sufficient time for rehearsal. In this regard, speechmaking is much like athletics. If you assure yourself that you have carefully prepared and practiced, you will do the kind of job of which you can be proud.

3. **Try to schedule your speech at a time that is psychologically best for you.** When speeches are being scheduled, you may be able to choose the time. Are you better off "getting it over with"? If so, volunteer to go first. Will listening to others make you feel better? Then try to schedule your speech near the end of the class period.

4. **Visualize successful speaking experiences.** Visualization involves developing a mental strategy and picturing yourself implementing that strategy. How

many times have you said to yourself, "Well, if I had been in that situation, I would have . . ."? Such statements are a form of visualization. Joe Ayres and Theodore S. Hopf, two scholars who have conducted extensive research on visualization, have found that if people can visualize themselves going through an entire process, they have a much better chance of succeeding when they are in the situation (Ayres and Hopf 1990, p. 77). By visualizing, people not only seem to be able to lower general apprehension, but they also report fewer negative thoughts when they actually speak (Ayres, Hopf, and Ayres 1994, p. 256). Successful visualization begins during practice periods. For instance, if during a practice you not only say, "So, you can see how the shape of the wing gives a plane lift," but you also see members of the audience nodding, you are visualizing successful response.

Finally, as you walk to the speaker's stand, continue to visualize success. Remind yourself that you have good ideas, that you are well prepared, and that your audience wants to hear what you have to say. Even if you make mistakes, the audience will profit from your speech.

5. **Pause for a few seconds before you begin.** When you reach the stand, stop a few seconds before you start to speak. Take a deep breath while you make eye contact with the audience; that may help get your breathing in order. Try to move about a little during the first few sentences; sometimes a few gestures or a step one way or another is enough to break some of the tension.

Persistent Nervousness

When is speaker nervousness a real problem? When it becomes debilitating—when the fear is so great that a person is unable to go through giving a speech. Unfortunately, many of those students respond by dropping the course. But that is not an answer to speech anxiety. In all areas of life, people have to give speeches—they have to get up before peers, people from other organizations, customers, and others to explain their ideas. Although it is never too late to get help, a college speech course is the best time to start working on coping with speech nervousness. Even if your fears prove to be more perception than reality, it's important to take the time to get help.

To start, see your professor outside class and talk with him or her about what you are experiencing. Your professor should be able to offer ideas for people you can see or programs you can attend. You may be able to find a program in **systematic desensitization**, which repeatedly exposes people to the stimulus they fear, associating it each time with something pleasant, or in **cognitive restructuring**, which helps people to identify the illogical beliefs they hold and provides individualized instruction in formulating more appropriate beliefs.

But before you get overly concerned, keep in mind that there are very few speech students who have been so hurt by fear that they can't deliver a speech. The purpose of a speech course is to help you learn and develop the skills that will allow you to achieve even when you feel extremely anxious.

OBSERVE AND ANALYZE

Controlling Nervousness

Interview one or two people who give frequent speeches (a minister, a politician, a lawyer, a businessperson, a teacher). Ask about what is likely to make them more or less nervous about giving the speech. Find out how they cope with their nervousness. Which behaviors do you believe might work for you?

TEST YOUR COMPETENCE

Presenting Your First Speech

1. Prepare a three- to five-minute informative or persuasive speech. An outline is required.

2. As an addendum to the outline, you may wish to write a specific plan for adapting the speech that discusses strategies for (a) getting and maintaining attention, (b) facilitating understanding, (c) and building a positive attitude toward you and your speech.

3. Criteria for evaluation include the essentials of topic and purpose, content, organization, and presentation. As you practice your speech, use the diagnostic checklist to ensure that you are meeting the basic criteria in your speech. A sample student outline and speech follow.

Check all items that were accomplished effectively.

Content

_____ 1. Was the goal of the speech clear?

_____ 2. Did the speaker have high-quality information?

_____ 3. Did the speaker use a variety of kinds of developmental material?

_____ 4. Were visual aids appropriate and well used?

_____ 5. Did the speaker establish common ground and adapt the content to the audience's interests, knowledge, and attitudes?

Organization

_____ 6. Did the introduction gain attention, gain goodwill for the speaker, and lead into the speech?

_____ 7. Were the main points clear, parallel, and meaningful complete sentences?

_____ 8. Did transitions lead smoothly from one point to another?

_____ 9. Did the conclusion tie the speech together?

Presentation

_____ 10. Was the language clear?

_____ 11. Was the language vivid?

_____ 12. Was the language emphatic?

_____ 13. Did the speaker sound enthusiastic?

_____ 14. Did the speaker show sufficient vocal expressiveness?

_____ 15. Was the presentation spontaneous?

_____ 16. Was the presentation fluent?

_____ 17. Did the speaker look at the audience?

_____ 18. Were the pronunciation and articulation acceptable?

_____ 19. Did the speaker have good posture?

_____ 20. Was speaker movement appropriate?

_____ 21. Did the speaker have sufficient poise?

Figure 16.5

Evaluating a speech: diagnostic checklist.

Based on these criteria, evaluate the speech as (check one):
_____ excellent, _____ good, _____ satisfactory, _____ fair, _____ poor.

Criteria for Evaluating Speeches

In addition to learning to prepare and present speeches, you are learning to critically analyze the speeches you hear. From a pedagogical standpoint, critical analysis of speeches not only provides the speaker with an analysis of where the speech went right and where it went wrong but also gives you, the critic, insight into the methods that you want to incorporate, or perhaps avoid, in presenting your own speeches.

Although speech criticism is context-specific (analyzing the effectiveness of an informative demonstration speech differs from analyzing the effectiveness of a persuasive action speech), in this section we look at criteria for evaluating public speaking in general. Classroom speeches are usually evaluated on the basis of how well the speaker has met specific criteria of effective speaking.

In these last five chapters, you have been learning not only the steps of speech preparation but also the criteria by which speeches are measured. The critical assumption is that if a speech has good content, is well organized, and is well presented, it is more likely to achieve its goal. Thus, the critical apparatus for evaluating any speech comprises questions that relate to the basics of content, organization, and presentation. (See Figure 16.5.)

The diagnostic checklist in Figure 16.5 shows a series of questions that will be used in the analysis of your first speech.

Speech Outline: Home Schooling[1]

Specific Goal: I want my audience to understand the three legal categories into which home schooling can fall.

Introduction
  I. What do Winston Churchill, Theodore Roosevelt, Agatha Christie, and Albert Einstein have in common?
 II. They were all home schooled.
III. Parents have the constitutional right to teach their own children at home.

Thesis Statement: The three legal categories into which the 50 states fall are states with specific home school laws, states without specific home school laws, and states with "approval" requirements.

Body
  I. The first group of states have specific home school laws.
     A. Thirty-four states fall into this category.

---

[1] Presented in speech class, University of Cincinnati. Used with permission of Ruth Snell.

    B. In half of these, home schoolers have to file annual notice of intent.

    C. All 34 states require that certain subjects be taught.

    D. Half these states require regulated testing and evaluating to monitor progress.

    E. Students must receive 180 days of instruction.

(Now that we've seen the group of states that have specific home school laws, let us look at the second category into which states can fall.)

II. The second group of states have no specific home school laws.

    A. Twelve states fall into this category.

    B. These states say children must attend a public or a private school.

    C. Home schoolers in these states fit themselves into the private school category.

(In addition to the categories of states with specific home school laws and those with no specific laws, there is one final category to consider.)

III. The third group of states have "approval" requirements for home schooling.

    A. Five states fall into this category.

    B. In these states, home schools are not considered private schools.

    C. They require approval from their local school superintendents.

Conclusion

I. The three legal categories into which the 50 states fall are states that have specific home school laws, states without specific home school laws, and states with "approval" requirements.

II. If you decide to become your child's teacher, you now know the basic legal requirements that must be met.

Bibliography

Churbuck, David, "The Ultimate Choice: No school at all," *Forbes* (October 1993): 144–148.

Clark, Charles, "Home Schooling," *CO Researcher* (September 1994): 771–780.

Cray, Dan, "Home Sweet School," *Time* (October 1994): 62–63.

House, Karen, "Home Schooling—Legally Speaking," *Mother Earth News* (August 1993): 54.

Mayberry, Maralee, J. Gary Knowles, Brian Ray, and Stacey Marlow, *Home Schooling: Parents as Educators* (Thousand Oaks, CA: Sage, 1995).

Rawlings, Rebecca (a woman who home schools her three children), Personal interview.

Sample Speech and Analysis: Home Schooling

Speech

What do Winston Churchill, Theodore Roosevelt, Agatha Christie, and even Albert Einstein have in common? Well, the answer might surprise you at first. They were all home schooled. The U.S. Supreme Court determined in 1972, in the *Wisconsin v. Yoder* case, that parents do have the constitutional right to teach their own children. Now they base this on the First Amendment, which guarantees freedom of religion, and also on the Fourteenth Amendment, which guarantees the right to liberty. The Supreme Court determined that this also includes parental liberty.

Now since this ruling, all 50 states have legalized home schooling. And at this time, according to the Home School Legal Defense Association, more than 1.5 million children are now schooled at home; our own state of Ohio stands third in the nation, with some 46,400 children being schooled at home. I feel comfortable talking about this topic since both my sister-in-law and several of my friends are home schooling their children.

But in each state there are laws regulating home schooling that vary greatly from state to state. Now there are three separate legal categories that the 50 states can fall into. These categories are states that have some specific home school laws, states that do not have specific laws, and states that have approval requirements.

The first category of states are those that have specific home school laws. There are thirty-four states in this category, including such states as Tennessee, Florida, and our own state of Ohio. How do parents comply with the laws in these states? According to *Forbes* magazine, October 1993, in one-half of these states parents have to file notice of intent annually with the state to show them that they will be home schooling their children that year. There is also a requirement in all 34 states that certain subjects be taught in the home, such as history,

Analysis

Notice how Ruth gets audience attention with a question about four well-known people.

Recall that the opening is a good place for orientation. Here Ruth gives the Supreme Court ruling and the basis for that ruling.

Here Ruth adapts to her audience by giving Ohio figures.
This statement helps to build her credibility for discussing this topic.

Ruth previews the main points by giving her thesis statement.

Notice the clear complete-sentence statement of the first main point. Again, Ruth adapts to her audience by referring to "our own state of Ohio," immediately followed by a rhetorical question.

Notice her brief citation of Forbes. *This section includes the necessary information showing how parents comply with state laws.*

Speech

Analysis

mathematics, and English. And 180 days of instruction must be given to the students on a year-round basis. Half of these states require regulated testing and evaluation by the state to make sure that the student is doing well and to monitor their progress.

Well, now we've seen the group of states that have home school laws. Let's take a look at the second category that states can fall into.

Here Ruth uses a signpost transition to show that she will now present her second main point.

This second group of states have no home school law on record. There are 12 states, including our neighboring states of Kentucky and Indiana, that fall into this category. According to *CO Researcher* in September 1994, there is no written ruling on home school law. But they do have laws that state that a student must attend either a public or a private school during the school year. Now because of this law, the home schoolers fit themselves into the private school category, which allows them to operate in that state.

Another clear complete-sentence main point. Again Ruth adapts to her audience by mentioning two neighboring states that fall into this category.

After giving the citation to support the absence of a written ruling, she shows how home schools qualify as private schools in these states.

So, now that you've seen the two categories of states that do have home school laws and states that have no home school laws, let's look at the final category into which states can fall.

Her transition reviews the two previous points and previews the third.

This third group of states have what they call approval requirements for home schooling. There are five states that fall into this category, including Massachusetts and Utah. According to Dan Cray in *Time* magazine, October '94, there's no actual language in their state law that allows the home schooling parents to categorize themselves as a private school. So there is no home school law on record, but they do have to have approval by the state. Now this approval is met on a case-by-case basis, and it's determined by the local school superintendent. And the school superintendent has the authority to go into the home and determine whether this home is an appropriate place for the child to learn.

Again, the third point is a complete sentence.

Ruth gives a source for an important assertion. In the speech she only gives three source citations, but each one supports important information. In a three- to five-minute speech, you'll not usually want or need more than three source citations.

Now we've seen the three legal categories which states can fall into: states that have specific home school laws, states that have no specific home school

She begins her conclusion with a good summary. Her final statement reminds the audience of the potential importance of this information.

Speech	**Analysis**
laws but where they qualify as private schools, and the third category, states that have approval requirements. So, at any time if one of you decides that you are going to be your child's teacher, you now have a view of the basic requirements that must be met.	*A good first speech, with an introduction that gains attention and gives necessary orientation, three well-supported main points, enough audience adaptation to hold interest, and a good conclusion.*

Summary

Although speeches may be presented impromptu, by manuscript, or by memory, the material you have been reading is designed to help you present your speeches extemporaneously—that is, carefully prepared and practiced but with the exact wording determined at the time of utterance.

The verbal components of effective presentation are clarity, vividness, and emphasis. The nonverbal elements of presentation include voice, articulation, and bodily action.

Effective speaking uses verbal and nonverbal components to achieve a conversational quality that includes enthusiasm, vocal expressiveness, spontaneity, fluency, and eye contact.

To rehearse an extemporaneous speech, complete the outline at least two days in advance. Between the time the outline has been completed and the time the speech is to be given, you will want to practice the speech several times, weighing what you did and how you did it after each practice. You may wish to use brief notes, especially for longer speeches, as long as they do not interfere with your delivery.

All speakers feel nervous as they approach their first speech. Some nervousness is cognitive (in the mind), and some is behavioral (physically displayed). Rather than being an either-or matter, nervousness is a matter of degree.

Because at least some tension is constructive, our goal is not to get rid of nervousness but to learn how to cope with it. Even though nervousness is normal, you can use the following specific behaviors to help control it: (1) Pick a topic you are comfortable with. (2) Take time to prepare fully. (3) Try to schedule your speech at a time that is psychologically best for you. (4) Visualize successful speaking experiences. (5) Pause for a few seconds before you begin.

TEST YOUR COMPETENCE

Critiquing a Speech

Use the speech critique checklist in Figure 16.5 to evaluate a speech you have listened to in or out of class. Using the data on the checklist, write a two- to five-page paper explaining your evaluation.

If nervousness is truly detrimental to your performance, see your professor outside class and talk with him or her about what you are experiencing. Your professor should be able to offer ideas for people you can see or programs you can attend.

Speeches are evaluated on how well they meet the guidelines for effective content, organization, and presentation.

Terry Weathers is running for student body president and has asked her friend Megan to deliver the key speech of support at the All-University Candidates' Meeting. Being a good friend, Megan agrees.

Megan works several days developing the speech, and she believes that she has prepared a really good one. The problem is that although Megan can prepare excellent speeches, she suffers from stage fright. She is scared to death to give this one in front of such a large audience. So, she asks Donnell Gates, a guy in her speech class who wows audiences with his engaging manner, to deliver the speech she wrote at the event.

Donnell thinks about her request and then leaves the following message on her voice mail: "Listen, you know I'm not crazy about Terry, so I would never vote for her. But since I don't really care who wins this election, I'll give the speech. Hey, I just enjoy the power I have over an audience!"

1. Now that Megan knows that Donnell doesn't care for Terry, should she let him give the speech?
2. And what about Donnell? Should he give such a speech knowing that he wouldn't support Terry himself?

OBJECTIVES

After you have read this chapter, you should be able to answer the following questions:

■ What are the three goals of informative speaking?

■ What are the tests of presenting ideas creatively?

■ What can you do to increase your credibility?

■ How can you proceed to leave the impression that what you've said is new and relevant?

■ What are key techniques that you can use to emphasize information?

Informative Speaking

For several months, a major architectural firm had been working on designs for the arts center to be built in the middle of downtown. Members of the city council and guests from various constituencies in the city, as well as a number of concerned citizens, were taking their seats as the long anticipated presentation was about to begin. As Linda Garner, mayor and presiding officer of the city council, finished her introduction, Donald Harper, the principal architect of the project, walked to the microphone to begin his speech.

Scenarios like this one are played out every day as speakers struggle to help us increase our understanding of complex issues. In this chapter, we build on the action steps of general speech preparation by focusing on informative speaking.

As an informative speaker, your rhetorical goal is to present information in a way that holds interest, facilitates understanding, and increases the likelihood of remembering. We begin by focusing on principles of informing that you can use to consider (1) *how* to create interest so the audience will listen, (2) *how* to explain in a way that will help the audience understand, and (3) *how* to discuss the information in a way that will help the audience remember. Then we consider four methods of informing that effective speakers must master. We conclude the chapter with a sample informative speech that illustrates these principles.

Principles of Informing

You will be a more effective informative speaker if you apply principles of credibility, intellectual stimulation, creativity, relevance, and emphasis.

Credibility

PRINCIPLE 1

Audiences are more likely to listen to you if they like, trust, and have confidence in you.

Although we've already discussed the bases of credibility—knowledge/expertise, trustworthiness, and personality—we emphasize them here because building or maintaining your credibility is essential to your success. If your listeners have faith in you, they'll be more willing to learn. The following three points are mentioned as reminders of what you must do in your speeches.

1. **Demonstrate your expertise.** As an informative speaker, you must talk knowledgeably and fluently, with command of your information and without stumbling and misstatements.
2. **Emphasize your interest in audience well-being.** Likewise, you must show your listeners that you care about them and what happens to them.
3. **Look and sound enthusiastic.** Finally, you must show enthusiasm for your information.

You will probably see the cumulative effect of credibility during this term. As your class proceeds from speech to speech, some speakers will grow in stature in your mind and others will diminish.

Your credibility will be high if you talk knowledgeably, emphasize that you care about your audience, and look and sound enthusiastic.

Intellectual Stimulation
PRINCIPLE 2

Audiences are more likely to listen to information they perceive to be intellectually stimulating.

Information will be perceived as **intellectually stimulating** when it is new to audience members and when it meets deep-seated needs to know.

When we say *new*, we mean either information that most of the audience is not familiar with or information that offers new insights or twists on familiar topics. If you really have researched your topic, you are likely to have information that will be new to a majority of your audience.

But even when you are talking about a topic that most of the people in your audience are familiar with, you can uncover new angles, new applications, or new perspectives on the material. For instance, a football player's speech on field-goal kicking or blocking will be much more informative if he includes information that gives us some scientific insights than if he only gives us steps in the process. Likewise, a business student's speech on the Dow-Jones averages will be much more informative if she includes information on how companies were selected and why than if she just lists the companies.

But just being new is not enough. The information must also meet the audience's deep-seated hunger for knowledge and insight. Part of the informative speaker's job is to feed that hunger. Every day we are touched by ideas and issues that we don't fully grasp. But we often ignore these ideas and issues, partly because we don't have sufficient motivation to find additional information. For instance, several years ago scientists discovered an "ice man"—the well-preserved body of a man who lived between four and five thousand years ago, buried in a glacier of the southern Alps. When newspaper headlines announced the discovery, many readers were excited by the information, but most probably did not pursue study of the topic. The informative speaker would seize the topic and link this discovery to an understanding of our own history and development, thereby stimulating our natural intellectual curiosity.

Let's consider a more typical example. Suppose you are planning a speech on new cars. From just the data you could draw from the April issue of *Consumer Reports* (the month in which comparative statistics and ratings are given for all new cars), you could find information that would be intellectually stimulating. For instance, most of us are aware that over time Japanese-made cars have captured an increasingly large share of the American market, at least partly because of perceived quality issues. How are American companies responding to those issues? Are American-made cars achieving higher quality ratings? Are American-made cars "competitive"? Are sales increasing? Equally stimulating speeches could explore information on safety features, mileage data, and styling.

Audiences respond well to creative presentations and are more likely to remember what you said.

Creativity

PRINCIPLE 3

Audiences are more likely to listen to, understand, and remember informa- tion that is presented creatively.

Creativity can be defined as a person's capacity to produce new or original ideas and insights (Eysenck 1994, p. 200). Although you may be thinking, "I'm just not a creative person," all of us can be creative if we are willing to work at it. Let's see what steps you can take to become a more creative speaker.

1. **Gather enough high-quality information to give you a broad base from which to work.** Contrary to what many of us may think, creativity is more likely a product of perspiration than inspiration. If you have more quality information than what you really need for the speech, you have more flexi- bility and choices.

2. **Give yourself enough time for the creative process to work.** Many students finish their outline just in time to "go over the speech" once before they present it; then they wonder why they're not able to "be creative." Your mind needs time to reflect on your outline and information. This is why we recommended completing your outline for a classroom speech *at least* two days before the actual presentation. With that extra time, you're likely to find that the morning after an uninspiring practice you suddenly have two or three fresh ideas to work with. While you were sleeping, your mind was still going over the material. When you awoke, the product of unconscious or subconscious thought reached your consciousness. So, you can facilitate creatively simply by giving your mind time to work with your information.

3. **Be prepared to pursue a creative idea when it comes.** Have you ever noticed how ideas seem to come at odd times—while you are cleaning your room, mulching the garden, or waiting at a stoplight? Have you also noticed that when you try to recall those "great" ideas, they are likely to have slipped away? Many speakers, writers, and composers carry pencil and paper with them at all times, and when an idea comes, they make a note of it. Not all of these flights of fancy are flashes of creative genius, but some of them are good or at least worth exploring. If you do not make note of your ideas, you will never know whether they are good.

4. **Force yourself to practice sections of the speech in different ways.** Too many times, when we have finished our outline, we act as if it's cast in stone. Then we keep going over it the same way "to learn it." But if you do not take the time to practice in different ways, you allow yourself to be con- tent with the first way of presenting material that comes to mind rather than considering alternatives that might be better. If, however, you pur- posely phrase key ideas in different ways in each of the first few practices, you give yourself choices. Although some of the ways you express a point

may be similar, trying new ways will stretch your mind, and chances are good that one or two of the ways will be far superior and much more imaginative than any of the others.

Let's look at an example that gives you a chance to think about alternative choices. Suppose you are planning to give a speech on climatic variation in the United States, and your research has uncovered the data shown in the table in Figure 17.1. We will use these data to show (1) that one set of data can suggest several lines of development on the same topic and (2) that the same point can be made in many different ways.

City	Yearly Temperature (in degrees Fahrenheit)		Precipitation (in inches)	
	High	Low	July	Annual
Chicago	95	–21	3.7	35
Cincinnati	98	–7	3.3	39
Denver	104	–3	1.9	15
Los Angeles	104	40	trace	15
Miami	96	50	5.7	56
Minneapolis	95	–27	3.5	28
New Orleans	95	26	6.1	62
New York	98	–2	4.4	42
Phoenix	117	35	0.8	7
Portland, ME	94	–18	3.1	44
St. Louis	97	–9	3.9	37
San Francisco	94	35	trace	19
Seattle	94	23	0.9	38

Figure 17.1
Climatic data.

1. **Study your information and ask what's unusual or noteworthy and why.** As you look at the table in Figure 17.1, you might notice several unusual or noteworthy points. First, you might notice that yearly *high* temperatures in U.S. cities vary far less than yearly *low* temperatures. For instance, the yearly high was only one degree higher in Miami (96) than in Minneapolis (95), whereas the yearly lows were 50 degrees in Miami and –27 in Minneapolis—a 77-degree difference! Conventional wisdom would suggest that high temperatures should vary nearly as much as low temperatures. Ask yourself, why is this not so?

You might also notice that it hardly ever rains on the West Coast in the summer. Two of the three West Coast cities, Los Angeles and San Francisco, show only a trace of rain in July and a third, Seattle, often considered a rainy city, received only 0.9 inch in July—considerably less than any eastern city and almost 5 inches less than Miami. Why is there so little rain on the West Coast in July? Why is there so much more in the East?

Finally, you might notice that in the major cities cited in the East and in the Midwest, July, a month generally thought to be hot and dry, actually accounts for *more* than the average one-twelfth of annual precipitation. So why do we perceive July to be a dry month? And why isn't it?

Thus, as we study the data in this one chart, we can raise questions that suggest at least three different lines of development for a speech on climate: Why are highs so similar but lows so different? Why is there so much more rain in the summer in the Midwest and East than in the West? Why is July wetter in most cities than we would expect?

2. **Create different ways of making the same point.** Using only the information from the climatic data, let's consider two ways of supporting the point that "Yearly high temperatures in U.S. cities vary far less than yearly low temperatures."

    a. Of the thirteen cities selected, ten (77 percent) had yearly highs between 90 and 100 degrees. Yet four (31 percent) had yearly lows above freezing; two (15 percent) had yearly lows between zero and 32 degrees; and seven (54 percent) had low temperatures below zero.

    b. Chicago, Miami, Minneapolis, and New Orleans, cities at different latitudes, all had yearly high temperatures of 95 or 96 degrees. In contrast, the lowest temperature for Miami was 50 degrees, and the lowest temperatures for New Orleans, Chicago, and Minneapolis were 25, –21, and –27 degrees, respectively.

    Can you find another way of making the same point?

Relevance

PRINCIPLE 4

Audiences are more likely to listen to and remember information they per-ceive as relevant.

Rather than acting like sponges that absorb every bit of information, most of us act more like filters: We listen only to that information we perceive to be relevant. **Relevance** is the personal value that people find in information when it relates to their needs and interests. Relevance might be measured by an audience's "need to know."

Finding *vital* information—information the audience perceives as a matter of life or death—may be the ultimate in relevance. Police cadets, for instance, will see information explaining what they should do when attacked as vital. Similarly, students may perceive information that is required for passing a test as vital. A speaker who shows listeners that information is critical to their well-being gives them a compelling reason to listen.

Of course, information does not have to be vital to be perceived as relevant. But always ask yourself in what way the material you plan to present is truly

---

OBSERVE AND ANALYZE

Different Ways of Presenting Information

Which of these two ways, a or b, is better? Why? Create a third way that is somewhat different. Is the way you created even better? If so, why? If not, why not?

important to the audience, and emphasize that connection in your speech. For example, in a speech on Japan—a topic that may seem distant from the audience's felt needs and concerns—you can increase the perception of relevance by focusing on the importance of Japanese manufacturing to our economy, including local jobs; in a speech on the Egyptian pyramids, you can increase perception of relevance by relating their construction to contemporary building construction. In any speech you give, it is up to you to show how the information relates to the audience's needs and interests.

Although determining relevance is important throughout the speech, it is especially important during your introduction when audience members are sure to ask themselves, "Why should I listen to a speech on . . . ?" Notice how the following opening for a speech on high-speed rail transportation establishes relevance:

> **Have you been stuck in a traffic jam lately? Have you started what you had hoped would be a pleasant vacation only to be trampled at the airport or, worse, to discover when you got to your destination that your luggage hadn't? We're all aware that every year our highways and our airways are getting more congested. At the same time, we are facing a rapidly decreasing supply of petroleum. Today, I'm going to tell you about one of the most practical means for solving these problems: high-speed rail transportation.**

Emphasis
PRINCIPLE 5

Audiences are more likely to understand and to remember information that is emphasized.

Audiences will remember only some of the content presented in a speech; the rest is likely to be lost over time. Part of your challenge is to determine *what* you want the audience to retain and then to give that information proper emphasis. Toward this end, you must prioritize your information.

Ordinarily, the highest-priority information in your speech includes the specific goal, the main points, and key facts that give meaning to the main points. So, if you were giving a speech on evaluating diamonds, you would want to make sure the audience remembered

- the goal: to understand the four criteria for evaluating a diamond.
- the main points: The four criteria for evaluating a diamond are carat (weight of the diamond), clarity (purity of the diamond), color (tint of the diamond), and cutting (shaping of the diamond).
- important facts: A carat weighs 200 milligrams; clarity is marred by internal blemishes, such as bubbles, feathers, clouds, and inclusions, all of which detract from a diamond's purity; the most expensive diamonds are without color; and diamonds can be cut into six common shapes (emerald, oval, marquise, brilliant, heart, and pear).

Once you have prioritized your information, plan a strategy for increasing the audience's retention of these items. In previous chapters, we have discussed various methods of emphasizing information. Let's remind ourselves of the importance of visual aids, repetition, transitions, humorous stories, and one additional method, mnemonics.

1. **Use visual aids.** Recall that visual aids emphasize because we remember more when we can associate pictures with words. Especially for informative speeches, you will want to think very carefully about the kinds of visual aids that will work best for you.

2. **Repeat important words and ideas.** Recall that just because a word is spoken does not necessarily mean that we perceive it. One of the best ways of breaking through is sheer repetition. You may want to repeat a word, or you may want to restate an idea in a slightly different way. But bear in mind that when repetition is overdone, it loses its effectiveness. So, in your speech, repeating a few important words and ideas will pay dividends—but repeating too many words or ideas will backfire.

3. **Use transitions to guide audience thinking.** Since listeners cannot go back if they get lost, it is especially important for speakers to do what they can to help audiences see where they have been and where they are going. Thus, in the introduction of the speech, you tell the audience what you will cover: "In this speech, we will look at the four criteria for evaluating a diamond." Then, as you proceed through a long main point, you might remind your listeners where you are going by saying, "So we've seen that color of the diamond affects its value; now let's consider the conditions that affect color." And before the end of the speech you might review, "So, in this speech, we've looked at the four criteria of carat (weight), clarity, color, and cutting."

   The value of such clarifying structure is tremendous. Because listeners' minds may wander, you must exercise control in how you want the audience to perceive what you say. I have heard listeners swear that a speaker never stated the second main point of the speech when in reality the point was stated—but in a way that had no effect on the audience. Clarifying structure through transitions helps your audience recognize where you are in the speech and why your point is significant.

4. **Use humor to stress key points.** Our own experience shows that of all the forms of presenting information, we are most likely to remember information presented in humorous story form. For instance, suppose you were giving a speech on the importance of having perspective. Your main point might be that because a problem that seems enormous at the moment might turn out to be minor in a few days, being able to put events into perspective saves a great deal of psychological wear and tear. To cement the concept of *perspective*, you might tell the following story:

Audiences are more likely to remember information presented in a humorous story form.

> A first-time visitor to the races bet two dollars on the first race on a horse that had the same name as his elementary school. The horse won, and the man was ten dollars ahead. In each of the next several races, he bet on horses such as Apple Pie, his favorite, and Kathie's Prize, after his wife's name, and he kept winning. By the end of the sixth race, he was 700 dollars ahead. He was about to go home when he noticed that in the seventh race, Seventh Veil was scheduled in the number seven position, and was currently going off at odds of seven to one. The man couldn't resist—he bet his entire 700 dollars. And sure enough, the horse came in seventh. When he got home, his wife asked, "How did you do?" Very calmly he looked at his wife and said, "Not bad—I lost two dollars." That's perspective.

5. **Create memory aids for your audience.** You can help your listeners retain more of your speech by suggesting **memory aids**, formally called **mnemonics.** For instance, your audience might remember that the four criteria for evaluating a diamond are weight, clarity, tint, and shape. But they will be more likely to remember "carat, clarity, color, and cutting." Why? Because you've created a memory aid by having all four criteria begin with the letter C.

Mnemonics may be **acronyms,** or words formed from initial letters of each of the successive parts of a compound term (NATO, OPEC); common words made up of the first letters of objects or concepts (HOMES for the five great lakes); or sentences with the initial letter of each word standing for something (Every Good Boy Does Fine for the five lines of the musical staff).

Most memory aids are a form of association. An **association** is the tendency of one thought to stimulate recall of another, similar thought. Suppose you are trying to help the audience remember the value of color in a diamond. Because blue is the most highly prized tint and yellow or brown tints lower a diamond's value, you might associate blue tint with "the blue-ribbon prize" and yellow (or brown) tint with "a lemon." Thus, the best diamond gets the "blue ribbon," and the worst diamond is a "lemon."

Figurative associations like these fall into the two categories of similes and metaphors. Recall that a simile is a comparison using *like* or *as*: "A computer monitor is like a television screen." A metaphor states an identity: "Laser printers are the Cadillacs of computer printers." I still remember vividly a metaphor I heard in a speech more than twenty years ago. A student explained the functioning of a television tube by saying, "A television picture tube is a gun shooting beams of light." If you make your associations striking enough, your audience will remember your point as well as I remember that point about how a television tube works.

Methods of Informing

Your informative speaking strength will grow as you gain a mastery of the four major methods of informing: narrating, describing, demonstrating, and defining.

Narrating

Recall from Chapter 13 that a narrative is a story, a tale, or an anecdote (often humorous) that has a point or climax. A joke has a punch line; a fable has a moral; other narratives have some climactic ending that makes the stories interesting. Thus, the primary goal of a narrative is to make a point in such a unique or interesting way that the audience will remember it because of the way it was presented.

Suppose you were making a point about the costs to personal well-being of faulty listening. You might exemplify the point with a narrative statement:

> **Abraham suffered great personal cost by working all day to finish a report for the five o'clock deadline, only to find as he turned it in that he was a day early.**

This one-sentence narrative about Abraham can then be developed to be both more interesting and more memorable. Let's consider three major elements of narration and how they can be used to increase the power of this particular narrative statement.

1. **Narratives are built with supporting details.** A narrative can be long or short depending on the number and degree of development of supporting details. Supporting details build the story so that the point or climax of the story has maximum effect. For instance, in the narrative about Abraham's report, you could introduce such details as Abraham's getting to work at 6 A.M., more than two hours earlier than usual, to work on the report and turning down a lunch invitation from a man he'd been trying to see for three weeks about an important issue of company policy.

2. **Narratives usually maintain suspense.** Part of the power of the narrative can be increased by withholding the punch line until the end. If you can tease the audience, you will hold their attention. They will be trying to see whether they can anticipate what you are going to say. Vocally, a slight pause before delivering the punch line will heighten the effect:

   > **Abraham worked all day to finish his report for the five o'clock deadline, only to discover when he turned it in [pause] that it was one full day early!**

3. **Narratives include dialogue when possible.** A story will be much more enjoyable to an audience if they can hear it unfold through dialogue. Notice how our one-line story improves with this presentation:

   > **As Abraham burst into his boss's office with report in hand, his boss's secretary stared at him, dumbfounded. When he said breathlessly, "Here's the report, right on the dot!" she said, "Abraham, the report isn't due until tomorrow!"**

Describing

Questions like "What does it look like?" and "How do the parts fit together?" are answered by describing. As with any of the methods of informing, descriptions must be carefully worded to be effective. To describe effectively requires that you observe particular characteristics and create vivid ways to communicate those observations. Let's consider the characteristics of description and some means of revising creatively.

Characteristics of description. Vivid description is based on observation of size, shape, weight, color, composition, age and condition, and the relationship among various parts. Because the goal of description is to enable the audience to visualize, if some particular aspect is especially important, you might describe it in two or three different ways to make the image as vivid as possible.

How large is the place or object? If it's an object, how heavy is it? Both size and weight are most descriptive when they are presented comparatively: "The book is the same length and width as your text, but about twice as thick," "The suitcase weighed seventy pounds, about twice the weight of a normally packed suitcase."

What is the object's shape? What color is it? Simple shapes are easily described by words such as round, triangular, oblong, spherical, conical, cylindrical, and rectangular. Complex objects are best described as a series of simple shapes. Color, an obvious component of description, is difficult to describe accurately. Although most people can visualize black and white, the primary colors (red, yellow, and blue), and their complements (green, purple, and orange), very few objects are exactly these colors. Perhaps the best way to describe a color is to couple it with a common referent. For instance, "lemon yellow," "brick red," "green as a grape," or "sky blue" give fairly accurate approximations.

What is the object made of? What is its age or condition? A ball of aluminum does not look the same as a ball of yarn. A pile of rocks gives a different impression than a pile of straw. A brick building looks different from a steel, wood, or glass building. Whether an object is new or old can make a difference in its appearance. Because age by itself may not be descriptive, an object is often discussed in terms of condition. Well-read books become tattered, older buildings become dilapidated, land becomes eroded. Age and condition together often prove valuable in developing informative descriptions.

How does an object fit together? If the object you want to describe is complex, its parts must be fitted into their proper relationship before a mental picture emerges. Remember the story of the blind men who described an elephant in terms of what each felt? The one who felt the trunk said the elephant was like a snake; the one who felt a leg said the elephant was like a tree; and the one who felt the body said the elephant was like a wall. When it is relevant to your description, be sure audiences understand how the parts fit together.

Revising descriptions. Description can be improved with careful revision. For most people, vivid description does not come easily—we are not used to describing vividly in ordinary conversation. In practices, speakers have the opportunity to work on their language, revising general and bland statements to make them more specific and vivid. We can work with a single, simple idea to illustrate the revision process. Consider the following sentence:

> Several pencils were on Jamal's desk.

This statement of fact tells us that pencils (plural) were on a desk, but it gives no real description.

Revising this description begins with asking questions that relate to the essentials of description. If we ask, "How many pencils? What color were they?" specific descriptive details come to mind. The following revision answers those questions:

> Five yellow pencils decorated Jamal's desk.

Five is more descriptive than several because it is more specific; yellow begins a description of how they looked; decorated is more descriptive than on because it carries a mental picture. Now ask the questions "What condition were the pencils in? How were they arranged?" In the following two sentences, we get completely different descriptions of the pencils based on the answers to these questions:

> Five finely sharpened yellow pencils lined the side of Jamal's desk, side by side in perfect order from longest to shortest.

> Five stubby, well-chewed pencils of different colors, all badly in need of sharpening, were scattered about Jamal's desk.

These examples begin to show the different pictures that can be created depending on how you use the observed details.

Continued revision may lead to your trying to memorize the speech. As you practice, try to keep the essentials in mind, but try to use slightly different wordings each time to express your descriptions. By making minor changes each time, you will avoid memorizing the speech.

Demonstrating

Many informative speeches involve explaining processes—telling how to do something, how to make something, or how something works. A demonstration involves going through the complete process that you are explaining—for example, how to get more power on a forehand table-tennis shot, how to make fettuccine noodles, or how to purify water.

When the task is relatively simple, such as how to get more power on a forehand table-tennis shot, you may want to try a **complete demonstration.** If so, practice until you can do it smoothly and easily under the pressure of facing

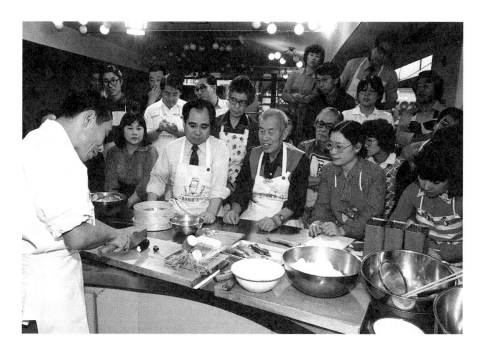

Demonstrations must be carefully prepared and organized if audiences are to retain the information.

an actual audience. Since the actual demonstration is likely to take longer than in practice (you are likely to have to make some modifications during the speech to enable everyone in the room to see the demonstration), you may want to make sure that the final practice is somewhat shorter than the maximum time limit you will have for the speech.

For a relatively complicated process, you may want to consider a **modified demonstration,** in which you complete various stages of the demonstration at home and do only part of the actual work in front of the audience. Suppose you were going to demonstrate construction of a floral display. Actually performing the construction from scratch is too complex and time-consuming for a speech-length presentation. Instead, you could prepare a complete set of materials to begin the demonstration, a mock-up of the basic floral triangle, and a completed floral display. During the speech, you would describe the materials needed and then begin demonstrating how to make the basic floral triangle. Rather than trying to get everything together perfectly in a few seconds, you could remove, from a bag or some concealed place, a partially completed arrangement illustrating the floral triangle. You would then use this in your demonstration, adding flowers as if you were planning to complete it. Then from another bag, you could remove the completed arrangement to illustrate one of the effects you were discussing. Conducting a modified demonstration of this type is often easier than trying to complete an entire demonstration in a limited time.

Throughout a demonstration, speak slowly and repeat key ideas often. We learn best by doing, so if you can include audience participation, you may be even more successful. In a speech on origami, or Japanese paper folding, you could explain the principles, then pass out paper and have audience members each make a figure. Actual participation will increase interest and ensure recall. Finally, through other visual aids, you could show how these principles are used in more elaborate projects.

Although your audience may be able to visualize a process through vivid word pictures (in fact, in your impromptu explanations in ordinary conversation, it is the only way you can proceed), you will probably want to make full use of visual aids in a demonstration speech. Perhaps more than with any other kind of informative speech, carefully prepared visual material may be essential to listeners' understanding.

Defining

Because of their importance in solving problems, learning, and understanding, clear definitions are essential for effective communication. Richard Weaver (1970, p. 212), a major twentieth-century figure in rhetorical theory, has labeled definition as the most valuable of all lines of development, primarily because of its role in helping audiences understand and relate to key concepts. In your informative speeches, you are likely to use both short and extended definitions.

Short definitions. Short definitions are used to clarify concepts in as few words as possible. Effective speakers learn to define by synonym and antonym, classification and differentiation, use or function, and etymological reference, and to supplement these definitions with examples and comparisons.

1. **Synonyms and antonyms.** Using a synonym or an antonym is the quickest way to define a word, enabling you to give an approximate, if not exact, meaning in a single sentence.

   Synonyms are words that have the same or nearly the same meanings; **antonyms** are words that have opposite meanings. Defining by synonym is defining by comparison; for a word that does not bring up an immediate concrete meaning, we provide one that does. Synonyms for *prolix* include *long*, *wordy*, and *verbose*. Its antonyms are *short* and *concise*. Synonyms are not duplicates for the word being defined, but they do give a good idea of what the word means. Of course, the synonym or antonym must be familiar to the audience, or its use defeats the purpose.

2. **Classification and differentiation.** When you define by classification, you give the boundaries of the particular word and focus on the single feature that differentiates that word from words with similar meanings. Most dictionary definitions are of the classification-differentiation variety. For instance, a dog may be defined as a carnivorous, domesticated mammal of the family Canidae. *Carnivorous, mammal,* and *family Canidae* limit the boundaries to dogs, jackals, foxes, and wolves; *domesticated* differentiates dogs from the other three.

3. **Use or function.** A third short way to define is by explaining the use or function of the object represented by a particular word. Thus, when you say, "A *plane* is a hand-powered tool that is used to smooth the edges of boards," or "A *scythe* is a piece of steel shaped in a half circle with a handle attached that is used to cut weeds or high grass," you are defining tools by indicating their use. Because the use or function of an object may be more important than its classification, this is often an excellent method of definition.

4. **Etymology.** Etymology is the derivation or history of a particular word. Because meanings of words change over time, origin may reveal very little about modern meaning. In some instances, however, the history of a word lends additional insight that will help the audience not only better remember the meaning but also bring the meaning to life. For instance, a *censor* was originally one of two Roman magistrates appointed to take the census and, later, to supervise public morals. The best source of word derivations is the *Oxford English Dictionary*.

5. **Examples and comparisons.** Regardless of which short definition form you use, most definitions need to be supplemented with examples, comparisons,

or both to make them understandable. This is especially true when you define abstract words. Consider the word *just* in the following sentence: "You are being *just* in your dealings with another when you deal *honorably* and *fairly*." Although *just* has been defined by synonyms, listeners still may be unsure of the meaning. To make it clearer, we might add, "If Paul and Mary do the same amount of work and we reward them by giving them an equal amount of money, our dealings will be just; if, on the other hand, we give Paul more money because he's a man, our dealings will be unjust." In this case, the definition is clarified with both an example and a comparison.

For some words, a single example or comparison will be enough. For other words or in communicating with certain audiences, you may need several examples and comparisons.

Extended definitions. Often a word is so important to a speech that an extended definition is warranted. An extended definition is one that serves as an entire main point in a speech or, at times, an entire speech. Thus, an entire speech can be built around an extended definition of a term such as *freedom*, *equality*, *justice*, *love*, or *impressionistic painting*.

An extended definition begins with a single-sentence dictionary definition or stipulated definition. For example, *Webster's Third New International Dictionary* defines *jazz* as "American music characterized by improvisation, syncopated rhythms, contrapuntal ensemble playing, and special melodic features peculiar to the individual interpretation of the player." This definition suggests four topics—improvisation, syncopation, ensemble, and special melodies—that could be used as the main points of a speech on jazz. The key to the effectiveness of the speech would be how well you explain each of these main points. Your selection and use of examples, illustrations, comparisons, personal experiences, and observations will give the speech its original and distinctive flavor.

TEST YOUR COMPETENCE

Informative Speaking

Prepare an informative speech. An outline and a bibliography are required. Criteria for evaluation include your means of building credibility and of ensuring audience interest, understanding, and retention of information.

As an addendum to the outline, you may wish to write a plan for adapting the speech to your audience based on predictions you made using the audience analysis checklist on p. 281. In this plan, include three short sections discussing strategies for (1) getting and maintaining interest, (2) facilitating audience understanding, and (3) increasing retention. Where appropriate, comment on use of visual aids and the role of language and delivery techniques for implementing your plan. See the sample outline, speech plan, and informative speech at the end of this chapter.

Criteria for Evaluating Informative Speeches

In this chapter, we have been looking at principles of informative speaking. Now let's apply those principles to evaluating and presenting informative speeches.

PRACTICE IN CLASS

Critiquing on Informative Speech

Write a critique for at least one of the informative speeches you hear in class. Outline the speech. As you outline, answer the questions on the informative speech checklist.

Check all items that were accomplished effectively.

Primary Criteria

____ 1. Was the specific goal designed to increase audience information?
____ 2. Did the speaker show creativity in idea development?
____ 3. Was the speaker effective in establishing his or her credibility on this topic?
____ 4. Was the information intellectually stimulating?
____ 5. Did the speaker show the relevance of the information?
____ 6. Did the speaker emphasize the information?
____ 7. Was the organizational pattern appropriate for the intent and content of the speech?

General Criteria

____ 1. Was the specific goal clear?
____ 2. Was the introduction effective?
____ 3. Were the main points clear?
____ 4. Was the conclusion effective?
____ 5. Was the language clear, vivid, and emphatic?
____ 6. Was the speech delivered enthusiastically, with vocal expressiveness, spontaneously, fluently, and with eye contact?

Evaluate the speech as (check one):
____ excellent, ____ good, ____ average, ____ fair, ____ poor.

Figure 17.2

Critiquing an informative speech: checklist.

Use the information from this checklist to support your evaluation.

Speech Outline: Improving Grades[1]

Specific Goal: I want my audience to understand three techniques for improving grades in college.

Introduction

I. We all know that good grades are a necessity whether we wish to go on to graduate school or get the best job possible.

II. Because I'm a returning student, I've felt even more pressure to do as well as I can in all my courses.

III. I want to share with you three methods for improving grades that I've tried to apply in my own work.

Thesis Statement: Three proven techniques for improving test scores in college are to attend classes regularly, develop a positive attitude, and study efficiently.

Body

I. The first proven technique for improving grades in college is to attend classes regularly.

---

[1] Presented in speech class, University of Cincinnati. Used with permission of Jennifer Howell Streyle.

A. The primary difference between A students and C students is regular attendance.
   1. A students average one absence a term.
   2. C students average four absences a term.
B. If your motivation lags, remember that each day of classes is worth $1,000.

(Now that we've seen the importance of attendance, let's consider the second technique.)

II. The second proven technique is to develop a positive attitude.
A. The mind has power over behavior.
   1. Go into class relaxed.
   2. Be confident.
B. Visualize success on the exam.
   1. Once the subconscious mind accepts an idea, it executes it.
   2. Use affirmations.

(Now let's consider the third technique.)

III. The third proven technique is to study systematically.
A. Read assignments thoroughly before each class.
B. Process information presented in class.
C. Review assignments after class.

Conclusion

If you attend class regularly, study efficiently, and prepare yourself psychologically for every class, you'll reap the rewards of an improved GPA.

Bibliography

Jewler, A. Jerome, and John N. Gardner. *Step by Step to College Success*. Belmont, CA: Wadsworth, 1987.

Kalish, Richard A. *Guide to Effective Study*. Monterey, CA: Brooks/ Cole, 1979.

Murphy, Joseph. *The Power of Your Subconscious Mind*. New York: Bantam, 1985.

Olney, Claude W. *Where There's a Will There's an A*. Paoli, PA: Chesterbook Educational Publishers, 1989.

Wipperman, R. P. Personal interview, 2 November 1992.

Plan for Adapting to Audience

1. **Getting and maintaining interest.** I plan to begin the speech by showing the monetary rewards of study. During the speech, I believe that my quotations and examples as well as my clear and vivid language will help maintain interest. Likewise, I hope to show the relevance of the topic for all of us—I will focus on all of our interests in improving grades. I will also use personal pronouns and rhetorical questions. I further believe that my enthusiastic delivery will help to maintain interest.

2. **Facilitating understanding.** Even though the class should perceive the techniques as relatively simple, I believe listeners will find the information

intellectually stimulating. I believe my listeners appreciate the clarity of the information that I present. I will also use repetition and comparison to help listeners see the information more clearly. Foremost, I will clarify structure with good transitions. I will also use repetition and comparison.

3. **Increasing retention.** My primary means of increasing attention will be emphasis through repetition and transitions. I will preview the three techniques in the introduction, state each clearly as main points, and then repeat them again in the conclusion. I also believe that by relating the techniques to their needs as students, they are likely to want to remember them.

Sample Speech and Analysis: Improving Grades

Read the following speech aloud at least once. Examine it to see whether information has been presented in a way that is creative, credible, intellectually stimulating, relevant, and emphatic. Most important, assess the speech for its informative value.

Speech

We all know the importance of good grades for either getting into graduate school or getting the best possible job. R. P. Wipperman, a section head for Procter & Gamble, told me that good grades "are the calling card that get you in the door."

Because I've been away from college for more than seventeen years, I've been particularly concerned about getting back into the studying groove, so I've been reading study guides looking for specific techniques that are most likely to help with my grades. Today I'd like to share with you three relatively easy, proven techniques for improving your GPA that I've learned from my study: attend classes regularly, maintain a positive attitude, and study systematically.

The first proven technique is to attend classes regularly. It sounds so simple, doesn't it, but it turns out to be really important. According to Dr. Claude Olney, who is highly regarded for his publications on grades, one of the most significant differences between and A and a C in a course is attendance. Olney did a study of eight hundred students and found that those who got A's missed less than one class per term, and people who got C's missed more than four classes per term. During class professors

Analysis

Notice how Jennifer begins with a statement that we will all agree with. Then she moves to a quotation that reinforces that statement.

She uses her thesis statement as a transition leading into the body of the speech.

Throughout the speech, the speaker leads us through the organization. She begins the body of the speech by identifying the first technique. Although the speaker has given the credentials for her authority, she has not cited the source from which the information came.

Here the speaker does a good job of developing the point that attendance makes a difference.

Speech

clarify difficult concepts, emphasize key information, and give insights that can't be gotten any other way. Regular attendance is important to learning in general and to doing well on tests in particular.

If you need further motivation to attend class, think of it this way: Every day you attend class is worth $1,000 to you—that's a thousand dollars! According to a Census Bureau study reported in a recent *Cincinnati Enquirer*, a college diploma hanging on the wall is worth $1,039 a month in extra pay (an average of $2,116 a month for college graduates compared with $1,077 per month for high school graduates). This $12,000+ a year comes to some $600,000 over a lifetime. Since here at UC we spend about 600 days in class over four years, that comes out to about $1,000 for every day we come to school.

Now that we've seen the importance of attendance, let's consider the second technique.

The second technique is to develop a positive attitude toward school in general and each class in particular. Bill Moyers just finished a public television series reemphasizing the power of the mind in all aspects of our behavior. To emphasize this relationship, I love the following quote from Dr. Olney: "If you think you can do it, you're right, and if you don't think you can do it, you're still right." Notice, whether you can do it or not depends a great deal on whether you think you can.

So, go into class each day relaxed, confident that you're ready for class, and you're ready to make the most of what the professor chooses to talk about or discuss during that class. This will help the mind work for you. Joseph Murray, who wrote *The Power of Your Subconscious Mind*, said, "Once the subconscious mind accepts an idea it begins to execute it." Remind yourself of how much you are learning and how that learning is making you a better-educated, more interesting person. On test days, say, "I'm ready for this test" or "I know this information." If you have a positive attitude, you'll get better grades.

Analysis

Good adaptation to audience needs and interests. Clear explanation of the basis for the assertion.

Here the speaker points out the source of the study and the source of the information.

Notice the clear transition summarizing the first point and leading us to the second.

Again the main point is clearly stated. She begins this section with a reference to a television series that had been highly publicized in the local and national media.

Notice that the speaker not only presents a relevant quotation but also points out the significance of the quotation.

This second documented source in the section helps to reinforce the importance of positive thinking.

Speech

Now let's consider the third technique.

The third proven technique is to learn to study systematically. Every one of the study sources I consulted suggested the importance of reading, processing, and reviewing.

First, read assignments thoroughly before going to class. Many of us figure that the professor will cover what we need to know in class, so we don't really have to read the assignment before class. But learning works a lot better if we have a good idea of the material when we get to class.

Second, process the information in class. When the professor lectures, take careful notes, and see how this information relates to material you have studied for class; during class discussions, ask questions in order to check definitions and review examples.

Third, and most important, review the assignment material after class. This is the key to systematic study. Keep in mind that without reinforcement, we forget half of what we've read within forty-eight hours, and 90 percent of what we've read within two weeks. If the information is reinforced, however, we can remember 80–90 percent of the information we have read. Reviewing assignment material after class provides this important reinforcement. So, tonight, before you begin reading information for tomorrow's classes, review information from today's classes.

So, by attending every class, thinking positively, and studying systematically (read, process, and review), you will improve your GPA.

Analysis

A clear transition to the third technique.

Notice that all three main points are stated with parallel wording: "The first (second, third) proven technique is. . . ." Also notice the way she previews the three subdivisions of the point.

This section shows good adaptation, as the speaker refers to a common behavior—waiting to read the assignment until after class.

After identifying the second subpoint, she mentions the specific behaviors that are necessary to process adequately.

Notice that here she tells her listeners that this third subpoint is the most important.

Here the speaker presents important information. It would have been a good idea to mention the specific source of these statistics.

Jennifer finishes her speech with a brief summary. Although a summary is appropriate, she might have used some additional concluding point to help leave the speech on a high note. This is a good example of a clear, generally well-developed informative speech.

Summary

Informative speeches are those in which the primary goal is to create understanding. As an informative speaker, your rhetorical challenge is to present information in a way that facilitates attending, understanding, and remembering.

To accomplish these goals, speakers can learn to incorporate several principles: Audiences are more likely to show interest in, understand, and remember information (1) if it is presented creatively, (2) if they like, trust, and have confidence in the speaker, (3) if they perceive the information to be new, (4) if they perceive it to be relevant, and (5) if it is emphasized.

Speakers are perceived to be credible if they are competent, have good intentions, and have a pleasant personality. New information has even greater impact when it is perceived as intellectually stimulating. Creativity involves using material in an imaginative way. Information is perceived as relevant if it is vital or important. Information is likely to be remembered if it is presented visually as well as vocally, if it is repeated, if it is introduced with external transitions, if it is presented humorously, or if it includes specific memory aids.

Methods of informing include narrating, describing, demonstrating, and defining. Narrating is telling a story, usually one with a point or climax related to the theme of the speech. Describing means creating a verbal picture through vivid descriptions of size, shape, weight, color, composition, age and condition, and the relationship among parts. Demonstrating involves showing how to do something, how to make something, or how something works. Both full and modified demonstrations are often enhanced by visual aids. Defining is giving the meaning of a word or concept through synonym and antonym, classification and differentiation, use or function, or etymology, and is enhanced with the use of examples and comparisons.

REFLECT ON ETHICS

As Jason was practicing his speech, he found that he had some statistics that were important to his point, but he couldn't remember where he had gotten them. He recalled that during the two hours he had spent at the library, he had found several articles from which he had taken information. He had tried to be very careful about identifying the sources from which specific information came. But as he looked through his notes, he discovered at least three sets of information for which there were no references. Fortunately, two of the three weren't that important, but this one set of statistics was. As he pondered the problem, he concluded, "I know I didn't make these up— I'm pretty sure I copied the statistics accurately," but of course neither the source nor the date of the statistics was included. He thought, "I could go back through all the sources I have written down, but this would take me a very long time, and I'm not even sure this particular set of statistics is from any of those sources."

The more he considered it, the more convinced he became that even though he hadn't written down the source, he knew the statistics were valid, so there was no reason why he shouldn't use them. He decided that he'd just say, "A recent magazine article included the following statistics."

1. Does Jason face an ethical problem here? If so, what is it?
2. If you had been in the same position, what would you have done? Explain why your solution would be a good one.

OBJECTIVES

After you have read this chapter, you should be able to answer the following questions:

■ What is the difference between affecting behavior and moving to action?

■ Why should you assess audience attitude toward your goal?

■ What are good reasons?

■ What kinds of material gives support to reasons?

■ What are some common fallacies?

■ What are typical persuasive-speaking organizational patterns?

■ What does a persuasive speaker do to motivate an audience?

■ What are some major ethical guidelines for persuasive speaking?

18

Persuasive Speaking

As she finished her speech, the entire audience rose in a body and cheered. Over the din, the chair shouted, "All those in favor, say 'aye,'" and as one, everyone roared "aye" as a testament to her lucid and persuasive argument. As she walked to her seat, people reached to pat her on the back, and those who could not touch her chanted her name: "Sheila . . . Sheila . . . !"

"Sheila! Wake up," Denny said as he shook her shoulder, "you're supposed to be working on your speech."

Perhaps you've imagined yourself giving such a stirring speech that your audience cheered wildly at your persuasive powers. Although everything works well in our fantasies, our real-life attempts to persuade are not always so successful. **Persuasive speaking**—in which a speaker presents a message intended to reinforce a belief, change a belief, or move an audience to act—is perhaps the most demanding speech challenge.

Now let us turn to some specific principles designed to help you increase the likelihood of achieving your persuasive-speech goals. Then we'll look at a sample persuasive speech.

Principles of Persuasion

The following principles focus on what you can do to increase the probability of being an effective persuasive speaker.

Writing a Specific Goal

PRINCIPLE 1

You are more likely to persuade an audience when you can articulate specifically what you want your audience to believe or do.

Persuasive speeches are designed either to establish or change beliefs or to move an audience to action.

If your speech goal is to establish or change a belief, your listeners may end up acting on that belief, but your primary emphasis is on having them agree with you that the belief you present is reasonable.

The following speech goals are written to seek audience acceptance of a belief:

> I want the audience to believe that the city should build a downtown entertainment center.

> I want the audience to believe that small schools are better for insecure students than are large schools.

> I want the audience to believe that the federal income-tax deduction for home mortgage interest should be abolished.

> I want the audience to believe that the speed limit on all interstate highways should be raised to seventy miles per hour.

Notice that in each case you are focusing on what audience members ought to believe—not on what they ought to do as a result of that belief.

Speeches that are designed *to move an audience to action* go beyond gaining agreement on a belief—they state exactly what you want your audience to *do*. The following are all goals that seek action:

I want my audience to donate money to the food-bank drive.

I want the members of my audience to write to their congressional representative to support legislation in favor of gun control.

I want my audience members to attend the school's production of *Grease*.

✞ Adapting to Audience Attitude
PRINCIPLE 2

You are more likely to be able to persuade when you direct your goal and your information to your audience's attitude.

You'll recall that an **attitude** is "a general or enduring positive or negative feeling about some person, object, or issue (Petty and Cacioppo 1996, p. 7). People's attitudes are usually expressed verbally as **opinions**. Thus, "I think physical fitness is important" is an opinion statement that reflects a favorable attitude about physical fitness.

Because much of the success of a speech depends on determining how an audience is likely to react to your goal, you must find out where your audience stands. As we said in Chapter 12, you make such judgments based on demographic information and/or opinion polls. The more data you have about your audience and the more experience you have in analyzing audiences, the better are your chances of judging its attitudes accurately.

Audience attitudes (expressed by opinions) may be distributed along a continuum from highly favorable to hostile (see Figure 18.1). Even though any given audience may have one or a few individuals' opinions at nearly every point along the distribution, audience opinion tends to cluster at a particular point. That cluster point represents the general audience attitude for that topic. Because it would be impossible to direct your speech to all the various shades of attitudes held by the members of your audience, you must classify audience attitude as predominantly "in favor" (already holding a particular belief), "no

---

PRACTICE IN SPEECH PREPARATION

Writing a Persuasive Speech Goal

1. Write a persuasive specific goal, and then rewrite it two or three times with slightly different wordings.
2. Identify your goal as one of establishing or changing a belief or as one seeking action. If at this stage you do not know what your audience believes, you may wish to hold off on the final wording of your goal until you have finished the next section on audience attitude.

Hostile	Opposed	Mildly opposed	Neither in favor nor opposed	Mildly in favor	In favor	Highly in favor

Figure 18.1
Opinion continuum.

opinion" (uninformed, neutral, or apathetic), or "opposed" (holding an opposite point of view) so you can develop a strategy that adapts to that attitude.

Now let us consider specific strategies for adapting to audiences. Suppose your goal is "I want my audience to believe that they should alter their intake of saturated fats." As you will see, your assessment of audience attitude may affect how you phrase your goal and how you select your information.

In favor. If you believe your listeners are already in favor of your belief, then you may want to change your goal to focus on a specific course of action.

For instance, if members of your audience already favor limiting their intake of saturated fats, it would be a mistake to focus on changing their belief. Since what is likely to keep people who have a favorable attitude from acting is lack of motivation, your job is to provide a specific course of action around which they can rally. When you believe your listeners are on your side, try to crystallize their attitudes, recommit them to a particular direction, or suggest a specific course of action that will serve as a rallying point. The presentation of a thoughtful and specific solution increases the likelihood of audience action.

Even when audience members are on your side, they may perceive what you want them to do as impractical. If so, they are likely to ignore your appeal regardless of its merits. For instance, if your goal is to have class members increase their exercise, taking the extra time necessary to exercise may seem

When you know that your audience is already leaning in your favor, you can focus your speech on a specific course of action.

impractical given their workloads. However, if your on-campus facility has a weight room, you may be able to show them how they can increase their exercise by using otherwise "wasted" time between classes or before or after lunch, in which case they may see the practicality of your goal.

No opinion. If you believe your listeners have no opinion, then you will focus on goals that establish a belief or goals that move the audience to action.

If you believe your audience has no opinion because it is **uninformed,** the strategy should be to give enough information to help your audience understand the subject before you develop persuasive appeals that are directed toward establishing a belief or that seek to move listeners to action. For instance, if you believe your audience is uninformed about the need to lower saturated fat intake, then early in the speech you need to define "saturated fat," talk about how cholesterol is formed, and share medical evidence about its effects on the human body. Be careful about how much time you spend on this informative part of the speech. If it takes more than half of your allotted time to explain what you are talking about, you may not have enough time to do much persuading.

If you believe your audience has no opinion because it is **neutral,** then you see your audience as being able to reason objectively and accept sound reasoning. In this case, your strategy will involve presenting the best possible arguments and supporting them with the best information you can find. If your assessment is correct, then you stand a good chance of success with that strategy.

If you believe your audience members have no opinion because they are **apathetic,** all of your effort may be directed to moving them out of their apathy. Members of your audience may know what saturated fat is, know how cholesterol is formed, and even understand the medical information of negative effects, but they may not seem to care. Instead of emphasizing the information with this audience, you would emphasize motivation. You will need less material that proves the logic of your arguments and more material that is directed to your listeners' personal needs.

Opposed. If you believe your listeners are opposed, then your strategy will depend upon whether their attitude is slightly negative or totally hostile.

If you believe your listeners are **slightly opposed** to your proposal, you can approach them rather directly with your argument, hoping that its weight will swing them to your side. If your audience is slightly opposed to lowering their intake of saturated fat, you can present good reasons and evidence supporting the proposal.

Another part of your strategy should involve presenting arguments in ways that lessen your listeners' negative attitudes without arousing their hostility. With a negative audience, take care to be objective with your material, and make your case clearly enough that those members who are only mildly negative will consider the proposal and those who are very negative will at least understand your position.

When speaking to an audience hostile to your viewpoint, adjust your speech to call for a more modest change of attitude. Otherwise, you lose your audience as this speaker has.

If you believe your audience is **hostile** toward your goal, you may want to approach the topic indirectly or to consider a less ambitious goal. To expect a complete shift in attitude or behavior as a result of one speech is probably unrealistic. If you present a modest proposal that seeks a slight change in attitude, you may be able to get an audience to at least consider the value of your message. Later, when the idea begins to grow, you can ask for a greater change. For instance, the audience may be comprised of people who are "fed up" with appeals to monitor their diets. If you believe your goal is important to them regardless of their negative attitude, then develop a more subtle strategy. Such a strategy will involve recognizing their hostility and talking about the topic in a way that will not arouse that hostility.

Figure 18.2 summarizes the strategy choices we have reviewed for audiences with different attitudes toward your topic. Principle 4 (p. 444) relates speech organization to audience attitudes and expected reactions.

Giving Good Reasons and Evidence

PRINCIPLE 3

You are more likely to persuade an audience when the body of your speech contains good reasons and evidence that support your speech goal.

Human beings take pride in being rational; we seldom do anything without some real or imagined reason. Since the 1980s, persuasive speech theory has focused sharply on persuasion as a cognitive activity—people forming cognitive structures to create meaning for experiences (Deaux, Dane, and Wrightsman 1993, p. 19). To meet this audience need, the main points of a persuasive speech are usually stated as **reasons**—statements that tell why a proposition is justified.

THINK CRITICALLY

Assessing Audience Attitudes

In reference to your specific persuasive speech goal, is your audience's attitude likely to be in favor, neutral, or opposed? What speech strategies could you use to adapt to that attitude?

AUDIENCE ATTITUDES	**STRATEGY CHOICES**	
If audience members are . . .	then they may . . .	so that you can . . .
Highly in favor	■ be ready to act	■ provide practical suggestions
		■ put emphasis on motivation rather than on information and reasoning
In favor	■ already share many of your beliefs	■ crystallize and reinforce existing beliefs and attitudes to lead them to a course of action
Mildly in favor	■ be inclined to accept your view, but with little commitment	■ strengthen positive beliefs by emphasizing supporting reasons
Neither in favor nor opposed	■ be uninformed	■ emphasize information relevant to a belief or move to action
	■ be neutral	■ emphasize reasons relevant to belief or action
	■ be apathetic	■ concentrate on motivating them to see the importance of the proposition or seriousness of the problem
Mildly opposed	■ have doubts about the wisdom of your position	■ give them reasons and evidence that will help them to consider your position
Opposed	■ have beliefs and attitudes contrary to yours	■ emphasize sound arguments
		■ concentrate on shifting beliefs rather than on moving to action
		■ be objective to avoid arousing hostility
Hostile	■ be totally unreceptive to your position	■ plant the "seeds of persuasion"
		■ try to get them to understand your position

Figure 18.2

Adapting persuasive speech strategies to audience attitudes.

**INFOTRAC
COLLEGE EDITION**

Using InfoTrac College Edition, under
the subject "attitude change," click
on periodical references. Look for
articles that discuss how audiences
process information. Make a special
effort to find an article or articles by
Richard Petty.

Finding reasons. Reasons are statements that answer *why* you should
believe or do something. If you have expertise in the subject matter, you're
likely to know some of the reasons. For example, if you're an exercise buff and
you "want the audience to walk two miles at least three times a week," you
know that three reasons for walking are (1) to help control weight, (2) to help
strengthen the cardiovascular system, and (3) to feel better.

For most of your persuasive speeches, however, you will want to do
research to verify and/or discover reasons so that you can choose the best ones
for your speech. For example, for a speech goal phrased "I want the audience to
believe that the United States should overhaul the welfare system," you might
discover these six reasons:

I.   The welfare system costs too much to maintain.

II. The welfare system is inequitable.

III. The welfare system does not help those who need help most.

IV. The welfare system has been grossly abused.

V.   The welfare system does not encourage recipients to seek work.

VI. The welfare system does not encourage self-support.

Once you have a list of possible reasons, weigh and evaluate them to select
three or four good ones, using the following criteria.

1. **Good reasons can be supported.** Some reasons that sound impressive can-
    not be supported with facts. For example, the fourth reason, "The welfare
    system has been grossly abused," sounds like a good one; but if you cannot
    find facts to support so strong a statement, either modify it or do not use it
    in your speech. You'll be surprised at how many reasons mentioned in vari-
    ous sources have to be dropped from consideration for a speech because
    they can't be well supported.

2. **Good reasons are relevant to the proposition.** Sometimes, statements look
    like reasons but don't supply much proof. For instance, "The welfare sys-
    tem is supported by socialists" may sound like a reason for overhauling it
    to people who dislike socialism, but it doesn't offer any direct proof that
    the system needs overhauling.

3. **Good reasons will have an impact on the intended audience.** Suppose that
    you have a great deal of factual evidence to back up the statement "The
    welfare system does not encourage recipients to seek work." Even though it
    is a well-supported reason, it would be an ineffective reason to use in a
    speech if the majority of the audience did not see "seeking work" as a pri-
    mary criterion for evaluating the welfare system. Although you cannot
    always be sure about the potential impact of a reason, you can estimate its
    possible impact based on your audience analysis. For instance, on the topic

of welfare reform, some audiences would be more concerned with costs, equity, and abuses of the system.

The accompanying Spotlight on Scholarship features Richard Petty's research on attitude change and behavior.

Richard Petty, Professor of Psychology, the Ohio State University, on Attitude Change

As an undergraduate political science major, Richard Petty got so interested in how people change their attitudes that he chose to minor in psychology so that he could not only take more courses in attitude change but also learn empirical research methods. He then decided to go on to graduate work in psychology at the Ohio State University, with a focus on studying attitude change and persuasion. As with many scholars, the subject of his doctoral dissertation—attitude change induced by persuasive communications—laid the foundation for a career of research.

When Petty began his research, the psychological scholarship of the previous forty years had been unable to demonstrate a relationship between people's attitudes and their behavior. Petty believed that the relationship between attitude change and behavior had been obscured by the complexity of the variables involved in assessing attitude change. Now, Petty is in the forefront of scholars who have demonstrated that attitude change and behavior are in fact related, but in a complex way.

During the past twenty years, Petty has published scores of research articles on his own and with colleagues on various aspects of attitude and

persuasion, seeking to discover under what circumstances attitude does affect behavior. His work with various collaborators has been so successful that he has gained international acclaim. Not only have many of his works been published worldwide, but the Elaboration Likelihood Model (ELM) that he developed in collaboration with John Cacioppo has become the most cited theoretical approach to attitude and persuasion.

Before presenting their theory, Petty and Cacioppo found that attitude change is likely to occur as a result of one of two relatively distinct "routes to persuasion." The first, central route is through a person's careful and thoughtful consideration of the true merits of the information presented in support of a claim. The second, peripheral route is via a simple cue in the persuasion context (such as an attractive source) that induces change without necessitating scrutiny of the central merits of the claim. Following their initial speculation about these two routes to persuasion, they developed, researched, and refined their ELM.

The ELM "is a theory about the processes responsible for attitude change and the strength of the attitudes that result from those processes." The ELM hypothesizes that what is persuasive to a person and how lasting any attitude change is likely to depend on how motivated and able the person is in assessing the merits of a speaker, an issue, or a position. People who are highly motivated are likely to study available information about the claim. As a result, they are more likely to arrive at a reasoned attitude that is well articulated and bolstered by information received via the central route. For people who are less motivated to study information related to the claim, attitude change can result from a number of less resource-demanding processes that do not require the effort of evaluating the relevant information. These people are affected more by information through the peripheral route, but their attitude changes are likely to be weaker in endurance.

How does Petty's research help speakers who seek to persuade? First, speakers must recognize that attitude change results from their choices of the means of persuasion in combination with the choices made by audience members as to how deeply they wish to probe into the information. Sound reasons and supporting evidence adapted to audience needs should effect attitude change when listener thinking is expected to be deep; apparent credibility and emotional images will be more likely to effect change when listener thinking is expected to be superficial. Moreover, the attitudes changed by considerable mental effort will tend to be stronger than those changed by little thought.

This complexity of attitude change suggests that a speaker must not only have the necessary information to form well-constructed arguments, but must also have the artistic sense to understand important aspects of the audience (locus of belief, time constraints, level of interest) and have the artistic power to, as Aristotle once said, use available means of persuasion effectively.

Where is Petty going from here? He will certainly continue working on aspects of attitude change, for as he says, "I never finish a project without discovering at least two unanswered questions arising from the research." In addition, he's interested in finding out how people behave when their judgments may have been inappropriate or biased.

Currently, Petty teaches both graduate and undergraduate courses in attitude and persuasion, research methods, and theories of social psychology. Petty has written scores of research articles and several books, all dealing with aspects of attitude, attitude change, and persuasion. For titles of several of his publications, see the References at the end of this book.

Finding evidence to support your reasons. By themselves, reasons are only unsupported statements. Although some reasons are self-explanatory and occasionally have a persuasive effect without further support, most listeners look for factual statements and expert opinion to support the reasons before they will either accept or act on them.

As we learned in Chapter 13, the best support for reasons are verifiable factual statements. Suppose, in a speech designed to motivate people to donate money to Alzheimer's research, you give the reason "Alzheimer's disease is a major killer." The statement "According to statistics presented in an article in a recent *Time* magazine, Alzheimer's disease is the fourth leading cause of death for adults" would be factual support.

Statements from people who have good reputations for knowledge on the subject represent expert opinions. Thus, expert opinion support for the reason "Alzheimer's disease is a major killer" might be "According to the Surgeon General, 'By 2050 Alzheimer's disease may afflict 14 million people a year.'"

Whether your evidence is a factual statement or an opinion, you'll want to ask the following three questions to assure yourself that what you present is "good" evidence.

Demonstrate an inconsistency
between audience members'
beliefs and actions, and
you'll have an excellent
tool to inspire change.

1. **What is the source of the evidence?** This question involves both the people who offered the opinions or compiled the facts *and* the book, journal, or source where they were reported. Just as some people's opinions are more reliable than others, so are some printed sources more reliable than others. If evidence comes from a poor source, an unreliable source, or a biased source, you will want to seek verification of it or drop it from the speech.

2. **Is the evidence recent?** Products, ideas, and statistics are best when they are recent. You must ask when the particular evidence was true. Five-year-old evidence may not be true today. Furthermore, an article in last week's news-magazine may be using five-year-old evidence in the story.

3. **Is the evidence relevant?** Make sure that your evidence directly supports the reason. If it does not, then leave it out of the speech.

Testing reasoning.   So far, we have concentrated on presenting good reasons and supporting them well. To test the validity of our reasoning more completely, however, we need to look at the relationship between the reasons and the evidence given in support. When you can do that, you can ask questions to test the logic of the reasoning.

Several kinds of reasoning links can be established between reasons and their evidence or between reasons, evidence, and the speech goal.

1. **Generalization from examples.** You are reasoning by generalization from examples when you argue that what is true in some instances (evidence) is true in all instances (conclusion). Generalization links are the basis for polls and predictions. Take, for example, the factual evidence "Tom, Jack, and Bill studied and got A's" and the conclusion based on it, "Anyone who studies will get an A." The reasoning link can be stated, "What is true in these representative instances will be true in all instances." To test this kind of argument, you should ask, "Were enough instances (examples) cited? Were the instances typical? Are negative instances accounted for?" If the answer to any of these questions is no, the reasoning is not sound.

2. **Causation.** You are reasoning by causation when your conclusion is presented as the effect of a single circumstance or set of circumstances. Causation links are one of the most prevalent types of arguments you will discover. An example is "We've had a very dry spring" (evidence); "The wheat crop will be lower than usual" (conclusion). The reasoning link can be stated, "The lack of sufficient rain causes a poor crop." To test this kind of argument, you should ask, "Are the conditions described by the data (evidence) alone important enough to bring about the particular conclusion? If we eliminate these conditions, would we eliminate the effect?" If the answer to one of these questions is no, the reasoning is not sound. You can also ask, "Do some other conditions that accompany the ones cited in the evidence cause the effect?" If so, the reasoning is not sound.

3. **Analogy.** You are reasoning by analogy when your conclusion is the result of a comparison with a similar set of circumstances. Although reasoning by analogy is very popular, it is regarded as the weakest form of reasoning. The analogy link is often stated, "What is true or will work in one set of circumstances is true or will work in a comparable set of circumstances." An example is "Off-track betting has proved very effective in New York" (evidence); "Off-track betting will prove effective in raising state revenues in Ohio" (conclusion). The reasoning link can be stated, "If something works in New York, it will work in Ohio because Ohio and New York are so similar." To test this kind of argument, you should ask, "Are the subjects really comparable? Are the subjects being compared really similar in all important ways?" If the answer to these questions is no, the reasoning is not sound. You can also ask, "Are any of the ways that the subjects are dissimilar important to the conclusion?" If so, the reasoning is not sound.

4. **Sign.** You are reasoning by sign when your conclusion is based on the presence of observable data that usually or always accompany other unobserved variables. If, for example, you see longer lines at the downtown soup kitchen, the presence of that condition (longer lines) is usually or always an

indicator of something else (a worsening recession), and we can predict the existence of the other unobserved variable. Signs are often confused with causes, but signs are indications and sometimes effects, not causes. Longer lines at soup kitchens are a sign of the worsening recession. The longer lines may be an effect of a recession, but they do not cause the recession. To test this kind of argument, you should ask, "Do the data cited always or usually indicate the conclusion drawn? Are sufficient signs present?" If not, the reasoning is not sound.

Avoiding fallacies. When you think that you have finished constructing reasons, you need to take a minute to make sure that you haven't been guilty of any of the following four common fallacies.

1. **Hasty generalization.** Because the instances cited should represent most to all possibilities, enough must be cited to satisfy the listeners that the instances are not isolated or hand-picked. A very common fallacy of reasoning is presenting a generalization (perhaps a reason) that is either not supported with evidence or supported with only one weak example.

2. **False cause.** A false cause is one that is not related to, or does not produce, the effect. It is human nature to look for causes for events, but identifying something that happened or existed before the event or at the time of the event and labeling it as the cause is often a fallacy. Think of the people who blame loss of money, sickness, and problems at work on black cats that ran in front of them, mirrors that broke, or ladders they walked under. We recognize these as false-cause superstitions.

3. **Appeal to authority.** Attempting to argue from authority can lead to a fallacy when the person cited is not an authority on the issue. For instance, advertisers are well aware that because people idolize athletes, movie stars, and television performers, they are likely to accept their word on subjects they may know little about. But when a celebrity tries to get the viewer to purchase a car based on the celebrity's supposed "expert" knowledge, the argument is a fallacy.

PRACTICE IN SPEECH PREPARATION

Selecting Reasons

1. Write the specific goal that you will use for your first persuasive speech.
2. Write at least six reasons that support your specific goal.
3. Place stars next to the three or four reasons that you believe are the best.

4. **Ad hominem argument.** An ad hominem argument is an attack on the person making the argument rather than on the argument itself. Literally, *ad hominem* means "to the man." For instance, if Bill Bradley, the former U.S. senator as well as former New York Knicks basketball player, presented the argument that athletics are important to the development of the total person, the reply "Great, all we need is some jock justifying his own existence" would be an example of an ad hominem argument.

Such a personal attack is often made as a smokescreen to cover a lack of good reasons and evidence. Ad hominem name-calling is used to try to encourage the audience to ignore a lack of evidence, and it is often used in political campaigns. Make no mistake, ridicule, name-calling, and other personal attacks are at times highly successful, but they almost always are fallacious.

Organizing Reasons to Meet Audience Attitudes
PRINCIPLE 4

You are more likely to persuade an audience when you organize your reasons according to expected audience reaction.

Statement of logical reasons, problem–solution, comparative advantages, criteria satisfaction, and motivational are patterns that you are likely to select for your persuasive speech organization. So that you can contrast the patterns and better understand their use, we will use the same proposition (specific goal) and the same (or similar) reasons. Moreover, for each pattern, we will describe it, discuss the audience attitudes for which it is most applicable, and state the logic of that pattern.

Statement-of-logical-reasons pattern. The statement of logical reasons is a straightforward organization in which you present the best-supported reasons you can find following an order of second-strongest first, strongest last, and other reason(s) in between. It will work when your listeners have no opinion on the subject, are apathetic, or are perhaps only mildly in favor or opposed.

> **Proposition:** I want my audience to vote in favor of the school tax levy on the November ballot.
>
> I. Income will enable the schools to restore vital programs. (second strongest)
>
> II. Income will enable the schools to give teachers the raises they need to keep up with the cost of living.
>
> III. The actual cost to each member of the community will be very small. (strongest)

In a speech using the statement-of-logical-reasons pattern, the logic of the organization may be stated as follows: When good reasons and evidence are presented supporting a proposal, the proposal should be adopted.

Problem–solution pattern. The problem–solution pattern provides a framework for clarifying the nature of the problem and for illustrating why a given proposal is the best one. The problem–solution pattern is often organized around three general reasons: (1) There is a problem that requires action. (2) The proposal will solve the problem. (3) The proposal is the best solution to the problem because it will have positive consequences. This pattern is also a straightforward presentation of reasons, so it is likely to work best for a topic that is relatively unfamiliar to an audience—one in which they are unaware that a problem exists—or for an audience that has no opinion or is mildly pro or con. A problem–solution organization for the school tax proposition might look like this:

Proposition: I want my audience to vote in favor of the school tax levy on the November ballot.

I. The shortage of money is resulting in serious problems for public education. (statement of problem)

II. The proposed increase is large enough to solve those problems. (solution)

III. For now, a tax levy is the best method of solving the schools' problems. (consequences)

In a speech using the problem–solution pattern, the logic of the organization may be stated as follows: When a problem is presented that is not or cannot be solved with current measures and the proposal can solve the problem practically and beneficially, then the proposal should be adopted.

Comparative-advantages pattern. The comparative-advantages pattern allows you to place all the emphasis on the superiority of the proposed course of action. Rather than presenting the proposition as a solution to a grave problem, it presents the proposition as one that ought to be adopted solely on the basis of the advantages of that proposition over what is currently being done. Although this pattern can work for any audience attitude, it works best when the audience agrees either that there is a problem that must be solved or, when no particular problem is at issue, that the proposition is superior to its competitors. For example, when people elect to eat out, they have a variety of choices, so a speech advocating Le Petit France restaurant would emphasize its advantages over its competition. A comparative-advantages approach to the school tax proposition would look like this:

Proposition: I want my audience to vote in favor of the school tax levy on the November ballot.

I. Income from a tax levy will enable schools to raise the standards of their programs. (advantage 1)

II. Income from a tax levy will enable schools to hire better teachers. (advantage 2)

Information presented in a pattern that is relevant to the interests and orientation of your audience will be most persuasive. Here, he's likely to use a comparative-advantages pattern to persuade his colleagues to follow his business plan.

III. Income from a tax levy will enable schools to better the educational environment. (advantage 3)

In a speech using the comparative-advantages pattern, the logic of the organization that shows the relationship between the reasons and the speech goal may be stated as follows: When reasons are presented that show a proposal is a significant improvement over what is being done, then the proposal should be adopted.

Criteria-satisfaction pattern. Criteria satisfaction is an indirect pattern that seeks audience agreement on criteria that should be considered when evaluating a particular proposition and then shows how the proposition satisfies those criteria. When you encounter audiences that are opposed to your propositions, you need a pattern of organization that will not aggravate their hostility. The criteria-satisfaction pattern is likely to work because it focuses on developing a "yes" response to criteria before you introduce the proposition and reasons. A criteria-satisfaction organization for the school tax proposition would look like this:

Proposition: I want my audience to vote in favor of the school tax levy on the November ballot.

   I. We all want good schools. (a community value)
      A. Good schools have programs that prepare our youth to function in society. (one criterion of good schools)
      B. Good schools are those with the best teachers available. (a second criterion of good schools)

  II. Passage of the school tax levy will guarantee good schools.
      A. Passage will enable us to increase the quality of vital programs. (satisfaction of one criterion)
      B. Passage will enable us to hire and keep the best teachers. (satisfaction of the second criterion)

In a speech using the criteria-satisfaction pattern, the logic of the organization showing the relationship between the reasons and the speech goal may be stated as follows: When a proposal meets a set of agreed-on criteria, it should be adopted.

Motivational pattern. The motivational pattern combines problem solving and motivation: It follows a problem–solution pattern, but includes a series of specific steps designed to heighten the motivational effect of the organization. Much of the thinking behind motivational patterns is credited to Allan Monroe, a professor at Purdue University. Motivational patterns usually follow a five-step, unified sequence that replaces the normal introduction–body–conclusion model: (1) an *attention* step, (2) a *need* step that fully explains the nature of the problem, (3) a *satisfaction* step that explains how the proposal solves the problem in a satisfactory manner, (4) a *visualization* step that provides a personal application of the proposal, and (5) an *action appeal* step that emphasizes the specific direction that listeners' action should take. A motivational pattern for the school tax proposition would look like this:

Proposition: I want my audience to vote in favor of the school tax levy on the November ballot.

   I. Comparisons of worldwide test scores in math and science have refocused our attention on education. (attention)

  II. The shortage of money is resulting in cost-saving measures that compromise our ability to teach basic academic subjects well. (need—statement of the problem)

 III. The proposed increase is large enough to solve those problems in ways that allow for increased emphasis on academic need areas. (satisfaction—how the proposal solves the problem)

 IV. Think of the contribution you will be making not only to the education of your future children but also to efforts to return our educational system to the world stature it once enjoyed. (visualization of personal application)

V. Here are "Vote Yes" buttons that you can wear to show you are willing to support this much-needed tax levy. (action appeal showing specific direction)

Because motivational patterns are variations of problem–solution patterns, the logic of the organization is much the same: When the current means are not solving the problem, a new solution that does solve the problem should be adopted.

Motivation

 PRINCIPLE 5

You are more likely to persuade an audience when your language motivates them.

Motivation—"forces acting on or within an organism to initiate and direct behavior" (Petri 1996, p. 3)—is often a result of incentives and emotional language.

Incentives. An **incentive** is simply "a goal objective that motivates" (Petri 1996, p. 185). Thus, if a speaker says that in addition to helping clean up the environment by collecting aluminum cans and glass and plastic bottles, you can earn money by turning them in to a recycling center, you might see earning money for your efforts as an incentive to recycling.

For an incentive to have value, it must be meaningful. **Meaningfulness** involves an emotional reaction. Eric Klinger (1977) suggests that people pursue those objects, events, and experiences that are emotionally important for them. Recycling would be a *meaningful* goal for someone looking for ways to participate in cleaning up the environment but not for someone who doesn't care about the environment or about earning small amounts of money. An incentive is most powerful when it is part of a meaningful goal.

1. **Force of incentives.** People are more likely to perceive incentives as meaningful if the incentives present a favorable cost/reward ratio. As we dis-

---

PRACTICE IN SPEECH PREPARATION

Selecting an Organization

Select a pattern of organization for your speech. Justify your selection on the basis of your audience analysis.

cussed in Chapter 8, John Thibaut and Harold Kelley explain social interactions in terms of rewards received and costs incurred by each participant in an interaction. Recall that rewards are incentives such as economic gain, good feelings, prestige, or any other positive outcome; costs are units of expenditure such as time, energy, money, or any negative outcome of an interaction.

Let's apply this idea to a speech setting. Suppose you are asking your audience to volunteer an hour a week to help adults learn to read. The time you are asking them to give is likely to be perceived as a *cost* rather than as an incentive. However, you may be able to describe volunteering in a way that it is perceived as a reward—a meaningful incentive; that is, you may be able to get members of the audience to feel civic-minded, responsible, or helpful as a result of volunteering time for such a worthy cause. If, in your speech, you can show that those rewards or incentives outweigh the cost, you can increase the likelihood of your listeners' volunteering their time.

2. **Using incentives to meet basic needs.** Many theorists who take a humanistic approach to psychology have argued that incentives are most powerful when they meet basic needs. One of the most popular needs theories is that of Abraham Maslow (1954). His theory suggests that people are more likely to act when a speaker's incentive satisfies a strong unmet need in members of the audience.

Maslow has devised a hierarchy of needs that is particularly useful in providing a framework for needs analysis. Maslow divides basic human needs into seven categories arranged in a hierarchy that begins with the most fundamental needs. These seven categories, illustrated in Figure 18.3, are physiological needs, including food, drink, and life-sustaining

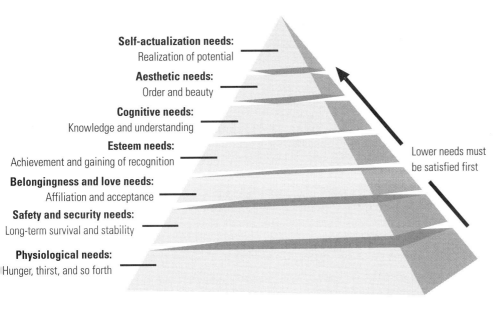

Figure 18.3
Maslow's hierarchy of needs.

temperature; safety and security needs, including long-term survival and stability; belongingness and love needs, including the need to identify with friends, loved ones, and family; esteem needs, including the quest for material goods, recognition, and power or influence; cognitive needs, including the need for knowledge and understanding; aesthetic needs, including the need for order and beauty; and self-actualization needs, including the need to develop one's self to realize one's full potential. By placing these needs in a hierarchy, Maslow suggested that one set of needs must be met or satisfied before the next set of needs emerges. In theory, then, a person will not be motivated to meet an esteem need of gaining recognition until basic physiological, safety, and belongingness and love needs have been met.

What is the value of this analysis to you as a speaker? First, it suggests the kinds of needs you may appeal to in your speeches. Second, it allows you to understand why a line of development will work on one audience and fail with another. For instance, in hard economic times, people are more concerned with physiological and safety needs and so will be less responsive to appeals to affiliation and altruism. Likewise, during a recession, fund-raisers for the arts will experience far more resistance to giving than they will in times of prosperity. Third, and perhaps most crucial, when your proposition conflicts with a felt need, you will have to be prepared with a strong alternative in the same category or in a more fundamental category. For instance, if your proposal is going to cost people money (say, higher taxes), you will have to show how the proposal satisfies some other comparable need (perhaps by increasing their security).

Arousing emotions through language. Even with good incentives directed to basic needs, to motivate an audience to act, you must appeal to their emotions. **Emotions** (anger, fear, surprise, joy) are subjective experiences triggered by actions or words that are accompanied by bodily arousal and by overt behavior (Weiten 1995, p. 711). Effective persuasive speech development entails both logical and emotional elements that act interdependently. Thus, we need to look for good reasons and for support that will, if properly phrased, arouse these emotions.

As you work on your speeches, you will want to determine the emotion(s) that you want to arouse, the kinds of information necessary to arouse the emotion(s), and how that information can be phrased for maximum effect. Let's consider each of these.

1. **What emotion(s) do you want your audience to experience as you make your point?** The emotion(s) you want to arouse will differ from speech to speech. For instance, in a speech calling for more humane treatment of the elderly, you may decide that you want your listeners to feel sadness, anger, grief, caring, or perhaps, guilt. In contrast, in a speech designed to get the audience to attend your school's production of a musical, you may want your listeners to feel joy, excitement, or enthusiasm.

2. **What information do you have that could be used to stimulate those emotions?** For the speech on the elderly, suppose you have determined that you want your listeners to feel sadness about their treatment in nursing homes. You might have interviews with elderly individuals in which their only talk of the future is the inevitability of death; or perhaps you have accounts of social workers saying that many old people live totally in the past and are reluctant to talk about the future; or perhaps you have information showing that many nursing homes do very little to give their clients anything to look forward to.

3. **Keeping ethical considerations in mind, how can you phrase your information to elicit those emotions?** How well you motivate your audience is likely to depend on how well you phrase your information.

   For instance, for the speech on the elderly, you might consider saying the following:

   > Currently, elderly people are alienated from society. A high percentage live in nursing homes, live on small fixed incomes, and exist out of the mainstream of society.

   But by adding a question and using language that creates more vivid pictures, you could make this statement much more emotionally powerful:

   > Currently, elderly people are alienated from society that they worked their entire lives to support. What happens to elderly people in America? They become the forgotten segment of society. They are often relegated to "old people's homes" so that they can live out their lives and die without being "a bother" to their sons and daughters. Because they must exist on relatively small fixed incomes, they are confined to a life that for many means separation from the very society they helped to create.

   You're likely to find that some of your best opportunities for using meaningful emotional appeals occur in the introduction and conclusion of your speech. Notice how emotional appeals heighten the power of the following introduction and conclusion in a student speech on euthanasia.[1] The speaker begins as follows:

   > Let's pretend for a moment. Suppose that on the upper right-hand corner of your desk there is a button. You have the power by pushing that button to quickly and painlessly end the life of one you love: your brother or father. This loved one has terminal cancer and will be confined to a hospital for his remaining days. Would you push the button now? His condition worsens. He is in constant pain, and he is hooked up to a life-support machine. He first requests, but as the pain

---

[1] By permission of Betsy Burke.

increases he pleads for you to help. Now would you push that button? Each day you watch him deteriorate until he reaches a point where he cannot talk, he cannot see, he cannot hear—he is only alive by that machine. Now would you push that button?

After giving reasons for changing our laws on euthanasia, the speaker concludes as follows:

> I ask again, how long could you take walking into that hospital room and looking at your brother or father in a coma, knowing he would rather be allowed to die a natural death than to be kept alive in such a degrading manner? I've crossed that doorstep—I've gone into that hospital room—and let me tell you, it's hell. I think it's time we reconsider our laws concerning euthanasia. Don't you?

Regardless of your beliefs on the subject of euthanasia, you would probably be inclined to experience sadness as you empathize with this speaker's feelings.

Building Credibility

PRINCIPLE 6

You are more likely to persuade an audience when they view you as a credible source.

As we have seen, maintaining credibility is important to speaker effectiveness in all types of speaking. In persuasive speaking, in addition to being knowledgeable, trustworthy, and personable, you must behave ethically. The following four guidelines are fundamental to ethical persuasive speaking.

1. **Tell the truth.** Of all the guidelines, this one may be the most important. Your audience is extending you its trust and expects that you will be honest with them. Consequently, if during your speech people believe you are lying to them, or if they later learn that you have lied, they will reject you and your ideas. But telling the truth means more than avoiding deliberate, outright lies. If you are not sure whether information is true, don't use it until you have verified it. Ignorance is seldom accepted as an excuse.

2. **Keep your information in perspective.** Many people get so excited about their information that they exaggerate its importance. Although a little exaggeration might be accepted as a normal product of human nature, when the exaggeration is perceived as distortion, most people will consider it the same as lying. For instance, suppose you discover that capital punishment has lowered the murder rates in a few states, but in many other states, the statistics are inconclusive. If in your speech, you assert that statistics show that murder rates are lower in states with capital punishment, you would be distorting the evidence. Because the line between some exaggeration and gross exaggeration or distortion is often difficult to distinguish, most people see any exaggeration as unethical.

3. **Resist personal attacks against those who oppose your ideas.** There seems to be almost universal agreement that name-calling and other irrelevant personal attacks are detrimental to a speaker's trustworthiness. Responsible listeners recognize that such tactics do not contribute to the speaker's argument and represent an abuse of the privileged status the speaker enjoys.

4. **Give the source for all damning information.** Where ideas originate is often as important as the ideas themselves, especially when a statement is damning. If you are going to discuss wrongdoing by individuals or organizations, or condemn an idea by relying on the words or ideas of others, provide the sources of your information and arguments. Moreover, since the mention of wrongdoing brings communication to the edge of what is legally defined as slander, speakers should be aware of the legal as well as ethical pitfalls of making damning statements without proof.

Gender and Cultural Differences

So far in this chapter we have discussed reasoning, appealing to emotions, and building credibility—three forms of proof that Aristotle, who wrote the first comprehensive treatment of persuasive speaking, called *logos*, *pathos*, and *ethos*. A legitimate question is whether women and people of other cultures use and appreciate these same forms of proof, which are based, after all, on male speaking in a predominantly Eurocentric culture. The answer is that in all cultures male and female public speakers use the same means of persuasion; the differences are in how women and people from other cultures *emphasize* each of these means. Whereas U.S. male culture relies on good reasons supported

---

TEST YOUR COMPETENCE

Persuasive Speaking

1. Prepare a four- to seven-minute speech in which you affect audience belief or move your audience to action. An outline is required.

2. As an addendum to the outline, you may wish to write a persuasive plan for adapting to your specific audience that includes

   a. How your goal adapts to whether your prevailing audience attitude is in favor, no opinion, or opposed.

   b. What reasons you will use and how the organizational pattern you have selected is appropriate for your topic and audience.

   c. How you will establish your credibility with this audience.

   d. How you will motivate your audience by using incentives or by appealing to their emotions.

3. For one or more of the speeches you hear during a round of persuasive speeches, complete the checklist in Figure 18.4 and then write a two- to five-paragraph evaluation of the speech. See the sample outline and speech at the end of this chapter.

DIVERSE VOICES

A Comparison of Arab and American Conceptions of "Effective" Persuasion

by Janice Walker Anderson

People from different cultures are likely to have different views about how to speak and write persuasively. In this excerpt, Janice Walker Anderson describes some differences in the ways Arabs consider persuasiveness.

Although mass media reports on events in the Middle East translate the words used by Arab leaders, the reports seldom explain the different cultural standards in Arab societies for evaluating reasonableness. "We can say that what is 'reasonable,' " intercultural communication scholars Condon and Yousef explain, "is not fully separable from cultural assumptions." This analysis indicates some of the differences between Arab and American cultural orientations toward what constitutes "effective" persuasion.

Before beginning the analysis, it is first necessary to acquaint American readers with some of the basics of Arab and Moslem orientations toward argumentation. "While only a small percentage (about 10%) of present-day Arabs are Bedouins," Gudykunst and Kim explain in *Communicating with Strangers*, "contemporary Arab culture holds the Bedouin ethos as an ideal to which, in theory at least, it would like to measure up. While values such as materialism, success, activity, progress, and rationality are featured in American culture, Arab societies revolve around the core values of "hospitality, generosity, courage, honor, and self-respect."

As H. Samuel Hamod indicated in "Arab and Moslem Rhetorical Theory and Practice," storytellers performed a vital function for the Bedouin tribes because few people could read or write: "Their tribal storytellers functioned as historians and moralists in recounting battles and instances of outstanding bravery and cunning." These storytellers, or what we today might call poets, performed important political functions by establishing a means for interpreting and directing action. As A. J. Almaney and A. J. Alwan

with factual information and expert opinion, other cultural groups may put more emphasis on credibility of the speaker or emotional arousal and expressiveness (Fisher 1988; Lieberman 1995; Friday 1995; see also the accompanying Diverse Voices on differences between American and Arab culture).

So, how should you proceed? Again, the advice of Aristotle, in his *Rhetoric*, is useful to any speaker. He points out that if an audience is truly homogeneous, then a speaker will want to use forms of proof, references, and examples that relate to their particular experience. But when an audience is heterogeneous, then a speaker will find it most useful to speak to what he calls "the golden mean"—that is, a composite that covers the majority of that audience.

explained, a poet's poems "might arouse a tribe to action in the same manner as . . . [a politician] in a modern political campaign. . . . He was both a molder and agent of public opinion." Some attributed magical powers to these storytellers because they controlled the power of language which could act upon the human emotions and rouse the people to action. To this day, poets are held in the highest esteem in Arab societies.

In addition, Arab cultures connect inspired language and religion. Arabic plays an important religious role in Islamic societies. All Muslims, regardless of their nationality, must use Arabic in their daily prayers. The language of the Quran is considered a miracle in itself because it was produced by the Prophet Mohammed, who was illiterate. Consequently, Muslims believe that the Quran cannot be faithfully translated into other languages.

The power of words lay not in their ability to reflect human experience, but in their ability to transcend it, to reach toward that which lay beyond human experience—the divine. To this day, the Quran stands as the ultimate book of style and grammar for Arabs. The cultural equivalent in the West would be using the King James Version of the Bible as our style manual.

The Arab's appreciation for the persuasive power of the rhythm and sound of words leads to a style that relies heavily on devices that heighten the emotional impact of a message. Certain words are used in speaking that have no denotative

meaning. "These are 'firm' words because the audience knows the purpose behind their use, and the words are taken as a seal of definiteness and sincerity on the part of the speaker." Other forms of assertion, such as repetition and antithesis, are also quite frequent. Emphatic assertions are expected, Almaney and Alwan explain: "If an Arab says exactly what he means without the expected assertion, other Arabs may still think he means the opposite."

Hamod explains the reasoning behind the Arab's emphasis on stylistic concerns. "He who speaks well is well educated; he who is well educated is more qualified to render judgments and it is his advice we should follow. Eloquence and effectiveness were equated." An Arab writer establishes credibility by displaying ability and artistry with the language.

Yet, given the vastly different assumptions about the role of persuasion in society, it is not surprising that misunderstandings occur between Americans and Arabs, even when the same "language" is used. Communicating across a cultural gap requires more than just a knowledge of respective vocabularies. It also requires an understanding of the different cultural rules for what constitutes "reasonable" political debate.

Excerpted from The Howard Journal of Communications, *Vol. 2, No. 1 (Winter 1989–90), pp. 81–114. Reprinted by permission of the publisher. Janice Walker Anderson is in the Communication Department, College at New Paltz, State University of New York.*

Presentation

PRINCIPLE 7

You are more likely to persuade an audience if you develop an effective oral presentation style.

Previous chapters have addressed characteristics of presentation that you must develop to increase your effectiveness, including the importance of practicing your speech until your presentation (language and delivery) enhances it. Although we will not repeat that information here, you must not forget that it is through your presentation that your listeners "see" your speech.

Check all items that were accomplished effectively.

Primary Criteria
_____ 1. Was the specific goal designed to affect a belief or move to action?
_____ 2. Did the speaker present clearly stated reasons?
_____ 3. Did the speaker use facts and expert opinions to support these reasons?
_____ 4. Was the organizational pattern appropriate for the type of goal and assumed attitude of the audience?
_____ 5. Did the speaker use emotional language to motivate the audience?
_____ 6. Was the speaker effective in establishing his or her credibility on this topic?
_____ 7. Was the speaker ethical in handling material?

General Criteria
_____ 1. Was the specific goal clear?
_____ 2. Was the introduction effective?
_____ 3. Were the main points clear?
_____ 5. Was the conclusion effective?
_____ 6. Was the language clear, vivid, and emphatic?
_____ 7. Was the speech delivered enthusiastically, with vocal expressiveness, spontaneously, fluently, and with eye contact?

Evaluate the speech as (check one):
_____ excellent, _____ good, _____ average, _____ fair, _____ poor.

Figure 18.4
Critiquing a persuasive speech: checklist.

Use the information from your checklist to support your evaluation.

Criteria for Evaluating Persuasive Speeches

In this chapter, we have been looking at principles of persuasive speaking. Now let's apply those principles to evaluating and presenting persuasive speeches by drawing together the criteria for evaluating persuasive speeches and then looking at a sample outline, speech plan, and persuasive speech.

Speech Outline: Limiting Exposure to the Sun[2]

Specific Goal: I want my audience to limit their exposure to the harmful rays of the sun.

Introduction
   I. How many of you have friends who spent spring break at the beach?

---

[2] Presented in speech class, University of Cincinnati. Used with permission of Elizabeth Helphinstine.

II. They probably did not come back and tell you about the jump start they got on premature aging of their skin or getting a head start on skin cancer.

III. You should limit your exposure to the sun because it causes premature aging and skin cancer, and because it is so easy to do.

Thesis Statement: Although exposure to the sun causes premature aging and skin cancer, it is easy to prevent premature aging and to lower the risk of skin cancer.

Body

I. Exposure to the sun causes premature aging.
   A. Sun damage occurs during your first 18 years.
   B. Premature aging is caused by the sun regardless of skin type.
   C. Sun damage occurs with as little as twenty minutes of exposure twice a week.

   (But premature aging is minor compared to the chances of skin cancer.)

II. Exposure to the sun causes skin cancer.
   A. More than 600,000 people will get skin cancer this year.
      1. All people are susceptible to skin cancer.
      2. Some people are at higher risk than others.
   B. Skin cancer is a major killer.
      1. Skin cancer is the #1 killer of women ages 26–32.
      2. The number of women dying of skin cancer is higher than the next four leading diseases combined.

   (The problem is great, but the cure is relatively easy.)

III. It is easy to prevent skin cancer.
   A. Limiting your hours in the sun is the #1 way.
   B. But if you want to be in the sun, take necessary precautions.
      1. Use sunblock.
      2. Wear a hat.
      3. Wear sunglasses.

Conclusion

I. Limiting your exposure to the sun will reduce premature aging and skin cancer.

II. Preventive measures can lengthen your life.

Bibliography

Balkan, Jodi. "Practicing Safe Sun," *New Woman*, May 1993, pp. 118–121.

"Everything You Thought You Knew About Sun Protection . . . But Didn't." *Glamour*, May 1994, pp. 216–223.

Farr, Louise. "Sunny & Safe." *Self*, May 1994, pp. 112–118.

Shapiro, Anna. "Taking Cover." *Vogue*, June 1995, pp. 194–196.

"Sunscreens: Everything New Under the Sun." *Consumer Reports*, July 1994, pp. 73–75.

Speech Plan

Audience attitude toward goal: During my preparation, I found that my audience was fairly apathetic about the sun and its harmful effects. I will attempt to build a positive attitude by making my information relevant to their lives.

Organization: I have organized my speech into three reasons, the first two showing the problem and the final one showing how easy it is to solve the problem. I will attempt to use transitions between points.

Credibility: I plan to build credibility by relating my own personal history of "sun worship." I will tell the audience about my grandmother's death from skin cancer. I will make reference to several sets of statistics from the American Cancer Society as well as from the American Association of Dermatology.

Motivation: I will try to motivate them by making safe sun easy for them. I will tell them that by limiting their exposure to the sun they cannot only save their skin, but also their lives.

Sample Speech: Limiting Exposure to the Sun

Read the following speech aloud. Then, analyze it on the basis of the primary criteria on the checklist in Figure 18.4: goal, reasons, support, organization, motivation, credibility, and ethics.

Speech	Analysis
How many of you have friends who spent spring break anywhere where it was fun in the sun on the beach? What did your friends come back and tell you the most about? What were they most excited about? Did they tell you about the jump start they got on premature aging of their skin? Or the head start on skin cancer? Probably not. My goal in this speech is to tell you three reasons why you should limit your exposure to the sun.	*Elizabeth uses a series of questions to get audience attention.* *Here she states her goal.*
Let's start with the first reason. The most common effect of the sun is premature aging of the skin. All of us are young, and we think, "Uh, I'm only 19, 21, 24, I don't have to worry about premature aging. That happens later in life." Not so. According to *The American Journal of Public Health*, 78 percent of all premature aging happens before the age of 18. Now we've all seen people who lie out by the pool all day, and we think, "I'll never look like them." Well, I've got news for you. This damage happened steadily over a number of years starting with their childhood. Now when I read that statistic about 78 percent of all	*Her first reason is stated as a complete sentence.* *Good direct audience adaptation: "All of us" and "we think."* *Good use of startling statistics to keep focus on relevance to this aged audience. Also notice use of personal pronouns.*

Speech

premature aging happening before the age of 18, that scared me. Because I remember as a little girl, my parents would send me off to summer camp every day without any sun protection. Not that they didn't care, but they really didn't know any better. So now, my sun damage clock is ticking every minute I'm out in the sun, adding another dose of aging to my skin. Many of my friends think that because they're African American or have naturally dark skin, they're exempt from the problem. And I thought the same way. But the sun doesn't discriminate—I don't care what nationality you are, what race you are, every one of you [pointing to each person in class] can be a victim.

Now you might be saying, "I agree with you on your first point, but I'll take my chances on aging." Well, if my first point didn't convince you, my next point should make you scared for your life.

My second point is that the sun causes skin cancer and, in many cases, death. According to the American Cancer Society, over 600,000 people this year alone in the U.S. will get skin cancer. Moreover, it's the number one killer of women ages 24 to 32. That's women like me and women like your sisters and your girlfriends. Well, you may say, but people with cancerous moles can go to their doctor and get them removed within an hour. But that's not true for everyone. When I was a little girl, my grandmother Helphinstine was the most vibrant, dynamic woman you would ever want to meet. She had a husband and five children. She would get her chores done, and then grab her tin of Crisco and go lie out in the yard for a couple of hours every day—she lived to tan. She died when I was seven. She died from a cancerous melanoma, a cancerous mole, that couldn't be removed—the cancer couldn't be stopped—it killed her.

I can't do anything about your vanity, but I can do something about your ignorance. Just by being here today, you now know the facts about skin aging and skin cancer. Aging and cancer are not something to be taken lightly—but there is something we all can

Analysis

Good use of experience that not only personalizes information but also begins to develop emotional appeal.

Excellent transition that also gives an emotional jolt.

Second problem reason is stated as a complete sentence. Notice, she not only presents statistical support, but she also relates information directly to the audience.

"Well, you may say," adapts by anticipating audience comment.

Another personal anecdote that continues to reinforce the strong emotional appeal of the speech.

Now that she's finished her two problem reasons, she lays the groundwork for the solution.

Speech

do about it. The other day Bryan told us about his mother's breast cancer. One of the lines in his speech struck a chord with me. He said, "My mother didn't do anything wrong, she couldn't prevent it, she didn't smoke, there was nothing she could do." But unlike that instance, there *is* something you can do to prevent skin cancer. According to the Academy of Dermatology, three-fourths of all skin damage can be prevented. Prevention cuts down on aging and cuts down on cancer. If you're cutting down on cancer, of course, you're cutting down on that chance of death.

My third point is that prevention is easy. Now I want to tell you about what I do on my fun-in-the-sun days. In this beach bag are a few things you can use to prevent premature aging and skin cancer. The first thing I pull out is a T-shirt. This is your basic T-shirt—it doesn't matter what it has on it or what color it is. A T-shirt has an SPF (a sun protection factor) of 15. This means that with it on you could stay out in the sun for 15 hours before you'd have the effects of 1 hour in the sun without it.

The next thing I pull out is my handy-dandy shark's hat. Now I'm not a real babe in this hat—not many women look good in a hat like this—but because it covers my head and has a full inch brim, according to this month's *Self* magazine, it cuts down on skin damage by at least 10 percent. Any hat will help—you can wear a hat like Jason has back there. Not only would his protect his face, but he could turn it around backwards and protect his neck.

Next I pull out my nifty sunglasses. Make sure yours have UV protection—ultraviolet protection for your eyes.

Finally, I pull out my sunblock. This one is a 35 sunblock—this means you'd have to be in the sun for 35 hours to get the same effect as 1 hour without any protection. Sunblock ranges from 2 all the way up to 45—so you can pick your level of protection.

Now you might say, "Elizabeth, how can you stand up here and tell us to stay out of the sun when you're standing up there with a complete tan?" That's my secret. My tan came from this bottle. Because I'm

Analysis

Good adaptation to words of a previous speaker.

Here we get the idea that she is going to be talking about how we can prevent skin damage and lower the risk of getting cancer.

Third reason is a complete sentence that emphasizes practicality of preventive measures.

So far speech has been quite heavy—here she begins to take a more lighthearted approach.

Good use of humor. By poking fun at herself, she makes her point that vanity is less important than safety.

Reference to Jason's hat is another example of direct adaptation.

Notice that each one of these measures is "easy," just as she had said earlier.

Here she adapts to a prospective audience question. Nice touch.

Speech

Analysis

still dedicated to having a tan, I put this on every day. Looks fairly natural, huh?

In conclusion—I've told you the sun causes aging—the sun causes cancer—and that prevention is easy. I hope that now that you have heard these three points you will limit your time in the sun, and when you are in the sun you'll take action. So, the next time you see a person with a great natural tan, realize that a great tan contributes to skin damage and may very well be the tan that kills.

She begins her conclusion by reviewing the reasons.

Her final sentence neatly reinforces the point of her speech. Throughout the speech Elizabeth blends logical information and emotional appeal quite well. This is a good persuasive speech that follows the problem–solution pattern.

Summary

Persuasive speeches are designed to establish or change a belief or motivate an audience to act. The principles governing persuasive speeches are similar to those presented for informative speeches, as are the steps of speech preparation.

First, write a clear persuasive speech goal, or proposition, stating what you want your audience to believe or do.

Second, analyze your audience's interest and knowledge levels and attitude toward your goal.

Third, build the body of the speech with good reasons—statements that answer why the proposition is justified. Support reasons with facts and expert opinion.

Fourth, create an organization for the speech that suits your goal and your analysis of the audience. Five organizational patterns for persuasive speeches are statement of logical reasons, problem–solution, comparative advantages, criteria satisfaction, and motivational.

Fifth, motivate your audience by reworking language to appeal to the emotions, especially in your main points, introduction, and conclusion.

Sixth, use your credibility advantageously. Especially in persuasive speaking, one of the most important ways of building credibility is to behave in an ethical manner.

Seventh, deliver the speech convincingly. Good delivery is especially important in persuasive speaking.

REFLECT ON ETHICS

Alejandro had decided that for his final speech, he would motivate the members of his class to donate money to the Downtown Food Bank. He was excited about this topic because when he was a senior in high school he had volunteered at the Food Bank, and he had seen first-hand the face of hunger in this community.

He planned to support his speech with three reasons: (1) that an increasing number of people in the community needed food; (2) that government agencies were unable to provide sufficient help; and (3) that a high percentage of every dollar donated to the Food Bank went to buy food. As he researched these points, however, he discovered that the number of families in need had not really risen in the past two years and that government sponsorship of the Food Bank had increased. Then, when he examined the Food Bank's financial statements, he discovered that only 68 percent of every dollar donated was actually spent on food. Faced with this evidence, he just didn't think his reasons and evidence were very strong.

Yet, because of his experience, he still thought the Food Bank was a cause that deserved financial support, so he decided to focus his entire speech on the heartwarming case of the Hernando family. Ineligible for government assistance, over the years this family of ten had managed to survive because of the aid they received from the Food Bank. Today, several of the children have graduated from college, and one is a physician working in the barrio. By telling this story of one family's struggle to survive, Alejandro thought he would be successful in persuading the class.

Would it be ethical for Alejandro to give his speech in this way? If so, why? If not, what would he need to do to make the speech ethical?

S E L F - R E V I E W

Public Speaking from Chapters 12 to 18

What kind of a public speaker are you? The following analysis looks at eleven specifics that are basic to a public-speaking profile. On the line provided for each statement, indicate the response that best captures your behavior: 1, never; 2, rarely; 3, occasionally; 4, often; 5, almost always.

_____ When I am asked to speak, I am able to select a topic and determine a speech goal with confidence. (Ch. 12)

_____ When I speak, I use material from a variety of sources. (Ch. 13)

_____ In my preparation, I construct clear main points and organize them to follow some consistent pattern (Ch. 14)

_____ In my preparation, I am careful to be sure that I have developed ideas to meet audience needs. (Ch. 15)

_____ When I speak, I sense that my audience perceives my language as clear and vivid. (Ch. 16)

_____ I look directly at members of my audience when I speak. (Ch. 16)

_____ My public-speaking voice shows variation in pitch, speed, and loudness. (Ch. 16)

_____ When I speak, my bodily actions help supplement or reinforce my ideas; I feel and look involved. (Ch. 16)

_____ I have confidence in my ability to speak in public. (Ch. 16)

_____ When I give informative speeches, I am careful to use techniques designed to get audience attention, create audience understanding, and increase audience retention. (Ch. 17)

_____ When I give persuasive speeches, I am careful to use techniques designed to build my credibility, prove my reasons, and motivate my audience. (Ch. 18)

Based on your responses, select the public-speaking behavior that you would most like to change. Write a communication improvement goal statement similar to the sample in Chapter 1 (page 24). If you would like verification of your self-analysis before you write a goal statement, have a friend or coworker complete this same analysis for you.

References

Abelson, R. P. 1976. Script in attitude formation and decision making. In *Cognition and social behavior*, ed. J. Carroll and T. Payne, pp. 33–46. Hillsdale, NJ: Erlbaum.

Adler, R. B. 1977. *Confidence in communication: A guide to assertive and social skills*. New York: Holt, Rinehart and Winston.

Ahladas, J. A. 1989. Global warming. *Vital Speeches*, April 1, pp. 381–84.

Ahles, C. B. 1993. The dynamics of discovery: Creating your own opportunities. *Vital Speeches*, March 15, pp. 350–52.

Alberti, R. E., and Emmons, M. L. 1995. *Your perfect right: A guide to assertive living*. 7th ed. San Luis Obispo, CA: Impact Publishers.

Altman, I. 1993. Dialectics, physical environments, and personal relationships. *Communication Monographs* 60: 26–34.

Altman, I., and Taylor, D. 1973. *Social penetration: The development of interpersonal relationships*. New York: Holt, Rinehart and Winston.

Andrews, P. H. 1992. Sex and gender differences in group communication: Impact on the facilitation process. *Small Group Research* 23: 74–94.

Argyle, M. 1991. Intercultural communication. In *Intercultural communication: A reader*, 6th ed., ed. L. A. Samovar and R. E. Porter, pp. 32–45. Belmont, CA: Wadsworth.

Arvey, R. D., and Campion, J. E. 1982. The employment interview: A summary and review of recent research. *Personnel Psychology* 35: 281–321.

Axtell, R. E. 1991. *Gestures: The do's and taboos of body language around the world*. New York: Wiley.

Ayres, J., and Hopf, T. S. 1990. The long-term effect of visualization in the classroom: A brief research report. *Communication Education* 39: 75–78.

Ayres, J.; Hopf, T. S.; and Ayres, D. M. 1994. An examination of whether imaging ability enhances the effectiveness of an intervention designed to reduce speech anxiety. *Communication Education* 43: pp. 252–58.

Bach, K., and Harnish, R. M. 1979. *Linguistic communication and speech acts*. Cambridge, MA: MIT Press.

Baeder, D. L. 1980. Chemical wastes. *Vital Speeches*, June 1, pp. 496–500.

Bahr, C. C. 1988. Sick companies don't have to die. *Vital Speeches*, September 1, pp. 685–88.

Bales, R. F. 1971. *Personality and interpersonal behavior*. New York: Holt, Rinehart and Winston.

Barker, L.; Edwards, R.; Gains, C.; Gladnes, K., and Holley, F. 1980. An investigation of proportional time spent in various communication activities by college students. *Journal of Applied Communication Research* 8: 101–109.

Bass, B. M. 1990. *Bass and Stogdill's handbook of leadership: Theory, research, and managerial applications*, 3d ed., New York: The Free Press.

Beebe, S. A., and Masterson, J. T. 1997. *Communicating in small groups: Principles and practices*, 5th ed. New York: Longman.

Berg, J. H., and Derlega, V. J. 1987. Themes in the study of self-disclosure. In *Self-disclosure: Theory, research, and therapy*, ed. J. H. Berg and V. J. Derlega, pp. 1–8. New York: Plenum Press.

Berger, C. R. 1994. Power, dominance, and social interaction. In *Handbook of interpersonal communication* 2d ed., ed. M. L. Knapp and R. Miller, pp. 450–507. Thousand Oaks, CA: Sage.

Berger, C. R., and Brada, J. J. 1982. *Language and social knowledge: Uncertainty in interpersonal relations*. London: Arnold.

Biagi, S. 1992. *Interviews that work: A practical guide for journalists*, 2d ed. Belmont, CA: Wadsworth.

Brilhart, J. K., and Galanes, G. J. 1995. *Effective group discussion*, 8th ed. Madison, WI: Brown and Benchmark.

Brown, P., and Levinson, S. 1987. *Politeness: Some universals in language usage*. Cambridge, England: Cambridge University Press.

Burgoon, J. K. 1994. Nonverbal signals. In *Handbook of interpersonal communication*, 2d ed., ed. M. L. Knapp and G. R. Miller, pp. 229–85. Thousand Oaks, CA: Sage.

Burgoon, J. K.; Buller, D. B.; Dillman, L.; and Walther, J. B. 1995. Interpersonal deception: IV. Effects of suspicion on perceived communication and nonverbal behavior dynamics. *Human Communication Research* 22: 163–96.

Burgoon, J. K.; Buller, D. B.; and Woodall, W. G. 1989. *Nonverbal communication: The unspoken dialogue*. New York: Harper and Row.

Burgoon, J. K.; Coker, D. A.; and Coker, R. A. 1986. Communicative effects of gaze behavior: A test of two contrasting explanations. *Human Communication Research* 12: 495–524.

Burgoon, J. K., and LePoire, B. A. 1996. Usefulness of differentiating arousal responses within communication theories: Orienting response or defensive arousal within nonverbal theories of expectancy violation. *Communication Monographs* 63: 208–30.

Burgoon, J. K.; Stacks, D. W.; and Burch, S. A. 1982. The role of nonverbal violations of expectations in interpersonal influence. *Communication* 11: 114–28.

Burgoon, J. K., and Walther, J. B. 1990. Nonverbal expectancies and the consequences of violations. *Human Communication Research* 17: 232–65.

Burgoon, J. K.; Walther, J. B.; and Baesler, E. J. 1992. Interpretations, evaluations, and consequences of interpersonal touch. *Human Communication Research* 19: 237–63.

Burleson, B. R. 1984. Age, social-cognitive development, and the use of comforting strategies. *Communication Monographs* 51: 140–53.

Burleson, B. R. 1994. Comforting messages: Features, functions, and outcomes. In *Strategic interpersonal communication*, ed. J. A. Daly and J. M. Wiemann, pp. 135–62. Hillsdale, NJ: Erlbaum.

Burleson, B. R. 1994. Comforting messages: Significance, approaches and effects. In *Communicating of social support: Messages, interactions, relationships, and community*, ed. B. R. Burleson, T. L. Albrecht, and I. G. Sarason, pp. 3–28. Thousand Oaks, CA: Sage.

Burleson, B. R., and Samter, W. 1985. Consistencies in theoretical and naive evaluations of comforting messages. *Communication Monographs* 52: 103–23.

Burleson, B. R., and Samter, W. 1990. Effects of cognitive complexity on the perceived importance of communication skills in friends. *Communication Research* 17: 165–82.

Butler, D., and Geis, F. L. 1990. Nonverbal affect responses to male and female leaders: Implications for leadership evaluations. *Journal of Personality and Social Psychology* 58: 48–59.

Cahn, D. D. 1990. Intimates in conflict: A research review. In *Intimates in conflict: A communication perspective*, ed. D. D. Cahn, pp. 1–24. Hillsdale, NJ: Erlbaum.

Canary, D. J., and Hause, K. 1993. Is there any reason to research sex differences in communication? *Communication Quarterly* 41: 129–44.

Canary, D. J., and Stafford, L. 1992. Relational maintenance strategies and equity in marriage. *Communication Monographs* 59: 243–67.

Cegala, D. J., and Sillars, A. L. 1989. Further examination of nonverbal manifestations of interaction involvement. *Communication Reports* 2: 39–47.

Centi, P. J. 1981. *Up with the positive: Out with the negative*. Englewood Cliffs, NJ: Prentice-Hall.

Clark, N. 1994. *Teambuilding: A practical guide for trainers*. New York: McGraw-Hill.

Clevenger, T., Jr. 1959. A synthesis of experimental research in stage fright. *Quarterly Journal of Speech* 45: 134–45.

Cloven, D. H., and Roloff, M. E. 1991. Sense-making activities and interpersonal conflict: Communicative cures for the mulling blues. *Western Journal of Speech Communication* 55: 134–58.

Cogger, J. W. 1982. Are you a skilled interviewer? *Personnel Journal* 61: 842–43.

Crutchfield, E. E., Jr. 1980. Profitable banking in the 1980's. *Vital Speeches*, June 15, pp. 535–37.

Cuomo, M. M. 1980. The family. *Vital Speeches*, February 15, pp. 268–70.

Cupach, W. R., and Canary, D. J. 1997. *Competence in interpersonal conflict*. New York: McGraw-Hill.

Curtis, D. B.; Winsor, J. L.; and Stephens, R. D. 1989. National preferences in business and communication education. *Communication Education* 38: 6–14.

Davitz, J. R. 1964. *The communication of emotional meaning*. New York: McGraw-Hill.

Deaux, K.; Dane, F. C.; and Wrightsman, L. S. 1993. *Social psychology in the 90s*, 6th ed. Pacific Grove, CA: Brooks/Cole.

Deavenport, E. W. 1995. Walking the high wire: Balancing stakeholder interests. *Vital Speeches*, November 1, pp. 49–51.

DeKlerk, V. 1991. Expletives: Men only? *Communication Monographs* 58: 156–169.

Demo, D. H. 1987. Family relations and the self-esteem of adolescents and their parents. *Journal of Marriage and the Family* 49: 705–15.

Derlega, V. J.; Barbee, A. P.; and Winstead, B. A. 1994. Friendship, gender, and social support: Laboratory studies of supportive interactions. In *Communicating of social support: Messages, interactions, relationships, and community*, ed. B. R. Burleson, T. L. Albrecht, and I. G. Sarason, pp. 136–51. Thousand Oaks, CA: Sage.

Derlega, V .J.; Metts, S.; Petronio, S.; and Margulis, S. T. 1993. *Self-disclosure*. Newbury Park, CA: Sage.

Dovidio, J. F.; Brigham, J. C.; Johnson, B. T.; and Gaertner, S. L. 1996. Stereotyping, prejudice, and discrimination: Another look. In *Stereotypes and stereotyping*, ed. C. N. Macrae, C. Stangor, and M. Hewstone, pp. 227–54. New York: Guilford Press.

Duck, S. 1987. How to lose friends without influencing people. In *Interpersonal processes: New directions in communication research*, ed. M. E. Roloff and G. R. Miller, pp. 278–98. Beverly Hills, CA: Sage.

Duck, S. 1993. Steady as (s)he goes: Relational maintenance as a shared meaning system. In *Communication and relational maintenance*, ed. D. J. Canary and L. Stafford, pp. 45–60. New York: Academic Press.

Duck, S. 1994. *Meaningful relationships: Talking, sense, and relating*. Thousand Oaks, CA: Sage.

Duck, S. ed. 1994. *Dynamics of relationships*. Thousand Oaks, CA: Sage.

Duck, S., 1997. *Handbook of personal relationships*, 2d ed. New York: Wiley.

Duck, S., and Barnes, M. K. 1991. Disagreeing about agreement: Reconciling differences about similarity. *Communication Monographs* 59: 199–208.

Duck, S., and Gilmour, R., eds. 1981. *Personal relationships*. London: Academic Press.

Duck, S., and Pittman, G. 1994. Social and personal relationships. In *Handbook of interpersonal communication*, 2d ed., ed. M. L. Knapp and G. R. Miller, pp. 677–96. Thousand Oaks, CA: Sage.

Duncan, S., Jr., and Fiske, D. W. 1977. *Face-to-face interaction: Research, methods, and theory*. Hillsdale, NJ: Erlbaum.

Durst, G. M. 1989. The manager as a developer. *Vital Speeches*, March 1, pp. 309–14.

Eisenberg, N., and Fabes, R. A. 1990. Empathy: Conceptualization, measurement, and relation to prosocial behavior. *Motivation and Emotion* 14: 131–49.

Ekman, P., and Friesen, W. V. 1969. The repertoire of nonverbal behavior: Categories, origins, usage, and coding. *Semiotica* 1: 49–98.

Ekman, P., and Friesen, W. V. 1975. *Unmasking the face*. Englewood Cliffs, NJ: Prentice-Hall.

Ellis, K. 1995. Apprehension, self-perceived competency, and teacher immediacy in the laboratory-supported public speaking course: Trends and relationships. *Communication Education* 44: 64–78.

Estes, W. K. 1989. Learning theory. In *Foundations for a psychology of education*, ed. A. Lesgold and R. Glaser, pp. 6–8. Hillsdale, NJ: Erlbaum.

Eysenck, H. J. 1994. The measurement of creativity. In *Dimensions of creativity*, ed. M. A. Boden, pp. 199–242. Cambridge, MA: MIT Press.

Fairhurst, G. T. 1993. Echoes of the vision: When the rest of the organization talks total quality. *Management Communication Quarterly* 6: 331–71.

Fairhurst, G. T., and Sarr, R. A. 1996. *The art of framing*. San Francisco: Jossey-Bass.

Fairhurst, G. T., and Wendt, R. G. 1993. The gap in total quality. *Management Communication Quarterly* 6: 441–51.

Fiedler, F. E. 1967. *A Theory of leadership effectiveness*. New York: McGraw-Hill.

Filley, A. C. 1975. *Interpersonal conflict resolution*. Glenview, IL: Scott, Foresman.

Fisher, G. 1988. International negotiation. In *Intercultural communication: A reader*, 5th ed., ed. L. A. Samovar and R. E. Porter, pp. 192–200. Belmont, CA: Wadsworth.

Forgas, J. P. 1991. Affect and person perception. In *Emotion and Social Judgments*, ed. J. P. Forgas, pp. 263–91. New York: Pergamon Press.

Forgas, J. P.; Bower, G. H.; and Moylan, S. J. 1990. Praise or blame? Affective influences on attributions for achievement. *Journal of Personality and Social Psychology* 59: 809–19.

Friday, R. A. 1995. Contrasts in discussion behaviors of German and American managers. In *Intercultural communication: A reader*, 7th ed., ed. L. A. Samovar and R. E. Porter, pp. 274–85. Belmont, CA: Wadsworth.

Gadzella, B. M., and Whitehead, D. A. 1975. Effects of auditory and visual modalities in recall of words. *Perceptual and Motor Skills* 40: 255–60.

Gillespie, P. P. 1988. Campus stories, or the cat beyond the canvas. *Vital Speeches*, pp. 235–38, February 1.

Gordon, T. 1970. *Parent effectiveness training*. New York: Wyden.

Gordon, T. 1971. *The basic modules of the instructor outline for effectiveness training courses*. Pasadena, CA: Effectiveness Training Associates.

Gorham, J. 1988. The relationship between verbal teacher immediacy behaviors and student learning. *Communication Education* 37: 40–54.

Gorham, J., and Christophel, D. M. 1990. The relationship of teachers' use of humor in the classroom to immediacy and student learning. *Communication Education* 39: 46–63.

Gorham, J., and Christophel, D. M. 1992. Students' perceptions of teacher behaviors as motivating and demotivating factors in college classes. *Communication Quarterly* 40: 239–53.

Gorham, J., and Christophel, D. M. 1995. A test-retest analysis of student motivation, teacher immediacy, and perceived sources of motivation and demotivation in college classes. *Communication Education* 44: 292–307.

Gorham, J.; Cohen, S. H.; and Morris, T. L. 1997. Fashion in the classroom II: Instructor immediacy and attire. *Communication Research Reports* 14: 11–24.

Gorham, J.; Kelley, D. H.; and McCroskey, J. C. 1989. The affinity-seeking of classroom teachers: A second perspective. *Communication Quarterly* 37: 16–27.

Gorham, J., and Zakahi, W. R. 1990. A comparison of teacher and student perceptions of immediacy and learning: Monitoring process and product. *Communication Education* 39: 354–69.

Grice, H. P. 1975. Logic and conversation. In *Syntax and semantics: Vol. 3, Speech Acts*, ed. P. Cole and J. L. Morgan, pp. 41–58. New York: Academic Press.

Gudykunst, W. B. 1991. *Bridging differences: Effective intergroup communication*. Newbury Park, CA: Sage.

Gudykunst, W. B., and Kim, Y. Y. 1992. *Communicating with strangers: An approach to intercultural communication*, 2d ed. New York: McGraw-Hill.

Gudykunst, W. B., and Matsumoto, Y. 1996. Cross-cultural variability of communication in personal relationships. In *Communication in personal relationships across cultures*, ed. W. B. Gudykunst, S. Ting-Toomey, and T. Nishida, pp. 19–56. Thousand Oaks, CA: Sage.

Gudykunst, W. B.; Ting-Toomey, S.; and Nishida, T. 1996. *Communication in personal relationships across cultures*. Thousand Oaks, CA: Sage.

Hall, E. T. 1959. *The silent language*. Greenwich, CT: Fawcett.

Hall, E. T. 1969. *The hidden dimension*. Garden City, NY: Doubleday.

Hare, P. 1976. *Handbook of small group research*, 2d ed. New York: Free Press.

Hattie, J. 1992. *Self-concept*. Hillsdale, NJ: Erlbaum.

Hawkins, K. W. 1995. Effects of gender and communication content on leadership emergence in small, task-oriented groups. *Small Group Research* 26: 234–49.

Hecht, M. L.; Collier, M. J.; and Ribeau, S. A. 1993. *African American communication: Ethnic identity and cultural interpretation*. Newbury Park, CA: Sage.

Helgesen, S. 1990. *The female advantage: Woman's ways of leadership*. New York: Doubleday.

Hennessy, B. 1985. *Public opinion*, 5th ed. Monterey, CA: Brooks/Cole.

Hill, C. T., and Stull, D. E. 1987. Gender and self-disclosure: Strategies for exploring the issues. In *Self-disclosure: Theory, research, and therapy*, ed. J. H. Berg and V. J. Derlega, pp. 81–100. New York: Plenum Press.

Hofstede, G. 1983. The cultural relativity of organizational practices and theories. *Journal of International Business Studies*, Fall, pp. 75–89.

Hofstede, G. 1991. *Cultures and organizations: Software of the mind*. New York: McGraw-Hill.

Hollman, T. D. 1972. Employment interviewer's errors in processing positive and negative information. *Journal of Psychology* 56: 130–34.

Infante, D. A.; Rancer, A. S.; and Jordan, F. F. 1996. Affirming and nonaffirming style, dyad sex, and perception of argumentation and verbal aggression in an interpersonal dispute. *Human Communication Research* 22: 315–34.

Jaksa, J. A., and Pritchard, M. S. 1994. *Communication ethics: Methods of analysis*. Belmont, CA: Wadsworth.

Jensen, A. D., and Chilberg, J. C. 1991. *Small group communication: Theory and application*. Belmont, CA: Wadsworth.

Johannesen, R. L. 1996. *Ethics in human communication*, 4th ed. Prospect Heights, IL: Waveland Press.

Jones, E. E. 1990. *Interpersonal perception*. New York: W. H. Freeman.

Jones, G. 1987. How deep are your convictions? *Vital Speeches*, June 1, pp. 492–94.

Jordan, J. V. 1991. The relational self: A new perspective for understanding women's development. In *The self: Interdisciplinary approaches*, ed. J. Strauss and G. R. Goethals, pp. 136–49. New York: Springer-Verlag.

Jurma, W. E., and Wright, B. C. 1990. Follower reactions to male and female leaders who maintain or lose reward power. *Small Group Research* 21: 97–112.

Kaplan, J., ed. 1992. *Bartlett's Familiar Quotations*. Boston: Little Brown.

Kellermann, K. 1992. Communication: Inherently strategic and primarily automatic. *Communication Monographs* 59: 288–300.

Kellermann, K., and Reynolds, R. 1990. When ignorance is bliss: The role of motivation to reduce uncertainty in uncertainty reduction theory. *Human Communication Research* 17: 5–75.

Kennedy, C. W., and Camden, C. T. 1983. A new look at interruptions. *Western Journal of Speech Communication* 47: 45–58.

Kerr, N. L. 1992. Issue importance and group decision making. In *Group process and productivity*, ed. S. Worchel, W. Wood, and J. A. Simpson, pp. 69–74. Newbury Park, CA: Sage.

Klinger, E. 1977. *Meaning and void: Inner experience and the incentives in people's lives*. Minneapolis: University of Minnesota Press.

Knapp, M. L. 1984. *Interpersonal communication and human relationships*. Boston: Allyn and Bacon.

Knapp, M. L., and Hall, J. A. 1992. *Nonverbal communication in human interaction*, 3d ed. New York: Holt, Rinehart and Winston.

Kolligan, J., Jr. 1990. Perceived fraudulence as a dimension of perceived incompetence. In

Competence considered, ed. R. J. Sternberg and J. Kolligan, pp. 261–85. New Haven, CT: Yale University Press.

Krannich, R. L., and Banis, W. J. 1990. *High impact resumes and letters*, 4th ed. Woodbridge, VA: Impact Publications.

LaFollette, H. 1996. *Personal relationships: Love, identity, and morality*. Cambridge, MA: Blackwell.

Leathers, D. 1992. *Successful nonverbal communication: Principles and applications*, 2d ed. New York: Macmillan.

Lieberman, D. A. 1995. Ethnocognitivism, problem solving, and hemisphericity. In *Intercultural communication: A reader*, 7th ed. ed. L. A. Samovar and R. E. Porter, pp. 178–93. Belmont, CA: Wadsworth.

Littlejohn, S. 1996. *Theories of human communication*, 5th ed. Belmont, CA: Wadsworth.

Luft, J. 1970. *Group processes: An introduction to group dynamics*. Palo Alto, CA: Mayfield.

Lustig, M. W., and Koester, J. 1993. The development and sex-related use of interruption behavior. *Human Communication Research* 19: 388–408.

MacArthur, D. 1968. Address to Congress (April 19, 1951). In *Speech criticism: Methods and materials*, ed. W. Linsley, pp. 337–44. Dubuque, IA: Brown.

Macrae, C. N.; Milne, A. B.; and Bodenhausen, G. V. 1994. Stereotypes as energy-saving devices: A peek inside the cognitive toolbox. *Journal of Personality and Social Psychology* 66: 37–47.

Mandler, J. M., and Ritchey, G. H. 1977. Long-term memory for pictures. *Journal of Experimental Psychology: Human Learning and Memory* 3: 386–96.

Markus, H. R., and Kitayama, S. 1991. Cultural variation in the self-concept. In *The self: Interdisciplinary approaches*, ed. J. Strauss and G. R. Goethals, pp. 18–48. New York: Springer-Verlag.

Markus, H. R., and Nurius, P. 1986. Possible selves. *American Psychologist* 41: 954–69.

Martin, M. M.; Anderson, C. M.; and Horvath, C. L. 1996. Feelings about verbal aggression: Justifications for sending, and hurt from receiving, verbally aggressive messages. *Communication Research Reports* 13(1): 19–26.

Martin, J. N., and Nakayama, T. K. 1997. *Intercultural communication in contexts*. Mountain View, CA: Mayfield.

Maslow, A. H. 1954. *Motivation and personality*. New York: Harper and Row.

McCormick, W. M. 1986. The American tort system. *Vital Speeches*, February 15, pp. 267–69.

McCroskey, J. C. 1978. Reliability and validity of the willingness to communicate scale. *Communication Quarterly* 40: 16–26.

McCroskey, J. C. 1978. Validity of the PRCA as an index of oral communication apprehension. *Communication Monographs* 45: 192–203.

McCroskey, J. C., and Neuliep, J. W. 1997. The development in intercultural and interethnic communication apprehension scales. *Communication Research Reports* 14: 145–57.

McCroskey, J. C., and Richmond, V. P. 1987. Willingness to communicate. In *Personality and interpersonal communication*, ed. J. C. McCroskey and J. A. Daly, pp. 129–56. Newbury Park, CA: Sage.

McCroskey, J. C., and Richmond, V. P. 1990. Willingness to communicate: A cognitive view. *Journal of Social Behavior and Personality* 5: 19–38.

McCroskey, J. C., and Richmond, V. P. 1993. Identifying compulsive communicators: The talkaholic scale. *Communication Research Reports* 10: 107–14.

McLaughlin, M. L. 1984. *Conversation: How talk is organized*. Newbury Park, CA: Sage.

Menzel, K. E., and Carrell, L. J. 1994. The relationship between preparation and performance in public speaking. *Communication Education* 43: 17–26.

Mruk, C. 1995. *Self-esteem: Research, theory, and practice*. New York: Springer.

Mullen, B.; Anthony, T.; Salas, E.; and Driskell, J. E. 1994. Group cohesiveness and quality of decision making. *Small Group Research* 24: 189–204.

Nickerson, R. S. 1986. *Reflections on reasoning*. Hillsdale, NJ: Erlbaum.

Nofzinger, R. E. 1991. *Everyday conversation*. Newbury Park, CA: Sage.

Noller, P. 1987. Nonverbal communication in marriage. In *Intimate relationships: Development, dynamics, and deterioration*, ed. D. Perlman and S. Duck, pp. 149–76. Newbury Park, CA: Sage.

Ogden, C. K., and Richards, I. A. 1923. *The meaning of meaning*. London: Kegan, Paul, Trench, Trubner.

Patterson, B. R.; Bettini, L., and Nussbaum, J. F. 1993. The meaning of friendship across the life-span: Two studies. *Communication Quarterly* 41: 145–60.

Pavio, A. 1979. *Imagery and verbal processes*. New York: Holt.

Pearson, J. C.; West, R. L.; and Turner, L. H. 1995. *Gender and Communication*, 3d ed. Dubuque, IA: Brown and Benchmark.

Petri, H. L. 1996. *Motivation: Theory, research, and applications*, 4th ed. Belmont, CA: Wadsworth.

Petty, R. E. 1995. Attitude change. In *Advanced social psychology*, ed. A. Tesser, pp. 195–255. New York: McGraw-Hill.

Petty, R. E. 1997. The evolution of theory and research in social psychology: From single to multiple effect and process models of persuasion. In

The message of social psychology: Perspectives on mind in society, ed. C. McGarty and S. A. Haslam, pp. 268–90. Oxford: Basil Blackwell.

Petty, R. E., and Cacioppo, J. T. 1996. *Attitudes and persuasion: Classic and contemporary approaches.* Boulder, CO: Westview.

Petty, R. E.; Haugtvedt, C. P.; and Smith, S. M. 1995. Elaboration as a determinant of attitude strength. In *Attitude strength: Antecedents and consequence*, ed. R. E. Petty and J. A. Krosnick, pp. 93–130. Mahway, NJ: Erlbaum.

Petty, R. E., and Wegener, D. T. 1998. Attitude change: Multiple roles for persuasion variables. In *Handbook of social psychology*, 4th ed., ed. D. Gilbert, S. Fisk, and G. Lindzey, Vol. 1, pp. 323–90. New York: McGraw-Hill.

Petty, R. E.; Wegener, D. T.; and Fabrigar, L. R. 1997. Attitudes and attitude change. *Annual Review of Psychology* 48: 609–47.

Phillips, G. M. 1977. Rhetoritherapy versus the medical model: Dealing with reticence. *Communication Education* 26: 34–43.

Phillips, G. M. 1991. *Communication incompetencies: A theory of training oral performance behavior.* Carbondale: Southern Illinois University Press.

Prisbell, M., and Andersen, J. F. 1980. The importance of perceived homophily, level of uncertainty, feeling good, safety, and self-disclosure in interpersonal relationships. *Communication Quarterly* 28: 22–33.

Pritchard, M. S. 1991. *On becoming responsible.* Lawrence: University of Kansas Press.

Reardon, K. K. 1987. *Interpersonal communication: Where minds meet.* Belmont, CA: Wadsworth.

Richards, I. A. 1965. *The philosophy of rhetoric.* New York: Oxford University Press.

Richmond, V. P., and McCroskey, J. C. 1989. *Communication: Apprehension, avoidance, and effectiveness*, 2d ed., Scottsdale, AZ: Gorsuch Scarisbrick.

Robbins, S. P., and Hunsaker, P. L. 1996. *Training in inter-personal skills: Tips for managing people at work.* Upper Saddle River, NJ: Prentice-Hall.

Roloff, M. E., and Cloven, D. H. 1990. The chilling effect in interpersonal relationships: The reluctance to speak one's mind. In *Intimates in conflict: A communication perspective*, ed. D. D. Cahn, pp. 49–76. Hillsdale, NJ: Erlbaum.

Rose, H. M.; Rancer, A. S.; and Crannell, K. C. 1993. The impact of basic courses in oral interpretation and public speaking on communication apprehension. *Communication Reports* 6: 54–60.

Roskens, R. W. 1989. Integrity. *Vital Speeches*, June 1, pp. 511–12.

Ross, M. 1989. Go, oh thoughts, on wings of gold. *Vital Speeches*, February 15, pp. 282–84.

Rubin, R. B.; Rubin, A. M.; and Piele, L. J. 1996. *Communication research: Strategies and sources*, 4th ed. Belmont, CA: Wadsworth.

Samovar, L. A., and Porter, R. E. 1995. *Communication between cultures*, 2d ed. Belmont, CA: Wadsworth.

Samter, W. 1994. Unsupportive relationships: Deficiencies in support-giving skills of the lonely person's friends. In *Communicating of social support: Messages, interactions, relationships, and community*, ed. B. R. Burleson, T. L. Albrecht, and I. G. Sarason, pp. 195–214. Thousand Oaks, CA: Sage.

Schutz, W. 1966. *The interpersonal underworld.* Palo Alto, CA: Science and Behavior Books.

Shaw, M. E. 1981. *Group dynamics: The psychology of small group behavior*, 3d ed. New York: McGraw-Hill.

Shimanoff, S. B. 1980. *Communication rules: Theory and research*, Beverly Hills, CA: Sage.

Sillars, A. L., and Weisberg, J. 1987. Conflict as a social skill. In *Interpersonal processes: New directions in communication research*, ed. M. E. Roloff and G. R. Miller, pp. 140–71. Beverly Hills, CA: Sage.

Spitzberg, B. H. 1990. The construct validity of trait-based measures of interpersonal competence. *Communication Research Reports* 7: 107–15.

Spitzberg, B. H. 1991. An examination of trait measures of interpersonal competence. *Communication Reports* 4: 22–29.

Spitzberg, B. H. 1993. The dark side of (in)competence. In *The dark side of interpersonal communication*, ed. W. R. Cupach and B. H. Spitzberg, pp. 24–49. Hillsdale, NJ: Erlbaum.

Spitzberg, B. H. 1997. A model of intercultural communication competence. In *Intercultural communication: A reader*, 8th ed., ed. L. A. Samovar and R. E. Porter, pp. 379–93. Belmont, CA: Wadsworth.

Spitzberg, B. H., and Cupach, W. R. 1984. *Interpersonal communication competence.* Beverly Hills, CA: Sage.

Spitzberg, B. H., and Cupach, W. R. 1989. *Handbook of interpersonal competence research.* New York: Springer-Verlag.

Spitzberg, B. H., and Duran, R. L. 1995. Toward the development and validation of a measure of cognitive communication competence. *Communication Quarterly* 43: 259–74.

Steil, L. K.; Barker, L. L.; and Watson, K. W. 1983. *Effective listening.* Reading, MA: Addison-Wesley.

Stewart, C. J., and Cash, W. B. 1991. *Interviewing: Principles and practices*, 6th ed. Dubuque, IA: William C. Brown.

Stewart, L. P.; Cooper, P. J.; Stewart, A. D.; and Friedley, S. A. 1996. *Communication and gender*, 3d ed. Scottsdale, AZ: Gorsuch Scarisbrick.

Stiff, J. B.; Dillard, J. P.; Somera, L.; Kim, H; and Sleight, C. 1988. Empathy, communication and prosocial behavior. *Communication Monographs* 55: 198–213.

Tannen, D. 1990. *You just don't understand.* New York: Morrow.

Taylor, D. A., and Altman, I. 1987. Communication in interpersonal relationships: Social penetration theory. In *Interpersonal processes: New directions in communication research*, ed. M. E. Roloff and G. R. Miller, pp. 257–77. Beverly Hills, CA: Sage.

Temple, L. E., and Loewen, K. R. 1993. Perceptions of power: First impressions of a woman wearing a jacket. *Perceptual and Motor Skills* 76: 336–47.

Tengler, C. D., and Jablin, F. M. 1983. Effects of question type, orientation, and sequencing in the employment screening interview. *Communication Monographs* 50: 253–63.

Thibaut, J. W., and Kelley, H. H. 1986. *The social psychology of groups*, 2d ed. New Brunswick, NJ: Transaction Books.

Tobias, R. L. 1993. In today walks tomorrow: Shaping the future of telecommunication. *Vital Speeches*, February 15, pp. 273–76.

Trachtenberg, S. J. 1986. Five ways in which thinking is dangerous. *Vital Speeches*, August 15, p. 653.

Tracy, K.; Dusen, D. V.; and Robinson, S. 1987. "Good" and "bad" criticism. *Journal of Communication* 37: 46–59.

Trenholm, S. 1991. *Human communication theory*, 2d ed. Englewood Cliffs, NJ: Prentice-Hall.

Tripp, R. T., comp. 1987. *International thesaurus of quotations.* New York: Harper and Row.

Vroom, V. H., and Yetton, P. W. 1973. *Leadership and decision-making.* Pittsburgh: University of Pittsburgh Press.

Watzlawick, P.; Beavin, J. H.; and Jackson, D. D. 1967. *Pragmatics of human communication.* New York: W. W. Norton.

Weaver, J. B., III, and Kirtley, M. B. 1995. Listening styles and empathy. *The Southern Communication Journal* 60: 131–40.

Weaver, R. 1970. *Language is sermonic.* In *Language is sermonic*, ed. R. L. Johannesen, R. Strickland, and R. T. Eubanks, pp. 201–26. Baton Rouge: Louisiana State University Press.

Weiten, W. 1995. *Psychology: Themes and variations*, 3d ed. Pacific Grove, CA: Brooks/Cole.

Whetten, D. A., and Cameron, K. S. 1995. *Developing management skills*, 3d ed. New York: HarperCollins.

White, R., and Lippitt, R. 1968. Leader behavior and member reaction in three "social climates." In *Group dynamics*, 3d ed., ed. D. Cartwright and A. Zander, pp. 318–35. New York: Harper and Row.

Williams, R. G., and Ware, J. E., Jr. 1976. Validity of student ratings of instruction under different incentive conditions: A further study of the Dr. Fox effect. *Journal of Educational Psychology* 68: February 1976, 48–56.

Wilson, J. 1989. *On the boundaries of conversation.* New York: Pergamon Press.

Wolvin, A., and Coakley, C. G. 1996. *Listening*, 5th ed. Dubuque, IA: Brown and Benchmark.

Wood, J. T. 1997. *Gendered lives: Communication, gender, and culture*, 2d ed. Belmont, CA: Wadsworth.

Zebrowitz, L. A. 1990. *Social perception.* Pacific Grove, CA: Brooks/Cole.

Zillmann, D. 1991. Empathy: Affect from bearing witness to the emotions of others. In *Responding to the screen: Reception and reaction processes*, ed. J. Bryant and D. Zillmann, pp. 135–67. Hillsdale, NJ: Erlbaum.

Index

Photo Credits